What Happened to Me

My Life with Books, Research Libraries, and Performing Arts

DAVID H. STAM

authorHOUSE®

AuthorHouse™ LLC
1663 Liberty Drive
Bloomington, IN 47403
www.authorhouse.com
Phone: 1-800-839-8640

Published by AuthorHouse   05/12/2014

ISBN: 978-1-4918-6149-3 (sc)
ISBN: 978-1-4918-6148-6 (e)

Library of Congress Control Number: 2014902483

CONTENTS

Preface ix

Chapter I   Not So Wild Oats,
                  1935 to 1958 1

A Brief Jacob Stam Family Profile 1
The Book of my Childhood 4
Summer Delights and Diversions 20
A Rebel at Wheaton College, Illinois 23
New College, University of Edinburgh 32
The Naval Interlude 41

Chapter II   Librarianship: its Duties and Rewards
                  1959 to 1967 60

The Career that Nearly Wasn't 60
Panacea or Precious Bane? 63
David V. Erdman, Master and Mentor 69
Training in Librarianship 74
My Introduction to Rare Books 75
"Less Mooning, More Bassooning" 77
Marlboro College, Vermont 94

Chapter III   Mid-Career: Four Research
                  Libraries and a Foundation
                  1967 to 1998 126

The Newberry Library and Chicago 126
Johns Hopkins and Baltimore 143
New York Public Library Revisited 160
The Research Libraries Group 165
Mixed Signals: Retrench and Grow—Two Leaders 174
The Schomburg Center and Its Vicissitudes 189

The Gladys Krieble Delmas Foundation 211
Another Transition: Syracuse University 221

Chapter IV "The Abbreviation of Time"
           September 1998 to December 2013 241

Busier than Ever 241
Amusements in Retirement 243
Greenland's Icy Mountains and Beyond 260
Friendships Predominate 264
Chamber Music America 278
More Amusements 280
Intimations of Mortality 284

Epilogue: The Origins of this Screed 285

Appendix I: Dramatis Personae 289

The Stam Family: My Grandparents and Parents
           Generation 289

Appendix II: Selected Publications of David H. Stam 293

Index 299

Dedicated to Deirdre Corcoran Stam
With love and gratitude

Preface

In a sense this entire memoir is an acknowledgment to the many people who have influenced the course of my life, in all the best senses, but including some of the adverse encounters that played their part in broadening my experience. For more direct stimuli on the composition of these autobiographical memories, please see the Epilogue: "The Origins of this Screed."

The reader may observe an undercurrent of what I would call a secular determinism, from the ambiguity of the title to the ending, and throughout. The title intends to convey a number of questions: Is this what really happened?; Holy smokes, did that really happen!; Who was responsible for what happened?

I was schooled in predestinarian Calvinism, and like other things in life (such as the Wheaton College pledge, q.v.), I retained only the parts congenial to my mind and heart. The free will/determinism debate is one of those motifs, partly as an ongoing family joke, more seriously as a poor excuse for avoiding responsibility, and most fundamentally as a search for causality and agency in my life. But what also sews this life together are the thin threads of chance, call them what you will: fate, providence, coincidence, luck, destiny, accident, or the wheel of fortune.[1]

Although presented here in a rough chronological order, I've written these memoirs as scattered memories came to mind, putting them in what seemed appropriate places. What started out as a series of sketches from memory for family and friends has grown into something bigger as I found that memory plays too many tricks, and I've had to verify and correct where I could. In several instances I've used the device of a bracketed Coda to provide a continuation and conclusion to a given subject without distorting the overall chronological order. Footnotes are also used to introduce digressions but also demonstrate a lifelong habit. When I use the first person plural, "we" usually refers to my wife Deirdre and me.

One of the readers of a draft of this memoir warned me of two pitfalls: pomposity and self-aggrandizement, another of the "garrulities of an old man." I would add ponderousness to the list. In writing, I've strived against pomposity; less so against self-aggrandizement, and I've not successfully avoided the ponderous. I've tried to include many of the things of which I'm most ashamed, and of endeavors that failed, but more things of which I'm proud or which gave me a great deal of pleasure or amusement. Achievements and mistakes are not in balance here, but in some cases memory works that way, for example in the way it has turned the misery of being a lowly sailor into a wholly positive experience "recollected in tranquility." I do plead guilty to name-dropping, including many people who will be unfamiliar to some readers. Some musicians

---

[1] It was not until I finished the manuscript of this book in late 2013 that I discovered by chance Ronald Dworkin's *Justice for Hedgehogs* (Cambridge, MA: Harvard University Press, 2011) and its central chapter on "Free Will and Responsibility" (p. 219-252). It struck me on a quick reading as a concise but thorough examination of the issues surrounding determinism: responsibility, control, freedom, choice (the decisions we make), causation, chance, duress, and justice, all leading to what he calls a "responsibility system." I'm sure I paraphrase him crudely by saying that his responsibility system is rather like my own, that though there is some force of determinism at work, we have to live our lives as though there is free will and take responsibility for our actions.

may not recognize the librarians and vice versa. By way of mitigation I can only say that each seems a part of my story as I remember it.

A number of readers have rescued me from many mistakes of memory or fact, of spelling mistakes and grammatical infelicities. Readers of the whole manuscript were Terry Belanger, Ed Bock, Joseph Mitchell, Robert Patten, Deirdre C. Stam, James Stam, and Daniel Traister, and to each I am heavily indebted. Several others have read some selected portions in which each was personally involved: Tom Ragle and others for the Marlboro College section; Donald Krummel re the Newberry Library; Richard Macksey on Johns Hopkins; Margaret Lioi and Louise Smith on Chamber Music America; and several others.

As I have been dredging in the "deep well of the past," I have been struck by the absence of any real boundaries between the personal and the professional parts of my life, between work and play, between family and friends, even between pleasure and pain. In what follows there are probably fewer than a dozen painful experiences and dozens of pleasurable ones. Like fellow ALS victim Lou Gehrig, I feel very lucky. I'd say luckiest if Gehrig hadn't preempted the term.

David H Stam
St. Cecilia's Day, 2013

Chapter I

Not So Wild Oats, 1935 to 1958

"My memory of what happened is not what happened."
John Cage. *Composition in Retrospect* (1993)

A Brief Jacob Stam Family Profile
1888 to 2012

Yield not to temptation, for yielding is sin;
Each vict'ry will help you some other to win;
Fight manfully onward, dark passions subdue;
Look ever to Jesus, He'll carry you through.

That seminal hymn of childhood brings out the darker side of growing up as fundamentalists. Sowing wild oats or skirting the boundaries of temptation was not what we did, at least not openly. Most of my six brothers and sisters were brought up in circumstances carefully protected from the evils of the heathen world. For all of us, primary and secondary education was all in sectarian Protestant schools, mostly in Dutch Christian Reformed schools (not to be confused with the quite separate Dutch Reformed Church). Two Sunday church services, Sunday schools, prayer meetings, week-long revival series, twice daily Bible reading, and daily chapel services in school—all of these were constant in our youth. Ours was a very sheltered environment, no closer to the real world than the smell of beer outside a tavern. Crucial scriptural texts of our education were "Be ye not unequally yoked together with unbelievers . . ." and "Come out from them and be ye separate . . ." (2 Corinthians 6: 14 and 17). Only the youngest, Bob, claims to have escaped the religious convictions that all my other siblings held at some point, and that four of seven retained throughout their lives. I imagine that each of us had some kind of secret life, hiding our temptations, but it was a long time before my brother Jim and I could talk about such things.

If there were to be another Civil War over the issues of our time (abortion, war, law, marriage, religion, social justice, etc.), it's possible that some Stams would be on opposing sides. Before our oldest brother Paul died the seven of us lined up much like the present Supreme Court with three evangelicals broadly defined, three left-wing liberals, and one swing vote to brother John (Juan) in Costa Rica who religiously is fairly conservative and politically more radical than the rest of us. None of these categories is airtight; for example, Mary belongs to evangelical groups dedicated to social justice and the environment. Juan can both explicate the apocalypse to Fidel Castro and explain Latin American missions to conservative supporters in the Adirondacks. My own scholarly output includes work on John Calvin, the American Seamen's Friend Society, and the American Bible Society.

Of the seven children of my parents, Jacob and Deana Stam, there was one scientist turned business executive and lawyer (Paul), three missionaries (Ruth, John, and Mary), and three educators (David, Jim, and Bob). All of the men received doctoral degrees, my own coming last in 1978. Both the women had bachelor degrees from Wheaton College, majoring in mathematics, and some further training, but no postgraduate degrees. The younger three brothers are all married to academics of varied religious backgrounds (see Appendix I for more genealogical details).

There is some disagreement as to where the parental views of religious fundamentalism, in which we were all well drilled, went awry. My father Jacob sometimes blamed it on me as the fifth and middle male and thus he saw me as an influential black sheep. I suspect I got some of the blame because I was the first to make an overt break when I returned from an abortive year in divinity school. The two younger men, Jim and Bob, understandably resented my father's view, claiming that they had souls of their own, that American individualism and its exceptionalism were at work, and that in any case our three views were no more homogeneous than those of our four seniors.

My recollection of the family lore about our grandfather Peter Stam was a publican, or tavern keeper, in Alkmaar, Holland, emigrated steerage class, somehow found and read a New Testament on the ship, and arrived in America a dedicated Christian convert ready to do the Lord's work. More recently I've learned that most of this is untrue, that his father (my great grandfather) was the publican who sent my grandfather to the United States (first class) to get the American bug out of his system, that his son Peter (my grandfather) became a successful contractor and house builder in Paterson where he started his large family and eventually founded a rescue mission in downtown Paterson twenty years later.

Whatever the real truth, it is certain that Grandfather Peter raised a family of missionaries, and those who were not missionaries were dedicated to the work of missions. Of his children, Peter Jr. was Director of the Conservatory of Music at Wheaton College and later an administrator of evangelical Faith Seminary near Philadelphia; Clazina spent most of her 103+ years at the Star of Hope Mission but sometimes as secretary to my father; Henry was a realtor from Pompton Lakes, New Jersey; our Dad Jacob was a lawyer serving many Christian clients and organizations; Harry was a missionary to the Belgian Congo and gave me my middle name; Catherine died at the age of 1; John was a missionary to China where he and his wife were killed, an event I will return to later; Cornelius was the founder of a schismatic church called the Berean Bible Society which believed in a rather convoluted doctrine of the end times known as hyper-dispensationalism; and Amelia married a banker. Cornelius had been Superintendent of the Star of Hope Mission but had to be removed because of his doctrinal divisiveness, a task assigned to and carried out by my father. The extended family of Peter's grandchildren added a number of other missionaries.

The next generation of the children of Jacob and Deana Stam, my children's generation, are variously called Stams, Stevens (children of Ruth), and also Brains (children of Aunt Amelia). This generation is much more diverse religiously, a rainbow coalition of conviction and dissent. It includes at least one each of Protestants, Catholics, Jews, atheists and agnostics, Buddhists, and none of the above. So far no Muslim spouses or converts have entered the clan that I know of. Perhaps indicative of the differences are the first two children born into this mélange (both children of Paul Stam, our oldest brother, now deceased): Karen Stam and Paul B. Stam, Jr. Karen is a Public Defender in Salt Lake City where she defends the defenseless. Skip, a former legislative aide to Senator Jesse Helms, is the Republican Speaker Pro Tempore of the North Carolina House of Representatives, where he has promoted right-wing legislation against Planned Parenthood, constitutional amendments against same-sex marriage, and laws against schoolyard swearing. His latest cause that I've heard involves 2013 Republican legislation in North Carolina to declare the state officially Christian, an idea that would have horrified his grandfather Jacob who firmly espoused the principle of separation of church and state: "render unto Caesar that which is Caesar's."

My six surviving siblings held a reunion in August 2012 at our brother Jim's home in Ijamsville, Maryland, a delightful conclave that was very helpful to me in testing my own memories, particularly of our parents, comparing notes from our varying perspectives. Another expanded reunion of all relatives took place in July 2013 in Costa Rica, with over fifty attending, although Deirdre and I could not attend. All cousins of all generations reported an harmonious few days together.

The Book of my Childhood
July 1935 to June 1951

The centerpiece of my childhood in a largely Dutch community in and around Paterson, New Jersey, was the Book, *The Holy Bible*. My father, Jacob Stam, was a lawyer primarily devoted to evangelical, non-denominational fundamentalist Christian causes. He was President of the Gideons (both nationally and internationally), an attorney for Billy Graham and Chair of the Billy Graham Foundation's Executive Committee in the early 1960s, Chairman of the Board of the Moody Bible Institute, a leader of the Pocket Testament League, and affiliated with any number of mission boards in Asia, Africa, and Latin America, over forty boards in all. His father Peter (my grandfather), started the Star of Hope Mission on Broadway in Paterson, right next to the local bus terminal, within walking distance of the Passaic Falls, and near the bars which provided some of the mission's clientele. The grandfather's patriarchal home at 146 North 7th Street was notable for its high cupola with an unobstructed view of the Manhattan skyline, twenty miles to the

East, with the Passaic River snaking through the City of Paterson in the valley below. Our house at 238 Jefferson Street was little more than a block away, nearer to 9th Street but lacking the view.

Our family was neither rich nor poor, neither luxury-minded nor ostentatious, solidly well-off in the middle class. Dad was extremely generous to his religious charities, except during his depressed periods when he earned less and gave less. We had the luxury of being well-fed and well-educated (if not broadly so). I remember some childhood envy of the fancier cars and more modern homes of my friends and even one friend's father who had so many more neckties than my father. My parents were conservative Republicans critical of FDR, occasional ballot splitters, very compassionate people, firm in their Christian faith.

A number of my father's siblings were missionaries and three of my own siblings were missionaries as well. Uncle Harry and Aunt Alma spent thirty years in the Belgian Congo; Uncle Cornelius started his own schismatic denomination as noted already; my father's younger brother John, and his wife Betty, were graduates of Moody Bible Institute who decided to join the China Inland Mission. Betty, who had grown up in China, arrived there in 1932 and John the following year when they married. Their child, my cousin Helen Priscilla, was nine months old when John and Betty were killed (decapitated) in Jingdezhen, Anhui Province, China, either by Communists (according to the Western press) or bandits (according to some Sinologists) after a $20,000 ransom demand was rejected. The child survived, protected by fellow Chinese Christians. One legend has it that a Chinese friend bartered his life for the survival of Helen Priscilla, a story we first heard when visiting the archives of the Baptist University of Hong Kong in 1998. Another version has the Chinese friend arguing with the communists not to murder John and Betty, only to join the other two in death.

I have the vaguest recollection of having met my cousin Helen Priscilla once in Virginia in our early 20s but that may be pure invention—her maternal and paternal families were never close that I know of, and she was raised by her mother's family. The fact that she was a direct descendant of John and Priscilla Alden of the *Mayflower* added to the public interest of the story, which was reported in a December 1934 issue of *Time*, no doubt adding to her diffidence about her early childhood. For years I owned a couple of Uncle John's books, "rescued from the loot," appropriately enough Bunyan's *Holy War* and a one-volume Foxe's *Book of Martyrs*, but alas now lost or more probably given to some library. All of this occurred in the middle of my own pre-natal period, seven months before I was born; since my father was very close to his brother, I cannot begin to imagine the harmful effects this had on my mother and her increasingly difficult pregnancies, or on me.

One attribute of most members of Jacob's family was a love of word play. It wasn't only The Word that was treasured but all words. Laughter was another, surprisingly for a basically serious family. Puns were the *lingua franca* of the Stam household, often defended by the repeated line, "the worse they are the better." The earliest joke I can remember was "They laughed when I stood up; I forgot I was under the table." Brother Jim may recall this differently, but I remember clearly a family laughing fit over the word circumcision as found in one of the mealtime Scripture readings from the Bible or *Daily Light on the Daily Path*. This may not qualify as a pun but one of Dad's letters from 1933 talks about grandfather's depression and a doctor's advice to my partially deaf Grandpa that he needed diversion. After several denials he firmly said, "No! No! I don't need a virgin."

Dad's clever use of language was most evident in his epistolary style, especially when he was defending his children, and at least some of us benefited from and inherited that quality until email crimped our style. Linguistic skill with foreign languages was unevenly distributed: Juan, Jim, and Bob certainly have it; I doubt that Jacob had it; I definitely do not, though our daughter Kathryn does. My own fragmentary studies of German, Latin, Greek, French, and Italian gave me what I needed for my library career, what is known in the trade as title-page languages, the ability to guess from minimal clues what a book is about and where and when published. I remember a visit in the early 1980s to the labyrinthine bowels of the Library of Congress where my host pointed out a rather large section of books, at least thirty shelves, marked "Books in Unidentified Languages."[2]

My father's legal probate work involved guidance for fellow believers towards appropriate bequests to religious charities. Rescue missions, foreign missions, Bible and tract societies, the Gideons, the Billy Graham Evangelistic Association, homes for unmarried mothers, and many others were all part of the scene. As I remember it, Christmas presents were usually opened in the morning after Bible reading and prayer, but infrequently, when the usual pre-Christmas tensions were getting out of hand, the opening would be late on Christmas Eve after family visits to a few of Dad's charities. Typical Christmas Eve or Christmas day visitations, each including prayers, a short homily (time was limited), and the unwrapping of gifts, would include the Florence Crittenden (now Christian) Home for pregnant single women (that was a sight for a six-year old), the Paterson jail, an Old People's Home, a hospital, and the Star of Hope Mission for a service followed by food distribution. Jim also remembers Christmas services at the Hawthorn Gospel Church but for me that's at best a repressed memory. After divinity school I claimed that by age twenty I'd attended enough church services for four score years and ten. Those services and sermons also encouraged any tendency I had toward attention deficits, my attention distracted by anything in the hall that could be counted, whether squares on the ceiling or tiles on the floor.

---

[2]   I asked Mark Dimunation of the Library of Congress about the status of that cataloguing backlog and learned that it had been renamed, according to this report from LCs Collection Policy Committee: "The Library's Lesser Known Languages Collection holds materials that were collected on a sample basis to document these languages. The materials are housed together in document preservation boxes in the custody of the Collections Access, Loan and Management Division. In 2008, a decision was made that no further items would be added to a language's document preservation box once it was filled with examples. In 2009, a decision was made to close the collection completely to new receipts. Materials in these languages will continue to be acquired, however. They will, for the most part, be cataloged individually and shelved as appropriate throughout the Library's collections, although this does not preclude some materials being added to pamphlet collections in custodial divisions."

I'm still a compulsive counter who needs to know how many ballerinas are on stage.

The day I was born, July 11, 1935, my father sent a night letter to Nicholas Bowman, my mother's father: "David Harry—born at two this morning—St. Joseph's Hospital Paterson—Dean well—sends love—Praise the Lord with us. At first glance baby looks like Helen Priscilla. Jake". Following that was a form letter announcing my arrival to my father's friends:

> Pray with us that our David will be a man after God's own heart, as David of old was; that he will be a faithful servant of God as his Uncle Harry in Africa is; pray too that he may grow in stature and wisdom and grow in grace and the knowledge of Christ.
> David means "beloved" as you know, and he is that to us already. He is the 5th grandchild on the Bowman side, but do you realize that he is the 20th grandchild on the Stam side! We call to remembrance Psalm 127 "Lo children are a heritage of the Lord—happy is the man that hath his quiver full of them."
> David weighs 9 pounds and 2 ounces, is [blank] inches tall, his skin is fair, his hair is dark and his eyes are dark blue.
> Yours in his blessed bonds,

Nothing fixed, soon enough my hair was blond and my eyes brown. As one of seven children, I liked to stay beneath the radar. I don't feel I knew my father terribly well (he was a workaholic when he wasn't suffering his sporadic but quite serious depressions); apart from word games he never played sports of any kind with us, and as I grew up I tended to avoid too much contact. Exposure to his legal world did introduce me not only to legal information sources but also to the concept of evidence and the importance of its discovery and retention. Much later he said to me that "As a librarian you'll get this: I may be an old number, but I'm not off the shelf." He also had an anti-materialist streak, which he passed on to his children. He was always slow to bill his clients, and then at the lowest rates the bar association would permit, or by bartering goods and services in kind, like the daily house call at the apartment of his barber, Moses Calabrese, or even Mo's home visits to cut our hair, I presume in exchange for legal services. Apart from such little luxuries, Jacob would have found the currently popular gospel of prosperity completely alien to scripture and the teachings of Christ.

There were plenty of books around our house, quite apart from boxes full of Gideon Bibles and pocket testaments. I once sent my father an article about a 17th-century Dutch Bible printer, Jan Fredericksz Stam (1602-1667), a commercial printer in Amsterdam and Middleburgh who published several English Puritan works and a number of Bibles. I told my father that I had had no idea how far our bibliocentric heritage went back.[3] One subject dear to his heart was the separation of church and state, a legal doctrine for which he was a staunch advocate, mostly out of fear of Roman Catholic penetration into the realms of Caesar. He had an annotated copy of the three-volume *Church and State in the United States* by Anson Phelps Stokes, and other legal books on the subject that he kept in a working closet just off our parents' bedroom. He did argue one case before the Supreme Court of New Jersey in support of a 1937 New Jersey statute that required the reading of five Old Testament verses every morning in public schools.[4] A divided court ruled against his argument, 6 to 3, I suppose as a violation of the separation doctrine in which he so strongly believed. Whatever books he had were heavily underlined, particularly his Bibles, but even newspapers would get the highlighting treatment. While in the Navy I bought an *Encyclopedia Britannica* on the

---

[3]   A. F. Johnson. "J. F. Stam, Amsterdam, and English Bibles," *The Library* (London: The Bibliographical Society, 1954) p.185-93.

[4]   Brother Jim, who worked in Dad's law office after dropping out of Wheaton, and while studying at Upsala College, sent me these recollections of dad's Court history: "Dad was 'introduced' to the U.S. Supreme Court (meaning he was eligible to argue)--I thought you attended that—but never in fact argued a case. He argued two cases before the NJ Supreme Court. He won one on reversal, the suit of Daphne Roberts Leeds against the Atlantic City YWCA, trying to force its liberalization. He lost the other on appeal, the Gideon Bible distribution case starting in the Rutherford (?) schools. That's when he had the colloquy with Justice Brennan (just how would you prove to a non-believer that they should read the Bible?), which set my agenda when I worked in Dad's office: to read and report on all of Brennan's relevant opinions. (Of course Brennan was later appointed to the U. S. Supreme Court)."

installment plan and left it at home. Several years later I was appalled to find the whole section on Bible societies heavily underscored. Ingrate that I was, I even found a churlish and embarrassingly immature letter to my brother Jim about it. Gratitude was a word I resented as a teen-ager as did my children when I threw the charge of ingratitude at them twenty-five years later. I still think it's an unjust verbal weapon.

My own childhood now seems an enigma: the happy youth of someone who would become a family black sheep; a born-again Christian who by college at age sixteen had been reborn rather too frequently at various revival meetings, the first being at age five, but none of my conversions seemed trustworthy by age twenty. Our church was the Gospel Tabernacle just around the corner on North 9th Street with a fine pastor and great family friend, Rev. Vernon Grounds, whom I remember fondly. By contrast, his successor, Enoch Moore, was a veritable Rev. Malaprop who in his offertory prayers often said "we give thee these gifts in lieu of our love" and for the hymns would enjoin us to lift our voices "into the girdles."

One Sunday at age five in the Gospel Tabernacle, I decided to accept Christ at Uncle Vernon's invitation, thinking this would please my mother. After going forward to be saved, I hurried home, raced up on the porch where she was nursing brother Jim, and announced that I had gone forward and been saved. The look of disappointment on her face was obvious and disappointed me as well since it had been done to gain her approval. She knew too well that I was not mature enough to make such a decision. (Jim reports a similar experience at a slightly later age.)

My father saw it quite differently. In an April 4, 1941, letter to my brother Paul (presumably at Wheaton), he wrote that "We were delighted when David came home to tell that he had opened his heart to let the Lord Jesus in. He told it in such a cute and naïve way that one of his older brothers or sisters, who should have known better, laughed. He lifted his face kind of sad and said to mother, "Did I do the wrong thing, Mother?" I had a long talk with him that night, and although he is real young I think he understands the transaction. It is a great joy to us that each of you children are not wandering away and rebellious, but that each one is opening his heart to the Lord and beginning to walk with Him early in life."

Our mother was a very loving and generous person who often counseled us "never to resist a generous impulse." Her great love was hymnody and she seemed to know hundreds if not thousands of hymns by heart, and a great deal of poetry. Much later "From Greenland's icy mountains" took on new meaning for me when I became obsessed with the Polar regions. She once told me that when people told her what a wonderful family she had she could weep, and she did weep throughout our wedding reception, presumably because I was marrying outside the faith which I had already left. After she died of a brain tumor on Thanksgiving of 1965, her seven children gathered around the kitchen table to reminisce and debate which one was the favorite. We thought it a real tribute to her that most of us claimed the distinction.

Something of a social misfit as the youngest person in virtually all my activities, I was a fairly precocious and copious reader who assembled covert collections of forbidden comic books (secretly purchased with funds often stolen from my father) but periodically disposed of by my mother. Something of a hypocrite, I enjoyed my reputation as the helpful son always volunteering to do the dishes, while secretly motivated by a desire to get away from the family's religious table talk—a memory that made it easy for me to understand what T.S. Eliot meant in *Murder in the Cathedral* when he wrote that "the last temptation is the greatest treason, to do the right thing for the wrong reason."

Perversely enough, my younger brother Jim and I spent a period at an early age as true biblio-kleptomaniacs—stealing Bibles from the Mission book and scriptural artifact tables at the back of the Mission auditorium. I suspect that it was the soft leather bindings that attracted us—it wasn't for the pre-highlighting in red of the words of Jesus nor was it for ostentatious display—we couldn't very well show off our stolen goods. Never caught, we hid the loot in the insulation of attic floor boards, where they may still remain, in proximity to the Korans of that now partly Islamic Paterson neighborhood.

Brother Jim, with the best memory among the surviving siblings, is serving as my fact checker and memory conscience on these memoirs, and he tells me that my memory is wrong, that we were caught by Aunt Nita (Clazina), our father's spinster sister who lived a good part of her life in the Star of Hope Mission and died at well over 100 with marbles intact and faith strong. According to Jim she was in charge of the scripturally-oriented gift tables in the Mission, and as Mission security she detected us and told our parents who then imposed a particularly draconian penalty, to memorize the book of Proverbs for recitation at daily breakfast devotions with my father. We both remember Bible memorization as punishment for transgressions, one of the worst being the longest Psalm but I no longer remember which Psalm it was (the 119th perhaps), much less the verses themselves. Nor can I bring a single Proverb to mind. (Jim also reminds me that our father was a compulsive ledger keeper, and seldom did cash thefts go undetected. He required us to keep meticulous records of any funds he provided us in college. No doubt some of our own ledgers had elements of fiction in them.)

[*Dear Reader: do not be misled to think that the revelation of such peccadillos and indiscretions will lead on to full disclosure of all my sins of commission and omission. There are plenty of actions and things of which I'm ashamed, actions either suppressed, brought to light by long-neglected archives, or recalled all too clearly during this exercise in memory identification, possibly hurtful events and words that are embarrassing at best, infelicitous, immoral, unkind, mean-spirited, and better not set down to burden others.*]

My first library was the Paterson Public Library on Broadway, about eight blocks east of the Mission and east of the Erie and Lackawanna tracks which led in turn to Hoboken, the Hudson River ferry, and the mysteries of New York City where I would eventually spend a good portion of my adult life. Images remain of the ice-clogged Hudson, the *Normandie* in 1942 lying on its side at an icy North River pier, double-decker buses going north and south on Fifth Avenue in front of the Public Library, and early visits to Wanamaker's department store, Wall Street, and shipping companies near the Battery.

Book III of William Carlos Williams's *Paterson* is called "The Library," a section of the poem that evokes some familiar images. When I graduated from the children's room to the adult collection of the Paterson Public Library, sometime during World War II, I resolved to read the entire library collection, starting with Dewey 001. Disillusion quickly set in; if I had only started at the other end I might have made a little more progress: at that stage of my life geography would have been more appealing than bibliography. My high school library at Eastern Academy augmented the public library eventually, and I have the sense that by graduation in 1951 I was already, in Coleridge's term, a library cormorant.

I began first grade in my grammar school (Fourth Street Christian School) at age five (sans kindergarten), compressed the second grade into one semester, and again the seventh grade, leading to completion of eighth grade while still 11 years old. My wife Deirdre contends that the lack of kindergarten caused my lack of any color sense or design skill. Both my grammar and high schools were operated by the Christian Reformed Church. Despite very strong Dutch Calvinist traditions, it was a bit too liberal for my fundamentalist family—e.g., its members were decidedly less rigid Sabbatarians, less evangelistic, and some of them even smoked and drank, if always in moderation. We seldom worshipped in their churches.[5] If my father had to use the telephone on a Sunday, he would apologize to the operator for causing her to break the Sabbath.

One of my high school friends once invited me to attend a Christian Reformed catechism session, I suppose out of a need for moral support, but I was asked to leave as a trouble maker. When I got to my own doctoral work, the dissertation included quite a bit on the publication of Calvin's catechism and its offspring.

While our Reformed classmates might be reading Sunday newspapers after church, including their sinful comics, we Stams were limited to multiple Sunday services and religious reading. By high school we were in the habit of buying an early edition of *The New York Times* on Saturday evening but saving it for Monday reading, though probably we had some covert ways of stealing a look. Its magazine was the only place young boys of my ilk could legitimately look for women clothed in little more than panties and brassieres, although there was always the trusty backup of the *National Geographic* around the Stam household. Yield not to temptation, indeed.

My first sign of incipient rebellion occurred on my first day of school in first grade. I had by then (aged 5) developed an incorrigible habit of whistling and I did so throughout the morning classes. After several warnings to stop, the teacher said "Thank you for your cooperation, Mr. Stam." I probably knew that she was being sarcastic so I replied in kind with "You're welcome." At that she told me to leave the class and

---

[5]   Jim believes that the point of contention was not a matter of liberalism but of evangelism: "They [Christian Reformed people] weren't evangelistic. I think it was because it was harder to make people into Dutchman than into Christians." Our favorite history teacher, Mr. Bontekoe, smoked in moderation but we admired him nonetheless. He once flustered me completely, aged twelve or thirteen, by asking: "Stammy Boy, what do you think were the causes of the Civil War?"

stand in the hallway. Soon the Principal, Gerhardus Bus (a short hulk of a man unaffectionately known as Bussy), came by and asked why I was being punished. "For being polite." That led to his office, some further discipline, and a call to my mother. An inauspicious start to my education.

I don't recall knowing any Roman Catholics before I graduated from college, other than players from Catholic schools we played against. True Sabbath breakers, what Catholics would do on Sundays was to us shockingly unthinkable: reading newspapers, going to movies, playing or observing athletic and sporting events, and probably other sins we'd never even heard of, no doubt including the kind of titillation we were secretly seeking. So much for our vaunted holier-than-thou pretensions. At our 2012 sibling reunion, I tried to canvas the other five on their recollections of our indoctrination in anti-Catholicism but came up with no good answer, though we all knew it was there. Ruth did say that 60 years in a Catholic country had all but eliminated any anti-Catholic prejudice for her because she early on realized that "we all worshipped the same God." I suppose anti-papist prejudice was just a common assumption within the family ethos that required little comment. By now, anti-Catholicism for me has morphed into a more general anti-clericalism towards most organized dogma. I confess to strong surprise at our son Julian's conversion to Catholicism, given our own attitudes towards hierarchical dogma.

We saw plenty of African-Americans at the Mission, both at the meetings and in sewing classes conducted by our mother, Deana, for black women. Mother once told Jim that the black mothers requested segregated classes because the white women didn't take the work seriously. Possibly the difference was that the black families were just poor and needed the help, while the white families were dysfunctional. We regularly walked comfortably through black areas of town between the Mission and our home on Jefferson Street, high on the hill northeast of the Passaic River valley where the city proper lay. And of course much of the family missionary activity was devoted to people of color in such places as Belgian Congo, Tibet, China, and Latin America. But there was also a subliminal assumption that we were superior to black people, an unfortunate but persistent white trait.

Proper handwriting was apparently an important part of the curriculum at the Fourth Street Christian School. In second grade, the handwriting teacher was Miss Burduyn, whose gloved wooden left hand was a wicked weapon against any violation of proper letter forms. By contrast, Miss Schilling was a beautiful favorite who once (sixth grade perhaps) caught me cheating on a test but the next year, when I picked up a pencil she had dropped on a staircase, said that there might be hope for me yet.

I have at hand what must be the earliest example of my childish handwriting, probably deserving a wooden slap on the wrist. It reads: "I love you and I will love you always until we are married and have a nice home in the country with 3 or 4 little children and we will be happy (for the (rest of the lives) and you and I will be happy for the rest of our loves [sic] Truly yours David." Date and age uncertain, intended recipient unknown, but on the verso is this note by my mother, probably to my Dad: "Cleaning attic turned this up. Don't know to whom written. Better not show David." Why not, one wonders? It seems innocuous enough.

After the War ended in 1945, when I was ten years old, my oldest brother Paul returned from his naval duties. He had been at Okinawa, where he survived, with serious burns, a kamikaze attack on his destroyer, the *USS Braine*. A wartime graduate of Wheaton College, in 1946 he married his Wheaton girlfriend, Jane Levering, and began doctoral studies in chemistry at Princeton University, some sixty miles south of Paterson. I was in awe of both Paul and Jane as a pre-teenager, and loved to visit them, to walk around the campus, to see the house down their street where Einstein lived, to go to Paul's work at the Textile Research Institute out on Lake Carnegie where he studied the chemistry of human hair, and to worship Princeton football players in what was to me then the immense Palmer Stadium.

Twice, in 1947 and 1948, at ages twelve and thirteen, I bicycled alone the 60 miles from Paterson to Princeton over fairly busy pre-turnpike public highways for weekends with Paul and Jane. Paul introduced me to the game of squash in the new Dillon Gymnasium, opened in 1947, and proudly showed me the magnificent new Firestone Library, opened in 1948.

[Coda: Twenty-six years later in 1974 I was a candidate for the University Librarian position at Princeton and I remember clearly the morning of my interviews, walking on Nassau Street on a crisp autumn day, feeling very much like Thomas Hardy's Jude the Obscure. Luckily, I didn't get the job. The University President, Bill Bowen, who soon became President

of the Mellon Foundation, ignored all of my self-serving advice about what Princeton's Library needed; the successful candidate lasted only a few years and four years later was a candidate for the position I moved into at The New York Public Library in 1978. Another lucky break in that I was not ready for a place as complex as Princeton and needed the years at Hopkins as experience for NYPL.]

My memory of high school and particularly grammar school is dim and blurred. In both I was too young for the social situation but hardly a misfit, though I was fairly shy and intimidated by the older girls in my classes. At one time late in grade school a friend and I started a club called the DeJack Club, after Jack Cauwels and me. We developed an obsession with basketball and occasionally we rented a small gym in Ridgewood, New Jersey. In high school my best friend, Bill Vermuelen, was the son of an undertaker who lived nearby. In his home in the late forties, I first watched television—it was forbidden at home for fear that it would distract brother Bob from his studies and might lead us down sinful paths. We eventually got television at home when Billy Graham began broadcasting in the mid 1950s. In the Vermuelen funeral home basement, I first saw a dead body, one of very few over the past seventy years. During high school I remember coaching Bill on the meaning of Gray's "Elegy on a Country Churchyard," a poem which was to figure in an impending examination. It only occurs to me now what an appropriate poem for an undertaker to be studying. His family firm presided over the funerals of both our parents and still exists in Franklin Lakes, New Jersey.

Sometime around age thirteen or fourteen an older friend took a couple of classmates to visit the burlesque house of Union City, New Jersey, about fifteen miles from home. The minimum age for admission was supposed to be eighteen, but there was no trouble about getting in. It was billed as family entertainment, but certainly wasn't meant for my family. Of course I was astonished at what I saw and heard, thinly clad women (or were they naked?) and a succession of corny and horny jokes. I felt guilty about such obviously forbidden activity, but that did not preclude a masturbatory marathon on getting home.[6]

---

[6]   For a fascinating comparison between 1940s burlesque and modern burlesque techniques today, see Joan Acocella, "Take it Off: the New-burlesque Scene," *New Yorker* (May 13, 2013) p. 68-70.

Often thought an antidote to such evils, sports became a major preoccupation when I made the varsity teams in basketball, tennis, and golf at Eastern Academy, all in my junior and senior years. Playing varsity basketball entailed physical training each autumn, one year with cross-country running, the second with soccer. I enjoyed all of these immensely, even when our best player was suspended from the basketball team for inseminating a lovely cheerleader, not that anyone told us what was going on.

[*Coda: Let me interject here a legacy of my high school years. I played a lot of intramural basketball in college, continued as a starter at the University of Edinburgh where the team played in the equivalent of an industrial league with trips to Manchester, Glasgow, St. Andrews, and in Edinburgh; a club team at Marlboro College composed of sober faculty and stoned students; and then pickup games for fifteen years before running up and down the court became too much for me. Squash took over from tennis as my major sporting activity in Chicago when I was in graduate school, partly because it was the most efficient form of exercise to fit into very busy days. I once sprained an ankle in the finals of a tournament in Baltimore, and lying on the floor intoned a "sic transit gloria mundi." My squash days ended at Syracuse when my best partner and good friend, Ambassador Goodwin Cooke, became lame and when I began to experience early but unrecognized symptoms of ALS. Over a long life, sports were the only part of popular culture that I didn't reject completely, if only to have something to say to my barber. An occasional injury would remind me of something attributed to Berthold Brecht, that "where sport begins health ends."*]

There was also a high school chess club which I enjoyed, some good teachers I admired, a youthful reading of Freud for one of them, one early acquisition being the Modern Library edition of Freud. Daily chapel in the gym took about twenty minutes, kept to that length by the fact that we had no auditorium and had to stand through the short service, a welcome alternative to Sunday sermons. I dimly recollect playing clarinet in the band, a music appreciation course, and editing some kind of high school magazine but have no memory of either process or content. My first publication was a prize-winning essay on the importance of oil in our society, written for a contest sponsored by the American Petroleum Institute and published in a collection of winning essays pandering to the energy lobby.

Two acronyms were important to me in my youth, one from high school and one from college. The first was TULIP, a concise summation of Calvinist doctrine:

T	Total depravity (original sin, sinners from the get-go)
U	Unconditional election (God elects, regardless of merit)
L	Limited atonement (Jesus died only for the elect)
I	Irresistible grace (the elect cannot resist God's call)
P	Perseverance of the saints (once saved, always saved)

These five points were the foundation stones of the doctrine taught in my Christian Reformed high school in Prospect Park, New Jersey, called Eastern Academy. They were also the received wisdom of my home, my local church, and the Star of Hope Mission. Good works were all well and good but they proceeded from faith, not the other way around. What I made of all this when I was fifteen years old is hard to imagine now, over sixty years later. The number of my conversions and spiritual rebirths belied the final P of the perseverance dogma and confirmed the initial T. What strikes me now is that none of those points captures my enduring sense of determinism that paradoxically requires free choice.

The other acronym I learned from a history teacher in my first term at Wheaton College, a mnemonic device intended to embrace the entire world of knowledge, PERSIA:

P	Politics
E	Economics
R	Religion
S	Social
I	Intellectual
A	Aesthetics

I only include it here as a useful device that proved helpful to me in facing the empty pages of examination blue books. It's hard to imagine where language might fit in that topology, if at all, nor would it be much use in a Latin test.

We had a Latin teacher at Eastern Academy who one year failed two-thirds of his Latin students, including me, probably in my sophomore year. That luckily forced me to take typing as an elective the next semester, an extremely useful skill for the kind of career that developed. *Felix culpa*, as John Milton and my former teacher might say. That unforgiving Latinist, on the other hand, was dismissed the following summer. I became a very skilled typist until my finger dexterity began its recent decline.

While I was destined to attend Wheaton College, Illinois, in 1951, most of my Eastern Academy classmates went to Calvin College in Grand Rapids, Michigan, I being the only exception apart from those few who didn't go on to college. My younger brother Jim attended Wheaton for only one year, and curiously, the youngest brother Bob, chasing skirts, chose to go to Christian Reformed Calvin with some of his classmates from our same Christian school, by then renamed Eastern Christian High School and relocated to a more spacious suburban campus. (I was always glad that I antedated that move because I felt that Eastern Academy sounded much more dignified than Eastern Christian on my resumé.) Bob's experience of Calvin College, not unlike mine at Wheaton, was far from totally positive, but somehow we both received sound if inevitably incomplete educations.

I've usually found it easiest to describe what Wheaton represented by saying it was Billy Graham's school, and it described itself as a college for non-denominational independent Christians. I always had the impression that Graham had dropped out of Wheaton before graduating, but not knowing whether it was to do the Lord's work, or because he failed at the academic work. Jim doubts the whole story and thinks Graham graduated the year before our brother Paul.[7] Whatever the truth, Wheaton has treated him well with an honorary degree and by housing and supporting the Billy Graham Archives. The school motto was "Christo et ejus Regno," "For Christ and his Kingdom." Wheaton was not usually associated with the radical right conservatism of universities like Bob Jones, Liberty, or Pacific, but as the reader will see, it would eventually prove to be too conservative for me.

---

[7]   One Internet source shows a 1943 Anthropology B.A. from Wheaton.

David H. Stam

Summer Delights and Diversions
1942 to 1951

From age six to sixteen my summers were mainly spent at evangelical boy's camps, one in Newfoundland, New Jersey, when I was quite young, but most frequently at Deerfoot Lodge near Speculator, New York, in the Adirondacks. Deerfoot featured a lively combination of outdoor activities which fostered my sporting enthusiasms: softball, archery, volleyball, badminton, tennis, marksmanship, swimming and other water sports, including water polo and canoeing. Overnight canoeing trips complete with portages to Indian Lake, mountain hikes and sleeping overnight in fire towers in the Adirondack Mountains, visits to other camps for competitive games of softball or tennis (one as far as Utica), all exciting adventures to most of us.

A good deal of the camp's programs mimicked a variety of Native American rituals and stereotypes. Deer spotting by canoe by moonlight and flashlight was a favorite activity, as was the annual snipe hunt. Evening campfire activities featured marshmallow roasts, mystery and horror stories, songfests, and inevitably the relentless religious focus, the call to spiritual renewal and rededication. I was used to that and mostly enjoyed my summers of physical and spiritual immersion. From the perspective of sixty-five years later, I now wonder whether there were pedophiles among the many counselors living in rather intimate surroundings with young boys, though I never experienced any such untoward behavior nor imagine any.

Another noteworthy experience of my high school summers was a trip from New Orleans to Ecuador via the Panama Canal in 1950. My father and my two younger brothers (Jim and Bob) met me in New Orleans where we eventually boarded a banana freighter bound for Esmeraldas, Ecuador. I had just turned fifteen. Earlier that summer I travelled by car with my older sister, Ruth, and her husband Ladoit Stevens, from Paterson to Wheaton, before the Pennsylvania Turnpike had been completed. In Wheaton we spent some time getting acquainted with my future college town before Ruth put me on the Illinois Central's *City of New Orleans* for the long trip down the Mississippi through the heart of America. That in itself was an eye-opening experience, not least for my first encounter with segregated facilities.

As it happened my father had a legal client who owned a Norwegian shipping company called Mosvold Shipping which operated banana freighters for the United Fruit Company, and we were to travel on one of their ships that was scheduled to pick up bananas in Ecuador. According to Jim,[8] Dad had settled the estate of Martin Mosvold's wife and felt that Dad had not charged enough for his services (rather typical of Jacob when he remembered to bill his clients at all). I guess this voyage was intended to even the tally. The ship was delayed in sailing from New Orleans by at least a week, so we spent a very hot and muggy August week in a Canal Street hotel and saw the sights of the city, the French Quarter, the harbor, the cemeteries and churches, as well as a couple of minor league baseball games at Pelican Park where the segregated colored bleachers were somewhat wrenching to our northern sensibilities.

Finally we boarded the ship, possibly the *MS Mosdaal*, a wartime Liberty motor ship converted to commercial use. We headed down the Mississippi with a handful of fellow passengers, some students from Brooklyn, a Swedish family, a couple of missionaries who disembarked in Panama City, and a couple of men who seemed to look quizzically at my father's prayers at mealtimes. The last I may be imagining, but if so it is a conflation of many other embarrassing prayer experiences over the years, my father's way of publicly witnessing to the Gospel. On the bridge, the Captain allowed us to steer the ship after the pilot disembarked; below decks the Norwegian cook was happy to chat for hours about life aboard ship and in Norway, and we all enjoyed watching flying fish and the rhythm of the sea. All very comfortable and friendly, apart from the hurricane which hit us in the Gulf of Mexico; nonetheless we were in the Panama Canal a few days later, sailing from west to southeast for the Pacific and Ecuador.

We went ashore in the small coastal town of Esmeraldas and saw our first real glimpse of poverty: shabbily dressed natives, emaciated cattle on the sandy beach, stray dogs everywhere. We did take a trip inland to see a rather lush banana plantation. On our return the cargo was being

---

[8]   The family joke about Jim is that he should be writing all our memoirs since he has by far the best memory, if not total recall. Without him, Google, and some extensive family archives, this memoir would have been easier to write and much less accurate.

loaded and I remember a worker trying to steal through our porthole for whatever he might find. By our return to the Gulf of Mexico the excitement had worn off, the stems of bananas hanging on deck had lost their novelty, and we were ready to head home. One pilot of the TWA Constellation that took us from New Orleans back to Newark and home, proudly told us that the plane had cost one million dollars (when that was real money). Ironically, after this seemingly idyllic vacation, our father suffered one of his longer bouts of depression that left him dysfunctional and unable to work for a period of months, and the household itself was rather less cheerful than usual during my senior year.

Hardly anything of my final high school year sticks in memory except the basketball team and a few girls who paid a bit more attention to a varsity player. Pizza at the Tree Tavern in downtown Paterson after a basketball victory was the height of macho excitement, but girls like Anna Jane and Lois seemed to involve long waits for buses to Midland Park and back. A good night kiss in the rain must have seemed worth it at the time. Ready or not, college beckoned.

My last summer before college (1951), I spent as a waiter, clarinet player, and all-round gopher at Camp of the Woods on Lake Pleasant in Speculator, New York, quite near to Deerfoot, and another evangelical stronghold. Visiting evangelists preached twice a day in services that included quite a good wind band. A spectacular trumpet player, Art Vasquez, from Chicago's South Side, became a friend who enlivened some of the religious services with his bravura performances. I visited him in Chicago throughout my college years but then lost touch. I remember Camp of the Woods as rough and rustic, late in the season breaking ice on the water needed for morning ablutions. Recent visits to Camp of the Woods to see my older brother Juan, whose missionary life in Costa Rica depended to some extent on support from prosperous donors at the Camp, indicated a shift to a gospel of prosperity, not something Juan could ever be accused of espousing. In fact, he told me that in the summer of 2012 he heard at the now posh Camp of the Woods a sermon preaching against that materialistic departure from the Gospel.

A Rebel at Wheaton College, Illinois
September 1951 to June 1955

I don't recall ever making a decision to attend Wheaton College, that fundamentalist bastion of Midwestern education, for which I left behind the all-Dutch milieu of Eastern Academy. It was a given that I would go to Wheaton: all of my older brothers and sisters and virtually all our cousins had attended Wheaton so why not me. When I arrived my sister Mary was a junior, and John (now known as Juan, English having become his second language) was in the graduate school of divinity. I started as a political science major (with dreams of the Supreme Court), enlisted in the college band first as a clarinetist and for a short period as a single-reed bassoon player, toured with the band throughout the Midwest and east during the spring break, most Sundays taught Sunday School classes in black churches on Chicago's South Side, and joined the staff of the *Wheaton Record* as a cub reporter. Works performed by the band and played on tour included the Polka and Fugue from *Schwanda the Bagpiper* (Weinberger) and the overture to *La Forza del Destino* (Verdi), as well as the perennial *Hallelujah Chorus* (Handel). At the end of that academic year I realized I could not pursue both music and journalism as primary extra-curricular activities, and I reluctantly chose the latter, jettisoning both the band and the Sunday School assignment.

During my first year I roomed with a cool well-dressed preppie from Grand Rapids named John Heetderks in a resident hall not far from campus. Between two dormitory buildings (as they were then called) was a non-descript white house with the first floor apartment of a favorite English professor. I think because of our musical interests he made his place freely available to us, whether he was there or not. The big attraction was his 45rpm record collection, not a big one, but it did include Mendelssohn's *Italian Symphony*, Beethoven overtures, some Berlioz, Tchaikovsky's *Romeo and Juliet*, and similar works. It was another step in my musical development, becoming well-acquainted with various warhorses. John's parents once invited us to dinner in nearby St. Charles. John was scheduled to announce a modern music program on the college radio station that night, so when I got home I turned on the college station only to hear some complex works by "Jesse James." I learned later that John, not knowing how to pronounce Prokofiev or Shostakovich, just substituted the easiest name he could think of.

At the end of the semester I returned home to Paterson, and though my father wanted me to get a summer job at the *Morning Call*, the local paper where he had some connections, I refused in favor of two courses in American literature at Paterson State College in nearby Haledon (now called William Paterson University in Wayne, New Jersey). The teacher was a Miss Greenaway and the courses opened my eyes to a vast new forbidden area of experience, especially in the naturalistic literature of Crane, Dreiser, London, Upton Sinclair, and others. Melville was Miss Greenaway's particular *bête noir*, and she once said that if she ever did something truly reprehensible her self-afflicted punishment would be to make herself read *Moby Dick*. It took me thirty years to get over her idle comment but I've now read the book three or four times, always with new appreciation.

Because of my recalcitrance that summer, my father refused to let me use the family car to get a driver's license, even though I had just turned seventeen. Again I fought this seeming tyranny, so every day I biked up the long hill to Paterson State, enjoyed my classes, and had an easy ride home, downhill all the way. When I returned to Wheaton I found that I needed a license to perform some of my newspaper duties and so was able to use the *Record*'s wood-paneled station wagon to take my test in Illinois. The real reason for Dad's opposition was less likely his desire for me to work than his fear of secular education—these were my first classes in a non-Christian environment, and in retrospect he had reason to be concerned.

During the summer of 1953 I did get a paying job as a counselor at an evangelical boy's camp on Lake Winnipesaukee in New Hampshire. In addition to presiding over a cabin of perhaps a dozen boys, I was the canoeing instructor, and had other varied duties including spiritual ones at Brookwoods Camp for Boys which now advertises itself as the best Christian camp in New Hampshire. It may be, but my own experience there would not have made them boastful. I went to New Hampshire with a classmate and the English teacher who drove us east in his spiffy convertible and who took us touring to hot spots like Kennebunkport and Portsmouth on our days off. I now wonder about his suitability for that job as a counselor to a dozen boys. At the end of the following year Wheaton let him go, not I think because of the quality of his teaching but more likely because of a suspect effeminacy. In retrospect it does seem that he enjoyed the company of young men, but what did I know. We liked him and learned a lot from his mature influence.

After camp closed for the season some of the staff were asked to stay on to prepare the premises for winter. My Wheaton friends had to get back but I stayed on to earn a bit more money. What happened next was a torrid if unconsummated liaison with the camp nurse who at thirty-six was more than twice my age, my own Mrs. Robinson. I had turned eighteen six weeks earlier so I suppose it was at least legal. It all started with a massage after a hard day's labor. My own cabin was unoccupied and she had her own cabin with nursing quarters and a bedroom and few people around. We worked all day, but after supper had our petting trysts in secluded places, including a trip in the camp motor boat to Wolfeboro, a quiet and prosperous town then but in the summer of 2012 much in the news with George Romney's presidential candidacy. All this lasted only three or four days, a week at most, though we did meet at the George Washington Bridge early in September before I had to return to Wheaton for my junior year. On that occasion we drove up the west side of the Hudson to a public park north of Nyack where we saw the Tappan Zee Bridge under construction and already spanning the Hudson. Many years later, as Deirdre and I were passing that bridge on the New York-Syracuse Amtrak train, I said "My God, she'd be seventy years old by now." It then sounded very old indeed, but no longer. We did meet once more five or six years later, just before I met Deirdre, and the last I heard from her was a postcard from Buffalo saying "No little Stams!"

The *Wheaton Record* was my major preoccupation for three of my four college years. The paper attracted some of the more progressive students on campus. In a conservative college in a very conservative community (for example, House Republican Speaker, Dennis Hastert, was a Wheaton resident and graduate), in 1952 we were stuffing envelopes for Adlai Stevenson's unsuccessful Presidential bid, though we also covered Eisenhower's campaign visit to the Wheaton City Hall. We were cautiously critical of the Billy Graham culture and tradition of the place, and there was a certain degree of self-censorship by the editors. Though daily chapel was strictly compulsory, the editor of the *Record* had the authority to issue pink slips excusing staffers from chapel for editorial assignments, a perquisite that editors were careful to use without conspicuous abuse.

With excellent mentoring from the preceding Editors-in-Chief, Roger Kvam and Lorraine Hoey, I worked my way up the staff hierarchy and was elected by the Student Council as Editor in Chief for 1953-54. My term covered the Spring and Fall semesters of 1954, the latter intended to stretch into my final year. That spring term of 1954 was one of much adrenalin and little sleep. The weekly paper was printed in the college town of Naperville, about ten miles south of Wheaton. The editor's duties included two mid-week evening trips to deliver copy, assist getting it into type, help on the composing stone, adjust headlines, and put the paper to bed for Thursday delivery. The whole experience was my introduction to the mysteries of printing: selecting type sizes for various purposes, typesetting (on Linotype machines), design, page composition and makeup, and then the actual printing. It was part of my fundamental education for a life dealing with a wider world of books and print.

One of my editorials railed against apathy on campus, on one occasion illustrated by the poor attendance at a Lieder recital by Eleanor Steber. Subsequently I noticed that at both Johns Hopkins and Syracuse, student apathy was a recurrent motif in undergraduate journalism. Another editorial entitled "The Free Enterprise of Ideas" contended that under Senator Joe McCarthy's House Un-American Activities Committee the mere expression of ideas was an un-American activity and quoted a Michigan student saying "We can beat the radicals—in the sunlight." That editorial was picked up by a national student news service, *Parade of Opinion*, and given a new title, "The Attack on Academic Freedom." If that wasn't enough to upset the College administration, the final issue of the spring semester of 1954 really did. In it I published "An Open Letter to the Editor" by a staff member named David Carder, causing all hell to break loose. The letter attacked a local Red-baiter and McCarthyite named Edgar C. Bundy, class of 1938, and a former reporter for the *Wheaton Record*. Colonel Bundy was a military man, a militant Baptist minister, who ran a non-profit foundation in Wheaton "to fund his world travels preaching against Communism."[9] Carder's piece pulled no punches:

---

9   See http://a2z.my.wheaton.edu/alumni/edgar-bundy Wheaton History A to Z).

Through ignorance, or willful disregard of the facts, this man has condemned innocent Americans as communists on mere suspicions. A master of taking material out of context, he will invade a town condemning unsuspecting citizens with a briefcase of isolated facts gotten up by others, and without previous knowledge whatsoever of the background of the appointed victims. To call anyone a Red on information foreign to the accuser until the night before the accusations are made, is evidence of a cheap lust for notoriety or pitiful ignorance.

Others might be mentioned from this group, but the example of one of Wheaton's 'true sons' most concerns us. Fundamentalist leaders throughout the U.S. have spoken out in condemning these self-appointed teachers of discord . . . . Billy Graham has regularly attacked what he calls "ultrafundamentalism." Graham adds that "these dissensions in the ranks of evangelical Christians are a stench in the nostrils of God."

When called on the carpet in President V. Raymond Edman's Office, I defended publication of the letter and stood behind the masthead statement that opinions expressed in letters were not necessarily those of Wheaton College or of the *Wheaton Record*. He would have none of it and summarily fired me from the Editor's post, following up with a letter to my father, with a long apologia for his action, a lament on the difficulties of such decisions, and his assurance from the Dean that I was taking the sacking constructively. My father was good enough to send a letter of protest to President Edman, invoking freedom of speech, but it addressed a dead issue as far as Edman was concerned. (By chance, in my early years at Wheaton, Edman's son David became a friend and musical influence; in the basement of the President's house David introduced me with great excitement to the dissonance in Beethoven's *Third Symphony*. He went on to Divinity School and lived in New York when I was there in the early 60s and he eventually became an Episcopal priest in Scarsdale.)

I did get some praise for my editorship and even received a surprising letter on May 14, 1954, a few days before I was sacked, from the Director of the Wheaton Student Union, the Student Center where the *Record* had its office:

Dear Dave: Just a note to tell you how much we appreciate your keeping the RECORD office clean. This is the first time in the history of the M.S.C. that that office is orderly by student initiative and we want to commend you for it. Thanks so much for your cooperation.

There you can see the makings of a very proper ACL (anal compulsive librarian).

Curiously, I had misremembered much of the newspaper incidents until reading some of the documentation from my files. Although the Open Letter was mostly Dave Carder's, I now remember editing it with him, I imagine to strengthen the "stick it to them" message. I also now see myself at that time, aged eighteen, something of a puzzle that I can't understand or relate to: an odd combination of skeptical but believing fundamentalist, a left-leaning liberal, and an aspiring Navy officer with a clear trajectory for the next five years of military service.

Several kudos for my principled stance on free speech from a few professors and students were welcome, but I didn't much care. I had little to gain from another semester as Editor and had already learned as much as I possibly could from my work on the paper. I didn't try to get fired but it seemed a good opportunity to turn to other things. As a junior I had switched from political science to an English major, thanks to an inspiring professor named Clyde Kilby, a thoughtful and plain-speaking Southerner who taught a stimulating course in biography (Augustine, Montaigne, Cellini, Johnson, Boswell, etc.). He was also dedicated to the work of C.S. Lewis and his circle, and thanks to his efforts, the Wheaton College Library now has a major collection of materials on Lewis, Dorothy Sayers, Owen Barfield, Chad Walsh, Charles Williams, J.R.R. Tolkien, and others of that Oxford school.

Apparently I had been mulling over the change in majors for some time before taking Kilby's course; when I talked to him about the change, I remember telling him that I had only one problem, that I didn't particularly like poetry. "Not to worry, we'll take care of that." He was a kind and hospitable man, with a gentle southern drawl, and, I now remember, a fisherman who introduced me to Izaac Walton.

My freshman roommate, John Heetderks, was a jazz lover who for a time led me in that direction. In my junior year I wrote a paper for Kilby's biography class on *Really the Blues*, the autobiography of Mezz Mezzrow, a jazz clarinetist. That class was probably the single most inspiring course of my educational life, opening up new vistas just as Paterson State had. It's worth noting that to write on a jazz subject was considered quite innovative if not subversive at Wheaton, but Kilby encouraged that kind of unorthodoxy. After his junior-year course I wanted to devote my senior year to studies of poetry, fiction, criticism, and biography, and thanks to the end of my editorship I had more time to devote to studies.

Army ROTC was available on the Wheaton campus, but always a bit out of step, I joined the US Naval Reserve in 1953, attended weekly drills as an apprentice submariner at Navy Pier in Chicago, and spent two weeks in submarine school in New London, including a couple of near-disastrous dives in Long Island Sound, during the 1954 spring break, very near to where my future wife spent summers in Madison, Connecticut. Eight-week summer sessions at Officer Candidate School in Newport, RI, following my junior and senior years, would make me a Navy Ensign and commit me to a four-year tour of duty. During that winter of 1954-55 I began wearing glasses, something that would wreak havoc with those plans.

Because I changed majors late I felt the need to catch up and in each senior semester I took an additional literature course at the downtown Chicago campus of Northwestern University to supplement Wheaton's more slender offerings. One course taught by a Mr. Robinson that made a strong impression dealt with Victorian literature, especially Browning and the narcissistic hypocrisy depicted in "The Bishop Orders his Tomb at Saint Praxed's Church." Because of the time constraints, these courses would have been impossible if I were still editing the *Record*. After three years of editorial preoccupations and mediocre grades, I could at last devote myself to my studies and my senior-year grades were at least decent if not exemplary.

My roommate during the latter part of college was Lennart Pearson, a somewhat crusty transfer from City College in New York, with a satiric sense of humor and a superb editorial touch. When I was Editor of the *Record*, he was Editor of *Kodon*, the student literary magazine. His 1954 April Fool's issue was a spoof on the College yearbook, the *Tower*, in which pages of student pictures were replaced by pictures of various primates, the President's picture inverted, the Table of Contents beginning with Genesis, and other irreverent spoofs on sanctimony. He too ran afoul of President Edman, and unlike me, was actually suspended from the College for a couple of weeks and like me, removed from his editorship, I suppose for representing the College in an unfavorable light. For us, we now had a shared badge of honor. I recently obtained a copy of the 1955 *Tower*. It was full of the pieties Leonard was lampooning, but I was also bemused to find nothing about me in it, not a picture nor any reference at all. That I can't explain—perhaps I had just lost interest and had mentally moved on.

By this time in my senior year, I had little patience with the Wheaton tradition of revival week each semester when we had morning and evening religious services, attendance required twice a day for the whole week. Since I no longer had access to the pink excuse slips, I had to go, but I usually sat in the back pretending to read a book called *Ethics for Unbelievers*. One morning the German professor sitting behind me tapped me on the shoulder and told me to stop reading and pay attention to the speaker. I responded with "you can lead a horse to water . . . ." That afternoon Professor Gerstung called my brother John to tell him about my miscreant behavior. John's good advice to me was to cool it.

One thing neither Lennart nor I dared tackle editorially was the so-called Wheaton College Pledge, a list of proscribed activities which every student annually pledged to honor, although we were released from the pledge during summers. The proscriptions included none of the Ten Commandments nor anything about sex, but did demand abstinence from dancing, smoking, drinking, secret societies, cards and other games of chance, gambling in any form, theatre, opera, ballet, motion pictures, and just about anything that might have the smell and look of sin, "the stench in the nostrils of God." Brother Jim, who survived only one year at Wheaton, tells me that music majors could get waivers to attend opera— one wonders what they would have made of Mozart's libidinous plots.

I was fairly faithful to the pledge, and recall only a few personal violations. One was the movie of *The Caine Mutiny* for which some friends and I sneaked over to Des Plaines, Illinois. More telling was a performance in Chicago of a ballet of Rimsky-Korsakov's *Scheherazade*. I was on a double date with a beautiful junior named Ruth and that night we all had the same epiphany: "Oh, now we see why they won't let us watch that sexy stuff." But sex wasn't even on the pledge. One of my New York girlfriends from Wheaton, could have been technically observant when at Wheaton she had slept with our ethics professor, or so she claimed. (In my archives I have now unearthed a very complete set of my typed lecture notes of the Ethics course I took in 1955 with the said professor.) Of the whole list of sins and misdemeanors on the pledge, after sixty years, I retain my hostility only to gambling and secret societies, and have added my own prejudices: against jewelry and watches; messages on clothing; split infinitives, and rhetorical euphemisms such as passed away, moving forward, circle back, on the ground, thanks for having me, and other such cant, most of which has gone virile. The takeaway should be: please take away the takeaway. Like OK? Most of my other prejudices are matters of taste or aesthetics, certain composers with Wagner near the summit of my opprobrium, and almost all elements of popular culture except sports.

As I look back on my college years I am amazed at the variety of jobs I held in order to make a little money during periods of paupery: flower salesman (mainly corsages for college events such as the ersatz class proms sans dancing), railroad-crossing gateman, taxi dispatcher, waiter, library janitor, church maintenance worker, golf caddy, Christmas postal worker, and several others lost in memory. I even wrote occasionally for a fundamentalist Sunday school paper published in Chicago called *Power* where I published a few sports columns about Wheaton athletes for $5 or $10 per piece. One of my closest younger colleagues at Syracuse, Randy Ericson, told me years later that the weekly distribution of *Power* in his pre-teens was one of the delights of his suburban Chicago Sunday School in Uncle Neil's church.

During the Christmas holidays of 1954-55, I once again defied my father who wanted me to come home for the holidays. I chose instead to join a friend (Frank Yuan) on a trip to the west coast in his Nash Rambler in which two could sleep fairly comfortably. To share the cost we had some other passengers returning to their homes in California. I remember hearing Schoenberg's *Transfigured Night* while driving across the desolate but moonlit Utah landscape. From that same night I recall waking up in the back seat with my arms around a girl in whom I had no interest but who had conceived an interest in me from our cozy encounter. Our visit to her beautiful home in Berkeley became a rather awkward one.

Among other friends, we visited our former Wheaton English teacher who had relocated to Portland, Oregon, where he taught high school English. Crater Lake, Yosemite, and the Rose Bowl Parade were some high points of our trip. We heard the San Francisco Orchestra in their grand Opera House doing Albert Roussel's *Third Symphony*, a new discovery for me. I have the disquieting feeling that at the end of the trip I owed some money to Frank which I never repaid, probably straining our friendship. He had relatives in New York's Chinatown whom I once visited with him; last I read of him in an alumni magazine in 2012 was that he was still involved and supportive of the College. I was completely broke at the end of our trip and, too proud to ask my father for money, I spent my last semester with little food except what brother Jim (during his single year at Wheaton) could cadge from the dining hall, and free meals from the Bristols, a friendly and generous family in town, whose sons enjoyed Italian operas by what their father called "those spaghetti twirlers."

Music became an increasing preoccupation during the Wheaton years; Rafael Kubelik and then Fritz Reiner led the Chicago Symphony Orchestra during my four years, and I went into the city quite often. I remember one concert that consisted of Brahms *Second Symphony* and Tchaikovsky's *Sixth*, another when Isaac Stern broke a string in the middle of Tchaikovsky's *Violin Concerto*. He went offstage for a moment and he came back on stage, whispered something to Reiner and announced, "Due to the vicissitudes of wood and string, the show must sometimes stop; but the show must go on," with which he lifted his bow and they all came in on the recapitulation. My brother Jim was there and has helped shape my memory of that event.

Later when Deirdre and I lived in Chicago from 1967 to 1973, the CSO conductors were Jean Martinon and Georg Solti. It was in my experience always a superb ensemble. Particular concerts that remain in my memory are a *B Minor Mass*, Mahler's *Sixth Symphony*, and Jacqueline du Pré in the Dvorak *Cello* Concerto. The Fourth Presbyterian Church on Chicago's Michigan Avenue was another refuge of good choral and organ music that I visited as often as possible while I was an undergraduate. Fifteen years later our three children attended preschool in that same church.

New College, University of Edinburgh
August 1955 to November. 1956

I was still only nineteen years old on graduation from Wheaton in 1955 and destined for a naval commission and four years of active duty. Halfway through my second summer of Officer Candidate School in

Newport, Rhode Island, the naval Bureau of Medicine decided that my defective eyesight disqualified me from becoming a naval officer. Through a series of purely aleatoric happenings, I ended up a month later on the liner *United States* headed to the UK via Southampton and to New College, the Divinity School of the University of Edinburgh. Here is how it happened.

In late July of 1955, I was about to take an examination on naval boilers when I was summoned to the office of the Commandant of the School. Wondering what dreadful breach of discipline I might have committed, I cooled my heels for what seemed a long time before an orderly ushered me into the Commandant's office. His surprisingly apologetic, almost deferential message was that I was to be dismissed from the program because of deficient eyesight and unfortunately would have to leave immediately. He appeared embarrassed that the Bureau of Medicine had taken so long to review my physical tests from the beginning of the summer, especially since I had started wearing glasses that winter. Apparently concerned that I would react adversely or even suicidally to this news, he insisted that I pay a visit to the base chaplain for counseling before I departed. Frankly, I was relieved not to be taking an exam in naval boilers and happy to be released from the horrid regimen of OCS, but I followed my orders before heading home.

The chaplain, noting my religious background and my college degree from Wheaton, pointed out that I need not despair over the lost gold stripes but could easily become a naval chaplain and thereby a naval officer. All I needed was a divinity degree—there were plenty of openings. At that moment, I didn't take this too seriously and feeling liberated, I drove home to Paterson on a laconic summer day on coastal US Route 1 before the Connecticut Turnpike existed. Although I was relieved at my emancipation, I was clueless as to the impending future for which I had had a four-year commitment.

When I got home I contacted my former roommate Lennart Pearson, then living in the Bronx, but planning to attend divinity school at a Presbyterian seminary in Columbus, Georgia. He wasn't completely happy about that choice and was hoping to make a tour of Presbyterian seminaries in Ontario and Quebec, looking for a better alternative. When hearing of my newfound freedom, Lennart invited me to join his quest, with the further hope that I could borrow a family car. My long-suffering father's condition on the auto loan was that we stop en route to visit his friend, the Rev. Herbert Mekeel (1904-1980), minister of the First Presbyterian Church in Schenectady, New York, someone he knew through various evangelical organizations, including the China Inland Mission. We did stop in Schenectady and found Mekeel a sophisticated, urbane, sympathetic, and scholarly man; a 2007 Canadian newspaper writing about Mekeel's ministry called him "one of the most remarkable Presbyterian ministers of the Twentieth Century," and as recently as 2011 Mekeel Christian Academy in Scotia, NY, was named in his honor, twenty years after his death. At the time of our visit in August 1955 he was pursuing doctoral studies at the University of Edinburgh, work he never finished. For us as we began our journey, Mekeel was the consummate host who advised my friend on must-see schools, dined us at his country club, and asked only that we return to Schenectady after our tour of the Canadian divinity schools in Montreal, Toronto, Hamilton, Kingston, and in London, Western Ontario.

It was an interesting trip on which I was a rather passive but interested chauffeur. One recollection of how things were then and have changed completely was when we were sitting on a low wall next to the McGill University Library. A security guard demanded that we put our shoes back on or leave the campus immediately. On the other hand, we also went skinny dipping somewhere on the fairly deserted north shore of Lake Ontario without being harassed. When we returned to Schenectady a week or so later, it was Lennart who gave his reactions to the various schools. After that review, Mekeel dropped something of a bombshell by telling Lennart that those were all fine schools, but what he really should consider was the Divinity School of the University of Edinburgh, known as New College, where Mekeel was studying. After hearing a list of advantages of that plan, Lennart agreed to pursue the possibility. Then Mekeel asked if I would also be interested and I had to admit that it sounded intriguing, especially given my lack of any other plans for my life. Not to prolong this story, a telegraph wire went to Edinburgh that evening reading "ADMIT LENNART PEARSON AND DAVID STAM FOR FALL TERM ASAP STOP REFERENCES TO FOLLOW STOP".

We were admitted to New College the next day before heading back to Paterson and the Bronx. It was late August and plans had to be expedited, reservations made, passports acquired, and funding settled. (Tuition was not to be a problem: £50 for all three terms.) Three weeks later we were aboard the *SS United States* sailing to Southampton, along with a lot of Rhodes Scholars and Fulbright recipients. While approaching Southampton at twilight I was standing on deck with another passenger who told me to look carefully at the overcast sun because it would be the last sight of it for another six months. In my naiveté I took him seriously and a few months later I was relieved that the sun, although low in the sky all winter, did show itself occasionally in auld reckie. The man's name was Anthony Haythorne-Thwaite and I somehow fancy that he is the English poet, Anthony Thwaite, who later became executor of Philip Larkin's estate. I suppose it's possible or memory faulty.

New College was distinguished by a fine faculty, close connections to continental "neo-orthodox" theologians (Karl Barth, Rudolph Bultmann, Emil Brunner, and Oscar Cullman, for example), and a diverse international student body. Martin Buber and Dietrich Bonhoeffer were two of the New College heroes of the time. Before I left for Scotland I received a letter from my very conservative Uncle Peter warning me to be vigilant against the wiles of those neo-orthodox theologians who so distort the Word of God.[10]

While I enjoyed most of the courses at Edinburgh (except Hebrew which I was unable to master before quitting), their cumulative effect on me was not the result intended. A fascinating course in comparative religion, taught by the Principal of the College, Professor John Baillie, created enough doubt about my own evangelical beliefs that it planted the seeds of agnosticism, a view that has remained with me ever since. What I remember of Baillie's lectures in this course was a tolerance of all religions that was quite new to me (Uncle Peter was right—this was dangerous stuff for the dogmatists). I began to see one's religion as what I called "the luck of the draw," a determination made by where you were born and in what circumstances. Here was a real turning point, the root if not the beginning of anti-dogmatism as my personal dogma, although not without some surviving prejudices.

---

[10]   Uncle Peter once gave my brother Jim and me a tour of Faith Seminary, an evangelical divinity school near Philadelphia, then in the mansion of the Harry Elkins Widener Estate, he of Titanic fame. On the tour Uncle Peter showed us a safe in one of the library rooms where seditious works like Karl Barth's *Church Dogmatics* were kept, a danger to young students or the faithful. T. F. Torrance and other New College faculty translated some of those volumes.

[*Coda: a friendly reader doubts these remarks, arguing that, by my own account in this memoir, I show plenty of evidence of skepticism about the received religion I grew up with. He argues that Baillie's course was not the root but the flowering of my developing agnosticism. Brother Jim concurs and says it was for both of us a part of the rebellion before the break. I admit to the mixed messages, and will only say by way of comment if not rebuttal that it was my road to Damascus moment (Saul must have been going in the opposite direction), when it became clear what I did not believe, though with much yet to discover and ponder. It's too easy to use a* post hoc, propter hoc *argument here. What I would say for those relatives and friends who continue to pray for me is that though I tried very hard when young, I have never experienced the presence of God that they attest, either mentally, spiritually, or metaphorically before or since the Edinburgh year.*]

By the end of the first term it was fairly obvious that divinity was not my calling, so I spent much of my time in the next two terms taking the most interesting of the divinity courses while auditing English literature classes, reading all of Dostoyevsky, playing on the University basketball team, and forming wider musical tastes during that Mozart bicentennial year. On January 26, 1956, Lennart and I were singing with the University Orchestra and Chorus in performing Mozart's *Requiem* in the Royal Usher Hall on his 200th birthday. I could scarcely hide my tears during the "tuba mirum." On a later concert program we sang Vaughan Williams's *Dona nobis pacem* to poems of Whitman. Many of my meticulous lecture notes from both divinity and literature courses are now in the Archives at the University of Edinburgh.

We had met another passenger on the *United States*, a single man who invited the two of us to visit him for a weekend in Glasgow, a visit which we duly made that fall. To anyone who knows Glasgow today, the then blighted city of that time, almost sixty years ago, would seem intolerably poor and bereft of culture and humane touches—at least that is what we perceived from our visit. The man lived in a small apartment across the road from a cemetery and crematorium where we took walks on the two days we were there. Lennart and I shared his one bedroom. I doubt that it occurred to either of us that the gentleman might be gay, we were so clueless on such matters. Such are the dubious advantages of constant indoctrination or the avoidance of taboo topics.

During the Christmas holidays an American friend (a basketball teammate) and I drove to London to enjoy the city's offerings. In addition to the usual sightseeing, the trip included the Peter Brook production of Samuel Beckett's *Waiting for Godot* at the Criterion Theatre on Piccadilly Circus, quite an emotional experience for a disaffected divinity student. There was also Shakespeare's *Henry V* with Paul Scofield at the Old Vic (or was it Richard Burton?), a theatre I came to know well years later. The Scottish New Year and Hogmanay seemed rather tame after London.

Shortly after I returned to Edinburgh following my decision to drop out, I had a visit from Rev. Mekeel. I had to tell him my decision to withdraw and that the Christian ministry was clearly not to be my calling. He was not the least bit censorious or disapproving and I remember to this day his comment: "Whatever you do in life you will always be grateful for the values and work ethic given you by your parents." That may be partially true, and I have often felt as a librarian that I was something of a missionary whose message centered around the "word" if not the "Word." In retrospect I can see that despite the antipathy I often had towards my father, he was also the model for my own workaholic *modus operandi* (and possibly of my somewhat neglectful parenting). Edinburgh was in many ways a depressing but mind-expanding year for a late adolescent steeped in Dostoyevsky, questioning long-held beliefs, open to new experience, but still a churchgoer and teetotaler.

On the spring break a Swiss friend and fellow New College student, Christian Zangger, and I went hitchhiking around northern Scotland for a couple of weeks in late March. On only one short stretch in the highlands were we compelled to take public transport—forced to take a train from somewhere between Fort William and Mailag. Our itinerary included Glasgow, Loch Lomond, Mailag, Skye, Kyle of Lochalch, Loch Ness, Inverness, Aberdeen, St. Andrews, and Dundee. At a youth hostel in Inverness I pontificated to a group of South Asians on how a Roman Catholic could never be elected President of my country, less than five years before Kennedy was elected. My ignorance of US international relations, especially with South Asia, was also amply demonstrated.

Christian and I were dirty and unshaven by the time we arrived at the Seamen's Institute in Dundee, but determined to have a decent meal though quartered in that seedy, smelly hostelry. In a mirrored second floor restaurant (on what locals would call the first floor) we looked around and saw nothing but our scruffy selves, and proceeded to uncontrollable laughing fits. I returned to Dundee with Deirdre fifty years later to see the Discovery Center and Robert Falcon Scott's *Discovery* ship, famous for his first Antarctic expedition. I've never returned to northern Scotland but beautiful images of soft browns and grays against brilliant blue waters before the verdant spring remain.

[*Coda: fifty years later Deirdre and I visited Christian and his wife just south of Zürich on the west side of the lake. He had become a parish minister on Lake Konstanz soon after leaving Edinburgh. We found him delightfully engaging, with our left-leaning sensibilities, and a real wit. In 1957 he had written me from Konstanz that his lake was land locked and he was sorry my battleship would not be able to visit. In 2006 he told us that I was the only person he'd ever met who used aerosol deodorant, apparently on our Scottish trip, something I don't recall at all. It seems a pity that that friendship was allowed to languish. I remember him as a frail, Kafkaesque figure but he was thriving when we saw him in his seventies fifty years later.*]

For some reason now unclear, I decided to spend the short final term of the year on my own, deserting Lennart in the New College residence on the Mound, and taking a room and meals at a shabby £10 per week residence in Portobello on the North Sea coast east of Edinburgh where I was allowed one bath a week and sixteen meals, excluding weekday lunches. It was the town where Mendelssohn had stayed during a visit to Scotland and where he wrote *Fingal's Cave* and began work on his third symphony, the *Scottish Symphony*. I suspect that by that time Lennart and I had begun to get on one another's nerves but we remained friends for several years before we lost touch. He took a second year at New College, finished divinity school at Union Seminary in Richmond, Virginia, and took a parish in Winchester where I visited him in June 1959. He married our Wheaton classmate Carol Landon, daughter of the author of *Anna and the King of Siam*, Margaret Landon of Washington, DC, and of a Southeast Asian US diplomat.

Looking back to our Wheaton days, I remember that etched in the slats of the double bunk bed that Lennart and I shared were the immortal words, "Len loves Carol and hates Bartok." During our summer breaks we attended a few concerts at Lewisohn Stadium at City College in northern Manhattan, seeing some legendary performers of that era including Leopold Stokowski.

Eventually his study of liturgical works led Lennart to bibliography and thus to library school, and from there to the librarianship of Presbyterian College in Clinton, South Carolina, where he spent the rest of his career as librarian and professor of religion, retiring in 1997.

He is now Professor Emeritus of Library Science and Religion, a unique combination so far as I know, although plenty of Christian divines ended up in librarianship. He had an excellent voice and musical ear but I think never came around to appreciate the twentieth-century music that I increasingly enjoyed after moving to New York.

After the final short term at Edinburgh, I went back to London en route to Europe, and on May 14, 1956, I saw the London premiere of Vaughan Williams' *Symphony No. 8*, with the composer himself in the Royal box of the Royal Festival Hall. I retain to this day a deep appreciation of that symphony, first heard with Sir John Barbirolli conducting the Hallé orchestra. I spent three months in the summer of 1956 on the continent, visiting Amsterdam and Hilversum, Zürich and the Alps, Hamburg and northern Germany, before returning to Edinburgh, where I took in a few events of the recently established Edinburgh Festival, including an exceptionally interesting Georges Braque exhibit, and returned home aboard the *Carinthia* from Liverpool to Montreal, now without a deferment and facing the military draft.

That summer included a lengthy visit with relatives in Hilversum, a Jewish uncle named Leo Blom and his warm and generous wife, actually my father's cousin.[11] Leo was a Jew who survived the war in Holland in hiding, and after the war resumed his position as violist in the Dutch Radio Philharmonic. He took me to rehearsals, Concertgebouw concerts (John Browning playing Brahms Second), and *Fidelio* at the Holland Festival, plus museums, canals, windmills, and countryside trips to the seaside and the Zuiderzee.

---

[11]   Here are my brother Jim's notes about the Bloms: "Leo Blom married Dad's cousin (Katrina? Kaete? Stam), the one who, while in fifth grade or so, wrote a letter to her American cousins, one page in Dutch, one in French, one in German, one in English. He was a prominent violist and friend of Hindemith. I may have misunderstood what he said, but I believe Hindemith dedicated one of his viola sonatas (or something) to him. I tried accompanying him on their piano at home, but I was not up to what he had in mind. When I was there he was first chair with the Netherlands Radio Philharmonic in Hilversum. I went to a recording session about which they were all excited, because the conductor was a young Dutchman who had been abroad for a while—Bernard Haitink. They did the Shostakovich Piano Concerto #1 with trumpet and a Haydn symphony.

Next I traveled by train from Amsterdam to Zürich, incredulous that the beautiful German landscape had so recently been ravaged by war. In Switzerland I visited my Swiss travelling companion from New College, the aforementioned Christian Zangger, who lived with his violinist mother in Erlenbach, a small village northeast of Zürich on Lake Zürich. Christian loaned me his bicycle and planned for me a two-week roundabout through the Swiss mountains, the idea being one day's arduous climb "über die Grimsal," and then gently downhill the rest of the way, staying at Swiss youth hostels, and meeting countless fellow travelers. What was not calculated in the planning was a strong *Gegenwind*, coming up the Rhone valley in the opposite direction, slowing me down drastically. Nonetheless, the camaraderie and even the joint chores of the Jugendherberge were a delight. After my return, there was swimming in the lake just beyond the home of Carl Jung, or was it Thomas Mann? They both had lived in Küsnacht, the next village on the Lake. Mrs. Zangger gave a violin recital in a tiny country church near Erlenbach—cowbells joined the accompaniment—the program still lurks in some unsorted archive.

The final month of the summer involved three weeks of physical labor at a Lutheran retreat house in Schleswig-Holstein on the Grosser Plöner See near Kiel. Music was intertwined with all these activities, including an organ recital in Telemann's church in Lübeck and some Bach cantatas, possibly in Hamburg or Kiel. At the end of those few weeks I took a train-ferry from Denmark to Newcastle and train back to Edinburgh. After collecting a trunk full of my worldly goods plus the books accumulated during the year, I took a night train to Liverpool in time to catch the *Carinthia* in early September. When I arrived on board I found a telegram from Lennart simply saying "With love stony hearts will bleed. George Herbert."

It was a delightful trip up the St. Lawrence (one third of the entire voyage) with both solitude and congenial passengers, some delightful emigrants headed to the big sky country of western Canada. Brothers Jim and Bob met me in Montreal with my mother's car. We called home from Plattsburg, and when I told my mother that I had a beard she said that she had a razor. She never did like my beard, though Dad defended it. It came off and did not reappear until Antarctica, over a year later.

By the time I returned home I had developed a rather severe case of eucharophobia, or fear of the sacrament of communion as the Protestants called it. It wasn't the literal or metaphorical issue of transubstantiation that disturbed me. Rather it was that I had been so long drilled in human unworthiness (the T of TULIP without the I of Irresistible Grace) to approach the communion table, a logical extension of the doctrine of total depravity. I was rapidly losing my faith in all of these beliefs, while still maintaining a measure of respect for the family religion. The easiest way to deal with the issue, although very distressing to my parents, was to stop church attendance altogether, which I did when I returned home. Years later I found a short story by Glenway Westcott in his *Goodbye, Wisconsin* about a fellow sufferer of this phobia. That was a comfort.

I've repressed the details of the trauma for my parents on my return, my refusal to attend church, my depressed attitude as I waited for a plan to develop, and my final decision to volunteer for the draft through the US Naval Reserve. Around that time my father wrote to a friend, in a letter I happened to see much later, that he "didn't see that a year's divinity school did me one iota of good, and had made me a pretty unhappy person."

Although 1955-56 was a very formative year for me, helping me emerge from late adolescence and from the sheltered cocoon of our religion, it was still difficult for me and must have been very hard for my parents—and some subsequent events surely made it even more difficult for them. I think now that I was much harder on them than vice versa. I wonder if it could have been different. They were both loving and supportive parents to the end, however disappointed and disapproving at times of their three youngest sons.

The Naval Interlude
Thanksgiving 1956 to Thanksgiving 1958

Having lost my draft deferment when I dropped out of divinity school, I entered the US Navy as an enlisted man, in effect drafted for two years' service from Thanksgiving Eve of 1956 to Thanksgiving Eve of 1958, two years which included duty as a journalist on a battleship (*USS Iowa*), two cruisers (*USS Northampton* and *USS Galveston*), briefly on a destroyer, and three months on a cargo ship (*USS Wyandot*).

The two years began at the Brooklyn Navy Yard; for over a month I commuted with some fellow sailors from Paterson, performed menial duties including night parking guard just outside the base, and went through all the introductory rituals:

How much education you got?
Seventeen years.
Bullshit! Don't go that high!

My orders came through for the *USS Iowa* to serve as a seaman and journalist apprentice, assigned to the Admiral's staff of Commander Battleship and Cruiser Atlantic (COMBATCRULANT), commanded by Rear Admiral Lewis M. Parks. We boarded the *USS Iowa* (BB64) in Norfolk for an initial cruise to the Mediterranean with the Sixth Fleet. Known as X Division, the Admiral's staff moved with him when he temporarily flew his flag aboard the flagship, in this case the *Iowa*; as such he ruled the fleet but not the ship. His staff was separate from the ship's crew, and thus we were something of an elite class aboard ship, along with some Marines assigned to the Admiral, all of us assured of our superiority to the hundreds of ordinary swabbies among the 3000 sailors aboard. Essentially my work was naval public relations, with some duties on the flag bridge where the Admiral reigned. Above him, well above the Iowa's 16-inch guns, was the navigation bridge where the ship's captain was in charge. We had a spacious journalism office, complete with portholes, on the main deck on this long but low-slung and very sleek and beautiful ship.

Our first stop was Gibraltar, to me a fascinating place, evocative of my recent time in Britain less than six months before. There I had a harrowing experience in a local cinema. I had gone with Allan Lehtis, a naturalized Estonian immigrant and ship's artist, to a movie about an air battle of WWII. It was quite a tense picture and at one point I heard Allan breathing heavily. I looked at him and saw that he was sweating profusely, had a vacant gaze in his eyes, and was breathing with difficulty. I suspected it might be an epileptic seizure so I put my right arm around his shoulder and with my left hand tried to make sure his tongue wasn't making breathing impossible. After an agonizingly long time but probably no more than a few minutes he returned to normal, I removed my arm, and we watched the end of the movie.

We never talked about the incident, but later that summer four of us on liberty in Port of Spain, Trinidad, were having some refreshment at a resort hotel near the city square. As I looked at Allan across the table, that same vacant stare came into his eyes, and for ten minutes I desperately tried to get his attention until he began to recognize where he was. Again nothing was said. If we had talked, I imagined that he would be embarrassed and also that revealing his condition might threaten his naval standing and might even cause a dishonorable discharge for concealing his disease. Like me he moved to New York after the Navy, had a career in advertising illustration, made a name as an artist and muralist, and moved to Maine where he died in 2006. I did some cat sitting for him and his wife in New York in the early 1960s and we kept in touch until we both left New York after 1964.

The three-month battleship cruise was during a time of peace, and we showed the flag in Valencia, Palma de Majorca, Palermo, Istanbul, and Piraeus, the port of Athens. In all my Navy days I was seasick only once and that was while at anchor on a gently rolling sea near Valencia after a meal of SOS (aka shit on a shingle), a dreadful nautical delicacy of creamed chipped beef.

I have no desire to turn these memoirs into a travel journal, but the high points of the Mediterranean cruise for me were in Palma de Majorca seeing the fog enshrouded cathedral on sailing into port at dawn, visiting the home of Chopin and George Sand, and soaking up the atmosphere of Robert Graves' island. In Palermo I saw a Donizetti opera (*Linda de Chamonix*) from the family circle where one friendly family actually shared their meal with me on the family circle's hard benches; less friendly was a gang of kids throwing stones at me in a large piazza. In Istanbul one of our sailors fell into the swift currents of the Bosporus coming back from liberty, and was never found. We also had a sad walk around the red light district where the very pale incarcerated women on view in their shabby rooms were said to be state prisoners working off sentences. That at least was the scuttlebutt aboard ship. In Athens, most dramatic was the climb to the Acropolis and the blue eyes and blue smock dress of a young Greek girl standing in a doorway on a blindingly beautiful day, a picture of total innocence it seemed, though now I doubt that. In each of these ports there was a USO Center with free food, and often some form of local or American entertainment, somehow missing the point of being in a foreign culture, though it was a touch of home.

At sea there were many visual memories, sailing through the Strait of Messina of Scylla and Charybdis fame and under Mount Etna, recalling Arnold's "Empedocles upon Etna," a poem I'd discovered the year before in Edinburgh; the northernmost rocky islands of Malta where we had some deafening target practice with our 16-inch guns; and most spectacularly, the sight of four large ships turning to port in perfect formation on a dark-blue white-capped Aegean, not the Homeric wine-dark sea. On one moonlit night on the Admiral's bridge we were sailing from Istanbul to Athens when by the navigation charts I could tell we were passing the island of Skyros, seen in outline on the western horizon. Still a naïf, I mentioned to the bos'n's mate on duty that one of my favorite poets, Rupert Brooke, was buried there (author of The Soldier: War Sonnets No. 5, ". . . That there's some corner of a foreign field/That is forever England"). The obvious but still unexpected putdown came right back: "who gives a shit about poetry." A few years later I would be cataloguing some of Brooke's papers at The New York Public Library, though my taste for his rather saccharine poetry hadn't lasted that long.

By far the most irritating day of the Mediterranean cruise was near Crete when we were visiting a US naval support base at Souda Bay at the northwest end of the island. Early in the morning of another brilliant sunny day we weighed anchor and sailed half the length of the island to anchor near Heraklion. There a large group of officers took small boats ashore to indulge in a day's sightseeing, while the enlisted 3000 crew members like me stayed aboard staring at the mountains beyond the ancient city. When we did have liberty in the tourist venues, the fleet command would try to inform the crew of worthwhile places to visit, but in general the Navy clearly wasted many educational opportunities for its enlisted men while extending blatant but perhaps understandable favoritism to its officers—ass-kissing deference, civilized dining, duck hunting forays from the Admiral's boat into the creeks near Norfolk, no end of privileges.

Nonetheless, the *USS Iowa* and X Division brought together a quirky group of enlisted friends who constituted my circle: two ship's artists (Allan Lehtis and Mike Burgevan), another artist who ran the ship's library (Lou Eargle), and me, the journalist. In the artist's shack high up on the superstructure of the ship, Mike had an LP phonograph whose needle bounced with the ship but enabled us to listen to the classical recordings I was able to "borrow" from the Admiral's mess. (My job was to deliver the ship's newspaper there each morning.) Though it wasn't a large collection, it did include some classics we came to know very well:

Mozart's G minor *Symphony No. 40*, Prokofiev's *Third Piano Concerto*, Haydn's *Farewell Symphony*, and some Tchaikovsky. The *Iowa* was decommissioned in Norfolk that fall after NATO exercises in the North Atlantic. Since Eargle was responsible for closing the Library, he was able to deaccession quite a few books in our direction, a process I learned a lot about over the next forty years.

We had escaped the Mediterranean in time to miss the Sixth Fleet's 1957 deployment to Lebanon where hostilities had caused considerable tension. Meanwhile, I was enjoying several weekends of shore leave, including weekends at home. On one occasion I made my way from Norfolk via New York to my father's office in downtown Paterson to get a ride home for the weekend. He had some banking business at an outdoor kiosk, and while I was standing nearby in my Navy uniform a security guard approached and asked whether I was involved in Lebanon (obviously not) and whether I might be Jacob Stam's son (more obviously so). "I've known the Stams for a long time. It's a wonderful family. Why, I was even up at the house on 7th Street when your grandfather jumped out of the window." That was news to me but I pretended nonchalance and didn't mention it to my father on the way home. Grandfather Peter had died in 1940 and we had always heard that he had fallen out of a second-story bathroom window, a window we'd been warned about. In a sad letter following his father's death, Dad wrote that the day before he died Peter had spent time bouncing me on his knee and entertaining me with some games and toys. I was five at the time. Only much later did we learn about the genetic patterns of manic-depression in the Stam line, of which grandfather was a prime example, having suffered a "nervous breakdown" just at the point when the Mission was opening its new quarters on Broadway in 1919. It seems to me that the disease affects one in every four or five of our family, regardless of belief, including at least two of my siblings. Mercifully I've escaped, and Deirdre doubts that I've ever had a manic day in my life. Though I've certainly had depressing moments, they've always been episodic rather than fundamental. Even after five years since my ALS diagnosis, I've not been the least depressed over that sword of Damocles—frustrated occasionally but not depressed. After hearing and reading all the fund raising humbug over the years about "long battles with cancer," I'd like my obituary to read "after a long flirtation with ALS . . . ."

After two months ashore in the early summer of 1957, X Division moved to the *USS Northampton*, a new state-of-the-art communications cruiser, for an annual cruise designed for Naval Academy midshipman. I have the impression, probably from reading naval history or Patrick O'Brien, that by the time midshipmen were selected for Annapolis, they had learned of their innate superiority over enlisted men. It wasn't an attractive trait, an arrogance that my boss, Marine Colonel Aldridge, never demonstrated. Our itinerary included exercises off Puerto Rico and visits to Rio de Janeiro, Trinidad, and the US base at Guantanamo Bay. Images of anti-submarine warfare practice off of Puerto Rico remain, with exploding depth charges driving colorful but dead and bleeding tropical fish to the surface. There was also the brilliant sunny beaches and beautiful women of Rio, and the brutal tropical heat of Trinidad and Gitmo. I have no recollection of any useful work I did on these trips; although I must have been writing something, all I can remember is chipping paint, a dreadful necessity on all ships.

When we were not at sea, I actually had more work to do, partly covering local events with a 4" by 5" reflex camera, but mainly reading *The New York Times*. Stories and photo-ops that I covered included a high school student who had constructed a missile which he had sent up in his backyard. My profound press release, printed in a Norfolk paper, quoted one officer: "'It's an amazing thing,' said the Captain." Another piece I recall was for a self-promoting wannabe astronaut who needed some coverage for his aspirations, so found himself pictured in the kind of equipment those astronauts would soon be expected to wear. The intelligence part of my job, reading *The New York Times*, was more challenging and more fun. Aldridge was the Fleet Intelligence Officer, and my assignment was to compare *Times* articles about international affairs and national security issues with the daily confidential reports from naval intelligence, noting who got there first and how they differed. I don't know that the results were ever quantified but my impression is that the *Times* won hands down with more timely reporting and greater accuracy.

Our next assignment for the X Division was back on the *USS Iowa* for NATO exercises in the North Atlantic, a two-month expedition in September and October. Our first destination was Scotland, which I had left less than a year before. To avoid the usual restrictions on mufti for enlisted men, I carefully smuggled some civilian clothes ashore when we disembarked at the port town of Ayr in the North Channel of the west coast. I was able to get back to Edinburgh more or less incognito, visit Lennart, see a couple of girlfriends, and visit New College again. It was not until 1962 that I would return to Britain.

The NATO exercises in early October were interesting in several respects. As the largest ship in the fleet, the *Iowa* had the best medical facilities. One day off the coast of Norway, a sailor on a British cruiser required an appendectomy and had to be transferred by highline to our ship. This can be a tricky operation, the ships sailing in parallel with high transfer lines connecting them, and carrying a swaying gurney across the divide. Even moderate seas can complicate the operation. The same technique is used for refueling smaller ships from oilers. While the transfer was proceeding, three tuna between the ships executed their own perfect formation, leaping in unison between the ships until the ships parted. A stunning sight.

On that same day we were sailing north about sixty miles west of the Norwegian coast on a crisp late September day. What we saw to the east was a mirage of dramatic Norwegian mountain peaks, floating above a completely vacant horizon, an amazing mirage which I've not heard others describe. It now reminds me of explorers, like Robert Peary, who mistakenly identified nonexistent lands. But the real excitement was yet to come. We headed back in early October past the Shetlands and into a fairly rough sea, something a battleship can weather with equanimity but harder on the smaller ships. On October 4, 1957, we learned through the ship's public address system that the Soviet Union had launched Sputnik I in low earth orbit and that night we could see the luminescent red spot travelling across the sky. I'm not sure that battle stations were called, but there was something of a paranoid panic within our command, dramatic course changes to allow surveillance of rather simple looking fishing trawlers thought to be spy vessels, boats that we observed without flying our courtesy flags usually displayed when ships pass at sea.

Eventually we made it back to Norfolk, to my *New York Times* duties, and a couple of weekends at home. Shore duty meant a return to some musical life. Two concerts stand out: a visit of the Pittsburgh Orchestra to Norfolk for a concert that included Prokofiev's *Symphony No. 5*, and perhaps a Brahms symphony, and a program by the LaSalle String Quartet that provided my first live hearing of a Béla Bartók quartet, a real revelation to me.

About this time I met another sailor named Philip Gardner, a yeoman billeted ashore to work on early automation of Navy personnel records. He lived in Washington, DC, with his mother, and I stayed at their apartment a couple of blocks from the White House on several occasions before and after my discharge. These visits were organized around famous performers at the nearby George Washington University's Lisner Auditorium; a few that come to mind were Andrés Segovia, Dietrich Fischer-Dieskau, and Elisabeth Schwarzkopf, artists whose work I have enjoyed on recordings ever since. Under my benign influence Phil eventually became a librarian in the Montgomery County system, but our youthful friendship petered out in the 1970s.

During my New Jersey visits in 1957, I had become dangerously close to a slightly older married woman who shared my affection and whose husband actually encouraged our friendship by suggesting after my discharge that she and I jointly subscribe to the Poetry Center of the YMHA in New York. He worked a night shift in the aerospace industry and was unaware of the growing danger. It was a good time for some careful consideration of what was happening to me. When I learned of some temporary additional duty for a journalist needed on a trip to Antarctica departing from Norfolk in November 1957, I volunteered for duty on the cargo ship *USS Wyandot*. Its assignment that winter was to resupply a US base participating in the International Geophysical Year of 1957-58, part of Operation Deepfreeze II. The cargo included not only supplies, provisions, and construction materials, but also personnel known as winterovers, the sailors and scientists who would be spending the austral winter at Ellsworth Station on the Weddell Sea. We would also be picking up those men who had spent the winter there.

For me, the prospect of visiting Senegal, South Africa, Argentina, and Brazil was an added incentive. My job on the Antarctic cruise was to produce a daily 4-page mimeographed newspaper when at sea, mostly taken from wire services, to be delivered to the officers' mess by 6 am each morning. It was a minor job but for me an important and transformative assignment which has influenced my interests to this day, though I hardly realized it at the time. It was the ideal job for my heavy reading program, which included *War and Peace* in one of those compact and convenient

Oxford World's Classics editions.[12] Alas, I never saved copies of my seaborne newspaper, and a check of the National Archives about the ship's voyage turned up no copies.

As I recall it, the day before we reached Dakar, Senegal, in early December 1957, the crew was summoned to watch a survival training movie on the mess deck. The space was particularly hot, the room extremely smoky, and the movie bloody. I was standing on the second step of the ladder leading to open air, when I fainted dead away, fell onto a garbage barrel, broke a front tooth, lacerated my upper lip and eyebrow, and probably had an undiagnosed concussion. When I came to I was strapped to a gurney being hauled up the ladder to the sick bay where I spent a day or two, fortunately forfeiting the indignity of the "crossing the line" ceremony with its crass rituals. Actually I had already crossed the line when going to Ecuador as a teen-ager, was already a shellback, and thus qualified as one of Neptune's minions, but had no way of proving it. Over time I began to doubt the veracity of this memory of my accident, and also wanted to see whether the *Wyandot* archives contained my newspaper, so I went to the National Archives at College Park to look. All they retained on the history of that voyage were the deck logs. Alas, no newspapers, but the logs did describe my accident on December 12, 1957, with these reassuring words for both my memory and my sensibilities:

> 0800-1200 Underway as before. 0800 Mustered the crew at quarters. Absentees: none. 1000 Made daily inspection of magazines and smoking powder samples. Conditions normal.

---

[12] I have a note on the rear endpaper of my copy: "I bought this book in Rio de Janeiro in June of 1957. I started reading it after leaving Cape Town in December of that year en route to Antarctica. I reached the first epilogue in February 1958 when approaching Buenos Aires, but due to an acute attack of channel fever did not finish the book then. I've carried it around from home to home for over fifty years."

There is now a later note: "I have just finished rereading it in Feb. 2010, this time including the two epilogues. Tolstoy's discussion of free will and necessity throughout the volume now seem to be a long-forgotten influence on my historical thinking, at least subconsciously, though I think it had been largely forgotten. DHS 2/21/10"

During First Aid lecture, STAM, David H., 451 18 28, JO3, USNR fainted, striking GI can and deck as he fell, sustaining following injuries: Wound, lacerated, right eyebrow. No A or N involvement [alcohol or narcotics, I presume], and wound lacerated, upper lip. No A or N involved. Treatment administered by Medical Officer. Disposition: returned to duty. Injury not due to personal misconduct.

When we docked in Dakar a few days later we were given shore leave in the city. I was sitting in my summer white uniform alone on a park bench on a high promontory looking west over the sparkling Atlantic. I was reading Ayn Rand's *The Fountainhead*, of all things, when a wiry native woman with her baby sat down beside me. I smiled and went on reading only to be distracted when she withdrew from her blouse the most pendulous breast I have ever seen, lean and at least ten inches long roughly the shape of a pork tenderloin. It's still hard to reimagine that scene, with my white gob suit, the new gap in my front teeth, my odd choice of reading matter, and my covert glances on what was happening on the bench two feet away from me.[13]

A week or so later, in Cape Town on a Sunday, I went to a Presbyterian Church service (cannot explain why) and was soon adopted for the week before Christmas by a generous family of British immigrants which took pity on this lonely swabbie. They gave me tours of the entire Cape, took me to their various homes and to some holiday parties at beautiful hillside mansions under Table Mountain with their spectacular views of the harbor, the South Atlantic, and the miniscule-looking *Wyandot* at its waterfront. They took me to the Public Library, the University of Cape Town, the Cape vineyards, and showed off the naval base at Simonstown. There were jokes about the South African navy

---

[13]   Something is amiss in these memories. A simple look at a map shows Dakar 15º north of the Equator. What the deck logs show is that we were moored in Dakar from December 8 to 11, that my accident occurred on the 12th, and we crossed the line on the 13th. There was no gap in my grin when this encounter happened. Why we were watching a battle survival film en route to the Antarctic remains an unanswered question, probably some naval regulation rigidly followed. A film on hypothermia would have seemed more appropriate.

(two crews but only one ship) and serious political discussions of what a dangerous powder keg they were sitting on. And no joke, I even heard a local symphony play Mozart's *Ein musikalischer Spass*. One other memory was the open hostility of Afrikaans speakers to English speakers like me, despite my Dutch pedigree and my reformed credentials. Yet along with Rio de Janeiro, Portree (Skye) in Scotland, and Palma de Majorca, Cape Town is one of the most beautiful ports that I've been lucky enough to visit.

We left Cape Town for Antarctica on Boxing Day, 1957, with new supplies of fresh fruit and meat, Christmas gifts from home received and variously stowed, including a fruit cake from my mother, placed on a safe shelf above my desk in the Executive Officer's outer cabin where I usually worked. About 1300 miles south of Cape Town, after passing the remote Norwegian island of Bouvet with its high mountains shrouded in mist, we ran into a frightening hurricane with troughs far deeper than the height of the ship which itself was rolling to 45 degrees. There was little we could do but retreat to our primitive hammock-like bunks and hang on for dear life. When things had cleared up we surveyed the damage, including one landing craft mechanical (LCM) that had been stowed across the width of the ship under the boom. It broke loose during the storm, shifted 40 feet to port, and was saved only by its rear cabin being snagged on the cargo boom. Collateral damage was the disappearance of my fruit cake. One officer told me that the tin had fallen from its perch during the night, broken open, and these officers ate the contents. I was pissed but powerless to protest.

By the time we entered the Weddell Sea icepack, there was 24-hour daylight, and my *modus operandi* was to work for a few hours after dinner, assembling most of the day's news and typing up pages two to four and mimeographing those pages in advance. Then I would do whatever I pleased, mostly reading, for the rest of the night. At 5 am I would return to the radio shack, pick up any late breaking news, type up and run off page 1, staple the four pages, and deliver the paper to the officer's mess by 6 am. The morning call to "commence ship's work" was my signal to hit the rack, often to the sound of obscenities from the reveille rituals. One morning I lost my cool and yelled out: "fuck, fuck, fuck, fuck, fuck. All I hear all day long is fuck, fuck, fuck." It was ultra-tedious and against my character, since I seldom let it be known what I thought. After that outburst I overheard someone say, "Whatever got into Stam?"

Enlisted men's bunks were lined up as racks, five high, two abreast less than a foot apart divided by upright supports, and clearance of no more than 20 inches, no place for claustrophobics. There were probably up to eighty men in our compartment, with no light for reading. The highest bunks were uncomfortably close to outdoor hatches and whenever one was opened below the Antarctic Circle, very frigid air rushed in to screams of "shut the damned hatch" or worse. There was a rudimentary library of popular paperbacks on a lower deck with a few shabby but comfortable chairs. Movies were shown daily either on the mess deck or on the fantail in the tropics when it was dark before 1800 hours. In the tropics it was extremely hot below decks and we tried to spend as much time as possible above decks.

In retrospect, the lack of environmental concern at that time is now appalling. At the fantail rail was a 2 feet by 2 feet chute through which all the ship's garbage passed, both in the tropics and within the Antarctic Circle. Seagulls and albatross would hover over our wake awaiting their next meal. Today the requirement is that everything brought into Antarctica, including human waste, must be brought out again. I have no idea what happens to garbage after it returns to temperate waters.

In Antarctica I enjoyed the "daytime," often leaning over the bow and watching the stem of the *Wyandot* slicing through icepack and growlers (through leads already opened by our accompanying icebreaker, the *USCGC Westwind 281*), observing phlegmatic seals lazily roll from their icy perches as we came near, watching killer whales watching us, and marveling at the larger icebergs, the only signs of color in the pack. Before reaching the mooring ice for Ellsworth Station, we went ashore on the very landing craft we almost lost off Bouvet Island, to visit an immense emperor penguin colony near Halley Bay, a noisy and smelly affair where a few of our intrepid sailors managed to get wrists broken by penguin flippers. The pack did cause some significant damage to one of our propellers, and as I recall temporary repairs were made by scuba divers.

What do I remember of Ellsworth Station and what have I learned subsequently? I remember visiting the *Westwind*'s dentist to get a temporary repair for my broken tooth and to have a wisdom tooth removed. I recall a beer party on the ice next to the ship. I visualize crisp, blue sunny days at freezing or below, but there was little by way of scenery: the mountains of the Antarctic Peninsula were too far away and the weather produced no mirages such as we'd seen off Norway. The base was about two miles up a gradual slope of the barrier from the ship; we once went in small groups by Sno-Cats to visit the base. One thing I remember vividly was a complex group of communications machines, with many dials and devices, intertwined with cutouts of *Playboy* centerfold bunnies, rendering ludicrous to the rest of us the claims of some winterover personnel of over a year of auto-erotic abstinence. Where I gained my sense of Antarctica's overwhelming silence is another mystery. We were always within hearing of the throbbing of ship's engines or base generators, as well as transport noises. But that feeling of complete silence is palpable, and when I hear it described by other visitors I recognize it. The stop at Ellsworth was also much shorter than I remembered, only one week according to the deck logs. I would have said nearly a month.

Ellsworth Station and its austral winter of 1957 is probably the best-documented of all the Operation Deepfreeze stations, not least because it was the most fraught and problematical. The leader, a well-known Norwegian explorer named Captain Finne Ronne, on his fourth or fifth expedition, was reputedly detested by most of the winter men for his authoritarian and dictatorial manner, his megalomania, his capricious direction, and his conflicts with both scientists and enlisted men. He tried to ban Jennie Darlington's *My Antarctic Honeymoon*, a book critical of Ronne and his wife, from the base library, not knowing that other copies were in personal collections and much in demand.

Despite his best efforts at secrecy, news of the troubles at the base easily leaked out, and the Navy sent with us on the *Wyandot* a small team of psychologists to interview the entire staff of the base on their way home. Five officers, nine civilians (scientists), and 25 enlisted men, each had at least one, and sometimes multiple, interviews. The psychologists particularly wanted to improve screening practices for selecting personnel for Antarctic duty, hoping to avoid a repeat of what happened at Ellsworth. When I told Dian Belanger, the excellent historian of *Deep Freeze* (2006), that I had been on the *Wyandot* in 1958 she merely said, "Ah, you were with the shrinks."[14]

---

[14]   See Charles Mullen and H.J.M. Connelly. "Psychological Study at an IGY Antarctic Station" *United States Armed Forces Medical Journal* (March 1959) 290-96.

There is no point in repeating the story of Ellsworth Station here but I do recommend the works of Dian Belanger, John Behrendt, Edith Ronne, Jennie Darlington, and the various autobiographies of Ronne himself to get a fairly complete picture.[15] I'll only add that on the trip from the ice to Buenos Aires on a couple of occasions I was on the bridge when Ronne asked me to get him some coffee. I knew little of the story that eventually emerged until I read much later publications, but back then he struck me as a very lonely man who'd been through some kind of hell.

[*Coda: Ronne's daughter Karen was a participant at a June 2012 conference on Antarctica held in Jaffrey, New Hampshire. She and her late mother Edith Ronne were faithful defenders of the Ronne legacy and Karen still had his voluminous archives and was looking for a suitable institutional home for them. She seemed interested in the Byrd Polar Research Center at Ohio State University as a possible home but said Byrd and her father became staunch enemies. When I told her of my brief meetings with her father she did not invite conversation on the topic.*]

On the return from the ice as the dark night resumed from the austral summer, we passed near the Falklands and stopped first at Buenos Aires where I had enough liberty to take a hotel room for four or five days, listen to classical music on their fine radio stations, go to an outdoor opera (Donizetti again, I would guess), and enjoy dining alone on the

---

[15]   Dian Belanger. *Deep Freeze: the United States, the International Geophysical Year, and the Origins of Antarctica's Age of Science* (Boulder, CO: University of Colorado Press, 2006); John C. Behrendt. *Innocents on the Ice: a Memoir of Antarctic Exploration, 1957* (Boulder, CO: University of Colorado Press, 1998); Jennie Darlington. *My Antarctic Honeymoon: a Year at the Bottom of the World* (Garden City, NY: Doubleday, 1956); Edith Ronne. *Antarctica's First Lady: Memoirs of the First American Woman to Set Foot on the Antarctic Continent and Winter-over as a Member of a Pioneering Expedition* (Beaumont, TX: Clifton Seaboat Museum, 2004); Finn Ronne. *Antarctica, My Destiny: a Personal History, by the Last of the Great Polar Explorers* (New York: Hastings House, 1979); Finn Ronne. *Antarctic Command.* (Indianapolis, IN: Bobbs-Merrill, 1961); Finn Ronne. *Antarctic Conquest: the Story of the Ronne Expedition, 1946-1948* (New York: Putnam's, 1949). The Syracuse University Library holds the archives of Admiral George Dufek, the commander of Operation Deepfreeze.

world's best steaks, away from all the guys I'd been stuck with for the last two months. A good number of them went AWOL for a few days, not surprising after a rather long deployment, and one of them was killed in an auto accident.

Next stop was Santos, Brazil, an important port near Rio and near some spectacular beaches. Since no paper was needed while in port, I took advantage of liberty days to take the small railroad through lush tropical vegetation to the nearby city of Sao Paulo (reminiscent of Villa Lobos and his *Little Train of the Caipira*). A few days in another hotel continued the restorative process, and soon we were headed back to Norfolk. When we arrived in Norfolk on February 29 I was reassigned to my former billet with Colonel Aldrich.

For most of my two years' duty with X Division I reported to a Navy lifer from Lubbock, Texas, a yeoman third class, a real redneck ("I hate my mother because she's a civilian"), with a coarse sense of humor who would return from liberty with stories of sexual conquests at low prices. Mostly I worked for Marine Lieutenant Colonel Frederick Stokes Aldridge, the Intelligence Officer of COMBATCRULANT, and public relations coordinator for the Fleet. A graduate of Colgate and Harvard Business School and a later PhD in history from American University, the Colonel was an affable and urbane man who didn't seem the least bit hung up over hierarchical status. In the Mediterranean in early 1957 on the *USS Iowa*, for example, he introduced me to visiting Senator Henry "Scoop" Jackson from Washington and allowed me to stay for the conversation.

I only saw the Colonel angry once. On May 25, 1958, during a period of shore duty, several of us in X division boarded the *USS Canberra* for an unusual day at sea. The ship was chosen for a ceremony of burial at sea and we were along to help publicize the event. The Tomb of the Unknowns at Arlington Memorial Cemetery did not yet have representatives of World War II or of the Korean War. Somehow three unidentified bodies had been sent on three separate ships to rendezvous with the *Canberra* off the Virginia Cape where the body from Korea and one of the other two were destined for burial at Arlington after lying in state at the US Capitol.

The whole thing was something of a P.R. dream and I was on duty that day helping to guide dignitaries and their wives (it was always unusual to have women aboard in those days and they were always dressed to the nines). The three bodies were transferred aboard by high-line from the rendezvous ships and lined up on the quarter deck where a medal-of-honor winner made the choice between the World War II casualties from the European and Pacific theaters of war. The one not chosen was buried at sea with all the solemnity of that ritual. One of the reporters aboard that day was Bob Considine, a well-known and sometimes controversial cold-warrior correspondent of the time. It was he who angered the Colonel by writing in his story that "one unknown soldier was chosen for honored glory in Arlington today, and the other was fed to the fishes off the Virginia Cape." "Anybody can be cynical," the Colonel told me, "what good is that?"

On checking out this memory I searched on Google for Bob Considine and was amazed to find that his personal papers were in my own Syracuse University Library, donated by Considine in the 1960s when SUL was collecting personal archives almost indiscriminately.[16] In Considine's archives I found a copy of his syndicated article as published in *The Bakersfield Californian* on May 27, 1958, with the offensive sentence missing, replaced by an innocuous "The one he rejected would be buried at sea." Could it be that we'd only seen a draft of his article? I don't suppose we'll ever know whether naval censorship, persuasion, or a sharp-eyed editor played a role in this redaction.

On all of my Navy travels, from Scotland to Cape Town, from Istanbul to Rio, from Trinidad to Guantanamo Bay, I had followed my

---

[16]   When I told Robert Warner, then Archivist of the United States, that I would be taking over the Syracuse University Library, he warned me that I'd probably have to do some weeding, that the University's archival collection policy used the vacuum cleaner approach called A and E: Anything and Everything. It is true that for a time the main collection tool was *Who's Who in America*, and we took materials from anyone listed there. Subsequently we have tried to find homes for some of the more inappropriate archives in our collection: 30,000 Norman Vincent Peale prayer letters to his Center in Pawling, New York; Michigan rail archives to Ann Arbor; minor state legislators; more recently New York Central Railroad Archives to the Mercantile Library in St. Louis. But some very important and useful collections came into the wide net thrown in the 1960s under Chancellor William Tolley: Arna Bontemps, Benjamin Spock; publishing archives of Grove Press and Street and Smith, to name a few.

old habit of visiting libraries wherever I found them. In Mediterranean cities I enjoyed the libraries of the United States Information Agency and buying up the highly subsidized American publications which the USIA flooded into some of those countries, especially Turkey. I particularly remember using the base library at Gitmo, as every sailor called it, and wonder if any of that sizable collection is available to detainees there now.[17] My last Navy assignment as journalist was on the cruiser *USS Galveston*, a magnificent but ageing ship being converted in Philadelphia into a modern missile cruiser. With vast cost overruns, planning disasters, and sailors facing what were then called morals charges, the last thing the ship needed was publicity. During that period I advanced to JO2, journalist second class.

In the summer of 1958 my long life in libraries began—by accident: the ship's chaplain took pity on this underemployed sailor and put me in charge of the ship's library, a tidy one-room collection of about 3000 volumes. Since we were mostly in port for my five months' duty (except for two days of sea tests) my only clients were prisoners from the brig, allowed to use the library for writing letters to their parents, partners, and "sweethearts and wives" (the traditional toast of Polar ceremonial dinners, usually concluded with a cynical, "may they never meet").

At the end of one weekend liberty in Paterson I missed my train from Newark to Philadelphia. I was loitering on the platform wondering what to do while waiting, when in pulled the all-reserved Broadway Limited, the night train to Chicago. An engineer climbed down from the diesel locomotive and struck up a conversation with me. When told where I was headed he invited me to join him in the cab. It was one of the most exciting train journeys of my life, before or since, a whole new perspective on train travel.

Shore duty in Philadelphia that autumn was really quite delightful. The library work was easy and liberty frequent. Sailors could get free tickets to the Philadelphia Orchestra's concerts at the Academy of Music, often conducted by Eugene Ormandy, and the Free Library of Philadelphia sponsored a free series of afternoon chamber music concerts which I

---

[17] A description of the library and library services at the Guantanamo Bay Base today appeared in *The New York Times Book Review*, June 16, 2013, p. 35. See also gitmobooks.tumblr.com

attended regularly with fellow sailors or some Wheaton friends. One acquaintance of that time was Philadelphia musician Harold Boatrite who later taught music for many years at Haverford College. He was a fairly prolific composer whose manuscript orchestral scores are now in the Fischer Collection of the Free Library. I doubt he would remember me, but I personally was very impressed by him as the first composer I'd ever met.

On New Jersey weekends at home I spent much of the time with my brother Jim listening to chamber music recordings from the East Orange Public Library, and it was from Jim that I initially learned the most about music and music history. Brahms's chamber music was then my favorite. After graduating from Upsala College in East Orange in 1958 Jim won an Austrian Danksstipendium for a year's study in Vienna, followed by a three-year National Defense Education Act fellowship (NDEA was one of the Congressional responses to Sputnik) for study at Brandeis University. We thought it amusing that he had chosen the history of ideas in general and the question of language origins in particular to help defend his country.

Jim's Viennese year must have been a lonely and somewhat depressing one for him, similar to mine at the same age in Edinburgh. His letters to me from the period are voluminous, often with two long letters a day. He was still studying in Europe when I was discharged from the Navy and had moved to New York and started work at NYPL. He returned in the summer of 1959 for a fellowship at Brandeis University where he studied History of Ideas with Herbert Marcuse and Frank Manuel, but those are stories for his memoirs.

Brother Jim was and is a pianist, still practicing and playing regularly at 75. During high school or earlier he got roped into playing for evangelistic services, often with a "chalk artist" who was well practiced in the art of depicting the perils of hell in vivid pastels. I'm sure Jim turned cynic about such things at an earlier age than I did, but he still seems to bear the stigmata of that experience, thankfully now healed.

In retrospect, I would have to say that I enjoyed my naval adventures much more in hindsight than I did in living through them. The discomfort, close proximity, the aggravation of chipping paint, the tedium of bureaucratic regulations (e.g., being finger-printed on every payday), the make-work to maintain the appearance of productivity—all that fades more rapidly than the beauty of tuna in formation between two ships off the Norwegian coast, entering Palma de Majorca at a misty dawn, the extraordinary sight of colorful tropical fish being blasted to the surface by depth charges in the Caribbean, or the stark beauty of the Antarctic icepack.

I also have come to think that my service as a Navy journalist was largely a wasted opportunity, that for the most part I squandered. My newssheet usually just parroted the wire services, and I now think I should have been more assertive in covering more of what was going on, especially in Antarctica.[18] The short period when we were on the ice was the precise time when Vivian Fuchs and Edmund Hillary concluded their historic but troubled Trans Antarctic Expedition (TAE 1955 to 1958), completing their continental crossing in what one Polar historian called "the greatest polar expedition ever forgotten."[19] I would have learned a great deal more if I'd been more aggressive reporting, not that the Navy would have welcomed strong initiatives from an enlisted man.

Distance had not cooled the romantic connection with my friend and we saw each other several times before my discharge at Thanksgiving Eve of 1958 and regularly for the next year with our subscriptions to the 92nd Street YMHA's Poetry Center, before the affair ended in near-violence and sadness all round in November of 1959. The worst and most painful event of the liaison was when her mother called my mother and reported what was going on. I denied any wrong-doing, but the damage was done, and it must have been devastating to my parents. It is still a painful memory.

---

[18] On one occasion I exercised my imagination on the paper, causing anger from the Chief Signal Officer. One evening in Antarctica the wireless reception was particularly bad to the point of illegibility. I took the liberty of reproducing some of it just as it was received, all scrambled and unintelligible, for the lead article. Little did I think that he could take this as a personal affront and it was some time before he settled down and perhaps even forgave me.

[19] David Haddelsey. *Shackleton's Dream* (Stroud, UK: The History Press, 2012) p. 251.

Chapter II

Librarianship: its Duties and Rewards 1959 to 1967

"I declare that the library is endless."
Jorge Luis Borges. *Collected Fictions* (1998) p. 112-13.

The Career that Nearly Wasn't
December 1958

On leaving active duty in the Navy the day before Thanksgiving, 1958, I had no idea what I wanted to do with my life other than to live in New York City. It was close enough to home in Paterson, New Jersey, to be able to exploit parental support, but far enough to be totally independent. Sometime in December, my future sister-in-law, Liga Ziemelis, then studying for an MLS in the Graduate School of Library and Information Service at Rutgers University, suggested that I apply for a job at The New York Public Library and it seemed as good an option as any.

Although planning to spend some weeks helping Mike Burgevan and his wife renovate an old farmhouse in upstate Hillsdale, I first went to 42nd Street for an interview in the building where I was to spend over thirteen years of my working life. Lennart Pearson was with me and spent the time of my interview at the Automat at Park Avenue and 42nd

Street. In 2012 in the now beautifully restored Gottesman Hall, the Library exhibited a section of a surviving Automat, as part of a show on Lunchtime in New York. The interview took place in that same room on the first floor of the 42nd Street building, then an ugly rabbit warren of offices for the staff nurse, labor relations, business offices, and personnel. The testing was hardly rigorous—evidently my Wheaton B.A. in English Literature sufficiently qualified me for the proffered job of clerk-typist at $2750 a year. A bit of banter, a typical wise-crack about my pride in failing accounting in college, a brief description of duties, and the job was mine. I requested a starting date three weeks off, January 15, 1959.

Right after Christmas spent in Paterson, I went off to help Mike fix up his new house just north of Hillsdale, New York, on Route 22, just south of the border near Great Barrington, Massachusetts. It was quite a primitive farm house with no electricity or running water, some form of firewood heating, plus the warmth of active exertion. I don't remember other details of the visit—this friendship folded when he and his wife became Jehovah's Witnesses, a surprising development for someone who served as ship's artist on the *USS Iowa* and who was something of a classical music lover.

When I arrived at the Library on January 15, a Friday as I recall, I was immediately accosted by my new supervisor of the Card Preparation Division, a Mrs. Hannah Friedman, who accused me of getting myself hired under false pretenses, having applied when clean shaven but then growing a beard while awaiting the new job. She told me that I could return the following Monday without a beard or I need not bother to return at all. It was my first beard since Antarctica, where the Navy was more tolerant than my new employer. I mulled over the decision during the weekend and then on Sunday night reluctantly cut off the beard so necessarily hatched in Hillsdale. Having heard no news and read no newspapers during those three weeks, I was completely unaware that the Cuban Revolution had culminated during that period and that for some, beards had become political statements. To this day I have no idea whether that played a part in Mrs. Friedman's summary decree. The whole episode was a chancy throw of the dice, or should I say a close shave.

[Coda: exactly eighteen years later, in Dec.-Jan. 1977-78, I was interviewed twice for the position of Andrew W. Mellon Director of the Research Libraries of The New York Public Library, a role I assumed in July of 1978. Out of some perverse impulse I grew a beard between my December

and January interviews to test whether NYPL mores might have changed. No one ever mentioned the new beard and in due course I was formally welcomed at a party in the Trustee's Room. There I was able to recount this felix culpa *in the presence of Mrs. Friedman, by then Head of Acquisitions, who professed not to recall the incident.*]

The duties I assumed in January included the typing of headings at the upper left margin of 3" x 5" catalogue cards (red for subject headings, black for other entries), the designation of those cards to the Library's complex set of catalogues, and the alphabetizing of these cards for inclusion in the various catalogues. A catalogue entry for a complicated book might have as many as ten cards, and often these sets might be designated to just as many catalogues. Subsidiary tasks included such exciting diversions as gluing the bottom edges of these sets to keep them together, and then slicing them apart so each set could go to its assigned catalogue without re-collating. At this time (1959), libraries had scarcely begun experiments with automation, and for us in Card Prep as it was called, our only taste of automation involved a Remington alphabetizing machine which could take a fairly large pile of catalogue cards or sets placed in a kind of basket for alphabetizing. Over the pile was a magnifying glass and a suction cup at the left end of the machine, a conveniently placed keyboard near the magnifier, and an attached contraption with twenty-six receptacles ready to receive the cards as they were sorted and directed by the keyboard to whichever letter had been pressed on the keyboard. The next step was to take all of the cards in the first receptacle and go through the same process with the second letter— about, accrue, agony, arrange, attack, etc. The machine was in a small caged office on the top floor of the Library stacks, overlooking Bryant Park, a space that would disappear in the 2012 Central Library Plan. One lesson of our experimentation was that the machine was efficient at most to the fourth letter—anything beyond the fourth letter took too much time to distinguish, and some fellow workers didn't do well beyond the third letter.

By the end of February I had made some good friends in the Library but realized that the job itself was completely dispiriting and that I had to get out. Eight hours a day of typing, sorting, alphabetizing, and gluing soon became not only boring but loathsome. By comparison, the Navy was paradise. I resolved to quit as soon as I found something else and began to apply for other positions in the Library. After a few rejections (the American History division had no interest in someone who claimed no interest in American history), I was fortunate enough to win a position as Editorial Assistant in the Library's Office of Library Publications. Often when in despair of the human condition, I think back on that job in card preparation and my faith in the possibility of human progress is partially restored, just by knowing that that job no longer exists, thanks to the noble Library tradition of innovation in library automation.

Panacea or Precious Bane?
1959 to 2006

At home and at school through my college years, all use of tobacco was verboten and held little attraction to me, despite some sporadic attempts to pretend enjoyment. Three childish one-shot experiments at sophistication are memorable. The first was probably while I was still in grammar school when I smoked my first cigarette in nearby Haledon. I was sitting on a tree branch about 15 feet off the ground, and nearly fainted. Another was while cycling to Princeton from Paterson at age twelve when I paused in Montclair to try a cigarette—that had the same dizzying effect. I thought I might have to return home on that trip, but my head eventually cleared up and I went on. Much later I saw a letter I'd written from my brother Paul's house in Princeton, chiding my mother for being anxious about her 12-year old son's independence. The third was actually quite terrifying: one Monday I was with four or five boys smoking in a wooded church lot near home when one of them said he knew a girl nearby who would be glad to show us her breasts. We went to her house and indeed she was very agreeable and allowed each of us to feel one breast. As I recall we had to scramble when a parent arrived. Later that week my mother asked me what I had been doing the last Monday evening. Breaking into a cold sweat, I pretended nonchalance and said "nothing in particular." She pressed harder and got me to admit that I had been smoking. Nothing further. What a relief!

There was another occasion probably before high school when a couple of us kids were smoking under the wooden porch steps when my mother came home and mounted the steps. Unfortunately out of sight did not mean out of smelling distance for our ever vigilant mother. Caught again.

But I didn't become an habitual smoker until after my year in Britain and the Continent, and after two years in the Navy. It was arrival at NYPL in 1959, aged 23, which brought the change, probably through the peer pressure of my new friends. Many claim to regret ever having started to smoke—I can't agree. Given the camaraderie of smokers that I have known, even after smokers had achieved pariah status in our society, I look back on the friendships around the shared ashtray as an important part of my maturation and success. I'll single out a number of fervent smokers: Robert Allen (NY Public Library reference librarian), Bill Towner (Newberry Library President), Richard Polacek (Johns Hopkins Medical School Librarian), Ernie Siegel (Director of Baltimore's Pratt Library), Michael Smethurst (British Library); Edward Shaw and Jim Michalko (Research Libraries Group Presidents), George Rochberg (American composer), and Gladys Krieble Delmas (philanthropist and library trustee), all of whom influenced my life in wonderful ways; I am grateful for what helped bring us together. And there were many others: Richard Landon, Dan Traister, Jean Paul Delmas, Bernie Wilson, etc. I should also point out that most of them are now dead, some from lung cancer. When I asked Gladys if her doctor gave her a hard time about her heavy smoking, she said, "Listen, David, I pay my doctor very well." She was still smoking on her sickbed and I was still a smoker when I visited her shortly before her death.

There is more of a book connection here than one might imagine. Probably the greatest collection of books and materials on the topic of tobacco is the George Arents Collection at the NYPL. One of my editorial duties at the Library in the early 1960s was to help prepare for publication *Tobacco: A Catalogue of the Books, Manuscripts, and Engravings Acquired since 1942 in the Arents Tobacco Collection at the New York Public Library, from 1507 to the Present.* Compiled by Sarah Augusta Dickson, this was a series of twelve supplements to a monumental earlier catalogue, and I was involved in seeing two or three of them through the press. George Arents became wealthy as a manufacturer of cigar wrappers, and he used some of his wealth to collect everything he could on tobacco, not just the subject of tobacco but anything that so much as mentioned it. A snuffbox mentioned in Oscar Wilde's *The Importance of Being Earnest* was enough to qualify the typescript of the play for inclusion in his collection; similarly, the works of Shakespeare and Sir Walter Raleigh's *History of the World* (1614).

The inside joke about George Arents was that he once took a subway just to see what it was like. I never met Arents (he died in 1960, the year after my arrival at NYPL), but I feel that I followed him around. He was a trustee of both NYPL and Syracuse University and had major influences on the collections of each. The title of this section, "Panacea or Precious Bane," is borrowed from a book subtitled *Tobaco* [sic] *in Sixteenth Century Literature* by Sarah Dickson (Curator of the Arents Collections, someone I met often during her last and my first years at NYPL); the copy I found in the Syracuse University Library was given to us by George Arents, stolen by John Mayfield, and subsequently returned by Georgetown University.

[*Coda: I've only stopped smoking recently, about five years ago in 2008. It was occasioned by a humiliating sermon from my cardiologist, Jim Longo, who argued that there was no safe minimum and that I wasn't worth his investment if I kept smoking. I'm proud to say that it was the only time I quit, but by then I was down to four or five cigarettes a day and tired of concealing my habit from others, and the camaraderie I'd experienced early on was disappearing amidst a sea of disapproval. That day I went home, had two stiff drinks and two last cigarettes, and quit completely. The half-finished pack still sits hidden in an unused ashtray in my living room, a challenge to my resolve which has never wavered and which now seems irrelevant. For some time I occasionally had a troubled dream of starting again.*]

While on the subject of the so-called vices, I might as well interject here a word on alcohol. My very first drink, no more than a few sips, was at Christian Zangger's home near Zürich when his mother offered a glass of red wine, on or about my 21ˢᵗ birthday. I'd heard so much for almost twenty years about the evils of alcohol that I thought I might collapse on the spot and I recall heading to the bathroom to check in the mirror whether I was still all right. That was in July 1956 when I appeared to be an adult, but it was not until January 1958 that I had another, again no more than a sip of beer on the ice of Antarctica next to our ship moored to an ice peer, a lower section of the glacial ice barrier. The temperature was about 0°F and the beer too cold to taste.

When I settled into New York City and found a circle of friends at New York Public Library in addition to the new habit of smoking, I began to drink regularly. Whether this was a conscious casting off of old inhibitions and proscriptions, or just a natural development I cannot say. The next forty years of my library career and then beyond have been fairly well lubricated, seldom to the point of danger but no doubt more than needed.

Another topic I'd like to address is the homosexual culture of libraries in general and NYPL in particular. I've already intimated that Wheaton gave me no understanding whatsoever of gay life and the Navy only what was regarded as the criminal nature of homosexual acts as seen in the morals charges against the sailors on the *USS Galveston,* my patrons in the library. It was not long before I was taking coffee and lunch breaks at NYPL with a number of new colleagues, primarily men who were interested in the cultural matters that interested me, literature and music, theatre and dance, opera and all the other performing arts. Some were straight and some gay, not that I often knew which.[20]

One of the first was Bob Allen, a reference librarian from Ohio who was a natural born mentor in the arts, an hospitable host, and a superb cook then living at West 62nd St. and Columbus Avenue in a small second floor apartment above a fragrant hotdog stand garage. Most of his walls were lined with long playing records, his major teaching tool in introducing handsome young men to the wonders of classical and some popular music, especially of jokesters like Anna Russell, wannabe divas like Florence Foster Jenkins, or masterpieces of the zarzuela literature. He and his Italian colleague and friend, Camilla Fabris, travelled the European and northern African world together, and often entertained as a couple in Bob's apartment. A typical evening would be an hour's drinks, a hurried dinner, a rush to Carnegie Hall for Arthur Rubenstein, City Center for the City Ballet or New York State Opera, or farther afield, one

---

[20] One such person was Donald Seibert, then a music cataloguer at the Juilliard School who was later the Music Librarian at Syracuse when I arrived there in 1986. I have a distinct recollection of having him to dinner at our West 115th Street apartment in 1963 or so, but neither Deirdre nor Donald remembered the event. In any case, shortly before his death in 2011 Donald gave me a copy of his unpublished autobiographical memoir, "Music, Dance, Sex and Friendship: The memories of a gay man of his life in New York City in the 1950s." His inscription read "For David Stam my favorite former library director Thank you for the many times you have encouraged me as a writer." He was a fine writer whose essays, reviews, and interviews were chiefly about Tchaikovsky.

of the Broadway theatres for *Beyond the Fringe* or a Tennessee Williams play.

The Metropolitan Opera at West 39th Street was much less convenient to Bob's apartment and usually involved supper near the Library. I remember best a performance of *Wozzeck* in 1959; for years I stupidly claimed that of all opera, I only enjoyed Mozart and Berg. I remember standing outside the Met stage door on 39th Street to get a close view of Victoria de Los Angeles. By the time Deirdre and I left New York in 1964, a good deal of Lincoln Center across the street from Bob's apartment was already completed. Apart from my brother Jim, Bob was really the biggest influence on my aesthetic development, and when we decided to leave New York for Vermont his farewell present was a foot-high stack of LP records; like a typical New Yorker (transplanted from Ohio), he assumed we were leaving civilization. Bob Allen was still at the Library when we returned in 1978 but died of cancer and alcoholism a few years later. I felt privileged to conduct his memorial ceremony in Room 315, NYPL's Reference Room. The reference desk where he spent most of his working life served as the bar. In my tribute to Bob on that occasion, I said that he'd taught me three things: never to trust an administrator, how to drink a martini, and most of what I then knew about music, theatre, and dance.

After a few experiments with the gay life it was clear to me that my own orientation was heterosexual, not for lack of exposure to the alternative. On one of Bob's annual trips with Camilla, this one to Morocco, he had lent his apartment to a mutual gay friend, Fred Randy Muhleman, whose company I mostly enjoyed but whose interest in me I was uncertain about. One night in the fall of 1960, when returning from Rutgers, I was mugged in a subway tunnel under Times Square. I made my way home to East 64th Street and called Randy who told me to take a taxi to a party at an old loft on Cointes Slip. It was the loft of American painter Jack Youngerman and his then wife Delphine Seyrig, the heroine (if that's the word) of Alain Resnais's *Last Year at Marienbad* (1961). I met Ellsworth Kelly there, but from his description of what he did I took him to be a house painter. Richard and Jeannette Seaver of Grove Press fame were also there but I have no recollection of others. Not long after, some of these people attended the US premiere of *Marienbad* at the Carnegie Cinema under Carnegie Hall, where Zankel Hall now lies, two levels below Seventh Avenue.

Shortly after that Randy and I took the Seaver's three-year-old daughter, Nathalie, for a ride on the Staten Island Ferry as part of a baby-sitting assignment. As we returned to Manhattan she uttered the memorable words, "The Statue of Liberty is going out to sea." Not long after I had a "date" at the Central Park Zoo with the beautiful Delphine, just before she returned to France to pursue her movie career. She must have assumed that because of my friendship with Randy I was gay and safe. The Youngerman Cointes Slip loft was in an old brick building, soon to be condemned to make way for the massive skyscrapers now lining that section of Lower Manhattan. One sad day we all gathered on the sidewalk across the street to watch the wrecker's ball bring down their loft. Throughout all this Randy helped me recover from the street-paranoia I briefly experienced from the mugging. But it didn't help that he tried to trick me into pot use, a line I was unwilling to cross.

In October of 1960 Bob and Camilla took one of their typical European vacations to Spain and Italy. Randy was staying at Bob Allen's place during that trip, partly for cat sitting, but he used it to commit suicide by gas oven. His body was found by Delphine's friend Jeannette Seaver, wife of Richard Seaver of the Grove Press, my occasional tennis partner that year. I must have learned of his death from her, and it was my sad duty first to inform Bob of the death, and later to meet Bob at the police station, get the keys to his padlocked apartment, and take him home. I have a postcard dated October 16th from Bob in Palermo which essentially was his will in case of a plane crash, including a flight insurance policy for Randy, the recordings to two friends and me. "Camilla should have any thing she wants or will take. Not cheerful, but I'm managing."

When we got to Bob's apartment, we found that one of his two cats had been locked in the apartment for several weeks and was near death. Nursing the cat back to life was helpful therapy for Bob in his natural state of shock at Randy's death. I don't mean to imply in any of this that Randy's death had anything to do with our relationship—I have no evidence one way or the other, though I doubt any connection given his past history. (Jim Stam reminds me that Randy had made an earlier suicide attempt when Jim had to feed the cats.) Bob had to move in the early 1970s when his building was torn down and replaced by the honeycombed high rise now occupying the old site on Columbus Avenue. He never quite recovered, having had to leave the environs of Lincoln Center and the New York State Theater which had meant so much to him, especially for Balanchine's New York City Ballet, the company I've followed since he introduced me to it in 1959.

During the holidays of 1959-60 Jim and I took a trip, again with mother's car, to an Ohio campus where a friend was a visiting professor for the year. While there I met a teenage daughter, and it's fair to say there was a mutual instant attraction. When her family returned to New Jersey in the summer we got together, even though there was a substantial age gap of six or seven years. She spent most of that summer as an *au pair* girl for a rich family in Maine, a family that she mocked in our frequent telephone conversations that summer and in the one long and childish letter from her that survives in my archive. She terminated our affair a year later when she found another lover, but it left its mark, presumably on both of us. From Jim's correspondence I know that my associations with his friend's wife and his mentor's daughter were acutely painful for him, and created some acrimony between us, but he let both affairs take their course with little direct interference. He lived with me in New York in the summer of 1959 while he was working briefly at one of NYPL's bigger branch libraries.

David V. Erdman, Master and Mentor
April 1959 to December 1962

This lengthy diversion has taken me well beyond my new editorial job that began on April 1, 1959, with a salary of $4000, enough to let me move on April Fool's Day from one room in a dark and gloomy railroad apartment on West 114th Street to my own two-room flat on East 64th Street, a fairly easy walk home from the 42nd Street building.

My new boss was David V. Erdman (1915-1998), a noted Romantic scholar of Blake, Coleridge, Byron, and Wordsworth. At the time we met he was editing Coleridge's *Essays on His Times* for the Bollingen edition of Coleridge's works published by Princeton University Press, a three-volume work that did not appear until 1978, almost twenty years later. Erdman was one of the most fascinating characters I have ever known; for four years he was my mentor and I his ever-present colleague, student, and primary sounding board. [He was not one of the smokers described above.]

For me it was an apprenticeship in writing, editing, printing, and in librarianship, involving as it did contact with almost all units of the 42nd Street library, including all of the special collections at NYPL as well as nearby libraries. If Erdman needed a Blake manuscript collated at the Morgan Library he would send me to do it. He seemingly knew everyone in the world of Romantic scholarship, and most came knocking at our door. I even once fetched a Blake biography from the stacks for Anthony Blunt, before he was knighted and later be-knighted. If a special project needed a courier to get a unique item to the Meriden Gravure Company in Connecticut, I got to do that and to see their collotype machine in action, as I once did with Whitman's *Blue Book*, Melville's own annotated copy of the 1861-1862 *Leaves of Grass*. The Library's facsimile (1968) is a tour de force of the printer's art that I was privileged to help put through the early stages of production.

During the McCarthy period Erdman was fired by the University of Minnesota before he took up an appointment there, suspect because of his editing of United Auto Workers publications, including *The Bomb*, during World War II. Whether he was a communist or not I never learned, but he was definitely of the far left if undemonstrative about it. His *Blake Prophet against Empire* is a classic but whether it was Blake's art or radical ideology that brought him into the Anthony Blunt orbit I don't know. David was lucky to get the job at the Library, as it rescued him from the opprobrium of his McCarthyite condemnation, and gave him a stable life after some years of uncertainty. Our office was responsible for all library publications from *Staff News* to *The Bulletin of The New York Public Library*, specialized bibliographies of library holdings, lists of science and technology acquisitions, the publications of the branch libraries, exhibit catalogues, and very special publications from the Arents and Berg collections and the performing arts collections.

The Library had its own printing facilities, a composition shop of three Linotype machines, a Heidelberg press, and a typographic genius named Paul Arbucho, Chief of the Composing Room. I spent a great deal of time in the Library basement printing offices, working on our routine publications, but also special projects like the Whitman *Blue Book*. I helped to put to bed, for example, works such as the supplemental volumes of the *Catalogue of the Arents Tobacco Collection* (noted above), Margaret Hills' *The Bible in America*, and Richard Wolfe's bibliography of *American Secular Music, 1801-1825*. Deirdre proofread the Wolfe bibliography over the next nine months while awaiting our first son. We also published new editions of Virginia Woolf's *The Waves*, George Gissing's *Letters*, his *Commonplace Book*, and many similar works, both separately and in the *Bulletin*.

In my new job I got to meet and work with many people then famous in the book world. Publisher B.W. Huebsch, who first published James Joyce and D.H. Lawrence in the United States, came visiting as an octogenarian when working on a Bowker lecture that we were responsible for printing. He also published the first edition of *Winesburg, Ohio* in 1919, before his firm merged with the Viking Press. Another visitor was Dan H. Laurence, editor and bibliographer of George Bernard Shaw.

One particularly famous book designer and typographer who visited us was Thomas M. Cleland. In 1960 the Library was featuring an exhibition of Cleland's work as a fine artist. For the occasion the Editor's Office reprinted a 1915 speech of Cleland's called *Printing as a Fine Art*, a rousing talk that was first delivered to the American Library Association at its annual meeting in Berkeley and published by ALA in its *Bulletin*. In reprinting the work as designed by Cleland himself, we had to be sure to do it in a way that satisfied the criterion of the title. Cleland was 80 at the time and I remember guiding him cautiously down the steep steps to our office. He was known in the trade as a curmudgeon, difficult to work with, and he did give us a hard time about a few points but he was pleased with the product.

[*Coda: fast forward almost twenty years to 1978 when, as Director of the Research Libraries, I was asked to represent NYPL in accepting a posthumous honor for Cleland from the Art Director's Club, initiating him into their Hall of Fame at their annual dinner. Working up my acceptance speech was a delight in that Cleland was a brilliantly sardonic and irreverent writer and it was easy to quote him to good effect. I can't find the talk I gave in his honor but I know I quoted from an address he gave to the American Institute of Graphic Arts in 1940 called* Harsh Words. *After 36 pages of very caustic disparagement of graphic designers and typographers, the very people who were now honoring him, he claimed to be looking for something constructive to say:*

And this constructive suggestion reminds me that I ought, perhaps, to temper this hurricane of destructive criticism with some further helpful hints. At the moment I can think of only two that might relieve the dreadful situation that I have pictured.

One is that we organize a pogrom of all type designers—a little hard on them perhaps, but they would gain martyrdom to a cause—and the other that we establish a concentration camp in which to intern all those who think up or think they think up new ideas in typography for such time as it would take them to recover from their delusion. There they can while away many hours in the company of the men who invented paper towels, pasteboard milk bottles, and beer in cans.[21]

The award was a polished glass cube which I brought back to NYPL where such realia is not always appreciated unless it is an Oscar, Tony, or Grammy. It's the only posthumous award I expect to receive.]

During my first year in the Editor's Office we received a manuscript called *Wordsworthian Criticism, an Annotated Bibliography, 1945-1959*, by Elton F. Henley, supplementing an earlier Wordsworth bibliography by James Venable Logan. Since it fit in well with Erdman's vision of NYPL publications as a prime locus of Romantic scholarship, Erdman accepted the manuscript and asked me to prepare it for publication. Alas, the manuscript was riddled with mistakes, bibliographical, grammatical, descriptive, and otherwise, and it required a major overhaul. When ready for publication in 1960, Erdman thoughtfully added to the title-page a byline, "with the Assistance of David H. Stam." He wanted it clear that the intellectual responsibility for the work was a shared one. I never learned what Henley made of this intervention, or of the two subsequent versions whose title pages read "By Elton F. Henley and David H. Stam," for which in fact I had sole responsibility. This and a brief bibliography of Harry Miller Lydenberg (as Director of the Research Libraries, I would later be his successor as Chief of the renamed Reference Department, four or five times removed) and an edited volume of *Turgenev in English* gave my resume some early publications and a misleading reputation as a Romantic scholar. With the first publication of *Wordsworthian Criticism*, Erdman told me that I would always henceforth be labeled a Wordsworth man.

---

[21] T.M. Cleland. *Harsh Words: an Address Delivered at a Meeting of the American Institute of Graphic Arts in New York City February 5, 1940....* (New York: American Institute of Graphic Arts, 1940) p. 36-37.

The Lydenberg piece did get some attention that surprised us. In Edinburgh I had started a lifelong habit (sometimes sporadic, always in arrears) of reading the *Times Literary Supplement*. The Lydenberg bibliography, really a modest supplement to an earlier bibliography, appeared in the May 1960 issue of *The Bulletin of The New York Public Library*, an issue that *TLS* reviewed anonymously on July 29, 1960, along with several other American library publications. The author it turns out was John Carter. The last paragraph is perhaps worth quoting in full:

> But the place of honour belongs to the brief tribute by the present librarian, Dr. Edward G. Freehafer,[22] and the bibliography by Mr. David H. Stam, which fittingly mark the recent death of Harry Miller Lydenberg, perhaps the greatest librarian in the New York Public Library's history. Although it is close upon twenty years since that able, learned, open-minded, open-hearted, humorous and lovable man retired from Fifth Avenue, he has left an indelible mark not only there but on the whole library world, and an equally indelible one on the memory of anyone who had the luck to know him.

Between 1916 and 1921 Lydenberg, my able and learned predecessor, had been contributing chapters on the history of NYPL to the *Bulletin*, tracing the evolution of the Library from the Astor and Lenox libraries through the consolidation with the Tilden Trust, to the opening of the new building in 1911, and the difficult recovery from the nearly

---

[22]   When Freehafer retired in 1971 the Board of Trustees appointed its first paid President, Richard W. Couper (1971-1981). He was succeeded by Vartan Gregorian (1981-1989), Timothy S. Healey, S.J. (1989-1992), Paul LeClerc (1993-2011), and Anthony Marx (2011-). None of these men, all academics, had any qualifications in librarianship except as users. All believed they had the best interests of the New York Public Library at heart, though it would be difficult to argue that any of them embodied the service ethos of the true librarian. By contrast, all of the pre-presidential Directors were trained librarians as were all of the six Andrew W. Mellon Directors of the Research Libraries. During Freehafer's tenure the Library was comprised of the Reference Department (renamed Research Libraries in 1973) and the Circulation Department (renamed Branch Libraries in the same year).

disastrous effects of WWI. These essays were brought together as one large volume, *A History of The New York Public Library*, by Harry Miller Lydenberg, published in 1923. It bears on the title-page verso the legend "Printed and Bound at The New York Public Library." To my mind, Lydenberg remains "the greatest librarian in the New York Public Library's history."[23] None of the post-1971 Presidents is in the running.

Training in Librarianship
September 1959 to June 1964

Meanwhile, in September 1959, I began a master's program in library science at Rutgers University and proceeded slowly to set some kind of record for length-to-degree in librarianship. One course per term, and sometimes none, was a pace that suited my New York City life. One course in library administration I dropped at the first break, turned off by the eminent professor's opening gambit that "the reason that America is the greatest country in the world is because we know how to organize." Since it was a required course, I had to take it and eventually did so with an equally fatuous teacher.

My hero on the faculty was Paul S. Dunkin who had been Head Cataloguer at the Folger Library in Washington before coming to Rutgers. I took three of my required ten courses from Dunkin and considered

---

[23]   Some have argued that Lydenberg's greatest contribution to the Library and the world of scholarship was his obsession in collecting as deeply as possible the ephemeral and fugitive publications of pamphlet literature, and these collections at NYPL are in fact very extensive. One story about Lydenberg that I've heard but cannot now document was that in the years just before the US entered World War II, the Library administration was debating which Library treasures were the most important to protect by moving them to remote and safe storage. Some argued the incunabula, others all special collections, but Lydenberg argued that the pamphlets would be the collection most difficult to replace. The unhappy part of this story is that for over six decades tens of thousands of these pamphlets were placed in so-called "pamphlet volumes," anywhere from five to fifteen per volume, and then oversewn into strong black buckram bindings. These are now generally in very bad condition and constitute one of the Library's greatest preservation problems.

him something of a mentor for my future work in technical services. His short book on *How to Catalog a Rare Book* is a little gem of practicality, as was his course in descriptive bibliography.[24] His balanced approach to rare book cataloguing, to tell the catalogue user what readers need to do their work but not to do their work for them, proved useful to me as a library administrator, though some scholars regarded his book as too rudimentary for the sophisticated descriptive bibliographer. There were other notable faculty at Rutgers whom I saw less often, particularly Ralph Shaw and Richard Shoemaker, well-known in bibliographical circles for the Shaw-Shoemaker catalogues of *Early American Imprints* from 1801 to 1829.

For the most part I found many of the courses boring and the literature of librarianship turgid and dull beyond words. What I did enjoy was working on substantial research reports, in my case involving analyses of important functions in NYPL's Reference Department. Two that I remember were studies of periodical check-in systems in the library, and another on my own Editor's Office. A third I found buried in my archives, a paper written for my first course in the fall of 1959, taught by Richard Shoemaker. I had forgotten the piece but it was called "The Research Library," a topic to which I would devote most of the rest of my life, when not running them using them. I can sum up part of this period by saying that I eventually received a library degree from Rutgers University (1962) but achieved the greater part of my education in librarianship from The New York Public Library. It was the MLS that opened up doors that would otherwise have been closed, as did my later doctorate.

My Introduction to Rare Books
June 1959

Early in my time in the Editor's Office, about May 1959, I was talking with Erdman in our little mezzanine office when the now legendary Lola Szladits of the Berg Collection came in and asked Erdman

---

[24]   Paul Shaner Dunkin. *How to Catalog a Rare Book* (Chicago, IL: American Library Association, 1951) 85 p.

if he would be sending me to Charlottesville that summer. Neither of us knew what she was talking about, so she explained that it would be the first meeting of the Rare Books and Manuscript Section (RBMS) of the American Library Association (ALA), that the Library would pay half my cost, and that I might find it useful in my editorial work with the special collections curators. I was all of twenty-three years old and as naive as any sheltered late adolescent could be, even after two years in the Navy. A month later I found myself on a bus to Virginia, where I would meet several people who would become future colleagues and close friends, people like Stanley Pargellis and Jim Wells of the Newberry Library in Chicago, Marjorie Wynne of the Yale University Library (before its Beinecke Library had opened), Eleanor Nichols of the Pforzheimer Keats-Shelley Collection, and Lewis M. Stark, Chief of Rare Books at NYPL. It was an exciting conference for a neophyte, and I learned a great deal about special collections, no thanks to Lola Szladits who generally snubbed me during the conference. Fortunately, Mr. Stark was particularly kind. I could not figure out why Lola had wanted me to attend, but I remain grateful.

A few years later I worked for Lola as a cataloguer in the Berg Collection as part of an internship I had arranged after graduation from library school. Fifteen years after that I became her boss as Director of the Research Libraries, an interesting role reversal, as any who knew her would guess. She was a dictatorial and mercurial boss and a conspiratorial subordinate, always testing the limits of control until the appropriate limits were established. For example, in 1979, Mel Edelstein, Librarian of the J. Paul Getty Trust and an old friend from Baltimore days, asked me to lunch at the Century Club to report that Lola had been bad-mouthing me in New York circles and beyond, thus undermining my administration. After lunch I returned directly to the Berg Collection, told her what I had heard, that only she would know what was and was not true, that whatever it was it was bad for me, worse for her, and worst of all for the Library, and it had better stop. That rather severe slap on the wrist, reinforced by a stern memo, seemed to work, and led to a much more productive working relationship, which suffered briefly when Vartan Gregorian arrived in 1981 and she saw a possible wedge between Greg and me. In 1989 she stayed with us in Syracuse, gave an indiscreet talk to our Friends group about Berg's acquisition of the W. H. Auden papers, and enjoyed the freedom and space of our home and being away from

New York City. Shortly after her return she was diagnosed with cancer. By the time she died in 1990 we were good and mutually respectful friends and on her hospital bed she told us that her recent visit to Syracuse had been her last good day.

I can now add that while reading through some documentation about the first RBMS conference on the occasion of the fiftieth anniversary of its first Charlottesville conference, I ran across a memo from April 1959 from the conference organizers, expressing concern that the conference had received so few registrants and those planning to attend should drum up some more business if they really wanted to meet. At last, an explanation if not a very flattering one.

"Less Mooning, More Bassooning"
September 1961

In August of 1961 my girlfriend jilted me very suddenly and now I think for good cause, though I never knew what her cause was other than another man. My mistake, as I later speculated, was to be far too possessive, and determined to have her all to myself. There may have been other mistakes, and we were both fairly immature, but that was the clearest reason to me after the tears dried. I had once read a line from Goldsmith, "he drew the bonds of friendship so tight that they broke," and had applied it to one of my erstwhile NYPL friends, Gabriel Austin, only to find that it applied equally to me. At some point I vowed not to repeat that mistake.

In some despondency and through odd circumstances, I decided to buy a bassoon. One weekend during that fall of 1961 I was visiting brother Jim in Cambridge and during my visit he and his fellow Brandeis graduate student, Victor Wallis, were playing piano/cello duets. When amidst my depression I expressed some envy for their collaborative experience, Victor asked why I did not get a cello for myself. Harking back to my half-year of playing a single reed bassoon in college, I chose the bassoon instead. One of the Music Division librarians, Sidney Beck, with help from composer, oboist, and music publisher Josef Marx found a new Puchner bassoon which I bought for $425, partly thanks to a $125 loan from my ever-generous father. The Puchner was a very good German-made bassoon distributed in the US by the first bassoonist of the Detroit Symphony Orchestra, Hugh Cooper. It has a soft and sweet sound, but is a level below the Stradivarius of bassoons, the Heckel.

I threw myself into mastering the instrument with weekly lessons from Jane Taylor, constant exercises, even using the occasional sick day for four or five hours of practice. Within six months I had joined the New Cecilia Chamber Orchestra, an amateur orchestra that rehearsed at St. Mark's in the Bowery, conducted by oboist Henry Schuman. I was lucky with my teachers, starting with Jane of the recently-formed Dorian Quintet, a person of exquisite musicianship. She was the embodiment of the Dorians and only retired after their 40th anniversary, and after they had played in all but one of the United States. She had auditioned for Stokowski's American Symphony Orchestra and played with the ASO for over forty years until forced out by Leon Botstein a few years ago. I was nominally on the Dorian Quintet Board for forty years, but its first meeting did not occur until after she retired, and I never got to meet Elliott Carter and some other Dorian-commissioned composers with whom she papered her Board. She died rather suddenly in April 2012.

Other teachers were Robert Cole, first bassoonist of the New York City Ballet Orchestra, much diminished by alcohol but better than most with only 10% of the effort. There was a memorial concert for him at NYU that included Dvorak's *Serenade for Winds*, Op. 44, with Leonard Hindel and me on the bassoon parts. Not an easy second bassoon part, I wonder now how I had the courage to participate. Lenny Hindel spent his career, first with the Metropolitan Opera Orchestra, and then with the New York Philharmonic from which he retired a few years ago. The post-concert reception was at the home of Newell Jenkins, founder of the Clarion Chamber Orchestra and strong partisan of early and often obscure works. Another teacher was Morris Newman, a New York freelance musician who combined his bassoon with recorders and krumhorns, and worked with early music ensembles sometimes including countertenor Russell Oberlin. It's worth recalling that this period in New York saw regular performances of New York Pro Musica directed by Noah Greenberg, featuring LaNoue Davenport and Oberlin, and regular visits to Town Hall[25] of countertenor Alfred Deller whose LPs were all the rage, and whose recording of Purcell's *Ode to St. Cecilia* affected many of us when Kennedy was killed on St. Cecilia's Day, 1963.[26]

To return to August 1961, when the Berlin Wall went up my very young girlfriend called it quits (on the same day), within a few months I found solace in my new bassoon. That year was also a year of sexual searching, including the girl from Wheaton, a western Caribbean classmate from the Rutgers Library School, the camp nurse redevivus, a brief and unsatisfactory encounter with my Edinburgh friend in London, an African-American lesbian whom I unsuccessfully tried to seduce despite her apparent willingness, and a few other more fleeting acquaintances.

I was particularly saddened by the parting with my Rutgers classmate. She lived with relatives in Brooklyn. We had met at my apartment a few times, and I had accompanied her home a few times. We came back to New York by train after our last class at Rutgers in the spring of 1962. I was very tired and when she begged me to accompany her to Brooklyn I refused, saying she was very welcome to spend the night at my place but she too refused. We were both adamant and parted very unhappily. Earlier I had promised to send her some comments on a paper she'd written and

---

[25] Town Hall, on West 43rd Street, was a beautiful but now much-neglected classical music venue that had been a very active one in the 1960s. In addition to concerts by the Deller Consort, New York Pro Musica, Beverage Webster, and assorted quartets, the most exciting concert I remember there was Stravinsky conducting his own *Les Noces* in December 1959, with Samuel Barber, Aaron Copland, Elliott Carter, and Lukas Foss as the four pianists. See the website of composer Michael Colgrass for a hilarious description of that rehearsal and performance: http://colgrassadventures.com/2011/12/

[26] In the summers of 1964 and 1965, when I was at Marlboro College, I studied briefly with one of the Marlboro Music Festival bassoonists, Joyce Kelley, a delightful woman who lived in Greenwich and I believe played in the New York City Opera orchestra. In the Marlboro summers I had the Library to myself and occasionally practiced in my office, sometimes finding visitors to the campus listening outside. Once I noticed a group of these tourists listening intently to a recording I was playing of Mahler's *Resurrection Symphony No. 2*!

a few days later I did so. It was returned unopened and that was the end of that.

One of my critical readers has suggested that in this period I was spending an inordinate amount of time chasing skirts. I don't really think so, but think rather that it was one of several preoccupations. I look back and see myself as a very busy young man preoccupied with his job, his studies, his growing musical commitments, and his personal life. In any case, all that minor league philandering ended when I finally finished library school at Rutgers in the summer of 1962. I took my new Puchner bassoon to Detroit for conditioning, and then took a long vacation in Europe that included visits to friends in England, an awkward reunion in London with my Edinburgh girlfriend, going on to see my brother John who was studying patristics in Basle, and eventually joining an Italian friend, Aldo Giacchino, someone I'd first met in of all places the NYPL Card Preparation department where we commiserated about our miserable job. In Basle I remember a beautiful day at a public swimming pool where I saw a tabloid headline reading "Marilyn Monroe ist tot." There I borrowed my brother's VW van, met Aldo and his girlfriend and future wife Priscilla in Rimini, and drove from there to Dubrovnik, via Venice, Trieste, Split, etc. (not without car troubles or intestinal tribulations), then by boat across the Adriatic to Bari, and up the coast back to Rimini where Aldo's parents had a summer retreat from Milan. Aldo's father was a violinist in La Scala Piccolo. With no Italian to speak of, I kept wondering who "lui" referred to in our conversations until I came to realize that it referred to me. This trip gave me my first view of that part of the world, except for 1957 port visits with the *USS Iowa* to Palermo, described above. After that I never got closer than Switzerland until the Delmas Foundation brought us a new concentration on Italy.

In the fall of 1962, two new bassoonists joined the orchestra, a delightful Danish doctor named Jørgen Gliemann, then a visiting researcher at the Rockefeller Institute, and Deirdre [pronounced *dodd-dra*] Corcoran, just out of Radcliffe and a new Egyptology graduate student at NYU's Institute of Fine Arts. Deirdre had been a bassoon student of Sherman Walt, first bassoon of the Boston Symphony Orchestra. She spent her high school years in Hopedale, Massachusetts, a communitarian society,[27] beginning a fascination that has lasted into her retirement years and her present role on the Board of the Oneida Mansion House in upstate New York. But her real obsession was music; at fifteen she joined the musician's union so that she could play with the Worcester Symphony Orchestra as second bassoonist. At Harvard, although starting out as a mathematician (she had been admitted to MIT as a mathematician, but chose Harvard instead), she migrated over to Fine Arts with a senior thesis on Odilon Redon, the French symbolist artist. At Harvard no credit was given for performance, so her very heavy music schedule was over and above her academic work—work which she claims took a back seat to the enjoyment of her music-cum-social life in Cambridge. Those activities included the Harvard-Radcliffe Orchestra, the Bach Society Orchestra, the Gilbert and Sullivan Players, and any number of chamber groups needing a bassoonist. For a time she was President of the Harvard-Radcliffe Orchestra, sometimes known as the Pierian Society.

Since Deirdre is woven into the entire fabric of my life from this point on let me take a few pages to give a brief overview of some highlights of her life and career. Raised in New England in a somewhat fractured Irish-Catholic family, Deirdre chose a secular path. As a serious bassoonist from the age of 11, she was particularly drawn to circles of musical friends, many of whom were Jewish. During an early conversation, she expressed surprise that I was not, given the ambiguity of my name and my deep involvement in music.

Deirdre's father graduated from and played football and basketball for Ohio State University, graduating in 1931 in the midst of the Depression. He quite quickly found a job with the W.T. Grant Company and, appreciating the security it offered him, stayed with that company during his entire working life. He served in the Navy during World War II while he completed an MBA program at Babson Institute and Harvard University. This connection probably affected Deirdre's choice of Radcliffe/Harvard for her own undergraduate education. Her father was a sociable person, a devoted father, and a doting grandfather. Deirdre's

---

[27]   See her "The Role of Women in Hopedale, a Nineteenth-Century Universalist-Unitarian Utopian Community in South-Central Massachusetts," *American Communal Societies Quarterly* VII (July 2013) p. 115-137.

mother, Kathryn Walsh Corcoran, was a graduate of Brooklyn's Pratt Institute in textile design. She was a stylish, sophisticated and often charming woman, but not demonstrably affectionate, even towards her husband who I thought, looking at the situation from the male perspective, deserved better, or her children. She was an archly amusing raconteur of mostly sad tales, some of which were Irish and others that may as well have been. Like Nixon she maintained an active enemies list which for her included Nixon himself, along with those many Republicans whom she considered selfish and uncouth, as well as most British royalty and Prime Ministers. She was basically an independent in every sense of the word.

On our first date in late September 1962, hot chocolate after a rehearsal, Deirdre asked whether I edited real books or just bibliographies; also whether I was always in the habit of straightening out my silverware. (Yes, to both.) We survived that introduction and have been together for fifty-one years, my sharpest critic and best friend. In October she broke up with her Harvard boyfriend and we began to share more time together; a Schubert chamber concert at the YMHA, a November trip to Cambridge and Mount Monadnock, Thanksgiving with the Erdmans in Princeton, and fairly soon a decision to marry in May 1963.

Deirdre completed a full year of studies at the Institute of Fine Arts in 1962-63, and started her Masters' Thesis on Egyptian Group Sculpture, eventually completing the thesis and degree after we moved to Marlboro College, Vermont. While at Marlboro she taught Western Art 101 and Buddhist Art, among other courses. She did some graduate work at Northwestern University when we lived in Chicago, but completed her next two Masters degrees while we were in Baltimore, one in education from Johns Hopkins, and another in Library Science at Catholic University in Washington. In Chicago she was an administrative assistant to the Director of the Art Institute of Chicago, Charles Cunningham, and later Assistant Curator of Classical Art. In Baltimore she taught art history at the Bryn Mawr School, pursued her degrees, and spent one year as a reference librarian at the Baltimore County Public Library in Towson, just north of Baltimore. She was also busy with three young children at home.

The timing of our return to New York and NYPL in July 1978 was perfect in at least one respect: it was the year of the Metropolitan Museum's blockbuster exhibit on Tutankhamen and Deirdre the Egyptologist was immediately hired as "liaison" between the Met's

Egyptian Department and the exhibition designers. After a year as a librarian at SUNY-Purchase she went on to complete doctoral studies at Columbia. She was teaching at the Columbia School of Library Service when I moved to Syracuse in March 1986, Deirdre following in June.

This irregular pattern of employment is often the fate of a trailing spouse, and especially one with children, to follow the primary breadwinner. That pattern was at last broken when we came to Syracuse University, she as Assistant Professor in the School of Information Studies (now known as The ISchool), and I as University Librarian. A reorientation of the School with appointment of a new dean led to her resignation after two years. She next took a position, housed in the same school, of Executive Director of the Museum Computer Network for another two years, followed by three years of teaching at the Catholic University Library School, where she had earned her own first degree in librarianship. Then followed a one-year leave of absence during which she helped run the Skaneateles Chamber Music Festival, three years as Syracuse University's first webmaster, and then two difficult years as University Librarian at Drew University while I remained in Syracuse. She had remarkably diversified experience and a formidable publication list in several fields, all before I retired from the Syracuse University Library in 1998. Her last job, organizing and running a program in rare book librarianship at Long Island University from 2002 to 2011, was probably the most rewarding in her mind and to her many students.

But to return to my account of our early life together: for a short time we had in common a particular kind of bassoon. Deirdre's was a Polisi, a German bassoon distributed by a well-known New York bassoonist, William Polisi of the New York Philharmonic. He was famous for a recording of *Le Sacre du Printemps* in which Polisi played the opening bassoon solo. Since my bassoon was being voiced and serviced by the US distributor of Puchner bassoons, Hugh Cooper of the Detroit Symphony, I had to rent another. That one turned out to be a Polisi which I picked up at Polisi's home in Flushing, Queens. His son Joseph, also a bassoonist, is now President of the Juilliard School. For forty-five years we were a two-bassoon family, mildly debating the virtues of our two instruments. When I was diagnosed with ALS in 2008, I had not played for ten years. It was clear that I would not play again, and so we sold Deirdre's Polisi and the Puchner remains at home if she ever wants to return to it.

Shortly before we met in 1962 I had finished my library degree and soon would have to make a decision about how to use it. Not wanting to commit myself, with typical tergiversation I asked Harold Ostvold, the Director of the Research Libraries (then called the Reference Department), if I could create an internship using my new degree if not new skills in a few Library departments. The Library internship program had been moribund for a number of years but with his encouragement I asked for a year's worth of assignments in the Information Division, the Music Division, the Berg Collection of English and American Literature, and the American History Division.

The last declined my services (as they had in 1959; ironically, I was responsible twenty years later for closing American History as a separate division) but I spent all of 1963 in the other three departments. The first six months of my internship were devoted to the Information Division in Room 315, the central catalogue room for the Reference Department then still consolidated in the 42nd Street building, and the gateway to NYPL's great Reading Room. It was a baptism by fire in one of the world's most comprehensive reference services where I was mentored by a great librarian (Archibald DeWeese, a pianist with whom I played some bassoon duets at his apartment on 57th Street), from whom I learned a great deal. I remember those months in Room 315 as both mentally and physically demanding, the most tiring job I ever had, but extremely rewarding.

Since younger readers can hardly imagine what reference service was like in pre-automation, pre-Google days, let me outline a typical work day of eight hours with no computers: three hour-long sessions of information desk work, mostly standing; two hours of telephone reference (seated except when fetching appropriate reference works); one or two hours of work on reference letters; and the remainder in breaks and miscellaneous assignments (e.g., shelving books in the grand Reading Room). The reference desk was the easiest since it was primarily decoding the reference question and then interpreting the catalogue to the user in order to find the right book to answer the question. These were face-to-face interactions which, apart from a few hostile readers, usually helped us to figure out what the user needed. One reader asked me if I could recommend a book on the fall of Franco in 1940. I had to say that I didn't know that he had fallen in 1940 and asked to see the source of her question. It turned out to be a mimeographed course syllabus in which the crossbar of the letter 'e' in France had been obscured. Another legendary question was whether we had a copy of *Oranges and Peaches*. A little sleuthing showed it to be Darwin's landmark work.

Telephone reference was a different matter since you never quite knew what or whom you were dealing with. One woman called to ask whether it was appropriate for her husband to use the word 'crud' in a formal report. So I reached for a dictionary of American slang and read through a number of definitions, one of which was "semen left on the outside of a man's pants after intercourse." With this she howled with laughter and presumably persuaded her husband to find another word. We had a time-limit policy for telephone reference questions: after five minutes or so we had to ask the caller to come in to the Library for help. Brother Jim reminds me that one user wanted to learn something about extra-sensory perception. He claims that when the time had run out, I referred her to the Mental Telepathy Society, suggesting that "if they're any good, they're already looking up the answer."

Another policy was to decline questions related to crossword puzzles. They were easy to spot since several of the librarians would have already done the morning puzzles, and the word went around. But when I told one inquirer that we didn't provide crossword information she became irate and demanded my name so she could talk to my supervisor. Here I was insolent and said we didn't provide that information either but she could find it in the telephone book. And the flow of reference letters could be a challenge—there was a constant stream of them and we could choose which we wanted to do. Some were easy, some provided interesting mini-research ideas, and the really difficult ones would sometimes languish for months. Weekend duty in the Reading Room was often a good time to work on difficult reference letters. Back in 1963 the Library was open every day of the year from 9 am to 10 pm, except for Sundays and holidays when we were open from 1 pm to 9 pm. Those were great days, though I must say the exhaustion from Reference Department work fully justified our two-week honeymoon in June.

Deirdre and I courted very steadily from September 1962 until we married the following May. Our first formal date was an all Schubert chamber music concert, including the *Trout Quintet*, at the 92nd Street YMHA. Our second was the opening week of the new Philharmonic Hall on September 24 when John Browning premiered Samuel Barber's *Piano Concerto*, Op. 34, with the Boston Symphony and Erich Leinsdorf. I am amazed that I had the wit to suggest that date to hear a work that has become a favorite.

In November Deirdre and I met in Cambridge on the steps of the Fogg Art Museum where she handed me a carton of Marlboros, a guilt offering after bumming cigarettes from me for a couple of months. She quit six months later, a week after we married, and as far as we could tell a few days after her first pregnancy began. That weekend I met some of her Harvard friends, including one of her former roommates, as well as Ted Wendell. Ted was a Harvard soccer player and math major. We were very surprised to find him teaching math at Marlboro when we arrived there a year and a half later. Our twin son Wendell is named after him. We also took a trip to New Hampshire with Victor Wallis, the cellist friend of Jim's who originally encouraged me to take up an instrument. We had climbed Mount Monadnock that November day and were admiring the cloud filled valleys beneath some visible mountain peaks above when the always left-leaning Victor observed that "a nation conceived in liberty would be illegitimate." That trip pretty much sealed our relationship and I proposed in some slightly ambiguous way on the promenade in Brooklyn Heights. She said she was wondering when I would get around to asking. Today, neither of us can give a good answer to the question of why we married, other than intellectual compatibility and physical attraction.

We married on May 15th of this internship year, and already had taken an apartment on West 115th Street, one which shared an airshaft with my bassoon teacher's apartment where the Dorian Wind Quintet often rehearsed. The day we were married was also notable for the space launch of L. Gordon Cooper of Project Mercury, and for the award to Peter, Paul, and Mary of their first Grammy (not that that would have registered on my celebrity scale). When I went to work that morning I left Deirdre studying hieroglyphics on the fire escape, on a bright and beautiful spring day. We met at one o'clock in Bryant Park, took the subway to City Hall, and were married by a lisping J.P. who turned me into an "awful wedded husband." Deirdre's aunt Doll Miller was a witness and later we met her Uncle John, Doll's husband, who drove us to a minimalist reception insisted upon by brother Paul and Jane Stam in Kinnelon, New Jersey. Two of Deirdre's Radcliffe classmates came, one her New York City flat mate, but it was a low-key, alcohol-free affair. We had decided to avoid a large family event because of the strong and discordant religious traditions that we both had abandoned. We made an unusual group of Catholics, ex-Catholics, Protestants, and agnostics, of teetotalers and drinkers, all cautious about desecrating any shibboleths. My mother cried through most of it, I suppose over her lost son or her backsliding Catholic daughter-in-law. Uncle John dropped us off on 42nd Street at the No. 1 subway at around midnight and we went home to start our new life.

We delayed our honeymoon until the first two weeks in June when we borrowed a car and made a circuit of New England, starting in Madison, Connecticut, at Deirdre's parent's summer cottage, but mostly in New Hampshire where we had a near disastrous climb up one of Deirdre's favorite Sandwich mountains during black fly season. More successful was our visit to Dartmouth College Library and Evelyn Stefansson and the Stefansson Collection of Polar materials. Vilhjalmur Stefansson (1879-1962) had been an important but controversial explorer, one of the greatest collectors of Arctic books ever, a collection he sold to Dartmouth along with himself and his wife Evelyn. In the Navy I had read his *My Life with the Eskimo* and wanted to know more about this man who had dominated the field of Arctic Studies and had published another influential book called *The Friendly Arctic*. His general thesis was that the Arctic was safe and manageable if the explorer would only abandon his Western prejudices, eat plenty of blubber, and learn from the natives. Despite the death of her husband the year before and the uncertainties of her life, Evelyn could not have been more gracious to her visitors interested in her husband. Many years later when we reminisced with her about our visit, Evelyn told us that that period was the most difficult of her life.

We spent part of the summer in Madison, had visits there with Deirdre's parents, with the Danish Gliemanns (Jørgen had joined the orchestra at the same time as Deirdre), with Victor Wallis and his new wife Joan, played bassoon duets on the back patio overlooking the Hammonasset marshes, and took a trip with Aldo Giachinno and Priscilla Smith, Aldo's future wife, spending a night at her family home near Amherst and attending a concert at the Marlboro Music Festival, a visit that would have lasting ramifications. We were also surprised to learn that Deirdre was pregnant, an unexpected development requiring some serious planning of what to do after I finished my internship and she completed a second year at the Institute of Fine Arts.

In July 1963 I moved to the Music Division at NYPL where I did reference duty of a much more specialized nature. Among other duties was a project consolidating orchestral performance files in the Music Division under Frank Campbell, Chief of the Music Division. These were indexes for programs and program notes from most of the leading American symphony orchestras, for which we had complete runs of bound volumes. These lists were on typed 3" by 5" cards, listing the dates for the program notes in each volume (for example the dates when the New York Philharmonic played Brahms's *Fourth Symphony* or Fauré's *Requiem*). The task was to combine those dates with other performances of those works. It seemed to be a good idea at the time but it would better have waited for a computer app. Twenty years later I asked the archivist of the Philharmonic about a performance of the Fauré *Requiem* that I had attended in Carnegie Hall in February of 1962, memorable because Nadia Boulanger had conducted the piece in a concert in memory of Bruno Walter who had died that morning. Not only did the archivist tell me the exact date, but she also gave me a recording of the concert.

The Dance Collection was then a part of the Music Division, run fairly independently by Gigi Oswald, and there were several other librarians with whom I'd worked closely while I worked in the Editor's Office. On one occasion Campbell invited me to lunch with Samuel Baron, the founding flutist of the New York Woodwind Quintet, an exquisite group that premiered many contemporary works, including one of our own favorites, Samuel Barber's *Summer Music*. The discussion with Sam Baron concerned a grandiose scheme I'd developed to spend my next three years on grant funds from the Library to compile a comprehensive bibliography of chamber music for winds and other combinations of instruments. I worked hard on that proposal but it was rendered moot when other employment beckoned. On another occasion when Campbell was busy he asked me to join Sidney Beck in entertaining Julian Bream for an hour. I don't know that I did my job but he certainly entertained us, talking about his life as a concert guitarist, his repertoire, and his preference for the lute. He said he concertized with the guitar for money in order to enjoy the pleasure of the lute. Or so I remember. Frank also persuaded me to write book reviews for *Notes*, the journal of the Music Library Association.

My musicalische Sommer[28] concluded at the end of August and I moved on to the Henry W. and Albert A. Berg Collection of English and American Literature for the final four months of my internship. The Berg is one of the great treasures of NYPL, well-known for its printed and manuscript collections of English and American literature. There were good collections of earlier English literature, including manuscripts of John Donne, the Shakespeare Folios, etc. But the prime collections of greater research value were the manuscripts of modern writers like W. H. Auden, T.S. Eliot, the WWI poets in the Edward Marsh papers, and Virginia Woolf. The job itself was rather schizophrenic in that I loved the work and materials I was processing, but John Gordan was aloof and Lola was difficult to work with, not one of those smokers I enjoyed being around. *Horribile dictu*, at that time we could smoke at our desks, even while working on priceless manuscripts.

One of the literary collections I was fortunate enough to work on was the archive of Edward Marsh, editor of *Georgian Poetry*, publisher and friend of many of the WWI war poets, amanuensis and critic ("diabolizer") to Winston Churchill, and all-round polymath. Among the papers I processed were letters of Rupert Brooke, Siegfried Sassoon,

---

[28] This is an inexcusable pun on Susan 'Suki' Sommer, a colleague and friend in the Music Division, a brilliant and an extremely funny librarian. I knew her first during my internship and when I moved on from Music to the Berg Collection, I offered and she accepted a tour of the collection. Years later when I returned to NYPL she was still in the Music Division, in charge of its Special Collections. She then told me that the tour of Berg changed her life in giving her an appreciation for the raw materials of research. She was a pushy Smithee, sometimes loud and embarrassing with a heart of gold. Two anecdotes: I was once traveling from California to Syracuse via St. Louis, and was sitting toward the front of the plane. Suki got on in St Louis, and spotting me said in a loud voice to the crowded plane, "Why aren't you back in the smoking section? I always sit back there—you meet much more interesting characters there." When we moved to Marlboro in 1965 we somehow transferred our West 115th Street apartment to another NYPL music librarian, Neill Ratliff, who was still there when we returned to New York in 1978. Soon after our return, Suki and Neill threw a welcoming party for us in our old two-room apartment—about 200 people came. My age, she died in 2008 at 72, much loved to the end. One obituary called her the "spiritual leader" of the Music Library Association.

Isaac Rosenberg, Wilfred Owen, all in the Marsh papers, as well as other manuscripts of Padraic Colum, Arthur Hugh Clough, Lady Gregory, and several others. Among the Sassoon papers, if I remember correctly, were letters from the war and post-war periods which covered material also included in two of his autobiographical works. It was fascinating to see firsthand how memory molds or distorts the record to shape one's self-image. That lesson has stayed with me today as I continue to wonder whether I might somehow have shaped my own memory of Sassoon's variants. It might not have been Sassoon at all, but the papers are there to prove whatever might be made of them.

One problem that troubled me in the Berg Collection was that the very catalogue which reported what it owned was locked inside the room where the collections could be used. Thus the user had to know both what he was looking for and that Berg owned it. Five or six years later I read that the G.K. Hall Company was publishing a photo-facsimile of the entire Berg Card Catalogue and at last the world would know and be able to find what was behind those forbidding doors on the third floor. I was so thrilled by this news that I wrote a letter of congratulations to Jim Henderson, Chief of the Reference Department, little dreaming that someday I would hold the same office and face similar decisions. Thanks to my experience in the Berg Collection, making manuscripts accessible became my silent mission.

Deirdre was growing large and my work gave us a potential boy's name, Julian, after Julian Symons whose papers I was cataloguing, and Julian Bream whom I had met that summer. It seemed that her pregnancy was not welcomed by her Institute of Fine Arts professors and because of it she sadly lost out on an archaeological dig in Egypt. There were other affecting moments as well during late 1963. One November day I was returning from lunch in the new elevators at the northern end of the 42nd St. building. One of my Berg colleagues mentioned that the American sense of humor was not dead, that a rumor had started that the President had been shot. He was mortified when he learned that it was true. It was a shockingly emotional period, and I've not watched so much television since, no matter how great the crisis.

But it was a fascinating period. We still had orchestra rehearsals and performances, including one read-through of the *Marriage of Figaro*, with Bethany Beardslee and Ara Berberian, two excellent singers of the time. We scraped together various chamber combinations, rehearsed at our flat, or for Beethoven or Mozart quintets with someone who had a piano. I'd like to say that I attended the New York premiere of Benjamin Britten's *War Requiem* that Fall, simply because I had catalogued some of Wilfred Owen's poems from the Edward Marsh papers. I didn't, but my boss John Gordan did, making me further jealous by leaving the program in his waste basket. John Gordan was an elegant and courtly Virginian whom I did not and could not know well. To me, he always sounded and looked like my father's friend, Billy Graham.

Fifteen years later, on my return to the Library, his widow Phyllis was a very welcoming Trustee, an active member of the Committee on Research Libraries, a truly generous person as well as a most knowledgeable collector of incunabula, and one who truly cared about the Library staff. When the Chief of our Science and Technology Division, Robert Krupp, had a near-fatal train accident requiring two leg amputations she was the first to visit his hospital in Summit, New Jersey. Even while coping with Parkinson's disease late in life, she was extremely faithful to her Trustee duties, social, intellectual, and philanthropic.

In the bibliographical and typographical world, 1963 was noted for an important exhibition called *Printing and the Mind of Man* at the British Museum and at Earl's Court London, with Stanley Morison as the prime mover, and John Carter as editor of the catalogue (not to be confused with the massive book-length *Printing and the Mind of Man* published in 1967). A fine prospectus for the book was produced and distributed during the exhibition, and one visitor to John Gordan at the Berg Collection during that period was the same John Carter, a rare book dealer and author famous for his *ABC for Book Collectors* and many other bibliophilic accomplishments. One day in late 1963 I was talking with Gordan at his reading room desk when Carter arrived and Gordan graciously introduced me to the great man. As we stood there, Carter suddenly leaned over and pulled from Gordan's waste basket a copy of the prospectus of the catalogue, the clear and critical implication being that this was a piece of printing worth keeping.[29]

My period in the Berg Collection ended on New Year's Eve and I was and am grateful to the Library for the experience I gained during that very formative year. By that time, Deirdre was well along in her pregnancy and Julian Jacob was born on February 23rd at New York Hospital, nine months and eight days after we were married (who was counting, other than my mother?). Early that morning after seeing the movie of *Lawrence of Arabia*, having tea and stuffed dates with our Armenian neighbors, the Sassanians, we prepared for a trip to New York Hospital. (Mr. Sassanian was a violinist in the Radio City Music Hall and for us composed a brief piece for violin and two bassoons.) After an improvised breakfast, we took a taxi over to New York Hospital on the East Side. I noticed that the driver's name was Piper, so I could not help launching into a poem from *Songs of Innocence*, much of which I remembered:

Piping down the valleys wild
Piping songs of pleasant glee
On a cloud I saw a child,
And he, laughing, said to me:

"Pipe a song about a Lamb,"
So I piped with merry cheer
"Piper pipe that song again"
So I piped, he wept to hear.

"Drop the pipe, the happy pipe
Sing the songs of happy cheer,"
So I sang the same again
While he wept with joy to hear.

---

[29]   In 2013 we heard our friend Nicolas Barker, who in the early 1960s worked on the selection of titles for the PMM exhibition, lecture at the Grolier Club and again at Wells College on the history of the exhibition; despite the repetition he was able to bring differing insights into that epochal work on the history of printing and its influences on Western civilization.

"Piper please sit down and write
In a book that all may read"
So he vanished from my sight
And I plucked a hollow reed,

And I made a rural pen,
And I stained the water clear,
And I wrote my songs
Ev'ry child may joy to hear.

Julian was born later that day, after a long labor, and we named him after Julian Symons, a British crime writer, poet, and popular historian. My father asked about the name, confessing that he was afraid Julian had been named for the Apostate, so I was able to reassure him in this case if not in others.

During this period we had been seriously considering a move from the City and one possibility was Marlboro College in Vermont where not long afterwards we received joint job offers. While we were considering the jobs at Marlboro I asked John Gordan for his advice. He didn't dissuade me from going but only said that it would take me out of the mainstream and it would be very hard if not impossible to return. By the time I did return in 1978 he had died.

I hardly remember the blur of the next five months before we moved to Vermont. We had accepted the Marlboro jobs, Deirdre as part-time art historian and me as librarian and teacher, by the New Year, with a joint salary of $6,000 per year. Although I had resigned, Erdman gave me some wage-paying projects, including a supplement to *Wordsworthian Criticism*. One undated memory sticks out from that period, probably before Julian was born, a performance of Mozart's *Piano Concerto No. 23* in A major, K. 488, played by the Virtuosi di Philadelphia, the top players of the Philadelphia Orchestra, probably conducted by Eugene Ormandy. What struck us so strongly from the upper balcony at Carnegie Hall was the playing of bassoonist Bernard Garfield. The work, especially the second movement, became our song and still we hear it as such. A friend recently asked me who had played the piano in that performance but I could only tell him the name of the bassoonist. We used to joke that the Mozart piano concertos were actually bassoon concerti with *piano obbligato*.

Not having enough to do, another diversion was a degree program in English that I started at City College during that first year of marriage. I think I took four courses including one on Elizabethan revenge tragedy, another on seventeenth-century English prose writers (especially Thomas Hobbes), another on the Metaphysical Poets, and yet another on John Milton. After Julian was born, every evening during breast feeding time, I would read aloud one third of a book of *Paradise Lost* until both mother and child were asleep. The next evening always began with a brief summary of what they'd slept through. The experience was a good one for me but suggested the need for some training in reading aloud, especially when we learned that I'd be teaching some courses at Marlboro. My successor in the Editor's Office was poet William Coakley whose partner, Robin Prising, for a time gave me weekly lessons in dramatic reading. I was sorry to abandon the City College program when we moved to Vermont, but it and teaching at Marlboro were valuable experiences in moving my attention not away from literature but towards its historical context. It was my City College and Marlboro experience that caused me later to choose history for my doctoral work.

When we decided to move on from New York, I returned to the Director's Office, then held by James Henderson after Harold Ostvold had left to become Librarian at the California Institute of Technology in Pasadena. I was afraid Henderson might be critical of my leaving without the library benefitting from my internship, although I could rationalize that I'd worked hard and contributed substantially to the three departments where I'd done time. He had no such reaction, but merely said "Good people come and go. Good luck." Fourteen years later I moved into that same office when Jim Henderson, after twenty-three years at the helm of the Research Libraries, took on a huge project to transform the deteriorating main catalogue into an 800-volume book catalogue, eventually published by G.K. Hall.

Marlboro College, Vermont
April 1964 to August 1967

It happened that the man who found my bassoon for me was Sidney Beck, musicologist, early music editor and performer, husband of harpsichordist Blanche Winogren, and curator in the NYPL Music

Division where I worked during the summer of 1963. He had a summer home in Guilford, Vermont, very near Marlboro, and he mentioned to me in the autumn of 1963 that Marlboro College was looking for a librarian. We had been to a Marlboro Music Festival concert that summer and liked what we had seen and heard. A move could not have been further from our minds, but with a child on the way, the opportunity seemed worth exploring, especially since we were already immersed in chamber music, and we both could teach part time while I ran the Library. We interviewed on a visit to the College in November 1963 and when offered the jobs agreed to come in April 1964 when Deirdre would have had her baby and after we had concluded any academic obligations.

When we arrived, there were fewer than one hundred students, and for years we claimed that we left three years later when it had grown too large at 180, or that we had wearied of the same cocktail party where we knew everyone's opinion in advance. But that was later and though the Library was a pretty modest one-person affair with a few work-study students, and an occasional part-time assistant, it did give me the opportunity to do everything a librarian does while gaining a good deal of experience from my mistakes.

We left New York for Marlboro after midnight on April 21, 1964. The date and time are easy to recall because New York City taxi drivers had declared a city-wide stall-in that day to disrupt the opening of the New York World's Fair. Primary target was to be bridges and tunnels. Our mover, Al Daley, was a friend and he was glad to move the pickup time to the previous evening so we could beat the traffic jam. We got off soon after midnight, and arrived at the Vermont border, stopping to sleep in the first rest area of Interstate 91 with dawn approaching and during a heavy rain. Julian at two months slept right through. We arrived at the College mid-morning and our moving van later in the afternoon. At supper in the dining hall a call for help went out and about fifteen students unloaded the truck in record time, an encouraging start.

Our first apartment in Marlboro was on the ground floor of Hendricks House in the middle of campus, near the dining hall and laundry, and a short walk up the hill to the library in Dalrymple Hall. Sharing the upstairs of Hendricks House when we arrived were Nicholas Barber from Oxford's Wadham College, our first classics fellow, and Ted Wendell, then teaching math. They vacated for the summer to make way for musicians from the Marlboro Music Festival. Ted took the next academic year to get a master's degree in mathematics at the University of Washington but returned in September 1965 as Dean of Students. For that second year we moved to a one-bedroom apartment in a girl's dormitory called Halfway House, an experiment which could not end soon enough, and we moved back to Hendricks House and adult company the following spring.

In September 1964 Geoffrey Fallows, just out of Wadham College, stepped right into this friendly environment as our second classics fellow. We all had free meals during term times, as well as free housing. It was a very compatible group that expanded to include a few other faculty members, and the college nurse, the lovely Rusty Keating, now long dead of cancer. A few students became part of this inner circle, but mainly we were concerned with their instruction, not their extracurricular activities. Although our salary was small, it was a long time before we again had such easy spending money, with little to spend it on. In 1965 we took an eight-week European vacation which we could easily pay for, and we also bought a new Saab with cash.

In all but academic matters, the College was governed by a prototypical New England Town Meeting; in effect the community was managed by a board of elected selectmen, and the membership consisting of the whole body of students, faculty, and staff. The Town Meeting was a gathering of the whole community in the dining hall. Its deliberations in this avant-garde of the drug culture and the sexual revolution could be pretty bizarre. Most of the faculty and students were left-leaning liberals, with a couple of Republicans and more than a few radicals as the outliers. At one particularly raucous Town Meeting in which the college administration was trying to introduce so-called parietal rules to govern when the sexes could mix in dormitory rooms, our British economist, Charles Grailcourt, managed to get the floor and shouted, "Goddamn it, I'm an anarchist too, but there gotta be some rules."

For some reason tiny Marlboro College at fewer than 100 students was well-connected to the New England world of books and printing. The President, Tom Ragle, was at heart a bookman, obsessive about English and American poetry, and ideally supportive of the Library. Walter M. Whitehill, Director of the Boston Athenaeum; Carl Janke, Comptroller of Harvard University; Peter Elder, Dean of the Graduate School at Harvard; and David McCord, informally known as Harvard's poet-laureate, were all Trustees of the College, and they all took particular interest in the

Library. Three former students of Ray Nash, printing and design guru of Dartmouth College, visited or taught at Marlboro while we were there: Sinclair Hitchings of the Boston Public Library, Dana Atchley, film producer of *The Making of a Renaissance Book*, and David R. Godine, publisher, were all people we first met at Marlboro College.

Walter M. Whitehill (aka Mr. Boston) had taken an interest in my appointment and even interviewed me in New York the previous autumn, after I had given him a tour of the Berg Collection. After our first summer at Marlboro, he and his wife Jane Coolidge Whitehill invited us with Julian for a September weekend that included a tour of the Boston Athenaeum, an introduction to Philip Hofer at Harvard's Houghton Library, two nights in their North Andover home, and a visit to a Beverly estate whose library had been willed to the Athenaeum. Since most of the books were duplicates for the Athenaeum, I had the privilege of picking what I thought would be useful at Marlboro, an impressive haul which we loaded into Walter's VW van. Walter was somewhat given to occasional paroxysms of laughter and coughing which could be quite unsettling, rather like an overdose of snuff. This ride took place during the Johnson-Goldwater campaign of 1964. I had read somewhere that Billy Graham was prayerfully considering whether to run for President, so I told Walter of my terror that Graham might select my father as his designated Attorney General. At that Walter had one of his attacks and had to pull off the road to recover.

Since the Whitehills knew that Deirdre was completing her MA in Egyptology, that weekend they kindly invited the Curator of Egyptian Art at the Boston Museum of Fine Arts, William Stevenson Smith, author of the Penguin book of *The Art and Architecture of Ancient Egypt* (1958), for a Saturday evening dinner in their baronial barn, complete with martinis[30] in pewter cups (served in the horse stalls that were now book alcoves), and a meal of red meat of Henrician proportions. Come to think of it, Walter himself was of Henrician proportions, weight somewhat better managed, but with a commensurate beard [he claimed he grew it to make himself more at home with Marlboro students and vice versa] and a commanding voice. We were touched by their hospitality and their easy tolerance of a

---

[30]   See Bernard de Voto, "For the Wayward and Beguiled," *Harper's* (1947) p. 68-71, reprinted Halcyon Books, 1964.

six-month old. The relationship proved very beneficial to the College. The new library, opened in December 1964, despite Walter's skepticism, in many ways bore his imprint: several small rooms with fireplaces and easy chairs all surrounded by books. It was spooky to find his recorded voice describing Boston from the observation deck of the Hancock Building a number of years after he had died.

One of the books in the Beverly bequest probably should have stayed with the Athenaeum but it ended up at Harvard instead. It was a three-decker copy of James Fennimore Cooper's *The Water Witch* (Dresden, 1830). When I got around to cataloguing the book, I thought to look it up in Jacob Blanck's *Bibliography of American Literature*, where I found only one copy listed, a rebound copy at Yale. Our copy was in the original boards and in excellent condition. It was a rare and valuable title that didn't belong at Marlboro, and since Harvard had been very good to the Marlboro Library, giving me free access to their duplicate collections before they went on sale, I suggested to Tom Ragle that we give the Cooper to Harvard for the Houghton Library. When he agreed, I brought the volumes to Cambridge for the presentation and lunch with Harvard University Librarian, Douglas Bryant. Our paths crossed many times after that during my long career, especially after Bryant's retirement when he started and ran the American Trust for the British Library. He also chaired a 1980 Evaluation Committee for the John Carter Brown Library in Providence on which I served.

President Ragle, after Exeter and Harvard, had done graduate study in English in Oxford at Wadham College where the legendary raconteur Maurice Bowra was Warden. When Tom became President of this fledgling and struggling Marlboro College at a very young age, he hatched the brilliant idea of inviting newly-minted Oxford classicists, preferably from Wadham College, to teach Greek and Roman language, literature, and history in Vermont. One of our major sources of grants in this period was the Mellon-related Old Dominion Foundation which supported this idea with a five-year grant of $20,000 for a Classics Fellowship. The salary for those years would be $4,000 per fellow, with free room and board during term time and a few other perquisites that made the program feasible. Tom has written about this program in *Marlboro College, a Memoir*, published by the College in 1999.

Permit a digression here to say that in Marlboro in 1964 everyone without exception was named and addressed by his or her first name.

That might not seem surprising to boomers and 21st-century youth, but at the time it was very unusual. In an age of greater deference most of my colleagues at NYPL, with the exception of close personal friends, were known as Mister, Miss, or Mrs. Ms was yet to be invented. One could say that the pendulum has swung too far and gotten stuck. In May 2013 I happened to hear an NPR interview in which during fewer than four minutes the interviewee mentioned the host's first name a dozen times.

The Old Dominion Foundation was one of the College's most useful connections and they helped the library acquire the entire list of Bollingen Foundation publications from Princeton University Press. Whitehill never claimed credit for the gift, but I have no doubt that he was behind it. It was an exciting day when that shipment of thirty boxes of beautiful and pristine books arrived. That Foundation also funded a Monday Night Lecture series which provided $200 stipends for faculty and guest speakers. There was another grant of $5000 from one of the Beinecke foundations to purchase the entire book catalogue of the Library of Congress's book collections, complete with the supplements to 1965. This proved extremely useful for my project of manual cataloguing of the Marlboro collection in the pre-automation era. We used to joke that it must have been the only LC catalogue in the country redeemed with green stamps, a bonus program of the time, and a source of Beinecke wealth. Another joke was on me, my claim at age thirty that I was too old for this new-fangled automation business, then just beginning in colleges and universities in Ohio. After another five years of avoiding the issue, I spent much of the next thirty years preoccupied with the subject.

Rudyard Kipling was something of a local hero in southern Vermont. He had lived from 1893 to 1896 with his American wife in a large house he built near Brattleboro, Naulaka, now a National Trust USA guest house. The College capitalized on this connection in two ways. It instituted a fellowship for illustrious visitors known as Kipling Fellows who typically spent the best part of a week on campus, lecturing, teaching, mingling with students, and puzzling through the Marlboro ambiance. I remember two from our time at Marlboro: Louis Lyons, a Boston television news personality who was on leave that year as a Nieman fellow at Harvard; and Russell Meiggs, a delightfully eccentric Oxford classicist who specialized on the ancient timber of Roman Ostia, and got on famously with our roughhewn forester, Halsey Hicks. We hosted dinners for both these guests, a stimulating privilege for Deirdre and me. After I left, the College Library began collecting Kiplingiana and it has built a considerable collection of Kipling books and memorabilia.

Deirdre and I overlapped with the first four classics fellows, the first two becoming our longest-standing British friends. Tom Ragle's *Memoir* includes brief profiles of Nicholas Barber and Geoffrey Fallows, two colleagues with whom we have kept in close touch for almost fifty years. Both were slightly younger than we were but were significant influences on our lives and tastes, not to mention their great loyalty to the College in general and the Classics program in particular. I doubt that the program would have succeeded without Nicholas and Geoffrey to set the way, and happily it continues today. Nicholas would want me to point out that he preceded me as acting college librarian, adding $1500 to his already munificent $4000 salary. His summer cross-country travels included the 1964 Republican convention in San Francisco's Cow Palace, where because of his accent he was fingered as a foreigner brought with Rockefeller's millions to disrupt the convention.

Nicholas went on to a career in the shipping business when it was moving toward containerization; he was later on the Board of the British Museum, and more recently was Chairman of the Board of the Ashmolean Museum in Oxford where he deftly presided over its monumental expansion in 2010. To illustrate the informality of the early 1960s Nicholas passed along this anonymous excerpt from an Oxford alumni magazine on how he landed the Marlboro job:

> My conversation with Nicholas Barber, Chairman of the Ashmolean 2003-10, started with a wonderful Oxford story about how he got his first job upon leaving Wadham, where he read Greats (1959-63), under its legendary Warden, Sir Maurice Bowra. "I was determined to go to the US after graduating," said Barber, "Bowra knew this and at a JCR dinner mentioned a post he'd heard about that very morning. By the time the port had been passed around and back to me I had got the job, a position to start a Classics department at Marlboro College in Vermont."

Nicholas continues: "In other words no formal process! Geoffrey likewise, on my say so. And I suspect Martin Cropp (also Wadham) went on Geoffrey Fallow's say-so, hence after Jane Emerson Tom [Ragle] felt something more formal was required!" Geoffrey continued his career as a classicist as he rose to Head of the Camden School for Girls, one of the top comprehensive schools in London, and for a long time edited *Omnibus*, a journal of classics for teen-aged students. After receiving his doctorate from the University of Toronto, Martin Cropp joined the Department of Greek and Roman Studies at the University of Calgary where he is now Professor Emeritus, and well-known for his work on Euripides.

[*Coda: in May 2013 Ted Wendell hosted a reunion of several of us who had been at Marlboro during the mid-1960s, including the first two classics fellows, Nicholas and Geoffrey. In addition to the present President, Tom Ragle was there, as well as Tim Little, then Dean of Students, and a few spouses. Tom Ragle was kind enough to refer to all of us as the finest group of faculty that he had worked with.*]

Two other colleagues and friends important to us were Edmund Brelsford and Bill Davisson. Edmund was a multi-lingual polymath, skillful in what seemed to be any language needed, and for us an important musical influence. Being a Mensa member, he didn't always wear his knowledge lightly. He and his wife Veronica joined the faculty soon after we did and we soon found mutual interests in chamber music, particularly in early music for recorders, harpsichord, and wind instruments. On the faculty were such stalwarts of the Marlboro Music Festival as Marcel Moyse and his son, Louis Moyse (two highly regarded flutists), and Blanche Honegger-Moyse (an accomplished conductor of Bach cantatas and passions). They represented the professional musical establishment of the college, and although we occasionally played with them, more enjoyable was our independent baroque underground coffeehouse ensemble. Led by Brelsford, we picked up players wherever needed, made the necessary accommodations (e.g., stuffing newspapers into a piano to simulate a harpsichord), and played wherever we could—schools, churches, the occasional wedding, and not least forming the pit band for a number of theatrical productions directed by our brilliant theatre teacher and director, Geoffrey Brown. Deirdre and I once toured several colleges in Vermont playing the trombone parts of Kurt Weill's *Three Penny Opera* on our two bassoons—we made excellent foghorns. In my Marlboro archives is a flyer announcing a "benefit concert" of baroque music, with a note saying "Your 25-cent ticket will help the completion of the Perrine building."[31] We also played in *The Beaux Stratagem* by George Farquhar, a good play for our limited baroque resources. Our oboist for one year was none other than Martin Cropp, the third Classics fellow. Edmund died suddenly in 2011 at age 80 although apparently very fit.

Will Davisson joined the College faculty a year later. In 1964 he and his wife Eyre left their patrician life in Paris to settle for the rest of their lives in rural Marlboro. They had found a house advertisement in the *New Yorker* and bought it sight unseen. It was a beautiful house about ten miles from the College, with a clear view looking east across the Connecticut Valley to Mount Monadnock, ideal for summer evenings and Will's mint juleps. Will's father had been a partner of J. P. Morgan and his inherited wealth, well-invested, allowed Will to devote himself to his passions of history, cartography, books, horses (including four-in-hand carriages), fine wines, and real estate. During our time in Marlboro, Will

---

[31]   I thought this a clever joke that I didn't understand, so I asked Tom Ragle, Marlboro's most reliable memory, for an explanation. Here it is: "Eddie Perrine was a student who died in a motorcycle accident on Route 9 to Bennington (scarf came up and covered his face). He was popular, and students got permission to raise money and build a woodworking workshop in his memory (The Perrine Workshop), woodworking not to be for credit. When Gilbert "Gib" Taylor was appointed to teach introductory art and help Frank Stout [painting and drawing teacher], Gib saw potential and started teaching woodworking there (fine carpentry, instrument making, wood sculpture, etc.). Very popular, woodworking finally received credit and even degree status. When Gib retired, sculpture was substituted in its place, but there are many alumni out there who are fine instrument makers, wood sculptors, and cabinet makers, including my son Tim, who went from Marlboro to the Rhode Island School of Design, where he took a graduate degree in furniture making under a noted Swedish teacher and now makes his living restoring old buildings, especially 18th-century houses."

had annual summer tenants in another of his nearby houses, Mr. and Mrs. Pablo Casals.[32]

Will was a Harvard ABD in history, a student of Franklin Ford, with a never-to-be-finished dissertation on eighteenth-century French road administration. To support his study he had acquired the archives of the French postal administration of his period, complete with manuscript route maps, schedules, architectural designs, landscaping plans, fiscal accounts, etc. To accommodate the archives and his growing book collection he built a new library across the road from his house, utilizing a Pennsylvania Dutch building plan, with quarters for visiting scholars, and with a lower level rathskeller where we once shared a bottle of Napoleonic era brandy.

Librarians think of themselves as connoisseurs of shelving systems and tend to appreciate the more idiosyncratic ones. One colleague in New York, Thor Wood, had thousands of LPs arranged by composer's date of birth. Will Davisson's was the most unusual I've encountered. In his new library he had one very large wall of bookshelves which he saw as a map of France in the 18th-century. Clockwise the books would proceed from the history of Paris upper central, to Alsace on the right hand, Marseilles and the Mediterranean Coast along the bottom, the Spanish border rising to the left, and onwards and upwards to Bordeaux and Normandy. It would drive me mad but I think he enjoyed the whimsy of it. Terry Belanger, founder of Rare Book School, tells me Alistair Cooke had a similar wall for the United States.

By the time we left for Chicago, Will and I had become very close friends, largely through the fellowship of books, a shared interest

---

[32] In our files is a thank you letter from Will, dated 19 June 1968, after a visit he paid to us at the Newberry Library in Chicago within a year of our moving there from Marlboro. The first paragraph, about one of his maintenance men, is quintessentially Vermont: Louis Brown asked Eyre the other day whether Pedro was coming this summer. "Who?" "Pedro—that guy that plays the harp and stayed in the Powers house last summer." (After a moment's reflection, he added that "Will took me down there last summer to do some mowing and I got a look at his wife. If I had a wife like that I wouldn't waste my time playing the harp.") Pedro of course was cellist Pablo Casals and his wife Marta Montañez Martinez, who later married Eugene Istomin.

in cartographic history, and regular trips in one of his Mercedes to Dartmouth or Williams for some library sleuthing. In hopes of keeping us connected to the Marlboro community, he offered us for $2000, twenty acres near the College (he was rumored to have bought 2500 acres of the town by then, and owned several houses), but we had no savings and had to decline the offer. His instincts were right and we did lose contact after a few years, only to learn that after thirty years in Marlboro he had died of cancer and that not long after Eyre died in a car accident. *The William P. Davisson Collection of the History of Transportation in France and Related Subjects* was sold at Christie's on April 19, 1999, and totaled $400,000. Unfortunately, we saw the Davissons only three or four times over that long period after 1967. For all the sophistication, intellect, taste, and money it was in many ways a tragic family, plagued by problems with children, with health and particularly cancer, and with depression for Eyre and her daughter. But we cherished our relationship with them and were so sorry to hear of its end after some years of neglect.

We spent most of our three and a half years at Marlboro living in Hendricks House in the heart of the campus. During term time the upstairs rooms were used by faculty while in the summer they were taken over by musicians. Among our summer neighbors were Samuel Rhodes, soon to join the Juilliard Quartet; Donald MacCourt, a bassoonist I first met in New York in the New Cecilia Chamber Orchestra and the long-time first bassoonist of New York City Ballet; flutist Sharon Robinson; and others. They were engaging people, and we sometimes joined their informal parties on the second floor hoping that Julian would remain asleep.

During the spring of 1965, Harold Hugo and John Peckham of Meriden Gravure Company, printers of choice to the nation's finest cultural institutions and friends from my recent NYPL days, stopped by the College on their annual pilgrimage to visit Ray Nash at Dartmouth and Rocky Stinehour and the Stinehour Press in St. Johnsbury, Vermont. With them was Robert Shackleton, soon to be appointed Bodley's Librarian at Oxford University. I had the pleasure of showing him our new Library and what we called our Rare Book. [The book was a Bruce Rogers Bible—the last time I visited the College it was nowhere to be found.] Shackleton remained a close colleague and friend for more than twenty years and, apart from Syracuse, kindly visited all of my subsequent institutions—Newberry, Johns Hopkins, New York Public Library—for lectures, meetings, or informal exercises in comparative librarianship.

A local resident was noted book designer Bob Dothard, who designed college catalogues for a living, but also designed many classic editions for The Limited Editions Club and for The Heritage Club, from the *Aeneid* to Parkman's *The Oregon Trail*. Bob very helpfully welcomed my class in printing to his home printing facility and helped us produce an eight-page guide to the Marlboro College Library. We were printing that work in his home studio the night of the great Northeast blackout of 1965.

Another famous typographer and designer, Rudolph Ruzicka of Hanover, NH, designed a bookplate for one of our donors, Howard Rice, Jr., of the Princeton University Library. Rice, wanted the two crossed tree leaves of the bookplate printed in color, a luxury I thought we couldn't afford. Instead we had an art-minded student worker brush in the 100 plates in a vivid green symbolic of Marlboro's rustic image.

It was at Marlboro that I began my sporadic and always troubled career in deaccessioning of library materials. When I arrived in April 1964 the Library occupied one floor of an old barn called Dalrymple, and held, as I recall about 14,000 volumes which seemed randomly collected from the detritus of all the attics of southern Vermont. There was a common misperception at the time that accreditation bodies paid more attention to the numbers of books in a library than the quality of the selections and their ability to respond to faculty and student needs. On the other hand, our drama teacher, Geoffrey Brown, argued that nothing could turn off a student from a great playwright more quickly than a poor edition or a miserable copy, and it was better not to have them. Nothing, he argued, not even a book, had the right to bore other people. When we were ready to move the collections a hundred yards up the hill to the new library, we had pared the library down to about 7,000 volumes. Numerous summer loads on Don Woodward's pickup truck went to the dump for burning, though there was some protest at the destruction of the sacred word and the desirability of finding good homes for discarded books. The issues involved are difficult and almost impossible of resolution, as later experience at the Newberry Library, Johns Hopkins, New York Public Library, and at Syracuse showed throughout my career and beyond; the same arguments recur with regularity. Let me just say in this instance that when our New England Association of Schools and Colleges Accreditation Team gave Marlboro College its first approval on its first try for accreditation, it praised the library for its work in creating a well-selected collection suited to the needs of our small community. Tom Ragle was kind enough to attribute the achievement of accreditation largely to my work on the library as well as to admission policies of the time that put quality selection over the anemic bottom line.

Construction of the new library began shortly after we arrived in April, and the building opened in December 1964. On December 15, a bright but cold day of gentle snow flurries, much of the student body turned out to move the collection, shelf by shelf, about a hundred yards up the hill. We had constructed about twenty wooden trays the length of the book shelves, with hand grips at either end: two-person teams loaded them, another two moved them, and a third pair unloaded at the proper shelf location. As I recall this method was Walter Whitehill's suggestion—he claimed it was the method used by Louis XIV to move his library. I never confirmed his assertion but it fits my belief that in many ways the Library bore Walter's imprint: a homelike atmosphere with several small rooms surrounded by books, most rooms with fireplaces, an art gallery near the entrance, many easy chairs, 24-hour access, shoes forbidden, and an honor system for borrowing. Usage was good and losses low once we retrieved books from the residences at the end of each spring semester. The site itself was and is spectacular with a commanding view of the valley and mountains to the South. It had the most beautiful office I've ever worked in. I kept cross country skies at the back door to make impromptu skiing trips into the woods whenever the conditions seemed right or a break from cataloging necessary.

According to the College website, the December 1965 issue of *Architectural Forum* said of the building that "Its barn-like form is at home among the converted farm buildings that form the core of the campus; inside it is designed strictly for reading (and 'thinking,' which Marlboro regards as the only major subject in its curriculum)." Anyone who visits Glimmerglass Opera in Cooperstown, NY, will see the same barn-like theme repeated twenty years later in 1987.

Of course mistakes were made [the passive tense is so useful in avoiding responsibility]. Let me rephrase that: I certainly made several mistakes of judgment, and was recently taken aback in reading on the web some reminiscences of our second classics fellow, Geoffrey Fallows, to the effect that his plans for retirement included the reading of his twelve-volume set of Gibbons' *Decline and Fall of the Roman Empire* acquired "during one of David Stam's library clear-outs." That work at least found a good home, but one can only wonder what other treasures might have got away. For example, an Eleventh Edition of the *Encyclopaedia Britannica*, much buckled and abused by holding windows open in the old library, went to my brother Jim. I would argue that all libraries have to get rid of materials, space is expensive, and locating new owners is staff intensive and costly. Deirdre likens the issue to a swamp that for any responsible librarian is hard to avoid.

Other mistakes in librarianship which I made at the College's expense involved cataloguing, shelving, and bookbinding. One consultant in planning the new Marlboro library was the venerable Keyes Metcalf, retired Director of the Harvard University Library, former Chief of the Reference Department of The New York Public Library (and thereby another one of my predecessors when I returned to NYPL as Director in 1978). I never saw his Marlboro report and it may only have been an oral one, but his firm conviction was that any Library that was unlikely to grow beyond 100,000 volumes should use the Dewey Decimal Classification numeric scheme, rather than use or shift to the more flexible Library of Congress alpha-numeric system. I followed that advice and at the end of my time at Marlboro I had catalogued every book and periodical in the collection according to Dewey subject categories. By then I could transpose almost any license plate number into a subject, for example 655 into printing arts, 822.3 into Shakespeare, etc. The problem comes with the convoluted Dewey call numbers needed in complex areas like genealogy or local history, the Bible, or even Shakespeare. Where for example would a student shelver put Henry Louis Gates's *Colored People, a Memoir*, classified in Dewey as 975.4/00496073 /092? I have no idea, nor was I aware of the problem back then. In LC classification it is more simply PS29. G28 A3. The issue would reemerge when I was a candidate at Duke University twenty years later. I see from the Internet that Marlboro College Library, now at 70,000 volumes, is still yoked to Dewey. I suspect it will come to regret my decision, if it hasn't already.

The second decision was an economic one and more easily excused, to use wooden shelving of a fixed 12 inches throughout the library, with one larger bottom shelf throughout for oversize volumes, rather than to buy more flexible but more expensive adjustable metal shelving. This is a minor point, but with the vast majority of books and periodicals measuring under nine inches tall, a good deal of space is wasted. My view was obviously shaped by my NYPL experience where in the closed stacks books were shelved by size, a system I later introduced at the Newberry Library, only to have it abandoned by a successor. Possibly the new planners of the Marlboro expansion made a wiser decision on shelf size, but Tom Ragle doubts it and defends what we did in 1964.

The third problematical issue was bookbinding. Across the Connecticut River in Walpole, New Hampshire, was a wonderfully knowledgeable bookseller named Robert Kolvoord of the Old Settler Bookshop. We occasionally drove over to share martinis, cigarettes, book talk, and sometimes a meal prepared by his lovely but frail wife, and to buy books. Robert often worked closely with retiring Dartmouth faculty when they were disbursing their collections. At one point I visited his shop and home shortly after he had made a large acquisition of all the major literary journals of twentieth-century America in complete and unbound runs, none of them in the Marlboro College Library. A few of the titles included were the *Paris Review, Hudson Review, Partisan Review, Antioch Review, Virginia Quarterly Review*, the *Yale Review*, and several others. Offered at a very good price that we could afford, I grabbed them up.

American bookbinding standards of the time were promulgated by a self-serving trade association called the Library Binding Institute. It had a vested interest in something called an "oversewing" machine, which combined the misleadingly named "perfect binding" (i.e., to "perfect" the inner margins of a book or periodical by guillotining the inner margins in order to create a uniform gluing surface) with oversewing (i.e., to stitch thread into the remaining margin), which when sewn, glued, and bound in buckram made a uniform appearance on the shelf and provided a very strong binding, strong enough to withstand the assault of undergraduates. There were two major problems with this system of bookbinding, first, that as a book ages the paper is often unable to resist pressure against the threads during use, often causing irreparable harm; second, that oversewn volumes often require two hands to open and be read. Most hard cover trade books published today are perfect bindings but seldom oversewn, and are a bit easier to handle because they have no threads to fight against, though many are still two-fisted affairs. For decades, well into the 1960s, NYPL had its own bindery utilizing these infernal machines; many of its preservation problems relate to the use of oversewing machines on acidic papers. To truncate this confession, I admit that I sent all these beautifully sewn periodical issues to an approved LBI bindery in West Springfield, Massachusetts, from which they returned uniform and colorful and nearly useless. When I moved to the Newberry a few years later I quickly learned the iniquity of that machine and the depth of my sin.[33]

However small the scale, I cannot emphasize enough how valuable the Marlboro experience was to me over the next forty years. It gave me experience in all aspects of librarianship, including the whole path of the book: selection, acquisition, cataloging and classification, reference, circulation, public service, weeding, and even security. If at Marlboro preservation and rare books were the least of these preoccupations, I would enter a steep learning curve when we moved to Chicago in August 1973. I was bemused and a bit incredulous when I read a March 18, 2013, letter from an alumna in the *NYTimes* saying that at Marlboro "we do have a great library." That seems a bit of a stretch but I'll gladly claim it as part of my legacy.

In the early 1960s, in an attempt to encourage scholarly activity among the faculty, the College established (as noted earlier) a Monday night lecture series for faculty as well as invited speakers. David Erdman was one of the latter. The stipend was a munificent $200 and in addition to outside speakers, any faculty member could apply to present his or her work. Each of the classics fellows participated, Nicholas Barber on Pericles and Geoffrey on a Latin subject, perhaps Seneca's letters. The fourth Classics fellow with whom we worked was Jane Emerson, a remarkable woman from Somerville College, Oxford, the first break in the Wadham

---

[33] On this paragraph I consulted Peter Verheyen, the Conservator at Syracuse University Library, who responded with these comforting words: "Interesting and would be happy to grant absolution if that helps. There are far worse binding sins. No real inaccuracies, but I think the confession is a bit off when one considers the options then available for the binding of periodicals and similar materials. Adhesive binding as practiced now was not an option and adhesives still unproven/unstable, machine sewing through the fold was also not always an option and would have required a very careful disbinding of those titles that were even sewn as issues, and then there is the paper . . . While no doubt self-serving, LBI did do some good by standardizing some of these practices, practices that have continued to evolve with technology and materials."

tradition. Jane later married our well-known philosopher of the pre-Socratics, John Robinson, and then became the head of the Northfield School for Girls in Massachusetts. She died at an absurdly early age of cancer.

Taking a cue from my earlier studies at City College, my own offering for the Monday night series was a study of the authorship of some puzzling 1602 additions to Thomas Kyd's revenge drama, *The Spanish Tragedy*, first produced in 1587 and first published in 1592. The subject was arcane enough but it gave me the opportunity to work at the Boston Athenaeum and make visits to both the Williams and Dartmouth college libraries. My tentative conclusion, based on comparison of word usage in both the play and its additions, was that these additions were by Kyd himself, and for all I know that is still the received wisdom.[34] But the real fun a week before the lecture was to put on a semi-staged version of the play, helpfully directed by Geoff Brown, and using actors from the whole community, including the proprietor of the local Whetstone Inn, Hubie Moore. The hero Hieronimo was played by our infamous anarchist, Charles Grailcourt, who somehow managed to bite out a false tongue as called for by the script. The final scene was pure chaos with six dead bodies flung around the stage. About forty members of our small community participated in the play. Overall, the whole exercise helped me keep focused on a life of scholarship and made me appreciate the difficulties of dramatic production.

As recounted below, I had interviews at the Newberry Library in Chicago in the summer of 1966 which led to a job offer that I accepted on Halloween of that year, a few hours before our twins, Kathryn and Wendell, were born in Brattleboro, Vermont. We had no idea two were coming. Deirdre's obstetrician was a ski doctor on off-season duty and completely missed the call, though one of the attending nurses thought she detected a second heartbeat. The doctor and hospital offered bargain rates which we remember as a total cost of $125. That night Tom Ragle

---

[34] What goes round, comes round! *The New York Times* of August 13, 2013, carried a front page article by Jennifer Schussler entitled "Much Ado about Who: Is it Really Shakespeare," offering tentative but compelling proof that Shakespeare played a role in writing the 1602 additions to *The Spanish Tragedy*. How excited I would have been fifty years ago when I was working on the topic.

was giving one of the Monday Night Lectures, on higher education. After a long day's labor by Deirdre and a long wait of my own, I arrived at the dining hall shortly before Tom's talk was to begin, in time to announce the new births to unusual campus buzz. I'm sure it took some wind out of Tom's usually full sails. We did not leave for Chicago until the following July.

Since October 31, 1966, represented what would be the completion of our family of five, this pause in the narrative seems a good point at which to say a few things about our three children, starting with Julian. When we arrived in Marlboro, Julian was one day shy of two months old, and he quickly became a student favorite, a point of amusement and diversion in the dining hall where we took most of our meals during the academic year. So it was something of a shock for him two years later when the attention shifted to the new double threat of Kathryn and Wendell. For a time he denied their existence, forgot his toilet training, only once tried to harm them, but gradually accommodated to his extended family before we left for Chicago eight months later. Of the three, Julian is the one with the happiest genes, despite that youthful funk. He was nine when we left Chicago, studied at Boys' Latin in Baltimore, and graduated from Pelham Memorial High School in 1982 when we were back in New York. Then he went on to Upsala College in East Orange, New Jersey, where my brother Jim taught for many years until it closed in 1995, two years after its centennial and nine years after Julian's graduation

After 1986 Julian held a few technical jobs at NYPL (my departure had negated any nepotism rules that had applied to us), work that led him to the University of Michigan School of Information where he received his MLS in 1988. During library school he married his Upsala girlfriend, Anja Plato, from Denville, New Jersey. Anja had emigrated with her parents from Berlin when she was a year old, and for a time after her graduation she worked as a translator of German scientific work. Julian's library career involved three years as a serials librarian at Wayne State University in Detroit, nine years in the preservation department at Harvard College Library, and then 2000 to 2004 as head of the preservation department at Boston College Library. In 2003 he was elected Chair of the Preservation Section of the Association for Library Collections & Technical Services (ALECTS), a division of ALA.

About that time he stunned us with a telephone call announcing his decision to leave the library field and their home in Littleton, Massachusetts, to settle in rural Wellsboro, Pennsylvania, start an email business of his own dealing with popular culture games (one of his lifelong interests), and spend more time with his growing daughters, Kristin and Maia. The parental reaction was not immediately supportive, and Julian and Kathryn tell a story about it at Deirdre's expense. When Deirdre heard this news apparently she said something to Julian about now having to worry about all three of our children instead of just two. When Julian told Kathryn about this reaction, Kathryn said that Deirdre had said the same thing to her when Kathryn told us she would be marrying Suthin, a resident of rural Northeast Thailand where Kathryn was serving in the Peace Corps. But our ability to adjust is strong, and we've enjoyed watching the growth of both Julian's business, now called Pop's Culture and including a retail outlet, and the growth of Kristin as a Susquehanna University graduate and now a teacher and track coach at her alma mater, and of her sister Maia, a junior at Goucher College in Baltimore and a dedicated modern dancer.

The twins represented a lot of work, and as we look back we don't know how we managed, physically or financially. We moved to Chicago when they were nine months old, to Baltimore when they were almost seven, to New York when they were twelve; they were both out of the nest when we moved to Syracuse in 1986. After Pelham High School where she played ice hockey, Kathryn pursued environmental studies at the University of Vermont, spent a semester in Nepal, and graduated in 1988. She played goalie for the UV women's hockey team in her freshman and senior years. I only saw her play one college game, but that one was a stunning overtime victory over Yale at Yale, 4-3. The Peace Corps (1988-1990) then began a series of Thai chapters in her life, interrupted twice by graduate studies in Syracuse, first by an MS in Forestry from the SUNY School of Environmental Studies (ESF) in 1993, and again with a PhD in Social Science from Syracuse in 1999, approaching a school record of four years to her degree, thus following her mother's example. After a post-doc and a miserable year at SUNY Morrisville with very heavy teaching loads, she hit the jackpot in 2004 at SUNYIT in Utica, NY, the state school of information technology where she has taught anthropology, sociology, informatics, and who knows what else—she claims thirty-seven different courses in eight years on her resumé. She also won tenure early, won her

Chancellor's award for excellence in teaching, and a Fulbright fellowship for four months in northeast Thailand, all in 2010-11.

Briefly, the Thai chapters center on the northeast region of Issan, the largely Laotian district (the poorest region of the country) where she lived near the city of Kalasin. In addition to the Peace Corps this period included AIDS prevention work in Khon Kaen, marriage to Suthin Munawet in 1991 in a festive rural setting, a son Terrin Munawet, born in Syracuse in 1997, the death of her beloved stepson Nook a few months later in Thailand, an amicable divorce, and a permanent return to the US in the late 1990s. Suthin, Nook, and Nook's sister Gai spent almost two years with us in Syracuse while Kathryn was working on her graduate degrees in environmental studies and anthropology. The family returned to Thailand in 1998 only to experience Nook's death at age fifteen in a stupid motorcycle accident. This was a sad time for all of us, since Nook had won our hearts with his irrepressible smile and his wonderful sense of life. It happened that I was in Venice and Rome on some foundation business three months after his death when I learned of a unique Thai commemoration of the dead, 100 days after a person's death. I was able to continue east to Bangkok and Kalasin for Nook's ceremony which involved a shaman-directed séance calling up the dead, learning the news from the other world, and the presentation of some gifts. Nook reported through the shamen that he was doing well in his afterlife, studying regularly, and playing soccer twice a week. I remember Terrin's grandmother holding baby Terrin in the shaded woods, fairly near the priest as the séance ended, shouting out to Nook to remember to study hard. Nook declined the gifts of various sports equipment, according to the shaman: "I'd prefer you give them to my friends in the real world," which is what I was called upon to do the next day at his old grade school. The 44-hour trip back to Syracuse, via Rome and New York gave me plenty of time to think about the experience and our love for Nook.

Terrin, who was born the year before my retirement, returned with Kathryn to live in Syracuse shortly after in August 1998. By default I served as something of a surrogate father for much of his first five years, a role I enjoyed immensely. Throughout we have watched him grow up to a six-foot sixteen-year old, an eclectic lover of music in most forms, and as one of the great joys of our lives and the most mature teenager I've ever met. He and Kathryn now live in New Hartford near Utica, New York, an hour's drive and very convenient for keeping in touch. Her major preoccupation now is the large Southeast Asian refugee community of Utica, especially the Bhutanese Nepali people for whose musicians and dancers she serves as *pro bono* impresario.

By contrast to Kathryn, Wendell has skipped around quite a bit; probably the brightest of all of us (and certainly the wittiest), he was blown around by some of the vicissitudes of popular culture in the 60s and 70s, sampled a number of prep schools before he dropped out to pursue physical activities of skateboarding, snowboarding, and mountain biking, while following the Rocky Horror Picture Show, the Grateful Dead, and other groups his parents only found bizarre. He lived at home off and on, and after getting his GED pursued a BA at Syracuse University, completed in the early 90s, including two very successful semesters abroad, in London and Strasbourg where he got his best grades. (When 35 Syracuse students were killed in the crash of Pan Am 103 in 1988, a year after his own London semester, Wendell said that at least they had died after the best experience of their short lives.) But his heart was and is in the West, on its slopes and trails, and he certainly has opened our minds to that vast landscape. He spent time in Telluride, Colorado, before settling permanently in the shadow of the Grand Tetons on both sides of the Wyoming/Idaho boundary in Jackson and Driggs. One attempt at a retail bike shop in Driggs, Idaho, foundered in a weak economy. Other odd jobs included cooking, catering, trailblazing, and resort publicity, but eventually he found his métier in a form of abstract art incorporating bicycle parts in anything from cheese platters to sconces to clocks to belt buckles. We think they are beautiful but we're prejudiced. We would say the same of his beautiful wife Rachel Mancoll, whom he married in what we jokingly called the largest Jewish wedding in the history of Idaho. It was a destination wedding in 2004 for a lot of folks from Rachel's home town of West Hartford, Connecticut, and a bunch of local outdoors types, their friends. Rachel, who has an engineering degree from Dartmouth and an MBA in accounting from the University of Texas, is now running her own accounting business in Jackson, as well as a knitting store which once won her the honor of being named a Wyoming Business Woman of the Year. Wendell is now an artist in Jackson, Wyoming, creating pieces of functional art incorporating bicycle parts. Their son Benjamin, who is now six, is no less of a handful than his father (whom he strikingly resembles) was at the same age.

All three of our children tolerated a steady diet of museums, libraries, concerts, travel, and rather steady relocations, three cities and seven different homes between 1964 and 1978. Deirdre, who suffers regret and imagines should-have-beens far more than I do, sometimes thinks that such moves were harmful to their development and education. None of them came to share our narrowly focused love for classical music, but we like to think that their constant exposure to art, books, music, and language in particular, had good effects. Wendell certainly thinks so. I take it all with a grain of salt and a dollop of fatalism.

In the summer of 1966, in addition to an interview at the Newberry in Chicago, I also interviewed for the position of head librarian at nearby Bennington College. Its big advantage was that it offered childcare, an attractive benefit even before we knew about the coming twins. It was an excellent place for the creative arts (dance, music, theatre and writing), and it had some famous faculty as well as a larger library, but it struck me as more of the same hippie culture that we were experiencing at Marlboro. My interview with the President, Edward J. Bloustein, seemed to be more about him than the candidate or the job, so I withdrew my application and moved on to the prospect of Chicago. (Bloustein later became President of Rutgers University. I spent a good bit of time with him on a Middle States Accreditation Committee visit, and I found him a more sympathetic character than at Bennington. He died suddenly in 1989 while still in office.)

During our final summer of 1967 in Marlboro we had the pleasure of introducing our nine-month old twins, Kathryn and Wendell, to Rudolf Serkin, founder and director of the Marlboro Music Festival. Although he did not predict brilliant piano careers based on examination of their hands, he made the appreciative noises about the twins of someone who as an older father of a young child called himself "a do-it-yourself-grandfather." Serkin was generous to the College Library, giving us a number of collected editions of major composers—Mozart, Schubert, and Mendelssohn come to mind. We spent most of four summers at Marlboro, often attending two or three concerts a week and occasional rehearsals as well. Although one could call the programming somewhat unadventurous (the most modern piece I remember from that period at Marlboro was Schoenberg's *Second String Quartet*, 1922), the manner in which they played the standard repertoire and the depth of musical probing was beyond most of what we'd experienced before.

We retain extremely vivid images of our Marlboro days: very cold winter walks under extremely bright stars transmuted by the occasional aurora borealis, amorous evenings in the autumn fields below the campus, shingled icicles from the roof cooling our drinks in Hendricks House, autumn volleyball at dusk behind the new library, cross-country skiing on the Ho Chi Minh trail beyond the library, the Wendell Cup cross-country skiing competition which Deirdre won in 1966 in the lone category of pregnant with twins but fourth woman overall, and Deirdre crying all the way from South Road to Wilmington, Vermont, on our way to a totally different life in Chicago. A true idyll.

Figure 1: Jacob Stam, father of David Stam. Paterson, NJ, ca. 1915.

Figure 2: Deanna Bowman Stam, mother of David Stam, ca. 1918.

Figure 3: David H. Stam, New College Divinity Student,
University of Edinburgh, November, 1955.

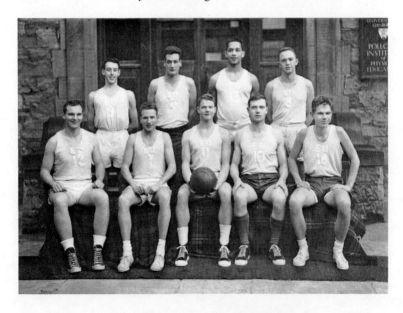

Figure 4: Edinburgh University Basketball Club, Season
1955-56. David Stam, second row, far right.

Figure 5: Journalist Third Class, USNR. Norfolk,
Virginia, Naval Base, November 1957.

Figure 6: David and Deirdre Stam family, Ontario, Wisconsin, Summer
1970: left to right Kathryn, David, Julian, Deirdre, Wendell.

To Dr. David Stam
With best wishes, Ronald Reagan

Figure 7: William Bennett, National Endowment for the Humanities,
and President Ronald Reagan, with David Stam, at White House,
December 1981, on announcement of preservation grants to all fifteen
members of the Independent Research Library Association (IRLA).

Figure 8: Alex Wilson, Director-General, British Library, and David
Stam walking on the moors of Northern Wales, ca. 1982.

Figure 9: My farewell party from NYPL, February 25, 1986. With me are Frances Anderson, Friend of the Schomburg Center, and Vartan Gregorian, President, New York Public Library.

Figure 10: Commencement ceremony in 1987 with Chancellor Melvin Eggers, Syracuse University, Carleton Sprague Smith (Recipient, Doctor of Humane Letters Degree, and former Librarian, Music Division, NYPL), and David Stam who presented Dr. Smith for the degree.

Figure 11: Engagement of our daughter Kathryn Stam to
Suthin Munawet in Northeast Thailand, 1990.

Figure 12: One of a series of library "baseball" card sets, devised by
Norman Stevens, University Librarian at the University of Connecticut,
for members of the Association of Research Libraries. 1992-1993.

Figure 13: David Stam on Venetian canal (1994), during one of several Delmas Foundation visits to Venice.

Figure 14: David Stam with daughters of Julian and Anja Stam, Maia and Kristin Stam. Mid-1990s.

Figure 15: First Lady Hillary Clinton with Board Member David Stam at Seward House Museum in Auburn, NY, July 15, 1996.

Figure 16: David and Deirdre Stam at Churchill, Manitoba, on Hudson Bay, June 20, 2002, as part of Polar Libraries Colloquy post-conference workshop.

Figure 17: David Stam reading with Grandson Terrin Munawet, 2000.

Figure 18: Fiftieth Wedding Anniversary Celebration in Syracuse, May 2013. Back row from left: Rachel Mancoll Stam and Son Wendell; Anja Plato Stam and Son Julian; and Daughter Kathryn Stam. Front row from left: David Stam; Grandsons Benjamin Stam and Terrin Munawet; and Deirdre Corcoran Stam.

Chapter III

Mid-Career: Four Research Libraries and a Foundation 1967 to 1998

"Hindsight is never 20/20."
David H. Stam, often.

The Newberry Library and Chicago
August 1967 to July 1973

By the summer of 1966, I realized that my learning potential from the Marlboro College Library was reaching a point of diminishing returns, and I began looking for other possibilities. Most of the re-cataloguing of the collection had been completed, and though I could very profitably have turned my attention to teaching, librarianship took precedence and we began looking elsewhere for new opportunities, of which at the time there were many.

In June 1966, I attended the American Library Association's annual conference in New York and visited NYPL's new Performing Arts Library at Lincoln Center to look up Frank Campbell in the Music Division. During my music internship at NYPL in 1963, Frank was already working on plans for the Music Division at Lincoln Center, and I was curious to see how the new building had worked out. Frank said he was busy for lunch but we chatted for half an hour before his luncheon companion arrived. We walked together to Broadway through a maze of construction; when I bid them farewell Frank's colleague suggested I come along to lunch. Uncertain of Frank's wishes, I declined but eventually was persuaded to join them. Frank's guest was Donald W. Krummel, Associate Librarian of the Newberry Library in Chicago, master music bibliographer, and grand music acquisitor. At that time he was searching for a Head of Technical Services at his renowned library.

The lunch did lead to interviews in Chicago (all conducted in sunglasses after I'd lost my normal glasses at the Toledo Zoo), an interview with the Library's Director and Librarian, Bill Towner, in Boston a few weeks later, and my eventual Halloween appointment as Head of Technical Services at the Newberry. I have always regarded that meeting with Krummel as the thinnest of strands that could shape a life, more peacefully than J.B. Priestley's *Dangerous Corner* (1932), where the treacherous plot hinges on differences in radio reception.

The offer from the Newberry came through on Halloween, October 31, 1966, the birthday of our twins. It was a full nine months before we arrived in Chicago on August 1, 1967, and a much different set of circumstances: enormous intellectual stimulation thrown out of balance by three children under four in a third-floor walkup, and complicated by feeling broke most of the time. It wasn't an easy time for Deirdre. Part of the rationale for moving to Chicago was the possibility of her continuing her Egyptological studies at the Oriental Institute at the University of Chicago. Eventually she found excellent employment at the Art Institute of Chicago, ending with the position of Assistant Curator of Classical Art, giving her fairly wide latitude since there was no full Curator. One of her acquisitions was an imposing Roman statue that for years stood on the staircase of the main hall of the Artstitute (as our childen called it) and known to her friends as Deirdre's torso.

Thanks to the Irving Apartment complex which the Newberry owned, one block from the Newberry, a real scholarly community thrived with the Library at its center. There were some apartments available for professors from the Associated Colleges of the Midwest, as well as visiting fellows who might come for a month or a year. There was a constant turnover of young dissertation writers and seasoned scholars, united by the need for Newberry collections. The Towners lived a block away, offering hospitality to the many visiting scholars. Heinz Bluhm of Boston College would visit frequently, working on pre-Luther Bibles. *Poetry* magazine occupied one of the seventy-two apartments; Henry Rago was the editor in our time at the Irving. Before the building was torn down in 1970, we lived above the well-known book dealer and famous bibliographer of Americana, Wright Howes, the compiler of *U.S.iana*. The elusive Allan H. Stevenson, the *eminence gris* of watermark studies, was seldom spotted outside of the basement laundry rooms. Richard Beeman, an American historian now retired from the University of Pennsylvania, lived there in our time, as did Thomas Schlereth, now retired from Notre Dame. A young Chicago architect named Patrick Shaw lived in the Irving, and the Irving garden included a boyhood sculpture of him. A number of Newberry staff lived in Irving apartments, including the Krummels, the Stams, John Dean and family, and Bernie Wilson. And often enough there were a few crabby old ladies resenting any child's intrusion in their garden. The whole exuded an atmosphere of faded gentility, adumbrated if not epitomized in Karl Shapiro's poem, "A Garden in Chicago":

In the mid-city, under an oiled sky,
I lay in a garden of such dusky green
It seemed the dregs of the imagination.
Hedged round by elegant spears of iron fence . . .

And one sweet statue of a child stood by . . .

Assuming that this garden still exists,
One ancient lady patrols the zinnias
(She looks like George Washington crossing the Delaware),
The janitor wanders to the iron rail,
The traffic mounts bombastically out there,
And across the street in a pitch-black bar
With midnight mirrors, the professional
Takes her first whiskey of the afternoon—

Alas, the garden no longer exists and the statue disappeared. We all had to vacate the Irving when, in 1970 during difficult financial times, the Newberry decided to sell the Irving apartments for two million dollars to a developer intending to build a luxury high-rise apartment with some surrounding town houses. Again I had the sad experience that I once had in New York, watching the wrecker's ball demolish the rooms of children in the interests of progress. I've often had a sense of guilt for voting with my colleagues in approving the sale, partly because of the memories and partly because we sold at the bottom of the market. As we Irvingites dispersed to various locations in the neighborhood and beyond, we felt that the scholarly community had been lessened.

In retrospect it seems, however, that everything about the Newberry was special and in a real sense signaled the beginning of my full involvement with special collections. The whole library has a great deal in common with any special collections unit, especially with its completely closed stacks and its enhanced security. During my time there Lawrence W. Towner and I were, it's fair to say, mentors to one another, he for tutelage in entrepreneurial librarianship: marketing, fund-raising, the relation of the library to the world of scholarship, and for sharing with me his prescience in recognizing the library preservation crisis ahead of almost everyone else. My contribution was regular and repeated indoctrination in the rudiments of library science, before the advent of OCLC, Inc., and the robust systems of library automation it helped develop.

Sometime in my first year in Chicago, Bill (as Towner was always called) asked me to join him on a trip to Grinnell College in Iowa. During that trip he told me that I would never run a major research library if I didn't get a PhD. That wasn't anything I was thinking about, but it seemed like a good idea and I asked what he had in mind. He thought I should continue in English literature to build on my studies at City College and my teaching at Marlboro. But teaching John Milton at Marlboro had sparked my interest in British history in its close connection to English literature, as had Dean Roland Boyden with whom I did some team teaching dealing with that connection.

Towner had a Northwestern PhD in history and knew Lacey Baldwin Smith, the British historian in the History Department at Northwestern; we were soon invited to meet Lacey at a typically bibulous Towner dinner in 1968. It all led to a partial leave of absence in 1968-69 for a year of full-time graduate study in history at Northwestern, a brief daily office visit to keep abreast of my library job, help from the GI Bill and a personal grant from a Newberry Trustee (Samuel Rosenthal), a home-front in the Library's Irving Apartments, with three children under five and too little help, and a spouse working part-time at the Art Institute of Chicago. I once estimated the reading load that year as twenty-five books and countless articles per week. What I realized during that period, especially after I was offered a promotion within the Newberry, was that doing the doctorate would be very good preparation for understanding the needs of scholars using research libraries.

It was not an easy year, but by the time it was over I had an approved dissertation proposal, Don Krummel had moved on to the University of Illinois via the Aspen Institute and a study leave in England, and I was appointed Associate Librarian, an ABD continuing to work at a more relaxed tempo on my doctoral work on the reception of Calvin's works in Tudor England. My topic was a bibliographical exercise in largely unchartered territory, but would not be completed for another eight years, in 1978. By that time Elizabeth Eisenstein, a fairly regular Newberry visitor, was about to publish her *Printing as an Agent of Change* (1979), and she even included a footnote about my work on the production of Calvin translations in Britain in her book. I also had the good fortune of choosing a minor field for my Northwestern studies, the history of printing, guided by the Newberry's own Jim Wells who had built and presided over the John M. Wing Collection on the history of printing, one of the finest such collections anywhere.

One welcome interruption to my dissertation work was a fortuitous acquisition by the Newberry of an extensive Leigh Hunt (1784-1859) collection, the gift of Robert Roloson of Lake Forest. Included in the collection was a bound volume of clippings of all of Leigh Hunt's anonymous contributions to a short-lived London periodical of the 1830s called *The True Sun*. The gift was so obviously in my area of interest that I took on the task of cataloguing the whole collection with special attention to this made-up volume. Identified only by his initials, it took quite a bit of sleuthing to determine that the compiler was none other than Alexander Ireland, Hunt's first bibliographer. I prepared for publication an introduction to Hunt and his journalism followed by a selection of social criticism from *The True Sun*. David Erdman published the piece in the *Bulletin of the New York Public Library* as "Leigh Hunt and *The True*

Sun, a List of Reviews, August 1833 to February 1834," in Summer 1974, after I had left the Newberry for Johns Hopkins.[35]

A number of fine scholars were helpful on my dissertation. Reformation historian William Monter was a strong influence; his book on *Calvin's Geneva* provided both inspiration and a title for my own work, "England's Calvin." Timothy Breen, a good friend already and a mentor, tore my dissertation draft apart, and helped me put it back together. Lacey Baldwin Smith, noted Elizabethan scholar and something of a popular historian, supervised my work and helped make it what he was so good at, creating a readable work. He was a bit cynical about librarians and once told me that the Northwestern librarians were clueless enough to classify *Lord Hasting's Indentured Retainers* in the Dental School Library. Yet he did take me on. Much later when I was writing a biographical essay about Bill Towner (2003), I saw a confidential reference letter about me in Towner's archives in which Lacey described me as a Scarlet Pimpernel, not an allusion I would have caught at the time and I'm still uncertain what he meant. It's hard to imagine that I came across as a patrician/aristocrat in his classes, but he would have caught a characteristic elusiveness.

The Newberry was and is a treasure trove of booklore. Monthly rare book luncheons at the Drake Hotel included such luminaries as Tom Tanselle (now the nation's premiere bibliographer, then at the University of Wisconsin); Harold Tribolet (Manager of the Department of Extra Binding at R.R. Donnelly & Sons in Chicago); Paul Banks,

---

[35]   In addition to the list of reviews, the article included excerpts from some of the more trenchant reviews, showing Hunt, twenty years after his imprisonment for libeling the Prince Regent, still a humanitarian radical, cynical about fire and brimstone Calvinists, a believer in good works, social justice, and equitable distribution of wealth.

I once found a signed copy of an offprint of this article for $8 in a bookseller's catalogue. Of course I had to know which one of my friends thought so little of the piece, so I bought it. It turned out to be a presentation copy for Mel Edelstein, Librarian of the Getty Research Institute. Obviously, he had been cleaning house when he retired and moved back to Rhode Island. I was glad to get it back since it's a hard piece to find.

Don Krummel, and Jim Wells of the Newberry staff; Ken Nebenzahl (an eminent Chicago map collector and a benefactor of the Newberry's cartographic center); Robert Rosenthal (Curator of Special Collections at the University of Chicago); and, many other distinguished bibliophiles and prominent visitors from the book world. I was too late to meet Stanley Morison (of Times New Roman fame), a frequent visitor whose spirit lingered on and whose protégé was Jim Wells (as was Nicolas Barker). Albi Rosenthal, A.N.L. (Tim) Munby, Helen Wallis, André Jammes, Lucian Goldschmidt, Walter Whitehill, David Diringer, William Bond, Ian Willison, David McKitterick, Fernand Braudel, and many other titans of the scholarly world paid stimulating visits, and some became lifelong friends. One visitor we got to know very well was the late Rhys Isaac, an Australian-American historian, whose book on *The Transformation of Virginia, 1740-1790* won a Pulitzer Prize in 1983, the only Australian to have won the prize. He and his family visited our Wisconsin farm on a couple of occasions. Walter J. Ong, S.J., of neighboring Loyola University, was a Newberry reader. He once chided me for a disparaging remark about Marshall McLuhan whose influence he thought I had underestimated. I of course had no idea that McLuhan had been Ong's thesis advisor at St. Louis University.

While at the Newberry I also met for the first time librarians Jim Haas of Columbia University, Richard DeGennaro from the University of Pennsylvania, Maurice Tauber and Lee Ash (library educators and consultants), all of whom served on a review committee on our technical services. Others were Herman Fussler of the University of Chicago, Tom Buckman of Northwestern University (and later the Foundation Center in New York), Sir Frank Francis of the British Museum (soon to be renamed the British Library), and other seasoned and esteemed librarians who made a strong impression on a young one. Both Haas and DeGennaro were particularly helpful in my subsequent career. It was all very heady stuff.

Midway through the Newberry years, Walter Whitehill came to Chicago for a talk at the Cliff Dwellers Club. In a taxi going to dinner Walter was grousing to Towner about genealogists as amateurs dealing with people "beneath the level of historical scrutiny." Much as I admired and appreciated Walter, I couldn't agree with that particular prejudice, especially since genealogists were among the Newberry's most numerous clientele. Soon after that we had another Boston visitor, William Bond of the Houghton Library at Harvard. I told him that story and his caustic reply was that Walter himself was beneath "the level of historical scrutiny." A witty response, but Whitehill still merits some scrutiny in these memoirs.

Another fascinating visitor was critic Malcolm Cowley whose papers we were in the process of acquiring. On one visit in 1970 with his wife Muriel, Deirdre and I were the designated hosts for dinner at the Tavern Club, other Library officers being otherwise occupied. The event included the Cowleys, the Stams, and Arthur Crook, then the editor of the *Times Literary Supplement*. Cowley was quite hard of hearing and didn't enliven the conversation very much. Muriel, seated on my left, was very attractive with a stunning neckpiece made for her by Alexander Calder. Crook, the second longest-serving editor of *TLS* (1959-74), was an excellent conversationalist, affable and sociable. He was an ardent defender of the *TLS* anonymity policy, a practice that ended when he retired. Soon after the wine was served Muriel Cowley, gesticulating rather carelessly, knocked her Chardonnay right into the middle of my lap. For the rest of the meal she kept stroking my left leg, seeking assurance that I was all right and not too cold. I merely purred.[36] The evening ended quite late on the 95th floor of the Hancock Building with Arthur flirting and dancing with Deirdre and Muriel while I, the non-dancer, tried to keep Cowley entertained despite the loud music. Crook expressed our own feelings when he wrote a few months later that "that was one of the most charming evenings I have spent in any city anywhere."

When Crook asked me that evening if I would write a piece for *TLS* on Leigh Hunt's journalism I disingenuously deflected him by saying that Hunt was just a hack writer. In fact I didn't believe that, but was simply intimidated at the thought of writing for that much admired journal. Now it wouldn't faze me at all and I wish I had responded positively then. The article I did write was the one published by Erdman in the NYPL *Bulletin* and would have made a good *TLS* Commentary piece.

Ten years later Gabriel Austin, my one-time friend who "broke the bonds of friendship" invited me for a drink at the Century Club in New York. Rather than choosing a table for two as was usual for private parties,

---

[36] Some cynical friends on hearing this story insist that the "accident" was clearly intentional.

he sat down at the common roundtable where unaccompanied members would sit in hopes of some entertaining company. We were soon joined by a gentleman whom I thought looked like Malcolm Cowley and so I told my host when the gentleman left us for a moment. He assured me that it couldn't be, but when the man returned Gabriel initiated the following conversation:

Friend: Has anyone ever commented on your likeness to Malcolm Cowley?
Cowley: No, never.
Friend: I hope you don't consider it an odious comparison.
Cowley: Consider it a damned libel!

But it was Cowley and he went on to say that he was recovering from a visit to his Connecticut home by a *Life* photographer who was preparing a picture essay on Cowley at 80. The article soon appeared and Viking turned it into a small and charming book called *The View from 80* (1980) when Cowley was 82. Five years later he published another article on "Being Old Old." The Newberry did acquire his papers and he was honored with a large dinner party at the Drake Hotel where John Cheever gave the laudatory address about Cowley's influence on his work.

Another delightful Newberry visitor was A. N. L. Munby, better known as Tim, a noted bibliophilic scholar and Librarian of King's College, Cambridge. Jim Wells once asked me to accompany Tim from the Newberry apartments to lunch at Jim's apartment on North Wells Street. I offered the scenic route along Lake Michigan, or an inland route through some Chicago slums. He chose the latter, and although uneventful he proved a very astute observer of another side of Chicago life. His signature joke was about a vintage car he once owned for which he had to improvise repairs using some vellum parchment to replace a defective gasket. That allowed him to say, when asked how old the car was, that parts of it went back to the middle ages. His most notable work was on Thomas Phillips, a venerable nineteenth-century collector—his *Phillips Studies* are well worth reading; it was a privilege to show Munby around Chicago.

I can't resist recounting one Newberry legend about the Shakespearean scholar, E. E. Willoughby, who had been on the staff of the Newberry as a senior assistant, but for whatever reason was terminated by the Library in 1929. The following year, the story goes, he began his practice of giving the Newberry a gift on each anniversary of his departure. These became increasingly valuable as time passed, culminating with the presentation on the twenty-fifth anniversary of his termination of an incunable rebound in the cloth from the tie he was wearing on the day of his dismissal. It must be true—nobody could make it up, and Paul Gehl, the current curator of the Newberry's Wing Collection, says he has handled the volume, although I don't remember ever seeing it. Willoughby was later chief bibliographer at the Folger Library and died in 1959. The mystery is why he was sacked.

In the same year as Willoughby's death, another great rare book cataloguer joined the Newberry staff, Bernie Wilson, who had been cataloguing *Short Title Catalogue* books at the University of Michigan. He had been arrested in Ypsilanti on some dubious charges, and though Michigan felt compelled to let him go, University Librarian Frederick Wagman helped arrange a job for him at the Newberry as a rare book cataloguer. A shy bachelor from Ohio, Bernie was constitutionally unsuited to administrative duties and it was to his and the Library's relief that I replaced him in his temporary post as head of Technical Services in 1967. He could be over-the-top on the amount of time he would spend on one book and locally was well-known for his multi-card catalogue sets. Until his death twenty years later he was part of our family and often accompanied us for weekends at our farm in southwest Wisconsin (about which more below). I can still picture him sitting on a far hill, reading, his silver mane flowing in the wind, always bringing to mind Wordsworth's opening line of *The Prelude*, "O there is blessing in the gentle breeze . . . ." He was one of those smoking friends described above in "Panacea or Precious Bane."

One of our more dramatic and troubling adventures at the Newberry involved a very capable cataloguer, in fact our Head Cataloguer, who was involved in an abusive relationship with her female partner. It was a bizarre case which involved the theft of books carried home in grocery bags, elaborate communist conspiracy theories with the Chairman of the Newberry Board as chief conspirator, and a good deal of physical violence. This cataloguer would often come to work with heavily powdered facial bruises but we were clueless about what was going on. One night I was working late and discovered that she had left a large number of photocopies on the office machine describing the conspiracy, hallucinatory reports of intrigues and collusions in high places. I can no longer reconstruct all of the details but they included taking her under our personal protection, confrontations with her abusive partner by both me at the Library and by Herman Dunlop Smith, Chairman of the Newberry Board, at his Presidential offices at the Marsh & McLennan Insurance Company, the recovery of some of the books, and in effect the kidnapping of our colleague, whisking her off to O'Hare Airport a few days later for a flight to her native state, dressed in some clothes provided by Deirdre. It was a nerve-wracking affair but I remember Bernie Wilson and my secretary Rita Fitzgerald saying "Thank God that David has nerves of steel." Ha.

I've neglected to describe the Wisconsin farm. During my year of full-time graduate work in 1969 a couple of our friends, John Tedeschi of the Newberry and Douglas Wilson of Knox College, had discovered the beautiful driftless area of southwestern Wisconsin and bought farms there. During the late spring we visited them, took a look at a number of available places, and found one we liked in Ontario, Wisconsin, thirty miles east of La Crosse, 80 miles northwest of Madison, and 250 miles from Chicago. It was forty acres with a stream coming down from behind the house leading to a wider stream in the valley, a broken down nine-room house, a picturesque ruin of a barn, two dilapidated out buildings, some rusting cars and farm machinery, and an affordable price of $5,000, mostly funds lent by a sympathetic colleague. The deal that gave us that low price was that we would provide barbed wire for fencing and the seller would maintain the fences and could continue to use the land to graze his cattle. That suited us very well because it kept the fields clear and maintained the look of a working farm without the labor. I doubt we paid more than $100 for barbed wire over the next five years. We had not been inside the house when we went to the closing, and the seller's last words when we signed the agreement were that "it's a funny way to do business but I hope you like it." Keith Calhoun turned out to be a good neighbor, always helpful to these city slickers, helping out in any kind of need.

Ontario was an ideal refuge from the city, 250 miles mostly on interstate highways, lush vegetation and salubrious surroundings summer and winter. The valley stream was fertile with watercress much of the year and we usually had a thriving garden if we were there enough to care for it. The children were young and I was obsessed with mowing enough lawn around the house to be able to throw or hit balls as far as possible without having them disappear into the burdock and nettles. A hilly county road crossed a corner of the property, and when the Vernon County Road Department wanted to expand and pave the road, we agreed to their purchase offer with the proviso that they use their heavy equipment to bury our unsafe barn. It was a simple operation, a long grave-like trench dug alongside the structure, the dilapidated barn crushed and pushed into it, and then covered with the trench dirt. Though the kids did like playing in the barn, they were nonetheless excited to watch its demise.

In 1969 a British geographer named David Woodward joined the Newberry as curator of maps. He had been doing graduate work at the University of Wisconsin, and when he and his wife Rosalind heard about our Wisconsin property, they came up to visit and ended up buying the adjoining forty acres from Keith Calhoun. They put a temporary mobile home on the property, and lived there until they built their own house. Their presence for our few summers there provided us with delightful companions for both adults and children. After we left Chicago, David moved to the University at Madison, the base from which he and J. B. Harley, another British colleague and friend, edited their monumental *History of Cartography* (University of Chicago Press, 1987—). In late 2012 *TLS* referred to David as the "late great" David Woodward. David did not live to see publication of his massive two volumes on Renaissance cartographic history, truly a living memorial. Both of these brilliant scholars died at relatively young ages, but their work continues, with the twentieth-century volume now being edited by my Syracuse colleague, Mark Monmonier.

This was a time when NPR was gaining traction nationally and the Wisconsin Public Radio version had very good coverage of news and music, both classical and jazz, interesting lectures, and readings providing diversions for farm downtime. Garrison Keillor from neighboring Minnesota was particularly appealing toward the end of our time in Wisconsin, especially when his monologues included a character named Wendell—it seemed he knew our son personally. On NPR we listened to Nixon's resignation and the Ford inauguration in our final summer in Wisconsin. The farm was a quiet place for me to attend to some of my administrative work, particularly budget preparation and service reviews, but also to entertain guests with a hankering for a brief touch of country life. It was also the place where I had one of my few confrontations with my brother Jim. Since he has reported this for at least thirty-seven years of AA meetings, I guess I can record what I told him, that he didn't give a damn about us but only about his next drink. Apparently it had an impact and on his second rehab program he stopped drinking (and smoking eventually) and has been sober for over thirty-eight years.

This country idyll came to an end when we moved to Baltimore. We did return for a month in 1974, but the farm was exactly 1000 miles from Baltimore, and the 1973 energy crisis caused a reduction in speed limits to 55 mph, making for a very long haul with three kids in those unconfined pre-seatbelt days. We put the place on the market and sold it quickly for something over $14,000, a welcome supplement to our strained house-poor budget in Baltimore. We did leave behind a large collection of books and serials and some pine shelving, but we told the Woodwards to help themselves.

Bernie Wilson and I took a trip to Britain at the Christmas holidays of 1972-73 when we went directly from the overnight flight from Chicago to Oxford and a tour of the Bodleian Library given by Bodley's Librarian, Robert Shackleton. Term had ended and dinner was an intimate affair at Brasenose College with only Shackleton and the librarian of Lincoln College. Dead tired, over coffee in the Senior Common Room, we both fell asleep in the middle of the conversation. Among other things we spent Christmas Eve at the Palace Hotel in Manchester where the Christmas present was a cheese knife, went to Oldham on Christmas for a meal with John Dean's family (see below), visited our Marlboro friend Nicholas Barber in Liverpool, and then his parents' home near Sheffield. Most spectacularly in London we saw *Cosi fan tutti* from the second row at Covent Garden. While I was sitting there falling in love with one of the sopranos, Pilar Lorengar, Bernie was laughing so hard that the pre-renovation row of seats was rocking. He also visited us in Baltimore and New York, and we were sorry to learn of his death at age 78. He left his piano and some rare Mozartiana to the Newberry.

As a graduate student in history, one of the privileges of being at the Newberry was meeting some of the great Renaissance and Reformation historians of the time. In addition to some named earlier were Natalie Zemon Davis, John Demos, Elizabeth Eisenstein, Max Savelle, Robert Shackleton himself, and Alexander Vietor. The list could go on and should include some of the noted scholars from the Newberry staff: Hans

Baron and Stanley Pargellis, both retired shortly before I arrived but very much present, and John Tedeschi and Jim Wells, both still very actively working for the Library when I arrived. Matt Lowman, not a scholar but an excellent bookman, presided over the Special Collections during my early years at Newberry before he moved to San Francisco to join Franklin Gilliam at the Brick Row Book Shop. One of the Newberry staffers much later told me that I had placed second to Matt in the lady's election of Newberry's best buns. He was an ideal colleague and news of his early death a few years after his move to San Francisco came as a shock.

Stanley Pargellis, a scholar of British history, whose *Bibliography of British History: the Eighteenth Century, 1714-1789*, was published by Oxford in 1951, was Librarian and Director of the Newberry from 1942 to 1962. In retirement he was a charming and avuncular raconteur, an outgoing scholar turned librarian. Hans Baron was the opposite, a shy and retiring man with no interest in the limelight, except for his considerable scholarship about which he was quite thin skinned. A German historian of the Italian Renaissance, his most famous work, *The Crisis of the Early Italian Renaissance; Civic Humanism and Republican Liberty in an Age of Classicism and Tyranny* (Princeton University Press, 1955), shaped the historiography of Renaissance humanism in the second half of the twentieth century. In his library position he helped build the Renaissance collections at the Newberry. Hard of hearing, he never gained oral fluency in English (his wife once told us that Hitler had stolen his language) and therefore his potential for teaching in the United States was limited. He was excessively grateful to me for finding him a study space after his retirement, and even initiated with me the German ceremony for switching from formal to familiar address (from Sie to Du), linking arms with drinks, a great honor.

During my Newberry years from 1967 to 1973, there was a good deal of ferment in the research library community on numerous issues, leading Towner and a number of other research librarians to form a group called IRLA, the Independent Research Library Association. This brought another group of prominent librarians to Chicago fairly regularly, people like Marcus McCorison of the American Antiquarian Society, O. B. Hardison of the Folger Shakespeare Library, Jim Thorpe of the Huntington Library, Art Gallery, and Gardens, Charles Ryskamp of the Morgan Library, Edwin Wolf of the Library Company of Philadelphia, and a number of others. The immediate purpose of this collaboration was to make independent research libraries eligible for the same kinds of federal grants which university libraries were increasingly receiving from the National Endowment for the Humanities, and to a lesser extent the Arts Endowment. The campaign succeeded and NEH projects and challenge grants became and still are the backbone of fundraising among these institutions and led to other cooperative endeavors as well.

[*Coda: Several years later after I had moved to NYPL, Marcus McCorison asked me to replace him as Chairman of IRLA; as such I was the chief speaker along with Ronald Reagan at a December 1981 White House event marking NEH preservation grants to all of our members. The White House sent some photographs to us, including one of me during my talk. Deirdre's caustic comment was "there he is, at the height of his career, and he still has his hand in his pocket." Another photo-op amused some of my siblings, sandwiched as I was between President Reagan and William Bennett, then Director of NEH, hardly the kind of political company in which I was comfortable. In the Oval Office Reagan recalled climbing the hill in Dixon, Illinois, to the Dixon Public Library: "Of course I didn't read what you guys read, Chaucer and Shakespeare; for me it was the Hardy Boys and Zane Grey." At this time all the Directors of the 15 IRLA libraries were male and a baker's dozen showed up at the White House, including my new boss, Vartan Gregorian, President of the New York Public Library. Today, more than half of the ARL librarians are female and until recently all three of Britain's leading libraries, Oxford, Cambridge, and the British Library, were led by women, including one American.*]

Part of the library excitement of the late 1960s concerned the many issues of library preservation, and the Newberry was at the forefront of the debate. When I arrived as Head of Technical Services in 1967, the Newberry was one of only two ARL libraries with preservation units dedicated to the survival of their collections, the other being the Library of Congress. Today preservation is a necessary organizational component of any moderate-sized library, but in 1967 it was hard to get attention to the decay occurring in our stacks. Bill Towner had hired Paul Banks as Conservator in 1964, a timely appointment because it preceded by less than two years the Florence Flood of 1966, a flood that inundated many rare Renaissance volumes in the libraries of Florence and led to international rescue efforts. Towner had the wisdom to lend Banks to that cause, and in turn the Florence Flood became a catalyst for action toward conservation of physical books, towards preservation by microform or other surrogates of materials incapable of repair, and of preventive measures to protect these resources.[37]

I think it's fair to say that Paul Banks was one of few leaders of this movement, if not the prime one. As a theorist of conservation, active in the American Institute for Conservation of Historic and Artistic Works (AIC), his 1969 paper on the preservation of *Moby Dick* was their first to deal with book conservation. Banks, who reported to Bill Towner through Associate Librarian Don Krummel, was a thoughtful and sensitive person who was less than effective as a personnel administrator. He was not much of a people person: he once asked me if it was reasonable for Krummel to ask him to say "good morning" to his staff every day. As I recall, he said it was hypocritical.

Like NYPL, Newberry had its own production bindery and that unit reported to me as one of the Technical Services, while Banks and a growing conservation team reported to Towner. In 1969, in hopes of boosting production in our bindery, we invited an English bookbinder from the Manchester Central Library, John Dean, to join us for three months on a provisional appointment. Dean was trained in the British apprentice tradition of bookbinding. When it came time to make his appointment permanent, Banks was opposed, I suppose on the grounds that Dean's methods of greater productivity violated two of Paul's primary principles, first that any conservation treatment must be reversible, and second, that "if in doubt, don't." John and I argued that some elaborate procedures were inappropriate for certain types of materials such as pamphlets, and that more efficient methods had to be found to deal with growing backlogs of preservation work. It was the typical tension between the purist and the pragmatist, the perfectionist and the practical. One case in point was a large collection of thousands of eighteenth-century pamphlets, bound up in the same pamphlet volumes that NYPL used, though fortunately on good paper and without heavy use or widespread deterioration. Paul believed they all should be disbound, deacidified, washed, and then rebound individually, all at considerably higher costs than the simple cloth binding that John Dean was recommending.

---

[37] For a fascinating *roman à clef* on book preservation after the Florence Flood, see Robert Hellinga, *The Sixteen Pleasures* (New York: Soho, 1994), in which a couple of Newberry staff are faintly recognizable.

John Dean had already proved his ability to increase bindery productivity. By this time in the fall of 1969, I was the Associate Librarian and in a position to make the appointment. My own view of Banks's opposition to John's appointment was partly that he was skeptical of Dean's success, and partly that it may have shown something of a class conflict between a practical and efficient English journeyman and a genteel aesthete. Both had their place and Paul and I co-existed until I left in 1973. Two years later I hired John Dean at Johns Hopkins in 1975 as Head of a new Conservation Department.[38] John went on to gain a library degree and a master of liberal studies degree from the University of Chicago and Johns Hopkins University respectively. Years later, before Paul's death, John publicly acknowledged his debt for Paul's help in his own career. Paul Banks and I may have been professional antagonists on occasion but we were always personal friends and shared many good times together, even after he moved to Columbia University's School of Library Service in 1981. There he organized the nation's first book conservation training program, later moving the training program to the University of Texas at Austin following the closure of the Columbia School of Library Science.

We had one embarrassing evening in Chicago when Paul planned a dinner party for a visiting scholar, David Diringer, a noted writer on the evolution of the alphabet. Paul's dinner plan included martinis, red wine, and prime beef, and only when the guest arrived did we learn that he was both teetotaler and vegetarian. Conversation was not easy. Much more fun was Paul's visit to our farm in Wisconsin, where he thrilled

---

[38] Peter Verheyen of Syracuse has written that "John Dean began binding at the age of fifteen as an apprentice in Manchester, England, and worked his way through the trade and became head of the conservation bindery at the Manchester Research Library before immigrating to the US where he led the bindery at the Newberry Library in Chicago. He established the Conservation Program at Johns Hopkins, which at that time also had a certified 5 year apprenticeship program based on that of the City and Guilds of London Institute. Until his retirement in 2003, Dean was Director of the Department of Conservation and Preservation at Cornell University and he continues to work at Cornell as Conservation Librarian. It was as a work-study student in the Conservation Program at Johns Hopkins that the author was introduced to and encouraged to pursue a career in conservation and the book arts." See www.philobiblon.com.

our children with rides through the countryside in his MG convertible. He died far too early in 2000, aged 66. He was posthumously honored with the establishment by ALA's Association of Library Collections and Technical Services (ALCTS) of the Paul Banks and Carolyn Harris Preservation award for achievements in the field of preservation. In a wonderfully ironic twist, the 2003 prize was awarded to John Dean, the award presented to him by our son Julian Stam who was then Chair of the Preservation Section of ALCTS.

[*Coda: Our friendship with John Dean has remained close to this day, despite fairly constant changes in our lives. In 1975 I hired him to start a new Conservation Department at the Eisenhower Library, much along the lines of the consultant's report he had prepared for that Library. His Department and his five-year apprenticeship program, based on British models, continued to thrive after I left Hopkins in 1978, but he became restless under my successor and in 1985 he moved to Ithaca to become the Director of the Department of Preservation and Collections Maintenance at Cornell University Libraries.*

Dean retired in 2003 but in his late years at Cornell he developed a keen interest in the preservation problems of Southeast Asia (a particular strength of the Cornell libraries), tropical countries where preservation issues are significantly different from those of Europe and North America. In the later part of his career and in retirement he helped set up preservation programs in national and university libraries in Cambodia, Vietnam, Myanmar, Laos, Thailand, Indonesia, the Philippines, and even Kabul in Afghanistan, where he spent six uncomfortable weeks in 2006. He also hosted training programs at Cornell for native librarians from some of those countries, created online tutorial programs for them, and as recently as 2010 returned to Vietnam for further pro bono consulting. In 2004 we co-authored a paper entitled "Arctic Survivals: the Restoration of Records Recovered from Lost Polar Expeditions" which I presented at the Polar Libraries Colloquy in Ottawa in 2004. In 2013 he was off to another job in Abu Dhabi.]

Johns Hopkins and Baltimore
August 1973 to July 1978

One day in the spring of 1973, Towner and I were talking in his office and no doubt smoking when his phone rang. I only heard his side of the conversation but it went something like this: Yes, I think the best one in the country is sitting in my office right now [Towner was prone to such hyperbolic posturing]. Pause. That depends on whether Hopkins makes it possible for him to finish [his dissertation]. Pause. You can't get him for less than $30,000. Pause. I'll tell him about it.

The caller was American historian Jack Greene, chair of the Johns Hopkins Library search committee, and to abbreviate this story let me just say that four months later I found myself the head of a major research library at a salary of $30,000. Towner's ambitions, not mine, opened the door that I then moved through. After a year and a half as Librarian of the Milton S. Eisenhower Library, Hopkins gave me an extended leave to work on my dissertation on the reception of Calvin's works in Tudor England. That summer I spent four months working mainly at Oxford, but also in Cambridge and London, and at other times at the Folger Library in nearby Washington. The dissertation itself was an exercise in book history long before the term became academically fashionable. The original impetus came from the acquisition by the Newberry of a 1584 Spanish edition of Calvin's *Institutes of the Christian Religion*, printed in London. My original question was "Why," who in England would need such a work. Then I broadened the question to all the works of Calvin's works printed in England during the Tudor-Stuart period. The whole project morphed into a prosopographical study of all the people involved in the production of the largest group of translations of any of the continental reformers: translators and editors, printers and publishers, patrons (actual or desired), and dedicatees. Called *England's Calvin*, that title itself was a takeoff on the work of my teacher, Professor William Monter, *Calvin's Geneva*. All of this was evolving during the early 1970s, and one irony is that I did not receive the degree until the very day in 1978 that we departed from Hopkins, the shrine of the PhD.

Thirty-eight was rather young to head such a library and I'm sure I was underprepared in many ways. I did have the advantage of the counsel and friendship of the Director of the Johns Hopkins Medical School Library, Dr. Richard Polacek. Richard was formerly the head of the Library at the University of Ulm in West Germany where he was an early innovator in library automation, interests he continued at Hopkins and nationally with his involvement in the automation of *Index Medicus*. He had served as Interim Director of the Eisenhower Library at Hopkins for the year before I arrived and knew most of the skeletons in the Library's closets. He was also a sailor and we often sailed from his Chesapeake Bay berth at Middle River, pure escapism, with or without our spouses. On one such trip, probably the first and just the two of us, I was confessing to him some of my insecurities in the new post. He listened patiently before giving his advice: "Those thoughts are fine here at the third buoy of Middle River, but leave them here—above all don't mention them on campus." It was a strong boost to my confidence, perhaps too much so.

For my dissertation leave from May to August of 1975 I joined Polacek on the *QEII*, sailing to France on May 1 and visiting libraries where he had some work, the Württemberg State Library in Stuttgart and his own University of Ulm which claimed a modern building and a well-preserved baroque library as well. I also had the odd experience there of seeing Benjamin Britten's *Albert Herring* sung in German by their provincial opera company. This quasi busman's holiday had to stop when my dissertation beckoned. After leaving Richard in Paris, I went on to England and Oxford to get to work. I was there for a good ten weeks, found a convenient B and B in North Oxford, rented a bicycle for my ten-minute commute and settled into a regular routine in Duke Humfrey's Library, using their rare Calvin editions during all its opening hours, always getting there early to assure a window seat where the light was barely adequate for reading. This routine was broken only by visits to the College libraries, with Bodley's liaison to the colleges, Paul Morgan, as guide. Late in July I did the same thing in Cambridge for a week with David McKitterick (then of the Cambridge University Library and now Librarian of Trinity College) as my cicerone. I also worked at the British Library before my family joined me in August for some true tourist travel: London, Oxford, Cambridge, Ely, Norwich, Lincoln, York, Peterborough, St Albans, etc.

It was an idyllic summer, one of heat, drought, rationed ice cubes, and perpetual sunshine for those very long days with twilight at 11 pm. One such evening Paul Morgan invited me to join him at the summer meeting of The Oxford University Society of Bibliophiles being held in the Warden's Rooms of All Souls College. The Warden, John Sparrow, arrived late and apologized, saying he'd been with some PNAs, a reference that meant nothing to me. The meeting itself was a round robin of members talking about recent personal book collecting coups, or books they had been reading. Poet Elizabeth Jennings read one of her poems, no doubt included in her posthumous *Collected Poems* (see *TLS* 10/12/12). I remember her as petite and frail, an image belied by her Web pictures and the *TLS* review. During the reception afterwards, Sparrow, well-known in Oxford and beyond as a book collector and bibliographer, approached me to ask whether I might have any interests that matched his collections. When I told him that I was working on John Calvin he said he surely had nothing on that subject. Was there anything else? I said that I had more than a passing interest in the Romantic poets. "Ah that's better, come with me" and he led me to the third floor of a house jammed with books. "Anyone in particular?" When I said Leigh Hunt his only possible response was "Oh dear!" and we soon retreated to rejoin the others. Riding our bikes home after the meeting, Paul asked me whether I'd heard Sparrow's opening remark and went on to explain that PNA stood for "perfectly nice Americans." I suppose we Americans should treasure our anodyne qualities in the light of such arrogance.

There were other diversions in Oxford that summer including a complete Beethoven Quartet cycle played by the Amadeus Quartet, the start of a long friendship with Colin Steele (then head of foreign acquisitions at the Bodleian), the hospitality of Robert Shackleton, Shakespeare in the Worcester College gardens, the Oxford commencement ceremony called Encaenia in the Sheldonian Theatre, where Dame Janet Baker received an honorary degree and our friend Alice Barwell Prochaska received her DPhil, the Oxford equivalent of the doctorate. I first met Alice in 1970 at the British Library Reading Room, at a time when she was about to marry Frank Prochaska, a fellow graduate student in British history whom I had known at Northwestern University. Frank and I were both writing dissertations under Lacey Baldwin Smith. Frank had gone to London in 1969 to complete his dissertation, and his friends marvelled that this ascerbic critic could find such a lovely and delightful spouse. Apart from one year teaching at the University of Missouri, and ten years at Yale where Alice was University Librarian (2001-2010), Frank never left London. He was never what the Australians call a *jafa* (just another fucking academic), his main job being to produce one well-received book after another, mainly on nineteenth—and twentieth-century British history and society, with particular emphasis on philanthropy and the monarchy. The latest in 2013 is a biography of Walter Bagehot in his own words.

Alice Barwell grew up in Cambridge in an academic environment, and read history at Oxford in Somerville College where she is now Principal. When we first met she had just moved from the London

Museum to the Public Record Office (now The National Archives). In 1984 she became Deputy Director of the Institute for Historical Research at the University of London where she served for eight years. From there on I can claim to have influenced Alice's career, first by sending a strong letter of recommendation on her behalf to my friend Michael Smethurst, Director General of the British Library in Bloomsbury. He once told me that my letter had been a great help in making Alice's appointment as Director of Special Collections at BL possible; she lacked the formal library qualifications but brought both scholarship and archival experience to the post. Nine years later I had the privilege of nominating Alice as University Librarian at Yale, a post she held for another nine years before moving to Somerville. Over forty years we have visited every Prochaska domicile and it has proved a rich and lasting friendship.

But to return to the summer of 1975, work came first, and during that summer in Oxford I completed most of the research and wrote much of two chapters of the dissertation. Together with a couple of week-long stints at the Folger Library I was ready to go back to work at Hopkins while continuing to polish the dissertation. It wasn't easy after a long day at the office so I decided to do the work in early morning before the children woke up and I did find a pattern not unlike Anthony Trollope's quota of words per day. Without that I might never have finished. In retrospect I believe that my dissertation made a minor contribution to Calvin studies, but a great contribution to my education in research librarianship. Despite the narrow subject, pursuing it gave me a much wider sense of how scholars of my time used their research libraries and I felt better able to serve them.

By 1975 after two years at Hopkins I turned forty and things seemed to be going very well: dissertation well on the way to completion; a leave of absence to finish research abroad and commence writing; the library running quite efficiently with a good team in place; increasing involvement in the national library scene; promising candidacies at other libraries, including Princeton, UCLA, and the Historical Society of Wisconsin (two near misses and one rejected offer, but all ego pleasers). Soon, right on schedule, came the predictable mid-life crisis, then a fashionable topic in the public prints. In a word, I had become so full of myself that common sense had no place. In retrospect, the details seem less important than the lesson that a good humbling was in order and duly received. The crisis was disruptive of family and work, including a separation of a couple of months, thus providing an unwanted but useful opportunity for full attention to Calvin. As a friend and mentor told me: "You can't do better than what you have already. Don't mess with it" or words to that effect. How could I have been so stupid? Just in time I realized that he was right.

Hopkins was famous as the birthplace of the American doctorate and a faculty paradise—heavy research support, easy teaching loads, small classes with smart students. The faculty was very distinguished, and I name only a few that I came to know quite well: John Baldwin, John Barth, William Coleman, Richard Goldthwaite, Stanley Fish, Michael Fried, John Higham, Richard Kagan, Hugh Kenner, Richard Macksey, Maurice Mandelbaum, Jerome McGann, Charles Newman, John Pocock, not a female among them, and for me personally, very few scientists. Frances Ferguson of the English Department, who arrived the same year I did, was an exception, one of few female faculty then, and someone who shared my interest in Romanticism in general and Wordsworth in particular. We've lost touch for many years but I remember her as a stimulating and delightful colleague.

I once told Hugh Kenner that one night over dinner our children argued over who were the true intellectuals they knew. Deirdre and I were dismissed out of hand, and they claimed to know only two, including Kenner. He of course wanted to know what company he was keeping (it was Frank Prochaska). Stanley Fish was a friend, a cutthroat athlete at both basketball and tennis (and sometimes a cutthroat academic), and a fascinating, provocative, and immensely knowledgeable scholar. I read the manuscript of his George Herbert book for him, and he once asked me to co-teach a course with him, though I left Hopkins before we could do that.

Obviously our children never got to know Dick Macksey, my favorite colleague during the time at Hopkins, and a good friend since. Probably the most knowledgeable and least pompous among the faculty, the ever garrulous Macksey wore his learning lightly and in his conversation always seemed to assume that you knew what he was talking about, though seldom with such insight as his. In my office at the Eisenhower Library I had inherited two rusty swords, perhaps left by my predecessor to suggest I abandon hope at my new situation. When Macksey first visited my office he spied the swords, and immediately speculated on what eighteenth-century workshops they might have come from. He knew a great deal about medicine and when he heard of my ALS diagnosis assumed that I knew as much about its pharmaceutical treatment as he did. He was an astute collector in any number of fields and Hopkins has a new room dedicated to him and his collection. His memory has been phenomenal, only fading minimally in recent experience; a native of Montclair, New Jersey, the last time I saw him he remembered more of my home town of Paterson than I do. I have savored our relationship and am grateful that it has continued for forty years.

Musically, Baltimore was a good place to be. The orchestra was a good one and we knew some of the musicians quite well, including the Associate Conductor, Andrew Schenck, one of Deirdre's classmates and fellow wind player at Harvard. Andrew recorded much of Samuel Barber's orchestral music with the New Zealand symphony; he died at age 51. Shriver Hall Concerts, the Johns Hopkins chamber music series, were exceptionally fine and I was honored to serve on its Board. Deirdre played regularly in the Goucher-Hopkins Orchestra. She and I continued to play our bassoons occasionally, but my doctoral work precluded putting much of my time into it. There was also a highly successful contemporary music series at the Baltimore Museum of Art, just next to the Hopkins campus, where we heard many new compositions for the first (and often the last) time.

One treasure of Baltimore was a lovely older man named Lester Levy, a successful merchant of straw hats and a stalwart of the Baltimore Jewish community. He devoted a good deal of his life to the collecting of American sheet music out of a love for American history, American music, and what I can only call a patriotic zeal. A 1918 alumnus of Johns Hopkins, he wished his collection to come to the Hopkins Library. My job of cultivation was to help keep that wish warm, to advise on cataloguing at a time of the onset of automated systems, and to help administer some of Lester's related ideas. One such idea was the start of a series of programs of American music and musicians. The first was in 1975 when we presented a performance in Shriver Hall of *A Lincoln Portrait* with the Peabody Orchestra performing and Aaron Copland as narrator. The performance was a fine one and his pre-concert dinner conversation delightful, but as we later learned Copland was entering his final dementia and managed to forget his beret in our Faculty Club dining room. "You are a genius" he declaimed when I returned it, poorly earned praise indeed from one who deserved the name. The next year

Lester presented his collection to Hopkins as a centennial gift. It then comprised 30,000 pieces of sheet music, as well as reference books on American music including his own publications on the subject. We attended his 80th birthday party at his home in Pikesville, at a time when he was scheduled for new hips. One of the speakers reminded him and us that Moses did his best work after he was 80, and in fact Lester did continue to develop and support the growing collection for the rest of his life.[39]

Another notable collection we acquired at Hopkins in the mid-1970s was the book collection of American objectivist poet Louis Zukofsky (1904-1978). Although Zukofsky's personal papers had gone to the University of Texas, this was an important collection of association copies of all his works. The deal was engineered by Hugh Kenner who helped honor the acquisition of the collection with a speech to the Friends of the Library entitled "What to Do until the Poet Comes." All I remember of that talk was Kenner's or Zukofsky's deconstruction of the floral word arbutus into "are but us." Much clearer is the memory of our visit to the Zukofsky home in Port Jefferson, Long Island, where Louis and his wife Celia had invited us for coffee, black coffee served with a square, frozen Sara Lee cake. There were lawn chairs for furniture: it seemed that their choice was an aesthetic of asceticism, with their very modest house near Stony Brook, Long Island. The décor was spartan in the extreme with one exception, a bedroom shrine to their son Paul Zukofsky, an extraordinary master of twentieth-century violin music whom they clearly worshipped. Louis's only novel, *Little*, was a *roman à clef* about Paul. We also met Paul a few times when he played with the Baltimore contemporary music group. Louis died shortly before we left Hopkins for New York.

I have some ambivalent feelings about Hopkins, partly because some of the five years we spent there included our personal problems, but more because it was not the kind of place that inspired intense loyalty. I attributed that, perhaps wrongly, to the unrelenting focus of this home of the American PhD on individual productivity rather than any kind

---

[39] See http://levysheetmusic.mse.jhu.edu/ where much of the collection will be found in digitized form. The Hopkins Library website includes a loving portrait of Lester and Eleanor Levy by Richard Macksey under the title "A Biography of Lester S. Levy."

of team spirit or collaborative endeavor (lacrosse excepted). It may have been different among the scientists but I really didn't get to know many of them, and often they were hostile to the Library. Undergraduates were tolerated but not catered to as the "customers" that now populate American campuses. The library was somewhat anomalous because book selection was based on faculty recommendations but the faculty seldom requested the bread and butter books that they bought for themselves. It was Hugh Kenner who pointed out that unfortunate consequence of the Hopkins collections policy.

The idea behind the Eisenhower Library was the consolidation of several departmental branch libraries into one central library building. I have no doubt that the departure of my predecessor was a direct result of the consolidation, though it's hard to know how much of it, if any, was his idea. The battle fought so long ago at Hopkins over centralized libraries is still being fought at places like Harvard, Syracuse, and even Oxford today, and will continue to take its toll; some librarians are likely to be sacked or quit, and the survivors will conceal their stigmata. Ten years after the Hopkins library consolidation, the Associate Provost took me on a tour of the former physics/mathematics library in Rowland Hall (I remember the name simply because Rowland Hall was the name of one of Calvin's English printers). It was a very large and high room completely surrounded by empty bookshelves from floor to ceiling, at least ten feet high. "We leave this here as a symbol of your guilt." Who knew that total depravity extended to the closing of branch libraries? In retrospect I can say that at Hopkins when I was there, the Library was not a high priority that could rise above individual faculty concerns. It did provide, however, excellent experience for a young and untested library director.[40]

Automation was another theme of the Hopkins years, a period when OCLC was expanding beyond Ohio into various regional

---

[40] Sometime in the late 1960s the Hopkins Department of Operations Research decided to work with some graduate students to create a new automated circulation system for the Library. They called in some consultants from the Library of Congress, one of whom told me several years later that after hearing their presentation she asked why the head of the Library was not represented at the meeting. "We don't want to bother them with it until we're ready to make it operational," was their response.

consortia created to broker OCLC services to colleges and universities. As noted before, Hopkins had experimented with the automation of its circulation system and developed a very rudimentary and awkward process of microfilming spine call numbers and then keyboarding those numbers four times, twice for circulation and again twice for discharging the circulated books when returned. In between one waited for the batch processing on a mainframe computer overnight or over the weekends. One of my decisions in the first year was to invite Richard DeGennaro to consult with us on the replacement of that system. He was then University Librarian at Pennsylvania but had been in charge of automating the circulation system at Harvard College Library. At one point he cynically said that it would be better to pretend to have a system than to keep the one we had. However, after a great deal of discussion and the necessary budget analysis we made our decision to purchase a turn-key system called CLSI (Computer Library Systems, Inc.) in early 1975, following DeGennaro's advice that a Library such as Hopkins should be one of the parasites, not one of the pioneers. It was a principle which stuck with me throughout my career, and kept me from some perilous temptations.

Next we turned our attention to the automation of technical services, those systems which control the acquisitions, cataloguing, classification, and preparation for binding, shelving, and circulation. This search was a long time before the ubiquity of the personal computer, and simply involved the installation of a few terminals to communicate with the OCLC data base to order catalogue cards for each book added, and when the cards came, to continue to do as we'd always done with card catalogues. Our regional utility for OCLC services was called PALINET in Philadelphia. Sometime in 1974 in anticipation of joining PALINET, the Hopkins Associate Provost, Richard Zdanis, two information technology people, and I drove up to Bucknell University to see the system in action. The demonstration was impressive enough to lead to a positive decision to join the network, but on the trip home Zdanis with real prescience said that the real problem with the system was quality control, that the locally edited records of diverse contributors was not likely to yield consistent data. It remains a problem today where the data base is strewn with redundant records. One should take any claim of two billion records, or any library statistics *cum grano salis*.

In 1976 we hired James Thompson from the University of Pennsylvania to head the overall conversion of the Library catalogues to automated bibliographical control. For my annual report of August 1977 he wrote a very helpful appendix which we called "The Coming Revolution in Processing and Bibliographical Control." It ended with this caution:

> At the same time, the Library must be prepared to accommodate the changes in scholarly use of its collections and services which will result from automation. For some scholars, these changes will be at best unsettling. The traditional card catalog to which we are all accustomed will be supplemented and eventually replaced by a new form of record. The changeover will be traumatic for some, and the need to adapt to new circumstances will present difficulties. Yet we hope to show through a vigorous program of instruction that these technological innovations offer important advantages to the scholar as well as to the librarian, not least in providing more varied approaches to information sources than a static card catalog has ever been able to do.[41]

His predictions proved remarkably perceptive and accurate, including user resistance, but despite some whinging faculty who accused us of inflammatory language in using a loaded term like revolution, the revolt was relatively peaceful except at the time of widespread removal of card catalogues from public view. Thompson went on to become University Librarian of the University of California at Riverside.[42]

There is no need here to go further into the complexities of library automation, the intricacies of authority control, or the history of the

---

[41] "Annual Report of the Librarian. Milton S. Eisenhower Library. Johns Hopkins University. Fiscal Year 1976-77. David H. Stam, Librarian" (August 18, 1977) Appendix I, 5 p.

[42] In addition to Thompson, a number of my Hopkins library colleagues went on to become University librarians, including Bessie Hahn (Brandeis), Shirley Baker (Washington University, St. Louis), Johanna Hershey (Johns Hopkins), and Sarah Thomas (Cornell, Oxford, Harvard).

OPAC, our now almost universal online public access catalogues. But I would like to recall one other incident. The mid-70s began to see the introduction of online catalogues and in 1976 Hugh Atkinson at the University of Illinois announced that on July 4th the University would close its card catalogue and move to an online system-wide replacement. I happened to mention this to my Northwestern mentor and friend, Tim Breen, who remonstrated that the move would be fine for a place like Illinois but not for a quality institution like Northwestern. I mention all this only to point out how primitive some of our efforts now seem, even though librarians were well ahead of the curve of similar institutions, e.g., museums and archives.

The Homewood Library at Hopkins, opened in 1964, was named for Milton S. Eisenhower who had served successively as President of Kansas State University, Penn State University, and Johns Hopkins (1956-67). Hopkins appreciated his regime and it was often said that Columbia University chose the wrong Eisenhower. When the JHU faculty engineered the departure of President Lincoln Gordon in 1971 after less than three years, Eisenhower was called back for interim duty to be succeeded the next year by Stephen Muller. Milton and I would get together at his home two or three times a year for martinis and conversation on everything from university gossip, to the iniquity of the electoral college, to the budgetary ignorance of Lincoln Gordon ("He knew as much about accounting as my daughter," were his biting words, words that now seem hopelessly sexist). One of his favorite stories was about an introduction he received for a talk he gave in Pittsburgh when the speaker kept referring to John Hopkins University, omitting the obligatory **s** at the end of Johns. Milton responded in kind saying what a pleasure it was for him to be there in Pittsburgh. My informal title of Eisenhower's Librarian pleased me as redolent of Bodley's Librarian.

One of our early visitors was in fact Bodley's Librarian, Robert Shackleton, whom I had known from our meeting in Marlboro in 1965, and again at the Newberry a few years later. I had asked him to give a talk on the Bodleian for our Friends of the JHU Library. Robert was a noted Montesquieu scholar whose fine personal collection of eighteenth-century books went by purchase to the John Rylands Library in Manchester after Robert's death; it is now part of the University of Manchester Library. His talk at Evergreen House was a great success in Anglophilic Baltimore, and he was separately lionized by two of Baltimore's true eccentrics, Douglas

Gordon and Clifford Truesdell. Both asked me to arrange separate visits to their homes and Douglas Gordon put up Shackleton for the few days of the visit. Both had large mansions in Guilford near the University.

Douglas Gordon (1903-86) was a Baltimore attorney of considerable means and an amazing collection centered in Renaissance French works and concentrated on Montaigne. At the perimeter of his collection was a first edition of Diderot's *Encyclopédie, ou dictionnaire raisonné des sciences, des arts et des métiers* (1751-72), including an extra volume containing many censored passages and personal letters. Its provenance was extraordinary: Andrè le Breton (one of the printers), Diderot himself, Catherine the Great, the Russian Government, a London book dealer (Maggs, as I recall), Douglas Gordon, and bequeathed with his death to the University of Virginia along with his entire library. It was a collection that many institutions envied, and Gordon used to brag that "they carry my bags in Cambridge, New Haven, New York, and Charlottesville."

He was good enough to put up Shackleton in Charlecote House, Gordon's Classical Revival dwelling now listed on the National Register of Historic Places. Although I had seen the collection before, I felt fortunate to join them for an afternoon of book talk. After Robert's talk at Evergreen House and a post-talk dinner at the Faculty Center, I drove Shackleton to the Clifford Truesdell mansion nearby for some post-prandial champagne. Clifford was Professor of Rational Mechanics at Hopkins, and a major figure in that mysterious field, at least by his own account, and he often made it clear that he felt without sufficient honor in his own country and university. Mostly he was a figure right out of Shackleton's eighteenth century. He had his own live-in wood-worker to recreate eighteenth-century styles in his beautifully renovated house. His tastes in art were largely baroque, as was his formal dress. His curvaceous second wife Charlotte was much on display at his musical soirees with such baroque eminences as Nikolaus Harnoncourt and Gustav Leonhardt, and they once had a baroque dance group of a dozen women and one man to perform a Rameau work in their large central hall. The festive buffet dinners which followed were nothing short of regal, and usually served 60 to 70 guests. For very special guests like Leonhardt the dinner table might be set for as few as ten.

Long before my time Truesdell had commissioned a large painting on the theme of Judith and Holofernes with Clifford and his wife as models, hard for me to imagine now because all the time I knew him he was bald, leaving no hair for Judith to hang on to. We left there rather late, and as we drove back to the Gordon house Shackleton wryly noted that it "was an extraordinary experience to see Mrs. Truesdell, first half naked in the flesh, and then fully naked in the paint." I once was toweling myself in the Hopkins gym when Clifford came by, looked carefully up and down my naked body, and finally said: "Oh David, I didn't recognize you without your glasses." He was antagonistic to almost anything the library tried to do for him, and it was always places like Oxford or European universities that did these things right, especially in their mathematics libraries. But he was personally friendly and wished me well when I went off to New York, assuring me that he didn't envy me my new city.

Another distinguished visitor in 1975 was historian Daniel Boorstin, newly appointed Librarian of Congress. In his new position he was trying to get a sense of the larger library community which he was charged to serve beyond the needs of Congress. I invited him to come to Baltimore for lunch with the Hopkins President, Steven Muller, and our Provost, Richard Longacre. John Y. Cole, who founded the Center for the Book at the Library of Congress, completed our luncheon party. At one point I was asked to describe the unique collections of the Hopkins Library. I talked about the holdings at Evergreen House, some of the important archives we held, the independent but unique holdings of the Medical School, and alluding to the impending possibility that Hopkins would take ownership and responsibility for the Peabody Library in downtown Baltimore. Boorstin's response was a bit of solipsistic arrogance: "Isn't it a shame that such treasures are scattered around the country when they should all be united at the Library of Congress." As I recall it left us all speechless.

Hopkins was my introduction to the Association of Research Libraries (ARL) and particularly its management program called MRAP, its Management Review and Analysis Program. MRAP was a system of participative management that tried to involve staff at all levels in debating the library issues of organizational structure, policy determination, problem resolution, and in practical procedural recommendations. In the first couple of years of the program when head librarians long in office were led to this new approach to library administration they often were also encouraged to retire or were sacked. I decided it was the better part of valor to do the program immediately before any battle lines were drawn. It was a useful program helping me to assess the strengths and weaknesses of the staff, and to give the librarians a better sense of how their work fit into the overall picture. Some of my older counterparts at other ARL libraries complained that MRAP was too labor-intensive to justify the results as thousands of hours went into endless meetings and report writing. There was truth in their claim, but at Hopkins every one of our quantitative measures of productivity, e.g. acquisitions, cataloguing, circulation, etc., increased during the year of MRAP. In my opinion it was the engagement of staff that made the difference.

From the perspective of the early twentieth-first century, MRAP now appears one of many acronyms assigned to cyclical attempts to instill new life into library administrators and their staffs. MBO, management by objectives, was next, followed by TQM, total quality management, and then LibQual, a system of assessment that I happily missed by retirement in 1998. By that point I was tired of the jargon and the formulaic nature of strategic planning, and might have escaped it altogether if most of my ongoing boards hadn't insisted on doing their own strategic plans. Presenters and facilitators actually make livings doing this stuff with their trusty and dusty PowerPoint presentations.

Although I gained excellent experience and enjoyed my five years at Hopkins for the most part, it was not then a librarian's paradise by any means. Some of those brilliant faculty members could be very difficult and arrogant. I remember one Faculty Library Committee meeting in 1974 where we were introducing the then incipient field of online searching for information and texts. The original offerings of journal holdings might have as little as the most recent three or four years of old and prestigious journals in physics, chemistry, or engineering. One clever scientist asked me if I was aware that serious work was done in those fields before 1970. I cheekily assured him that when the database purveyors could be sure of adequate sales they would convert far more, a gratuitous response to a gratuitous insult.

Baltimore is a rather conservative place and that conservative resistance to change was reflected in many of the staff that I'd inherited. MRAP certainly helped loosen up some of the more rigid "we've always done it that way" types, but for some, more draconian measures were needed from reassignment to termination. I did make a few bad personnel decisions along the way, but fortunately at Hopkins, like most of my other career moves, there was no way to go but up, thanks to the failed leadership of several of my predecessors. The exception was New York Public Library where it could go either way, and it has.

One problem did emerge at Hopkins just as I was leaving, and although I was not much involved in the case it was disquieting. It involved a problem known too well to all librarians, what to do with unwanted books. Apparently a graduate student worker was assigned by the Library to dispose of some discarded materials, books both at the Eisenhower Library and at the special library housed at Evergreen House. Rather than discarding certain books, a student named Roger Cox chose to take some of them to his graduate student office and developed a rather large collection, including some valuable books that he offered to the nearby Baltimore Museum of Art after appraisal by a local dealer. He claimed that these books were in boxes on a table marked for disposal though it was hard for me to believe that any library employee would not have recognized some of them as worth preserving. If there were any question he might have asked. I heard a little about the case before I left Hopkins in May 1978, but the story broke two years later with an April 1980 article in *Baltimore Magazine*, aptly entitled "Roger Cox and the Great Hopkins Library Mystery." Comments about me in the article were close to libelous, yet to me the case remains a mystery. I suspect but can't possibly prove that someone on the staff did enjoin secrecy for what should have been an open process and much more carefully monitored. But the issue of space and book disposal was a persistent one that came up in every institution I headed, and continues to trouble librarians everywhere.

In 1976 Dick DeGennaro, then President of the Association of Research Libraries, asked me to chair ARL's Preservation Committee, an assignment that was an accidental stepping stone for me to rather heavy involvement in library preservation and conservation issues in ARL, IRLA, and the Research Libraries Group (RLG) over the next two decades. At a preservation conference at the Library of Congress during this period I started a talk by saying that Penguin Books and I had been born in the same year (1935) and that I'd outlived many of them. Bill Towner was there and piped up from the second row that he had lots of Penguins in better shape than me. Sometimes preservation got to be a burden. The proponents were well-intentioned and able but their focus seldom reached the whole picture, fighting as they were for standing in a new profession. Many had what we called the "white glove" syndrome, where many things were thought too precious to be touched.[43] One of my friends at the Library of Congress later said that "the conservators have become our enemies," placing restrictions on both use and on exhibition loans, the antithesis of the open access many of us were striving for. I also remember telling myself at the end of a British consulting trip in 1983 that I never wanted to see another conservation lab. But my preservation preoccupation did last until the end of my career, including the chairing of the New York State Advisory Council on Conservation and Preservation of Library Materials. That group's most notable achievement was the drafting and passing of State legislation in 1984 to support major funding for preservation programs in the State's eleven research libraries, and smaller but vital grants for any of New York's libraries, historical societies and museums, and archives. The growth of awareness and action on preservation issues between my arrival at the Newberry in 1967 and the end of the twentieth century was gratifying to behold.

When I left Hopkins in June 1978 my final report was in fact a summary of my five years as Eisenhower Librarian, a summing up of achievements and failures, of problems and prospects. On rereading it 25 years later I was disappointed to find this rather jaundiced ending:

What we lack is the concentrated support of the faculty for excellent library services. Many years ago Paul Buck, Harvard's Librarian, said that "you cannot have a quality faculty without a quality library." Johns Hopkins has defied this dictum to a surprising degree but nonetheless the quality of its library reflects badly on the quality of its faculty. My own somewhat cynical view is that a faculty gets the library it deserves. Faculty support for the Library here has, with some notable exceptions, been generally grudging, invariably self-serving, and frequently self-defeating. As a result the University administration is under no great pressure from the faculty to support the Library adequately.

---

[43] See "Misperceptions about White Gloves," by Cathleen A. Baker and Randy Silverman. *International Preservation News* No. 37 (December 2005) p. 4-9.

Ergo, despite the rhetoric, it does not support Library Services adequately.[44]

What was clear by the time I was planning to leave Hopkins was that I had achieved a clear career path as a research library administrator and my name was in what Bill Towner called the "wind tunnel" of job candidates. It certainly wasn't by design but somehow took on a life of its own.

New York Public Library Revisited
July 1978 to February 1986

My two interviews for the Directorship of the Research Libraries at New York Public Library constituted the easiest search I'd ever experienced. Much of the two visits in December 1977 and January 1978 were more recruitment than evaluation. The Trustee Search Committee included President Richard Couper: Gordon Ray of the Guggenheim Foundation; Phyllis Gordan, widow of John Gordan and a collector and philanthropist; Jim Haas, then Columbia University Librarian; and Conrad Harper of the Simpson Thatcher & Bartlett law firm. It was a stellar group, but apart from Jim Haas and Gordon Ray, the group seemed to have little experience of search committees. My predecessor, James Henderson, told me in his farewell letter of advice and counsel that he was shocked that the Library had decided to use a search committee,

---

[44] David H. Stam. "Problems and Prospects of The Milton S. Eisenhower Library. Final Report of the Librarian 1973-78." (June 15, 1978) p. 32. I have no evidence that apart from some few Library staff and my interim successor, Richard Polacek, anyone ever read these gloomy words.

as it was the first.[45] One of the reasons the two-hour search committee interview was so easy was that Conrad Harper took an interest in my nearly completed dissertation on John Calvin called "England's Calvin," Fully an hour of the two-hour session was devoted to the subject on which at the moment I was the expert. The other hour seemed to consist of softball queries such as whether budget problems at Hopkins would be an incentive for me to come to New York. I laughed and said it was the reverse, that NYPL's epochal budget problems of the 1970s were an incentive to come, a challenge worth taking on.

When I was offered the position of Andrew W. Mellon Director of the Research Libraries at The New York Public Library, my friend Ernie Siegel, Director of Baltimore's Enoch Pratt Public Library, counseled me: "You can't not." The move to New York seemed almost predestined and so another major transition occurred in our lives. The President of Hopkins, Stephen Muller, had offered to match the $50,000 starting salary in New York, and though we would be losing college tuition benefits down the road, and would be house poor at that salary, we decided to make the move to a new venue and to seek new adventures. We found a comfortable house in the Westchester village of Pelham, half an hour by train to Grand Central Terminal, two blocks from my office. I started work informally on July 17, 1978, beginning with a few weeks of wall-to-wall interviews with division chiefs and department chairs, visiting the four research library buildings, and trying to get a sense of what I would be facing when my formal appointment became effective on August 1. Physically and organizationally the Library had changed a great deal since I left in 1964, but my past experience there was clearly an advantage.

Shortly after I arrived in New York, I attended a party at the Grolier Club where I met Francis Mason, then Deputy Director of the Pierpont

---

[45]   Henderson has written an appealing and insightful book of reflections on his career at NYPL called "Going Back: A Memoir of My Years at The New York Public Library," 1998. As far as I can determine it has not been published. Although he says little about my period as his successor, I was privileged to host a party in the Trustee's Room celebrating the completion of his massive post-retirement Project Retro, published as the *Dictionary Catalog of the Research Libraries of the New York Public Library, 1911-1971* (New York: NYPL; Boston: G.K.Hall, 1979-1983) 800 volumes.

Morgan Library, a suave and somewhat portentous diplomatic type, and a man influential in the world of dance. He was many things: an educator, critic, gourmet cook, gardener, cultural ambassador, and always a *bon vivant*. When we were introduced he said with a fierce glare, "It's a noble position you hold. I hope you do it honor." I have no idea what the deeper meaning behind that remark was, but it is what I tried to do. He was regarded by some as a pompous bloviator, but I respected him, enjoyed his company, learned a good deal from him, and was sorry to learn of his death in 2009.

My first task was to form my administration. The structure I inherited had about fourteen people reporting directly to me, partly because there was no unified leader of our numerous special collections, with separate reporting lines for each of the departments of Rare Books, Manuscripts, Prints, and the Arents, Berg, and Spenser Collections. From existing staff I was able to appoint Donald Jay Associate Director for Public Services, Paul Fasana as Associate Director for Technical Services, Juanita Doares as Associate Director for Collection Management and Development, and Donald Anderle, at that time the Chief of the Art and Architecture Division, as Associate Director for Special Collections. Together they constituted my initial Research Libraries Management Team until we recruited a Deputy Director, Arthur Curley, in 1979, and in 1981 brought Ruth Ann Stewart, assistant director of the Schomburg Center, to 42nd Street as Assistant Director for External Services. One special collections division chief, Elizabeth Roth of the Prints Division, was upset enough over reporting to Don Anderle rather than me that she resigned, not before orchestrating a resolution of protest against me from the Print Council of America. In the year or so that we overlapped, I remember only one time when she asked my advice, what color should be used in the third floor exhibition corridors, almost the last thing on which I could be helpful, as my family can attest.

The assembled team I thought quite a strong one, including such strengths and weaknesses as any such group might have. I tried to use annual retreats to unify the group and brainstorm our way to new ideas. Don Jay was articulate and competent but somewhat phlegmatic and non-assertive. Paul Fasana was our main technical expert, but disaffected by not having been appointed to my job and rather unsociable. Juanita Doares was the resident left-wing feminist with a heart of gold and at the outset preoccupied by managing the Schomburg building project, not completed until October 1980. Don Anderle was probably the smartest of the group, simultaneously innovative and conservative, with a short fuse and a caustic epistolary style.

Another key staff member was John Philip Baker, Head of the Conservation Department, and an old friend from my earlier NYPL times and the Bob Allen circle.

The flavor and diversity of my NYPL early days with Dick Couper is reflected in a fragmentary diary I kept during January 1980, I suspect the result of a New Year's resolution:

[January 1, 1980] Everyone slept late on New Year's Day so I was able to work for several uninterrupted hours drafting recommendations for NYPL's Board of Trustees for fiscal retrenchment. Although much of the work that went into the report was painful, cajoling staff into realizing the necessity for change while keeping a few of the Trustees from giving away the whole store, I nevertheless had a sense of exhilaration as the pieces of large-scale change in the institution fell into place. I hope it can be brought off smoothly without too many bruised feelings. The next three months should tell.

[January 2] Most of the work day revolved around the visit of a candidate for a high level job in the Library administration [probably the Vice President for Finance]. That involved me in a great deal of essentially introspective talk about the institution, the job he applied for, my role in it etc—tiring and probably tiresome. At times I had a strange sense of foreknowledge about great numbers of impending changes in the Library about which my colleagues were largely unaware but which I knew would occur.

The late afternoon meeting of the Executive Committee of the Board, discussing the Branch Library crisis related to City Budget cuts seemed a travesty, the folly of Committee approach to strategic problems. Mrs Astor looked incredibly well-preserved, expressed some conservative sentiments, but the meeting had little cohesion or leadership. Ended with a quick squash game with the boss.

[January 4] Before lunch I had the pleasure of fifteen minutes conversation with Lady Antonia Fraser who was working at the Library today on her next book on 17th century English women. She seemed as attractive as her publicity shots and extremely gracious and charming, full of praise for the Library and its services.[46]

Lunch with the Chairman of the Planning and Resources Committee [Bill Dietel] to review drafts of our final report. Most disturbing was his constant return to the subject of user fees as the way to protect the quality in our collections. We debated the issue from several angles but only reached an impasse. Otherwise he was impressed and supportive of the work I'd done.

That last sentence now seems too trusting. I wish I'd shown some discipline in keeping a diary or at least in keeping notes of significant events in my professional life. It would have been a much more efficient check on my defective and deceptive memory than searching through the haystacks of the archives.

Patricia Battin became the University Librarian at Columbia shortly before I came back to New York in August 1978. Her predecessor, Jim Haas, had recently left Columbia for the Council on Library Resources, and for much of the following period the three of us were involved in various collaborative activities such as the reorganization of the Research Libraries Group, the formation of what became the Commission on Preservation and Access, the NEH brittle books program, and other national and international initiatives. When Nicolson Baker's simplistic diatribe against preservation microfilming appeared as *Double Fold* (New York, 2001), I got off fairly easily and Pat (by this time President of the Commission on Preservation and Access) took the brunt of his criticism. I still believe those programs saved far more than was squandered, the loss of some color-printed newspapers notwithstanding, especially given the

---

[46] When I congratulated her on the success of her most recent book she said that sending a book off to the publisher was rather like sending a child to boarding school: out of sight, out of mind.

present ease of creating digital surrogates from those hordes of microfilm we diligently created.

The Research Libraries Group

The early days of the Research Libraries Group were among the most exciting of my forty-year career, not only for RLG's collaborative purposes focused on the specific needs of large research libraries, but also for the opportunity it gave for me to spend time in discussion and debate with some of the best minds in librarianship at that time. The founding members of RLG were Columbia, Harvard, Yale, and NYPL. Between my appointment and arrival at NYPL, Pat Battin had become University Librarian at Columbia and replaced Warren J. Hass on the RLG Board. Harvard had withdrawn from the organization (despite Doug Bryant's promises to me that he had no such intention), and the remaining RLG officers (at that stage two from each institution) faced the need to approve a replacement for Harvard, and to find an automated system that might be shared by the membership. Stanford University was an obvious contender to replace Harvard as a founding member since it had developed its own automated system and gave RLG the prospect of new leadership.

As the new blood on the Board, Pat Battin and I thought of ourselves as the founding step-parents of RLG II. Richard Couper and I became the NYPL representatives to the new governing body, called the Board of Governors and known not always kindly as the BOG. Stanford University made a strong bid but one that required adoption of BALLOTS, its automated bibliographical system. Despite a similarly strong proposal from NYPL and its ONLICATS system, diplomacy under Richard Couper as chair of RLG prevailed, and a new course was set for the organization. At a lengthy meeting at Columbia University in October 1978, Stanford was selected as a founding member and BALLOTS (soon to be renamed the Research Library Information Network, RLIN), was chosen as its bibliographic system. The original President of RLG, James Skipper, was forced to resign at that meeting, and as his replacement we elected Stanford's Ed Shaw, a heavy-smoking charismatic leader as our new head. I remember that meeting vividly because of Skipper's reaction on realizing that he had been fired: "Well in that case, who will take the minutes?" Someone determined that the alternate representative of the Board Chairman's institution would be Secretary. That was me, and very unexpectedly I had a new assignment. Another day-long meeting within a month involved RLG's own legal counsel, our new friend Noel Hanf, and attorneys from all four institutions. Although the meeting was intended to consummate the marriage of the four institutions, most of the discussion that day was about what would happen in case of divorce. It must have been a very expensive meeting.

At our first RLG meeting at Stanford in January 1979, I was surprised to be elected Chair of RLG's Collection Management and Development Committee, one primary focus of RLG aspirations. With Paul Mosher of Stanford as Vice Chair and John Finzi of the Library of Congress playing an equally active role, we formed a de facto executive committee for the CMDC. It was the Stanford Librarian, David C. Weber, who suggested that every committee have a Board of Governors member as chair, and he nominated me for the CMDC assignment. Our goal was to create a tool which would help research libraries allocate their resources to existing and prospective strengths, while leaving their lesser priorities to others through shared assignment of responsibilities. From the beginning I saw NYPL as the ideal place to fill in the interstices of collection development that research universities were unlikely to cover. The tool we developed was called the Conspectus, more widely adopted abroad than in the US, but a concept which caused a great deal of collection development introspection and controversy that continued even after its US demise. In good times the institutional narcissism (what one woman colleague called testosterone belly-bumping) would overshadow collaborations, only to return during fiscal difficulties. The fundamental issues addressed by the Conspectus have been affected but not resolved by the digital world. Someone should write its history before its principals die off—some, like the late John Finzi of the Library of Congress and Ross Atkinson of Cornell, already have, and others like Scott Bennett, Paul Mosher, and me have left the field.[47]

---

[47] The RLG Archives are in the Stanford University Library and have been carefully processed; the raw materials are ready for analysis, but the opportunities for oral history are rapidly disappearing.

In the absence of such a work, let me at least summarize my own recollections of the rise and decline of the Research Libraries Group. Following the reorganization of 1978, RLG began expanding its membership, adding another forty or so members within the next three years, including many of the major research universities in the US. We gained our first foreign member in 1982 with the British Library, and soon many of the British university libraries joined as a group. Each institution was represented on the Board of Governors and on the various committees, including the Collection Management and Development Committee. A hard-working group with some of the best brains in the business, its major agenda was the development of the Conspectus as a tool for shared collection responsibility, designed to assure comprehensive global coverage answering the resource needs of all scholarship going on within our member institutions and beyond. I personally saw the Library of Congress, an early member, and NYPL, as two unaffiliated institutions best placed to fill in the gaps of coverage not provided by university collections which always had to put priority on their specific scholarly needs and local priorities.

The Committee and the Board had exceptional staff assistance from John Haeger, a sinologist working under Ed Shaw. He stayed abreast of the technology and helped to develop the scholarly programs for art libraries, archives, and East Asian languages (CJK); shaped a major role for RLG in the online *English Short Title Catalogue*; and recruited new members from abroad. I often thought of John as the brains behind RLG, an incisive thinker who provided a healthy brake on some of the more irrational ideas sometimes proposed. The expansion included successful efforts to recruit the British Library, other UK National Libraries, and the major British university libraries as members, thanks to the initial efforts of Alex Wilson at the British Library, his successor Michael Smethurst, Denis Roberts of the National Library of Scotland, and a host of others. The RLG experience in Britain roughly mirrored the US experience—a burst of enthusiasm, a period of hard work and exhilaration, and then a decline of interest as economic conditions improved and the emphasis on collaborative interdependence diminished. But during this period I came to know many of these librarians very well in both professional and social settings, often as a home visitor (the Scots proved particularly hospitable).

From the beginning of RLG II (1978) there was considerable conflict and unnecessary tension between RLG and its most comparable but quite different entity, OCLC, Inc. (originally the Ohio College Library Center). By my lights, where I saw RLG as a helpful corollary to OCLC's own purposes, by contrast they viewed us as competitors. If RLG had successfully developed an efficient and economical cataloging and processing system, the competition might have been more fierce. That didn't really happen.

I saw our member libraries as providing the primary research resources for the publications that filled the shelves of OCLC's smaller college and public libraries. Some outside the organization unfairly pilloried us as the elite research libraries with lofty attitudes towards the great unwashed of the thousands of public libraries in OCLC's membership.[48] Some staff within member libraries felt threatened by the prospect of collaborative agreements that might detract from their own budgets, discretion and independence. When RLG began to put resources into automation of Chinese/Japanese/Korean records, OCLC felt obliged to duplicate the effort rather than collaborate with us. The conflict also showed up in the Association of Research Libraries where there were partisans of each organization, myself among them. I don't believe RLG ever enrolled more than half of the ARL membership, although it was quite successful in attracting the free-standing art museum libraries, law libraries, and members of IRLA, the Independent Research Libraries Association.

By 1985 the Conspectus had received a great deal of attention, with its expansion abroad in Britain, in Europe, and even in smaller libraries that wanted to develop sharing models. There was interest among smaller consortia, and Paul Mosher even helped develop a stripped down version of the Conspectus for the academic libraries of Alaska. There were other small successes: agreement on some periodical commitments among the members, and the creation of a new metadata field to indicate the intention to microfilm a given work so as not to duplicate the effort.

---

[48] See my "Elitism and the Common Cause," *American Libraries* (Nov. 1979) p. 586; Michael Gorman, "Network! or I'm Rational/ Mad as Hell and I'm Not Going to Take It Anymore," *American Libraries* (January 1980) p. 48-49; and "On Utilities, Elitism, and Democracy: Three readers respond to a portrait of OCLC as a 'bibliographic democracy' and RLG as 'an exclusionary group'" [David H. Stam etc.] *American Libraries* (May 1980) p. 278-79.

Mirabile dictu, the ARL membership also endorsed the scheme with its North American Collections Inventory Project (NCIP) to help its members and other libraries develop their coordinated collection profiles; it took over program administration as well, and produced a quarterly *NCIP News* for a few years. The methodology had its critics but I was not a close observer of its decline and apparent disappearance.[49]

The extensive travels to Research Libraries Group institutions, involving Board and Committee meetings around the country and occasionally abroad, gave me the chance to work in many special collections and to observe firsthand the practice of special collections while using them for my own research throughout North America and in Britain. Leigh Hunt, an often overlooked Romantic and Victorian English writer, was my subject of choice and a couple of RLG meetings in Iowa City led me to the incomparable Hunt resources at the University of Iowa. The best in the world, they happily survived the 2006 flooding of the library there. The University Librarian, Dale Bentz, knowing of my interest in Hunt, asked me to help celebrate Hunt's bicentennial in 1984 at Iowa along with such eminent scholars as Richard Altick, Carl Woodring, Charles Robinson, Donald Reiman, and Mary Carpenter. Mine was the after dinner talk. The Australian biographer of Hunt, Ann Blaney, was there, and after my talk she gave me a hug and a kiss, reminding me of Hunt's most famous poem, "Jennie kissed me when we met, Jumping from the chair she sat in." The proceedings were published by the University of Iowa Library and my own talk on Hunt as bibliophile was reprinted in *The Book Collector*.

I made one other important connection during this period with the newly formed Library of America at a meeting I had with its President, Cheryl Hurley, and co-founder Daniel Aaron. I suspect that Jim Haas had

---

[49]   In October 1986, after I moved to Syracuse and had left the RLG Board, I gave a talk at the 109th Membership Meeting of ARL in Washington, an entire session devoted to NCIP. My paper, entitled "An Informal Secret History of the Conspectus," was published in their *Minutes* (p. 7-10), and also by the National Library of Scotland in its *Conspectus in Scotland Newsletter* No. 5 (September 1987) p. 1-2. For a balanced critique see Virgil L. P. Blake and Renee Tjoumas, "The Conspectus Approach to Collection Evaluation: Panacea or False Prophet?" *Collection Management* Vol. 18 (1994) p. 1-27.

suggested the meeting, since he was a member of the LOA Board. Because I'd forgotten some of the details, I recently asked Cheryl Hurley why that meeting seemed important to her. Her response was a pleasure to my ears, an ardent reader of those beautiful volumes:

> What we got out of the meeting was not just enthusiasm for the idea of the series but a rare appreciation for what we were trying to do. You got it, in other words. You could envision the whole thing, and how it would change the landscape for American literature. Many other smart people were quite dubious of whether it was necessary, or they would get hung up on all the reasons why it wouldn't work. You offered support in the form of the prestige of your position endorsing the enterprise.[50]

That may be excessive praise, but it's fair to say that the program has been a successful answer to Edmund Wilson's complaint that the best of American literature was out of print, though many authors remain to be added to the series. When Jim Haas and Deirdre and I were invited to speak in 1984 at the Kanasawa Institute of Technology in western Japan, we took several of the initial volumes as gifts for the Library there. I gave a too long talk on "The Problems of Preservation," attempting to synthesize all my thoughts about the field. Deirdre gave a shorter paper on "User Studies and Preservation Planning," shorter partly because she nervously rushed through it, faster than the simultaneous translators could keep up. But the Japanese women in the audience clearly took courage from her performance, and one man, the President of a Japanese university who claimed to be a "failed kamikaze pilot" and knew some American argot,

---

[50] In reading a recent issue of *The New York Review of Books* (December 2012), I saw that February 2013 was the 50th anniversary of *NYRB*. It was founded during a period when *The New York Times* was on strike and writers were eager for a new outlet for reviews. Five years later Edmund Wilson published his *NYRB* article called "The Fruits of MLA," which I well-remembered reading sympathetically at the time. It created some controversy with the editors of scholarly editions, but eventually a successful consensus was reached and the series began, brokered in part by that sage of bibliographical description and textual editing, Thomas Tanselle.

told her "Good show, Joe." The reward for our efforts was a week-long holiday including a few days at a Noto Peninsula spa on the China Sea.

Another effort that Jim Haas got me involved in was the "Committee on Production Guidelines for Book Longevity of the Council on Library Resources." That name, which has appeared on the title page versos of tens of thousands of volumes published since the mid 1980s, represented an attempt to address prospective library preservation problems by providing guidelines for book permanence and durability. The Committee consisted of a fairly representative group who might be able to effect some change. Its chair was Herbert Bailey, Director of the Princeton University Press, and other members included Jim Hass, James Morris of the Mellon Foundation (with whom I lost contact after he joined the American Enterprise Institute and began work on the Clinton impeachment), and Leonard Schlosser, a paper manufacturer who later asked me to join the Board of the Conservation Center for Art and Historic Artifacts in Philadelphia. I attended the culminating event of the Committee's work, Commitment Day at NYPL on March 7, 1989, where a large group of authors and publishers endorsed our report and made their commitment to these paper guidelines. James McKeever of the Syracuse *Post Standard* wrote up the story from a Syracuse perspective on April 20, 1989, cleverly noting that as part of my lobbying in the cause of more permanent paper, I carried around a special pen to test the pH value of paper. "SU author-professor Tobias Wolff got the good word from Stam that his latest book, *This Boy's Life*, was printed on acid free paper . . . . Stam also tested Salman Rushdie's controversial novel *The Satanic Verses*, published by Viking—mildly acidic, as it turns out."

Other significant events of these eight years at NYPL included representing the Library abroad (in Japan, Great Britain, Ireland, Germany), chairing the Preservation of Library Materials Committee of ARL as well as the Committee on Collection Management and Development of RLG, consulting for the British Library on its preservation planning, some extraordinary tensions involving the Schomburg Collection in Harlem, and dealing with difficult policy issues in the Library relating to retrenchment, deaccessioning, charging for services, and union relations.

Somehow during this period I made it onto the library lecture circuit and for a time I cynically described my job as touring the country and abroad issuing opinions and then publishing them. Looking back I'm convinced that half of it was necessary bullshit of bromides and platitudes but some of it useful in stirring up debate on such issues as national collection building, practical collaborative approaches to cataloguing and preservation, NEH microfilming projects, library security, deaccessioning, and the importance of special collections. It was discouraging to see the collaborative initiatives fade during plush times, though they have reemerged during hard times since 2007, long after my retirement.

One interesting experience involved a speech I was asked to give at the University of Oklahoma where Librarian Sul Lee was celebrating acquisition of his library's two millionth book. There was nothing noteworthy about my talk, though I did make fun of the flawed statistics that created such celebrations. What was interesting was that the symbolic book, Gabriel Naudé's *Instructions Concerning Erecting of a Library,* translated by John Evelyn (London 1661), was formally presented at half-time of a football game in front of 70,000 fans, presumably a record for such events. I remember another talk I gave earlier, this one for the one millionth volume added to the Library at the University of Northern Illinois, DeKalb, where there must have been all of forty present to appreciate their new volume, Lord Byron's 1807 *Poems on Various Occasions.* My criticism in Oklahoma and DeKalb was that the statistics that led to such celebrations were bogus, did not account for stolen and missing books, and said nothing about the quality of the collections, emphasizing only their quantity. Further, that some of the statistics were willfully inflated to make an institution more impressive for accreditation purposes. James Cogswell, the first librarian of the Astor Library in New York, made some of the same points on January 7, 1854, in *The Home Journal,* shortly after the Astor Library opened. Complaining that the most frequent question he was asked about the new library was how many volumes it would contain, he too challenged the statistics. "To estimate the value of a library by the number of volumes it contains, is about as correct a mode as it would be to estimate it by the number of pounds they weigh." In the same vein, my stump speech when representing NYPL had this throwaway line: "It's true that at 18 million volumes, the Library of Congress has three times as many books as we do. The difference is that we selected ours." But the celebrations go on, aided and abetted by opportunistic development officers. Given the rate at which books are removed from some 21st-century research libraries there now should be celebrations when libraries go down to the next lower millionth-volume milestone.

Another talk was orchestrated by Daniel Traister who had been a colleague at NYPL and was in transition to the University of Pennsylvania. Dan was Chair of the program committee for the 1982 Rare Books and Manuscript Section (RBMS) preconference in Philadelphia in June. He asked me to serve as devil's advocate and lightning rod by preparing a keynote address on a library administrator's view of special collections, or "should the tail wag the dog?" He intended it to be provocative and to puncture the elite complacency of many rare book librarians. I have no idea whether that speech (which RBMS declined to publish) had any effect but I would say that for me it started a short string of periodic talks intended to force library administrator's to take their special collections seriously, and to encourage curators to work within their larger institutional framework. But the further point was to emphasize special collections as one of the few things that differentiated one research library from another, their general collections being largely duplicative and their programs similar. Two talks for ARL hammered the point home, one in Washington on the 60th anniversary of ARL in 1992, and another at Brown in 2001. All this and other encouragements eventually helped move ARL towards a permanent committee devoted to Special Collections, for some time chaired by our friend Alice Prochaska when she was the University Librarian at Yale.[51]

The Philadelphia conference preceded the 1982 annual meeting of ALA, a crowded affair that placed us in a hotel on the outskirts of Philadelphia. Making small talk on a long taxi ride, the cab driver said to me, "You won't believe it, but this town has just been invaded by 18,000 librarians and they're all women." I protested that they were probably 40% men and that I was one of them. "Really? Where you from anyway?" When I told him New York City he said "Oh well, that's different." Not sure what he meant but one can guess.

---

[51] *"Plus ça change . . .* : Sixty Years of the Association of Research Libraries. October 22, 1992," (Washington, DC: Printed and distributed by the Association of Research Libraries, 1992), reprinted in its 75th anniversary publication, and still found on its website, <www.arl.org>; "So What's so Special?" can be found at <http://www.arl.org/rtl/speccoll/building/stam.shtml>

By 1982 I had grown tired of ALA, its turgid politics and its glacial pace of reform, and so I resigned that year and seldom attended their conferences again except for unrelated business. The same was true of the New York Library Association which I thought was pricing itself out of the market and that they needed the likes of me more than vice versa. I suppose those resignations were the result partly of arrogance, partly of impecuniousness, and partly of boredom. Leaving those associations also saved some precious time for other work.

Mixed Signals: Retrench and Grow—Two Leaders

Two impressive though very different men served The New York Public Library as Presidents during my time as Director of the Research Libraries, Richard W. Couper until 1981, and Vartan Gregorian from then until my departure in 1986, followed by his own departure for Brown University in 1989. Although not always easy, it was a privilege to have known and worked with each. In very different ways their vanities matched their abilities.

In addition to the Board itself and various staff committees, the main venue for discussion of issues related to the Research Libraries was the Trustee Committee on the Research Libraries (CORL). Toward the end of Richard Couper's tenure and in my second year as Director, the NYPL Board of Trustees, then chaired by Richard Salomon, asked me to work with a subcommittee of CORL to outline steps needed for the major retrenchment then anticipated. The new committee was called the Planning and Resources Committee, but informally we called it the Retrenchment Committee. During the severe fiscal crises facing the City and the Library in the mid-1970s, one major principle motivating the thinking and decisions of the Research Libraries was that of reversibility, the idea that cuts would only be made in policies and actions that could be reversed. For example, staffing and hours of service could be reduced, but then expanded if financial conditions improved. On the other hand, gaps in acquisitions were never likely to be filled and therefore the book budget remained sacrosanct. The idea of deaccessioning, the selling of Library assets to raise operating funds, during that period would have been thought both foolish and reprehensible, certainly irreversible.

Much of that changed when the committee began its work. Its membership included several influential Trustees: the Chair was Rockefeller Brothers Fund President Bill Dietel. Other members were Proskauer Rose lawyer Sol Corbin, Simpson Thatcher attorney Conrad Harper, other trustees including Rhett Austell, Phyllis Gordan, and Samuel Woolley. There were also some external members including Martin E. Segal, a major figure on New York City's non-profit cultural scene and Chair of the Lincoln Center Board, and Edwin Holmgren, Director of the Branch Libraries. The retrenchment committee began its work in 1979 and proceeded to examine any possible means of cost reduction or revenue enhancement that anyone on the committee could think of, including reductions in acquisitions in selected subject areas, consolidation of service points, hours of service, setting fees for daily use, the sale of assets by deaccessioning, establishing for-fee priority services for business and industry, and other measures that I've probably repressed.

We did implement some of the recommendations as approved by the Trustees on March 25, 1980, but much of it was rendered moot by the arrival of Vartan Gregorian, Provost of the University of Pennsylvania, as President in March 1981.[52] We did eliminate the separate American History Division at the south end of the Main Reading Room, combining it with the Local History and Genealogy Reading Room at the north end, thereby reducing some positions, creating crucial swing space for anticipated renovations, and providing Gregorian with the first controversy of his new job. Though materials continued to be delivered through the Reading Room, the change was falsely misconstrued as the abnegation of our responsibility to collect comprehensively in US history, the opposite of what we intended. The proposal raised a ruckus among American historians of the AHA, the President of the Organization of American Historians, Gerda Lerner, and for me personally it made an unwitting enemy of Arthur Schlesinger who claimed it was detrimental to his scholarship. It was not an issue that our new President wanted to handle so I bore the brunt of Schlesinger's protest. Several other

---

[52]   "Report of the Planning Committee to the Board of Trustees… March 1980." Internal Library document. 17 p. + 6 appendices.

175

consolidations have occurred more recently but this was the Library's first that I know of.[53]

Richard Couper left the Library in late 1980, not very happily. Scuttlebutt alleged that he was forced out as not suave enough for Brooke Astor's social milieu or not up to the fund-raising demands coming from a newly reconstituted Board. He was underappreciated for all he'd done to help the Library survive through the City's and the Library's worst financial crisis since the Depression. He saw himself as something of a bureaucrat, given his experience as Acting President of Hamilton College and as Deputy Commissioner for Higher Education of New York State, and as a "51% man," i.e., a person willing to compromise to get something done, not exactly a charismatic stance. Several years later I was able to persuade Paul LeClerc, then President of the Library, to add a portrait of Couper to the second floor gallery of Presidential portraits, where his had been the only missing face.

Whatever Couper did, it was clearly not enough for Messrs. Richard Salomon, Bill Dietel, and Andrew Heiskell, who succeeded Salomon as Board Chair in 1980. You'll find no mention of Couper or any of the NYPL librarians in Heiskell's autobiographical account of the Gregorian

---

[53] It is puzzling to me that as a fully-credentialed historian, I had some of my more acrimonious library debates with fellow historians. In 1993, long after I had left NYPL, The Library of Congress asked me to appear before Congress's Joint Committee on the Library of Congress to support some security measures instituted by the Library that removed certain stack privileges available to historians but not to the general public. Having spent a good deal of my career in closed stack libraries (Newberry and NYPL), I defended the tightening in the interests of both security and better access. The Librarian, James Billington, read my testimony and told one of his colleagues that I had covered everything possible or needed to defend his position. My successor at NYPL, Paul Fasana, also testified at these hearings. Our opponent in this debate was Columbia Professor Eric Foner, then President of the Organization of American Historians, who apparently was so upset by our winning arguments that he refused to shake my hand afterwards. Curiously enough, my own political views were fairly close to his own but apparently not my library views about special privileges for his colleagues. The Hearing was published by the GPO as S. Hrg. 102-475, June 15, 1993, 103rd Congress, First Session. My testimony is on p. 22-31; Foner's is on p. 34-37.

era at the Library, roughly the penultimate decade of the twentieth century. What you will find is contempt for Couper's administration ("management not worth mentioning" I believe were his words) and that he was committed to find a new President even before he accepted the Chairmanship and before Couper knew that his days were numbered, and certainly before any of the Couper administration did.[54] But for me Couper's last year was among my most enjoyable and exhilarating at the Library despite the problems we encountered.

Among other things Dick and I were squash partners, a game I played quite seriously in the club leagues of Chicago and Baltimore. It always seems a bit odd that fierce opponents should be called partners, but we were fairly evenly matched on the court. I had a slight advantage in mobility in 1978, and he in shrewdness and what I called at the time "quick defensive moves." I once mentioned that to Gordon Ray of the Board and the Guggenheim Foundation (an avid sports fan), who remarked that Dick must have learned those moves in his ten years as President of the New York Public Library. The euphemism in our respective calendars for sneaking off to a squash match was "conference," and both our secretaries knew what it meant. An honest deception in fact—we did confer quite a bit, sweat and labored breathing notwithstanding.

Gordon Ray was a particularly helpful Trustee to me, always keeping in touch about new developments in scholarship as they might affect NYPL. We had lunch regularly and he took me to a few Yankees games. He probably understood scholarship better than any of the other Trustees (including the few academics and the ex officio Cardinals of St. Patrick's Cathedral), and he often sought my input for his writings on American scholarship. He once took me to lunch with Mary Hyde (later Lady

---

[54]   Andrew Heiskell. *Outsider, Insider: An Unlikely Success Story: The Memoirs of Andrew Heiskell,* with Ralph Graves (New York: Marian-Darien Press, 1998) p.234. Heiskell had been publisher of *Life*, CEO of *Time Inc.*, was married to Marian Sulzberger, and a member of several boards, including the Overseers of Harvard University and the American Academy in Rome. Thanks to the Sulzberger connection he seemed to exercise considerable influence with *The New York Times*. Curiously, Andrew's sister Diane had settled with her partner in Marlboro, Vermont, where we saw her quite frequently during our Marlboro years in the mid-1960s.

Eccles), hoping to get her more interested in NYPL, but I failed and her collection went to Harvard and her philanthropy to the Grolier Club.

There was one dramatic moment at a Trustee's meeting when historian Oscar Handlin was asked why he, as Harvard University Librarian, had led Harvard's withdrawal in 1978 from the Research Libraries Group, while, as a Trustee of NYPL, he had voted with the Board to continue our membership in RLG when Stanford became Harvard's replacement as founding member. Handlin hid behind some flimsy plea of poverty among the many and complex relationships of Harvard's nearly one hundred libraries. Ray's response was instant and unanswerable: "I must challenge Oscar's disingenuous claim of poverty in the Harvard libraries. Harvard faculty and staff are the most privileged library users in the world of academia."

After leaving NYPL, Couper spent ten years as President of the Woodrow Wilson National Fellowship Foundation before retiring to Clinton, New York, and his beloved Hamilton College where he indulged his hobby of amateur bookbinding. Shortly before he died in early 2006 I had the privilege of delivering the first Richard Couper Phi Beta Kappa Library Lecture at Hamilton College, a series which he endowed. In a talk entitled "An Army without Ammunition," I gave a brief history of the beginnings of the Hamilton College Library, based on some work in its archives. There I learned that Richard's grandfather had been the first paid employee of that Library, and his father worked there as well. The title was taken from the annual report of July 1865 by Librarian Anson J. Upson who compared an army without ammunition to "A College without Books." At the dinner after my Library talk I sat with Dick for what proved our final conversation. At the time he was still surviving a whole battery of diseases. I told him that I didn't know about the rest of his body but that his eyebrows were certainly flourishing. His wife Patsy later told me that when he had met Kim Novak at the Library back in the 1970s. Novak had complimented him on his lengthy eyebrows and after that no one could touch them.[55]

There were many exciting acquisitions for the Library in both the Couper and Gregorian administrations. Given my interests in music and

---

[55] See my Couper obituary in the *Proceedings of the American Antiquarian Society* (2007).

all the performing arts, and realizing that the Performing Arts Research Center at Lincoln Center had become something of a stepchild, out of sight and out of mind after it opened in 1965, I tried to pay special attention to their needs and problems. It was an interesting cast of characters, led by Thor Wood, Chief of PARC, and the Chiefs of the four divisions: Frank Campbell in Music, followed by Jean Bowen; Genevieve Oswald in Dance; Dorothy Sverdlove in the Theatre Division; and David Hall in the Rodgers and Hammerstein Archives of Recorded Sound. All were obsessively dedicated to their collections and services, and each a veritable missionary to the cause. David Hall was the evangelist of recorded sound who could decipher beauty in the scratchiest of recordings, as he did with the Metropolitan Opera's *Mapleson Cylinders* from the early twentieth century. Long after I left, PARC was renamed and reorganized as the Performing Arts Library, administratively combining the branch and research libraries.

Thor Wood once arranged a luncheon with William Schuman, composer and President of the Juilliard School, to discuss the gift of his archives to PARC, a successful lunch. Gigi Oswald twice asked me to lunch with Lincoln Kirstein just to keep him posted on library developments in general. I met with the daughter of Carlos Chávez, the splendid Mexican composer who died in 1978. Ana was a charming woman and I like to think our meeting helped seal the gift of her father's papers. Another luncheon with Thor Wood involved the presentation of the Joseph Schwantner score of *New Morning for the World*, Schwantner's 1982 tribute to Dr. Martin Luther King, Jr., presented by Robert Freeman, Director of the Eastman School of Music. Fascinating lunches were one of the perquisites of the position, yet I never gained much weight until the ALS diagnosis.

As Director of the Research Libraries I represented the Library on the Lincoln Center Council, the heads of all constituent members of Lincoln Center. Among the members were Lincoln Kirstein of New York City Ballet, Beverly Sills of the New York City Opera, Bernie Gerston from the Lincoln Center Theater after its rebirth in 1985, Charles Wadsworth of the Chamber Music Society, and a couple of others. Usually six or seven men attended in dark suits (Kirstein always in black), though I don't recall anyone from the Metropolitan Opera ever attending. For a time Beverly Sills was Chair of the Council. Once, when she arrived late, she announced, "Gentlemen, you are what I've always wanted, my own harem."

One of our most pleasing music acquisitions was the archive of a relatively obscure mid-western composer named John Becker who taught at Northwestern and died in 1961. He was one of the so-called American Five, along with Charles Ives, Carl Ruggles, Henry Cowell, and Wallingford Riegger, the scions of ultra-modern music of the mid-twentieth century, all better known than Becker. On one of my Chicago trips I was asked to pay a courtesy visit to Becker's widow Evelyn in Evanston who still had in 1980 all her husband's papers and musical manuscripts. We hit it off from the start and I made of habit of visiting whenever I was in Chicago. Becker was like Louis Zukofsky, quite obscure but enormously influential. On one of these visits Evelyn asked me to take a large envelope of letters back to New York as the first installment of her husband's collection. It was an unforgettable flight home as I read his correspondence with some of the major composers of his time. One of these letters remains in my memory, a letter from Charles Ives saying his wife had forbidden him to introduce their children to Henry Cowell because of the morals charges for which Cowell had been incarcerated.

Evelyn and I got on very well, and Deirdre and I also enjoyed getting to know her son Eugene, a New York fixture who had once served as Assistant Secretary of the Army, and was the keeper of his father's flame. In 1983 the Library hosted a splendid party in the Trustees' Room honoring Evelyn and the acquisition of her husband's papers, measured in the finding aid as 61 boxes.[56]

Feeding my interest in contemporary classical music was a chance 1981 encounter in Minneapolis during an Association of College and Research Libraries gathering. As chair of the RLG Collection Management and Development Committee I convened that Committee with an ARL task force on collection development to consider the Conspectus methodology. During the conference I took a half day off to visit the Walker Art Gallery. Beyond a closed door I heard the sound of a music rehearsal so I walked into a small auditorium where I found a subgroup of the St. Paul Chamber Orchestra, rehearsing works of Luciano Berio and György Ligeti, conducted by Bill McGlaughlin (now a regular

---

[56]   Writing about John and Evelyn Becker brings to mind one of my first tasks after joining the NYPL Editor's Office in April 1959, to see through the press *Some Twentieth Century American Composers: A Selective Bibliography*, by John Edmunds and Gordon Boelzner. Two Volumes (New York: NYPL, 1959-60). [Each volume contained impressive photo portraits of eight of the composers.] Reprinted from the *Bulletin of The New York Public Library* from July 1959 to July 1960, the volumes contained introductory essays by Peter Yates (Vol. I) and Nicolas Slonimsky (Vol. II). I remember having had the temerity to make editorial changes to the Yates essay, at which that Los Angeles music critic took umbrage. Edmunds was curator of the Americana Collection of the Music Division from 1957 to 1961, where Boelzner also worked. Boelzner was then a rehearsal pianist for New York City Ballet, rose to become a regular performer for both Balanchine and Jerome Robbins works, and then became the Music Director of NYCB. The next and last time I met him was when the Delmas Trustees paid a site visit to the City Ballet's music library in the bowels of the State Theater. He died in 2005 at age 68.

In his preface lamenting the NYC-centric nature of American contemporary composers, Edmunds said of John Becker: "Thus it happens that so strong and original a composer as John Becker (now well over seventy) is virtually ignored, being in the Midwest...." He also noted that my "editorial work has been indispensable." It's true that the manuscript submitted needed a lot of work, but it's hard for me to imagine that I learned the trade so quickly, the first installment published only three months after I joined Erdman. One error I didn't catch was that Twentieth Century in the title should have been hyphenated.

presence on NPR but then Associate Conductor of the SPCO). I sat there for over an hour, undisturbed, listening to them dissect and reconstitute these difficult works. This revelatory experience reminded me of Max Pollikoff's radical series called *Music in Our Time* to which I subscribed at the YMHA in the early 60s, and anticipated my later association with Neva Pilgrim and the Society for New Music in Syracuse.

Less successful on the musical front was NYPL's attempt to acquire the archive of Igor Stravinsky, a collection that had been on deposit at the Lincoln Center Performing Arts Library since shortly after Stravinsky died in 1971. In full expectation that it would come to us, we made a considerable investment in housing and serving, organizing, and preserving on microform the entire collection. But the collection was mired in controversy from the time of Stravinsky's death with litigation between his children and their stepmother, feuds with Boosey and Hawkes and Robert Craft over publication rights, not even ending when the archive was put up for private sale in a bidding war starting with the Library's reluctant offer of $1,000,000 dollars. We were outbid by Frederick Koch who offered $1,500,000 on behalf of the Morgan Library, only to be overtaken by an extraordinary bid of $5,250,000 from Paul Sacher, the Swiss conductor, commissioner of new works, and general musical philanthropist and impresario. We were in no position to compete and in fact we lost our whole investment including the microfilms of which we could not even keep copies. I told Gregorian that this would go down in history as the Koch-Sacher affair. It was a great disappointment, but a lesson in the perils of deposit collections, the blandishments of prospective donors notwithstanding. I don't believe I've allowed one since. After I left, the Library was able to seal the acquisition of another deposit collection (Arturo Toscanini's, complete with a collection of his batons), but we all would have preferred success with the Stravinsky.

Other important and always exciting additions in my New York period included the diaries and papers of Alfred Kazin, whose *New York Jew* includes in its first chapter an elegiac tribute to the Library, evoking the Library as I remembered it in 1959, open every day of the year for generous hours. That collection was acquired for the Berg Collection with a helping hand from me to Lola Szladits over another luncheon. In 1984 we acquired some manuscripts of Herman Melville, including the only surviving pages of the manuscript of *Typee*. Don Anderle was the point person for that acquisition which joined the Melville family papers in the Gansevoort-Lansing Collection in the Manuscripts and Archives Division, originally acquired by the Library in 1919.

One exciting development for which I received a good deal of credit was the development under Julie van Haaften of a separate section for photographs within the Library's Prints Division. This was a project that was brewing nicely before I arrived. After a number of years identifying the almost accidental wealth of photographs in our collections, Julie organized the Library's first major photograph exhibit. As a matter of policy going back to the opening of the Central Building in 1911, the Library had not collected photographs qua photographs, but only for their subject matter. Nonetheless there were many hidden treasures that were coming to light (pardon the pun), and an exhibition in 1977 called "Original Sun Pictures" was a successful start. On October 1, 2010, van Haaften reflected on the history of the collections with these comments:

> When a new Research Libraries director, David H. Stam, arrived in 1978, I told him of NYPL's rich but unwrangled photography holdings, and he invited Alan Fern, head of Prints & Photographs at the Library of Congress [and a personal friend going back to our Newberry Library days—DHS] to assess the Library's photographic holdings from a sampling I presented. His enthusiastic report helped secure funding, including Federal and private money from donors and trustees Phyllis Gordan, Sandra Payson and Bradford Warner. All together, the monies raised bought equipment and supported full-time positions for more than two years.[57]

Sandra Payson's was the lead gift that got the ball rolling and the success of the program was a factor in Sandra's ongoing connection with the Library, including her joining the Board of Trustees. Her largesse included occasional tickets for my family to Mets games with seats next to the dugout, quite a thrill for Julian in the early Daryl Strawberry days.

---

[57] "A Picture of Persistence: How a Photography Collection was Born," by Julia van Haaften, from an NYPL blog posted on October 1, 2010. <www.huffingtonpost.com/the./a-picture-of-persistence-_b_747187.html>

She was a patron of the arts and of the racetrack. She once told me she needed to name a horse in a hurry. At the time Arthur Houghton was disbinding for reproduction, and then for sale, his famous early sixteenth-century Persian manuscript of the *Shahnameh*, The Book of Kings, and she took my irreverent suggestion that she use the name. I last saw her when I was leaving the Kennedy Center restaurant fifteen years ago when she called out to me from her table. We had a pleasant chat and when I left, she called me back to say "By the way I've made good money on that horse, thank you very much." She died in 2004, I hope having no clue about how much I detested gambling.

Thanks to my apprenticeship in the 1960s with David Erdman, his publication of some of my work on Wordsworth and Leigh Hunt, and my interest in all the Romantics, I had a particular interest in one of the acquisitions that lay just beyond the horizon. That coup wasn't completed until after I left, but Couper and I worked very hard to assure the eventual transfer to NYPL of the Carl H. Pforzheimer Collection of Shelley and His Circle, in its own words "one of the world's leading repositories for the study of English Romanticism."[58] Pforzheimer was a conservative business man whose firm specialized in oil stocks just as America's love affair with the automobile was heating up. With prosperity he became a prodigious collector, in addition to his Shelley collection amassing a large collection of books and manuscripts, anchored by a perfect copy of the Gutenberg Bible, a Caxton, all four Shakespeare Folios, and other works of equal distinction. During the last eight years of his life, from 1949 to 1957, he was a Trustee of The New York Public Library.

When I became Director in 1978, his daughter-in-law, Carol F. Pforzheimer, was a much-respected member of the Board of Trustees. The negotiations to acquire the collections were not always smooth, with some conflicting demands on both sides. I lunched regularly with Donald Reiman, co-editor of *Shelley and His Circle*, and a member of the Pforzheimer staff, to discuss confidential matters, try to penetrate the transparent secrecy surrounding the project, and to help move

---

[58]   Stephen Wagner and Doucet Devin Fischer. *The Carl H. Pforzheimer Collection of Shelley and His Circle: a History, a Biography, and a Guide* (New York: New York Public Library, 1996) p. 8ff.

the prospect along. After Pforzheimer's death in 1957 the collections had been left to the Carl F. Pforzheimer Foundation, led by Carl H. Pforzheimer, Jr., and were then moved from his Park Avenue home to an office building at 42nd Street and Madison Avenue, with convenient proximity to NYPL. In 1978 the Foundation sold its Gutenberg to the University of Texas for $2.6 million dollars, and in 1986 the rest of the collection of 1,100 pre-1700 books and 250 manuscripts were again sold to Texas, this time through the good offices of Ross Perot. With a reported price of over $15 million, all this made possible the transfer of the Shelley collection, staff, and editorial project to NYPL late in 1986, with the requisite endowment to make the move feasible. The deal included the installation in the former Manuscript Division of the Brass Room which housed the original libraries in the Pforzheimer Park Avenue apartment. Richard Couper and I both rejoiced from afar to read of this acquisition in *The New York Times* on December 18, 1986, and to learn that the gift came with a $3 million endowment for the maintenance and growth of the collection.

On a more personal note I would add that during my eight years as Director under Couper and Gregorian, whenever I had meetings in the President's Office I would try to sit strategically with the best view of the Pforzheimer Collection's beautiful portrait of Mary Wollstonecraft. Apparently it was on loan from the Foundation as an adumbration of what was to come. With few exceptions, she was the most beautiful person in the room which also had portraits of Mary Shelley and Benjamin Franklin. They now hang more democratically in the Edna Salomon Gallery on the third floor.

The Library traditionally supported separate divisions for Rare Books and for Manuscripts. One of my hopes for the various consolidations planned was to unify these collections in one administrative unit, with seamless service between both types of materials, and cross-training of staff. After my time they were physically united in the Brooke Astor Reading Room, the former Local History and Genealogy Division, but my attempt to unify services was an abject failure, mainly due to staff opposition both during and after my time. Enter the Astor Room now and you will find two adjoining desks staffed separately and the reader takes his chances that the materials sought will be at a staffed desk, for seldom does one help the other. The same absurd situation was repeated in the Prints and Photograph Division, same desk but different people.

Why the Library has failed to follow the example of many successful consolidated units (e.g. Harvard's Houghton Library, and Columbia's Rare Book and Manuscript Library, or even Syracuse University's Special Collections Research Center) is a puzzle to me.

One odd result of Couper's departure from NYPL was that my evenings and even luncheon business schedules had gone from nearly impossible to very light, lacking even my "conferences" with Couper. Whereas Couper had been happy to share the duties of representing the Library with numerous staff, Gregorian preferred to accept as many invitations as he could, even when it meant four or five events per evening. Although I was still busy enough, this disconcerting development had a couple of salubrious results, first that I had more time for my own writing, and secondly I had more time to become fully engaged with the Grolier Club, an engagement that I have enjoyed immensely (especially during our Polar exhibition of 2005-2006), and which continues today.

Gregorian was welcomed to the Library as a messianic savior. Calvin Trillin said as much in a farewell poem called "Gregorian Saga" on the occasion of Gregorian's move to Brown University:

The place they loved was at the point
At which they quickly must anoint
A saviour who could save the joint.

Demeaning as that was to our former efforts and as often as we heard that things the library had done for decades were being done "for the first time" (we referred to the boast as FT^2), and however often I felt compelled to say that we were "standing on the shoulders of giants," it was still a period of renewal and real hope. We continued to make some exciting acquisitions and work on the building's badly deferred maintenance became a priority that saw a good deal of progress, starting with the renovated Periodicals Room that opened in Gregorian's first week, and not fully completed until the unveiling of the sparkling exterior for the 2011 centennial.

One embarrassing incident with Gregorian involved the Grolier Club's centennial dinner at the Colony Club in 1984. Greg had appropriately become a member on his arrival in New York, and although he seldom came to Grolier Club events and never was actively engaged in the Club's activities, he was asked to give the centennial after-dinner speech. It may seem a petty point but he upset many members, including me, by referring throughout his talk to the Grolier Society [sic], an encyclopedia publisher that had just been censured by the FTC for deceptive trade practices. It was also the name of a downtown nightclub of some notoriety. At the end of the talk, the Club President presented to Greg a copy of the Club's Centennial volume, *The Grolier Club, 1884-1984: Its Library, Exhibitions & Publications* (New York: Grolier Club, 1984). He immediately said that it should not be for him but for the Research Libraries and David Stam. So I got to lug it home for subsequent delivery to Rare Books.

In his defense I need to acknowledge that when Gregorian arrived a few years earlier, he didn't want to hear about retrenchment but rather rallied the Trustees to "Think Big," a refreshing change after a decade of cuts. One of the minor collecting recommendations of the Planning and Resources Committee had been to reduce the level of collecting of Armenian materials to a basic level, our minimal category. In making our staff recommendations on collections, my colleagues and I were attempting to utilize the newly developed RLG strategy of collaborative collection development in which the very large and independent research libraries such as NYPL and the Library of Congress would concentrate resources on subjects and areas not adequately covered by the consortium's university libraries. At the time we felt that Armenian studies were adequately covered elsewhere in our consortium, but in the wake of Gregorian's arrival, that was a change we quickly reversed.

Gregorian's success in fund raising is now legendary, and I find it interesting that after his academic career he turned to fund giving with his appointment as President of the Carnegie Corporation. It was similar to my own shift from beggar to giver with the Delmas Foundation, but his transition was on a much grander scale. I remember one family dinner in Pelham when I was describing to the children one of Greg's fund raising triumphs. At some point, our teenaged son Wendell interrupted to say "Now I know how a Gregorian chant goes: money, money, money."

To return to Library issues, I should discuss one controversial element of collections policy which absorbed a good deal of attention, what we might call high-end deaccessioning. Sometime around 1981 Richard Salomon, Chairman of the NYPL Board (and also Chancellor of Brown University), approached me to say that a friend of his was eager to acquire

Audubon's elephant folio *Birds of America* and was willing to pay $1 million for one of the Library's four complete copies. I tried to deal with the issue diplomatically, quieting down an outraged curatorial reaction that none of these copies could be considered a duplicate, and if one of these were to be sold what else might be considered fair game. I argued to Solomon that our copies were entailed by donor obligations such as to the Astor Library, that such a private sale might require NYS Attorney General approval, unlikely to be granted, and that in any case the only way to establish the fair market value of any of these copies would be to place each on the auction market. They were not in good condition and would probably have disappointed even the prospective collector as well as the needy Library.

That quest was abandoned but the issue continued to simmer. In June 1981, Brown University held an invitational conference on the subject of library deaccessioning, in anticipation of a sale it was planning of early medieval manuscripts deemed out of scope for the John Carter Brown Library whose entire mission dealt with the history of the Americas. I was asked to give the opening keynote address on the subject, probably because I told someone at Brown about the issue we were facing. I took the occasion to do some research on the history of library deaccessioning in general and at NYPL in particular. What resulted was a speech and an article published under the title "'Preserve All Things: Hold Fast to That which is Good,' Deaccessioning and Libraries," published the following year in *College & Research Libraries* (January 1982, pp. 5-13). It attempted to set the parameters of a conservative but not rigid deaccessioning policy, a policy which informally remained in effect through the Gregorian and Timothy Healey administrations. Without undue modesty I can claim the article as one of my best pieces of scholarly writing.

[Coda: I am distressed to record that the policy was abandoned and its procedures largely ignored in 2005 during the administration of Paul Leclerc when a number of significant paintings were sold, including Asher B. Durand's "Kindred Spirits," a great personal favorite and a regular stop on most of the many tours I gave as Director of the Research Libraries. At the time I shared copies of my article with my then successor David Ferriero and Paul LeClerc but by then the sale was a fait accompli *and you can now find "Kindred Spirits" in Bentonville, Arkansas. I have even dreamt recently about weeping over the loss of that painting, probably triggered by writing about it, and possibly because of the news in early 2013 that the Seward House*

Museum in Auburn, New York, would be divesting itself of a Thomas Cole painting, though I believe that case has a much better justification.]

The Schomburg Center and Its Vicissitudes
1980-1985

Another problematic chapter during my time in New York involved the Schomburg Center for Research in Black Culture, originally one of the branch libraries that became part of the Research Libraries in 1972 and therefore administered by what some considered the honky administration of 42nd Street. The present Schomburg website gives a brief description of its history:

> The Division of Negro Literature, History and Prints — the forerunner to today's Schomburg Center — opened in 1925 as a special collection of the 135th Street Branch library to meet the needs of a changing community. The Division first won international acclaim in 1926 when the personal collection of the distinguished Puerto Rican-born Black scholar and bibliophile, Arturo Alfonso Schomburg, was added to the Division. His collection included more than 5,000 books; 3,000 manuscripts; 2,000 etchings and paintings; and several thousand pamphlets. Schomburg served as curator of the Division from 1932 until his death in 1938. In 1940, the Division was renamed the Schomburg Collection of Negro Literature, History and Prints in honor of its founder. In 1972, the Schomburg Collection was designated as one of The Research Libraries of The New York Public Library and became the Schomburg Center for Research in Black Culture.

The collection was purchased through a grant from the Carnegie Corporation in 1926, at the urging of the Urban League. A further grant in 1932 allowed the Library to hire Arthur Schomburg as the curator of the collection which was then housed behind the Countee Cullen branch library. When I arrived in 1978, the Schomburg Collection and staff was in a rather derelict Carnegie branch library (albeit a McKim, Mead, and White building and a New York City Landmark) and in some administrative disarray, but construction was well underway for a large new building on the corner of Lenox Avenue (now renamed Malcolm X Boulevard) and East 135th Street, directly across from Harlem Hospital. Coordination of planning for the new building was delegated to a member of my staff, Juanita Doares, who seemed to be engaged nearly fulltime in the many details of quite a complex building which opened in 1979 and was dedicated in October of 1980.

Surprisingly, Juanita got less help than hoped for from the Chief of the Schomburg, Jean Blackwell Hutson (1914-98), its chief administrator from 1948 until 1980 when I created a new position for her and removed her from her leadership role. The protests in support of Jean Hutson were relatively muted compared to what followed.[59] Protests about the NYPL administration at the Schomburg outdoors dedication ceremonies, which I attended with my whole family on a crisp blue October Sunday in Harlem, were redirected towards Mayor Ed Koch who helpfully chose that week to call for the closing of nearby Sydenham Hospital, a venerable Harlem institution which did close soon afterwards. Tensions were high as pickets on 135th Street were marching against Koch. Amira Baraka (aka LeRoi Jones) delivered something of a diatribe on both topics, and Richard Couper delivered the official dedication remarks and acknowledgments to those who made the project possible. He broke the

---

[59]   There is a highly laudatory biographical entry on Hutson by Sharon Fitzgerald in the *Dictionary of American Library Biography: Second Supplement,* ed. Donald G. Davis. (Westport, CT: Libraries Unlimited, 2003) p. 134-38. She accurately glosses this change of assignment as follows: "Despite passionate community opposition, she was removed from her position at the Schomburg in 1980 and appointed the assistant director for Collection Management and Development, an administrative position within the NYPL. She retired from that position in 1984." Hutson was honored in a retirement party that year which I didn't attend, probably a mistake on my part that was criticized by some people but she and I had little mutual respect.

In that same volume you will find my own biographical account of Lawrence William Towner (1921-92), p. 214-16, reflecting some of what I've written above about the Newberry Library.

ice by saying there had been intense competition to avoid the honor of giving these remarks and unfortunately he had lost.[60] Of all the issues and problems we faced in my tenure at NYPL none was more intractable than the issues surrounding this library. Very curiously the subject doesn't come up in Vartan Gregorian's autobiography; you'll find me in the index but not Schomburg. Our attempts to provide Schomburg with responsible administration were not immediately successful. Despite a superb search committee and a national search we made what turned out to be an unworkable appointment. The committee recommended and I appointed Wendell Wray (1926-2003), an African-American professor of library science at the University of Pittsburgh and a former member of the Schomburg staff. Although clearly well qualified for the position his tenure only lasted from April 1981 to March 1983 when he returned to Pitt where he retired in 1988.

What follows is my reconstruction of the story from memory, without access to all the archives. The most important job to be filled at the outset of Wray's tenure was the appointment of a chief for the Center's Archives, Manuscripts, and Rare Books Division, the former white archivist having recently decamped for a good job at the Wisconsin State Historical Society archives in Madison, Wisconsin. Without my knowledge, Wray committed the job to a very well-qualified candidate, Dr. Robert Morris, a PhD who studied with John Hope Franklin. Wray announced the appointment to me as a *fait accompli*. Word soon spread around Harlem, no doubt abetted by the former Director, that a white man had been appointed to take charge of the history of blacks. I'm not certain whether I could have or would have blocked the appointment, but politically it was a disastrous mistake which Wray continued to

---

[60]   As a result of a 2010 Delmas Foundation grant to Columbia University Library for the processing of a portion of Amira Baraka's personal papers, Deirdre and I were invited by Michael Ryan to meet Amira over lunch at the Columbia Faculty Club. Although expecting to find a real firebrand we found a charming and rather modest man, still politically active in Newark but apparently mellowed with age. He and Philip Roth and I were all born in northern New Jersey within 20 miles of each other within a few years of one another but in three very different worlds. When I reminded him of our first meeting at the dedication ceremony in 1980, he merely said that "it seems so long ago." Baraka died in 2013.

defend despite rising hostilities from the more activist sections of the Harlem community. The appointment might have succeeded if some diplomacy had prepared the way, but there was none, in fact the reverse. I quickly learned that when people speak in the name of a community, they are speaking for only a segment of that community, just as when a presidential candidate says "the American people think . . . ," I usually know he or she is not speaking for me.

Nor at the outset did much of a highly divided Harlem community speak for me and certainly not for Wendell Wray, who outraged many in Harlem with abusive radio interviews castigating his black opponents. Regular picket lines formed, not only near the new building but also outside the home of Robert Morris in northern New Jersey. In November 1982 two black activists of the Black United Front, Preston Wilcox and Charles Burden, "were arrested in Harlem . . . in the latest incident involving protests against the appointment of a white man to head the archives section of the Schomburg Center for Research in Black Culture." *The New York Times* report of November 19th went on to say that 12 to 20 protesters had tried to remove Morris forcibly from his office, when the police responded to a complaint from Mr. Wray. At one point, Gregorian put Morris and his wife in a Manhattan hotel for a couple of days to let the situation simmer down.

The Black United Front was only one of the groups claiming to speak for the community. Somehow, a Committee of Five, calling itself the Schomburg Coalition, appointed itself to negotiate with the Library. The names I remember as being involved in various meetings at 42nd Street were John Henrik Clarke (1915-98), a Pan-Africanist professor from Hunter College who was closely allied with Jean Hutson; Alton H. Maddox, a Harlem lawyer and activist who later represented the discredited Tawana Brawley in her rape and abuse allegations; Frances Anderson, a community resident who lived near the library and who approved of the changes I was attempting to initiate; and Anna Hedgeman, a former mayoral cabinet member (and first woman to serve in such a post) under Mayor Wagner, a moderate diplomat in this conflict, and a true friend of the Schomburg and in the end of mine as well. As I recall, the Reverend Calvin Butts, then an assistant minister in the Abyssinian Baptist Church, appeared at one lengthy meeting.

Much of this occurred during a period in which the Library itself was undergoing its own transition to the new administration of Vartan

Gregorian, and the Schomburg meetings took place in his office. He sometimes described himself, an Armenian Caucasian from Iran, as a "person of color," although he also liked to joke that he was the only Caucasian among us. I think he genuinely believed that he could talk his way through some absurd allegations and impossible demands, including the illegal demand that only African-Americans could be employed at Schomburg. Another example was John Henrik Clarke's accusation that the Library's policies favored light-skinned black people on a kind of color spectrum that would exclude him as a very dark-skinned African-American. That charge I'm quite sure was directed towards one paler skinned African-American person on the Schomburg staff. I told Gregorian that he shouldn't dignify such arguments with a direct response, that the Library was a strong institution, and that we should negotiate from a conviction of strength, not weakness. In the end Gregorian came around to my view of the negotiations and even apologized. Somewhere in the library archives of my administration is a letter from Anna Hedgeman that I treasured, thanking me for my diplomacy in the Schomburg affair. Frances Anderson gave Deirdre and me a copy of her husband's photograph of pigeons perched atop the Library Lions. Through it all Robert Morris acted with great dignity and restraint, despite some horrid provocations. He did eventually resign to take a position with the National Archives at its facility in Bayonne, New Jersey.

In early 1983 Deputy Director Arthur Curley and I took Wendell Wray to lunch to negotiate his resignation. He quickly lost his appetite but did resign, ostensibly to "pursue academic research" and to return to Pittsburgh. The *Times* quoted Arthur accurately as saying "we are very sorry." We appointed a Schomburg staff member, Catherine Lenox-Hooker, as Interim Director, followed by John Miller, Chief of the American History Division when it was about to close. We then began a national search which concluded in early 1984 with the appointment of Howard Dodson, not without more demands and posturing from the "community," but beginning a period of 25 years of relative tranquility at the Center, at least to the best of my knowledge.

As an historian I don't believe that pure objectivity is attainable. It's a truism to say that all scholarship is autobiographical, but on the other hand the idea that one must be part of a group to assess and recount the history of that group, as the Schomburg critics claimed, is to me anathema. I can't play the oboe but I can appreciate or criticize someone who can. What the English called "The Indian Mutiny of 1857" South Asians call "The First War of Indian Independence." The danger to the truth of subjectivity, the narrowing of its pursuit to one group, red or yellow, black or white, is just too great. The scholar belongs in the study or the library, not in the church pew or on the hustings, and ideally will have some distance on his or her subject, even if a member of the group or relative of the organization or person is being studied. That is not to ignore the political and racial questions which in the end were what the Schomburg case was all about.[61]

One of the highlights of my eight years as Director of the Research Libraries and several years afterwards was my friendship with Alex Wilson, Director General of Humanities and Social Sciences at the

---

[61]   In searching the Internet I was surprised to have forgotten that a suit against Mayor Koch, the Library, and others by members of a Schomburg Coalition had not been adjudicated until June of 1985. An appropriate Internet search will reveal the following case:

RODGERS v. KOCH

111 A.D.2d 727 (1985)

**Madeline Rodgers, as President of The Schomburg Coalition, et al.,
Respondents,**

v.

**Edward I. Koch, as Mayor of The City of New York, et al., Defendants, and
New York Public Library et al., Appellants**

**Appellate Division of the Supreme Court of the State of New York, First
Department.**

June 27, 1985

Concur — Sullivan, J. P., Carro, Fein, Milonas and Ellerin, JJ.

The plaintiffs were dismissed with the following judgment:
Even under the expanded definition of standing, plaintiffs herein may not challenge a personnel decision on the part of the library, which is not even a governmental entity, simply because they would have preferred that the library appoint a different individual to head the Schomburg Center. This is particularly the case in view of the fact that in order to bring suit, plaintiffs must still "be within the zone of interest to be protected by the legislation and must suffer injury from administrative action or inaction." (Matter of Dental Socy. v Carey, supra, at p 334.) In that connection, the plaintiffs in the present litigation have asserted no specific pecuniary or other loss arising out of the purported wrongful conduct. Indeed, with one exception, they do not even allege to be users of the Schomburg facility but simply express a general unhappiness with the choice of a chief archivist.

British Library, i.e., the Bloomsbury British Library operations including the Round Reading Room, before they moved to their new St. Pancras building in 1996. Alex was a very modest man by temperament but self-confident and secure, the most brilliant library administrator I've ever met. He was a Scot who came from a public library career in the North of England (Preston, Chester). Very unusually for any British Library staff, he had no University degree; when asked about his London clubs Alex would say that he preferred to entertain in Italian restaurants. He and his wife Mary lived in Cheshire and he commuted weekly to London where he kept a small *pied-à-terre*.

We met Alex soon after his appointment in 1980 and we became fast family and professional friends, frequently staying in each other's homes in Pelham, Syracuse, Tattenhall, and London. Apart from shared interests in music (he an audio purist of high-end equipment, classical taste, and contempt for new-fangled CDs; me a more eclectic philistine), the basis of our friendship was the uncanny similarities of our individual responsibilities. The sources of funding for the BL and NYPL and the politics of funding were very different, but in most other areas of concern, collection development, administrative organization, public service in closed stack libraries, public relations, financial management, and not least in the field of preservation, the shared problems were found throughout our organizations. Both of us worked under non-librarian chief executives who required professional tutelage in the mysteries of our guild, and who thought those mysteries to be wilful obfuscations. Each of us was able to talk more candidly and confidentially to one another about our problems than we ever could or would in our home institutions.

The first order of joint business was maintaining the momentum for developing the online *English Short Title Catalogue*, a project run in the UK by a redoubtable bibliographer named Robin Alston, and in North America by the equally redoubtable Henry Snyder, then of Louisiana State University. It was barely underway when Alex came aboard, but it now includes 470,000 titles. It is described as follows in the Syracuse Library catalogue:

Descriptions and holdings information for letterpress materials printed in Great Britain or any of its dependencies in any language—as well as for materials printed in English anywhere else in the world. Coverage is from the beginnings of print to

1800 including all recorded English monographs printed between 1475 and 1700. The English Short Title Catalogue is updated daily.

What was then a dream is now an indispensable historical and literary tool, the product of some very dedicated and determined people. NYPL was a full participant and was in fact the site of a pilot project testing ESTC's feasibility before the project was formally launched; this participation, begun before I arrived, assured that our pre-1800 English titles were included from the earliest stage. Funding was always a struggle, since it was a labor-intensive project, but the National Endowment for the Humanities was a faithful sponsor, and when the Gladys Krieble Delmas Foundation began its library program in 1993, it too provided considerable assistance.

[*Coda: late in the twentieth century the commercial firm of Pro-Quest converted the microfilms of these ESTC titles and further collections of early titles, placing them online as digital page images in a package called* EEBO: Early English Books Online. *In 1999 ProQuest joined with the Universities of Michigan and Oxford to create the* Text Creation Partnership (TCP), *a collaboration funded by subscribing research libraries to create fully searchable online versions of EEBO texts. The partnership was based at Michigan and Oxford University, its work complemented by another online database, ECCO (Eighteenth Century Collections Online). The initial goal of converting texts for 25,000 ESTC titles has now been accomplished. I had the pleasure of serving on the TCP Board of Directors for its first seven years.*]

Soon after my return to NYPL in 1978, I learned from Lola Szladits that the former head of the Berg Collection and my boss in 1963, the late John D. Gordan, had the tradition of an annual luncheon with Marjorie Wynne, the manuscript curator of the Beinecke Library at Yale, on the Friday of New York's January Bibliography week. Book week is always scheduled for the last full week in January when many of the world's bibliophiles gather in New York City. I don't recall quite how it happened but I inherited John Gordan's role and for over thirty years Marjorie and I missed only two lunches, one because of weather, the other because of her declining health. Marjorie was the doyenne of special collections curatorship, widely known and much loved in the bibliophilic world, and was most instrumental in the creation of ALA's Rare Book and Manuscript Section in 1959. Our Friday lunches during Book Week were always a combination of personal and professional information, a certain amount of library gossip, and accounts of our travels. She was miffed with me for joining the Keats-Shelley Association of America Board of Directors, causing a calendar conflict that forced a move to Thursday lunches during the last four years of our traditional lunch. Only three friends spoke at her memorial service in the Beinecke Library: Alice Prochaska, Terry Belanger, and me. She was one grand lady.

Sometime in 1982, one of our best rare book librarians, Dan Traister, told me that he was considering a move to the University of Pennsylvania. I didn't want to lose him and arranged for us to meet with Gregorian in hopes that Greg would persuade him to stay. Gregorian made a strong pitch in his most appealing manner, but in the course of the meeting I told Dan that the important thing about his new job was that he go with sufficient authority to carry out his responsibilities, to which Greg rejoined that I had neither. Dan took it to be a light-hearted joke while I took it as an accurate assessment of Gregorian's view of my role in his Administration. Many years later Traister told me that he appreciated the meeting but that he had to leave his position because of physical problems related to his daily five-hour commute from and to Easton, Pennsylvania. I presumed also that his new salary would be considerably higher than our notoriously low pay scales. I'm very grateful that our friendship survived his move.

Early in 1983 Alex Wilson arranged for me to take a consultancy with the British Library Research and Development Division, a three-week study asking for a US perspective on national preservation planning in the United Kingdom. Following on some American initiatives in this field, the UK began its coordinated conservation efforts in the late 1970s, spearheaded by the University Librarian at Cambridge, Dr. Frederick Ratcliffe. Though Ratcliffe made clear his hostility to my visit and assignment, an intrusion on his personal fiefdom, I nonetheless spent three weeks in Britain in March 1983, visiting conservation operations in Oxford, Cambridge, the lending facility at Boston Spa where Maurice Line presided, Aberystwyth, Wales, Edinburgh, Scotland, and a number of London sites, including the House of Commons, the Public Record Office at Chancery Lane and Kew (now The National Archives), Lambeth Palace Library, the Wellcome Library, the London Library, and the Senate

House Library of the University of London. Unfortunately we couldn't fit Ireland into a very tight itinerary.[62]

The lunch with Ratcliffe was the low point of the trip. Robin Alston, one of the brains behind the online *English Short Title Catalogue* and an extraordinary bibliographer, publisher, scholar, and bibulous raconteur, joined us for the lunch and that ended all hope of getting any business done by avoiding any discussion of serious issues relating to preservation. I had known Robin for five years since we first met with Donald Richnell, Alex Wilson's predecessor, in 1978 to discuss the prospects for the *English Short Title Catalogue*, and NYPL's participation in the project. I enjoyed Robin's company immensely and this luncheon was all very convivial but useless for my purposes. Robin died suddenly in 2011 in Barbados, leaving behind a third wife and a rich legacy of historical bibliography and library history.

The high points of the consultancy were the national libraries in Aberystwyth and Edinburgh where the cooperation was unstinting and the hospitality magnificent. Nicolas Barker, editor of the *Book Collector*, and at that time head of the Conservation Service at the British Library, I suspect was also rather dubious about my assignment but slept through one of our BL meetings, as he had done in other meetings over the thirty-five years I've known him, allowing me to claim later that we'd slept together through a number of the same meetings. I intend no disrespect: he's a bibliographical wonder whose memory is breathtaking and he has my highest admiration. His collected obituaries, contributed over many years to *The Book Collector*, *The Independent*, and elsewhere, would make a fascinating volume for any book historian, to join his other distinguished

---

[62]   Ratcliffe deserves at least a footnote. He may have been something of a scholar-librarian but in my experience he was a self-important and narcissistic snob. Deirdre and I once sat across a dinner table from him at an RLG event at the Athenaeum in Pall Mall, London. At one point he referred to another British librarian at a far table as the second best librarian in the UK, and when he himself retired would be the best. Later in the evening he patronizingly told Deirdre that Cambridge was an excellent university. She disingenuously asked whether that university was the one with the cows in the back. Indeed, there are still cows in the Backs of King's College, but he had no idea that her comment was meant as a withering putdown.

books, including his biography of Stanley Morison, the typographic genius of Times New Roman and one of Nicolas's own mentors.

Since I would be very busy on returning to New York, I wrote the report while still in London at a temporary office on Sheraton Square, and it was issued that month as "National Preservation Planning in the United Kingdom: An American Perspective." *British Library R & D Report No. 5759*. London, March 1983. The report helped lead to the establishment of a National Preservation Office by the British Library Board in 1984, which continues now as the British Library Preservation Advisory Service housed at the British Library.

The consultancy was for me an extraordinary experience. For reasons I never understood, possibly because he was anticipating further Schomburg problems during my absence, Gregorian did not approve of my taking on the assignment, unconvinced by my argument that the prospective liaison with these institutions would be valuable to NYPL by enhancing our relations with several British libraries. In the end I simply took three weeks of vacation days of which I had far too many; nothing more was said on the issue, though it may have continued to rankle—and in fact the Schomburg situation did remain volatile while I was away.

Other friendships developed and blossomed because of my work at NYPL. We had known Marcus McCorison, Director and then President of the American Antiquarian Society (AAS) in Worcester, Massachusetts, since our Newberry days, but three things came together to strengthen our old friendship. In the late 1970s Marcus was President of the Bibliographical Society of America at a time when the BSA needed a new Executive Secretary. He asked Deirdre to take on the job, and for three years the organization operated out of our Pelham home and a Grand Central Station postal box. For that alone the McCorisons and the Stams were in regular communication. Marcus had also been Chairman of the Independent Research Libraries Association and asked me to take over as Chair, a job which entailed planning a couple of meetings per year, compiling statistics of the fifteen members, and on occasion testifying before Congress. (That was how I became the spokesperson for IRLA when we gathered in Reagan's Oval Office in the White House in December 1981.) And then too, AAS was one of the first independent libraries to join the Research Libraries Group, bringing us into regular contact during Board and Committee meetings.

It was an affectionate relation which continued until Marcus's death, with lots of self-deprecating and mutually insulting humor. I once heard his loud voice in the catalogue room of the Massachusetts Historical Society booming out "Who the hell let Stam in?" We once formed an HAA (Horse's Ass Association), with Marcus and Paul Mosher joining me as charter members. Some colleagues would no doubt applaud our self-knowledge, but we only had that one meeting at Stanford. Now we are all in various stages of enfeeblement, Marcus the first to quit our unremarkable Ass-ociation when he died early in 2013. Despite his gruff exterior he was really quite a sentimental character who treasured his friends.

In April 1983 the School of American Ballet was celebrating its 50th Anniversary with a dinner at the Performing Arts Research Center at Lincoln Center. At dinner Deirdre sat with Jacques d'Amboise, the celebrated New York City Ballet dancer, and I was seated with his wife, Carolyn George, a photographer. Speeches were mercifully short but the few comments by Lincoln Kirstein still echo down the years: "Our art is as fragile as a butterfly's wings, and the little that remains is here in the Library." On another occasion a Library gathering retired to Kirstein's apartment on St. Mark's Place where he and I discussed a photograph on his wall, an historic document of Mountbatten and Nehru at the moment of Indian independence. Also that evening Gigi Oswald introduced me to Suzanne Farrell. I'm sure Farrell has no memory of the conversation—for her it was an emotional time, shortly before George Balanchine's death on April 30, 1983—but I remember it vividly. She talked about many things, including her visits to Mr. B in the hospital, her idea of heaven (dancing *Mozartiana* with Peter Martins), and much else. Arthur Curley, my Deputy Librarian who later became Director and Librarian of the Boston Public Library, joined us half way through our long chat, and he was equally star-struck. As we walked away on our way home he said, "All right David, I'll work for nothing."[63]

Such events were indeed among the privileges of our positions in the Library, not least a parking space right beneath the State Theater, home of NYCB and the New York City Opera, an easy walk to the Performing Arts Library. Shortly after Balanchine died a few weeks later, on April 30, 1983, Deirdre and I happened to have subscription tickets to the program which would constitute his memorial. Suzanne was scheduled to dance Bizet's *Symphony in C* with Sean Lavery but insisted it be with Peter Martins and they danced that very sparkling work without a smile throughout. The end of the second movement that night was the saddest moment I've ever seen in dance. The *New Yorker* published a major piece about Balanchine and that performance soon after. We've seen *Symphony in C* many times since but no performance has matched the power of that evening.

The earlier conversation with Carolyn George eventually led to a luncheon invitation for Jacques and Carolyn to visit 42nd Street and survey some photographic collections. Among other things they were thrilled to see an early photograph of their own house on West 71st Street. The visit also led to one of the riskiest and probably most foolish things I did at the Library. At the luncheon in my office, a rather bibulous affair, were Jacques and Carolyn, Donald Anderle, the Chief of our Special Collections, a few others, and most importantly our impressive and irrepressible Chief of the Dance Collection, Genevieve "Gigi" Oswald. I had known Gigi for twenty years, when among other things I helped her edit a chronology of performances by Ruth St. Denis and Ted Shawn and

---

[63]   A few years later Gladys Delmas gave Peter Martins, Ballet Master of NYCB, one million dollars to commission a new ballet, to be called *Mozart Serenades*. By the time of the opening performance Gladys was too sick to attend, but we had a delightful intermission party in the Green Room. It only received a few performances and has not returned to the repertoire. At Gladys's memorial service I asked Martins about it. He said it was "resting."

see it through the NYPL press.[64] Conversation at lunch was sprightly, and somehow inspired me after lunch to invite Carolyn and Jacques, together with Anderle, to take a walk on the roof of the Library.

We mounted the spiral staircase in the large south column of the McGraw Rotunda and went out from there to the roof. Jacques was already on shaky knees and the most vertiginous of the four. Don and I carefully leaned inward as much as possible, but Carolyn was fearless, leaning over the parapet to take photos of the lions from atop, and many pictures of the roof against surrounding buildings, looking exactly like Margaret Bourke-White working for *Life* on the Chrysler Building. (We had no department of risk management then.) She did send me prints of her beautiful roof-scapes that are now in my archives. Carolyn, a former dancer with Mr. B and the City Ballet, died in 2009. I've seen Jacques a half dozen times since then and he is his warm and open self, always ready with a bear hug. I once asked Alex Wilson to give Jacques a tour of the British Library during an NYCB tour in London, something Jacques reminds me of periodically.

To return to the more difficult parts of my job, I should say that I was personally very fond of Gregorian and enjoyed our many conversations on academic as opposed to library matters, but he was not easy to work with. Publicly he was always full of praise and he referred to me to the Trustees and others as a "librarian's librarian," and described me briefly but graciously in his autobiography, *The Road to Home: My Life and Times* (New York: Simon & Schuster, 2003), as a very able librarian. But we had serious differences about a number of issues, most fundamentally over our differing visions of what the Research Libraries should be, and which of those visions should be the focus of our fundraising. My vision was of an NYPL at the center of a much wider world of scholarship and research libraries, mutually supportive and mutually dependent, the ideal of the Research Libraries Group of which NYPL was a founding

---

[64] Christina L. Schundt. *The Professional Appearances of Ruth St. Denis & Ted Shawn; a Chronology and an Index of Dances, 1906-1932* (New York: New York Public Library, 1960). When we moved to Syracuse in 1986 we began our custom of at least one weekend per summer of performances at Jacob's Pillow, the dance festival in Beckett, Massachusetts, founded by Ted Shawn eighty years ago. Its archivist, Norton Owen, has become a particularly good friend.

member. That was not the vision of the men, the Trustee troika, who apparently demanded the reorganization that caused my departure. Theirs was a single monolithic NYPL standing independent of that wider world. Perhaps I didn't articulate my vision well enough; perhaps it had to wait for the vastly changed world of the twenty-first century where moves toward such inter-dependency are more clearly perceived, are increasingly aided by technology, and are now sporadically occurring.

It seemed to me that the initial and much-puffed fund-raising successes of Gregorian and a new Board were doing little to enhance the budget of and thereby the actual public services of the Research Libraries. Major exhibitions were an added burden on already overextended staff. Fashionable parties and block-buster galas were striving all too obviously to enhance the status of the Library in New York society, with the legendary Mrs. Astor at the center, making it a locus of social climbing.[65] Like Willie Sutton, I do understand the need to raise money from where the money is, but I also instinctively wanted to protect the Library from overt social pandering. It didn't help that we had very few Development staff with any professional experience of libraries in general or of research libraries in particular. Typically, like many of the Trustees, they had little understanding of what the Library was all about and omniscient assurance that they did. They could be wowed by collections, but their eyes glazed over when it was time to discuss the nitty-gritty of library work, often the more expensive because labor intensive part. For all the glitz they were a rather unsophisticated breed. I remember attending a New York Philharmonic concert with one of them when a searing performance of George Crumb's *Ancient Voices of Children* evoked only a thorough reading of the Philharmonic's donor list in the evening's program. Or at a Library party when another told my wife that Mrs. Astor's kidskin gloves cost more than Deirdre's entire ensemble, a comment that my

---

[65] Apart from the insulting assertion in his memoirs that "The Library had a weak board of trustees and no management worth mentioning," Heiskell's most discouraging contention was that "It had no constituency except scholars, children and ordinary citizens who like to read." He was right that the Library had insufficient clout, but it should have been worth mentioning that those constituencies were those we existed to serve, not Mrs. Astor and the publicists for New York society. A weak Board was clearly one with too few billionaires.

wife, a thrifty New Englander, rather relished. I remember one meeting in Gregorian's office when a Development officer was seriously discussing whether we should tell the truth to one of our funders about how the funds being sought would be used. He said it was a question of whether the ends justified the means. I said I thought that Robert Moses had the last word on that subject, "if the ends don't justify the means what the hell does." The response was that it was good to be reminded of that! Bingo! It was a soul-destroying environment. Six months after I left, Deana Marcum, then of the Library of Congress, told me that with my move "we felt a soul had been saved."

(I should say parenthetically that all of our annual NEH preservation grants dealt with real library problems, and one grant received shortly after I left couldn't have been grittier—a million dollars from the Philip Morris Foundation to vacuum the general collection.)

The Library's success in capital funding was a different matter, and the beautification of the Library and the improvement of the infrastructure were majestic accomplishments, initiated by Couper who received little credit, continued by Gregorian, to a lesser extent by his successor Tim Healey, and completed in 2011 under Paul LeClerc with the centennial of the Central Building. Five decades earlier I was there for the 50th anniversary, when each staff member received a commemorative medal by Leonard Baskin. Back then the building was well on the way to the shabbiness that has now been rectified for the next generation or two. I felt mildly hurt not to have been invited to any of the centennial celebrations in 2011. When the newly cleaned building was unveiled for the centennial, the sight took my breath away.

[*Coda: that last paragraph has to be revised after the announcement on December 19, 2012, of the Norman Foster architectural plans for the Central Library. The plan includes the removal of the seven-story bookstack on which the third-floor Main Reading Room rests, to be replaced by a fairly large circulating library in a four-level atrium, a new children's room, completion of a large stack area under Bryant Park (in effect a sop to scholar-critics of plans to remove collections to remote storage), and a new center for teenagers. The* Times *coverage that day included a rather grandiose comment by Tony Marx, the President and CEO since 2011, that "At a time when people wonder about the future of libraries, we're going to create the greatest library the world has ever seen." Such hubris it seems to me marks the end of the Research Libraries as the jewel of the NYPL, the blurring of the necessary distinctions between research and popular use, and the end of my vision of its role as one pillar of a global collaboration. I can only think of Ozymandias.*][66]

Pat Battin and I once agreed that mega-libraries like NYPL, Columbia, or the Library of Congress are basically unmanageable but strong enough to survive whatever mismanagement might come along. Playwright and poet Archibald MacLeish when Librarian of Congress claimed that research libraries were far more complex than the Department of Defense. They are stressful institutions and just keeping the doors open is no mean accomplishment. After almost seven years at the helm of the Research Libraries, as noted earlier, I was beginning to show signs of restlessness and burnout; frankly I was depressed and yearning to devote my next years to a more manageable institution in an academic environment, away from a hierarchical structure that precluded effective management. At times I'd come home wanting to quit on the spot, but Deirdre would always say, "But David, the children," a good and necessary caution.

That reminds me of one staff member, a very helpful assistant in my office named Walter Zervas who retired on the day he became eligible after 25 years of service. Walter was an ideal employee, extremely helpful to anyone needing assistance, cordial and polite, and deferential to a fault. He once begged me not to make him use my first name as most of my colleagues did. A day or two before his departure, Arthur Curley and I took him out for a farewell lunch (he declined a bigger retirement party) where he indulged in three manhattans before we had this conversation:

Stam: Walter, you have been such a splendid staff member, always helpful when needed, always ready to go the extra mile.
Walter: Thank you very much, Dr. Stam.

---

[66]   Under intense public pressure the Library asked its architect, Norman Foster, to revise the Central Library Plan and to reevaluate the decision to sell rather than renovate the Mid Manhattan Library, the long-time flagship of the Branch Libraries. In October 2013 the Library announced that it would delay the announcement of new plans until well into 2014.

Stam: But there must have been days during those twenty-five years when you simply wanted to say to the administration, "shove it."

Walter: Dr. Stam, every day for twenty five years!

He retired to Maine, to work on some mysterious writing projects which he never divulged, at least to us. His formal thank you note for the lunch, dated October 2, 1984, was in his usual good form:

Dear Dr. Stam:
Concealed Dramatist that you are, you got me onto the Retirement Stage with all the skill of a Merlin, and got this poor player to feel like Prince Hal (iburton) Getting off to the Planet M (oosehead): Smooth Directing, indeed! Thanks — & I'm already peering through the mist: 'Where's the Moose?'!!!
Sincerely Walter

Although I remained productive through my last two years at NYPL, I was ready to throw in the towel. What precipitated my departure, however, was an overt decision by Gregorian in early 1985 to reinstitute a position called Director of the Library, to whom the Directors of the Branch Libraries (Edwin Holmgren) and of the Research Libraries were to report. The position had existed under the President until 1978 when the incumbent John Cory retired and it was only the disappearance of that position that made it feasible for me to come to New York. I would not have come otherwise. At that stage in my career I was willing to be No. 2 though in actuality in charge of the Library, but not No. 3. I told Greg that it was an additional level of bureaucracy and administrative expense that would be better used by providing the existing Directors with greater authority and accountability and better budget support. His justification I found hard to believe and still doubt it: "The Trustees made me do it." Ergo, I told him I would have to leave, and within the year I had interviews at Duke University, the Newberry Library, and Syracuse University. The new Directorship was advertised and I soon learned that my British Library colleague, Alex Wilson, was asked to apply, presumably by Gregorian or a search firm. There is a letter from Alex in my correspondence files saying he gave very careful consideration to "THAT JOB," that his wife Mary was fully supportive, but that he didn't believe he could do justice to the job and maintain a trans-Atlantic commute. He would have been miserable in it.

In 1987, after I'd left NYPL, Alex was President of Britain's Library Association and intending to preside over its annual conference, that year in Harrogate. He invited me to attend and speak on some aspect of preservation. He was unable to participate in the conference because of some serious medical problems, though I was able to visit him in his Chester hospital and then bring his greetings to the conference. We visited the Wilson home in Tattenhall, Cheshire, quite often during his retirement years and he remained a close friend and valuable advisor until his death in 2002.

In November of 1986, eight months after I had left NYPL, the new position was filled by Richard DeGennaro, an old friend and mentor of mine and someone whom Gregorian had known from Penn. The position was abolished three years later when Gregorian left for Brown and was replaced by Timothy Healey, S.J. DeGennaro went on to become the Harvard College Librarian, a position for which I was also recruited. I felt the abolishing of the NYPL position was something of a vindication, having seen it as unnecessary and wasteful in the first place. But who knows—it may have served some purpose in encouraging me to move on, and very unfortunately it has recently been reinvented as a Chief Library Officer in 2013.

How can I sum up my own feeling about the end of my NYPL career? I've come to believe that subconsciously at least but more probably overtly, Heiskell and Gregorian wished for and welcomed my resignation, may even have tried to cause it with their cumbersome reorganization, as the easy removal of a critic, avoiding the unpleasantness of a termination without cause as occurred with Couper. I had learned from working with Bill Towner years before that the hardest job of the Number Two is that of critic and naysayer, and I certainly was not deferential enough to have avoided expressing any unwanted criticism, whether it be misguided reorganizations, restaurants in the park, selling off Audubon folios, defending Schomburg against racist charges, or for simply arguing that for all the new achievements, we were all standing on the shoulders of giants who had left us a great institution to protect and at that we were failing.

As I've reviewed a great deal of correspondence and papers that survive in my personal archives and some in the Library's institutional archives, my further if immodest reflection is that my administration was a fertile period in the Research Libraries in support of scholarship throughout the country and internationally. On the other hand, despite the lip service to the bibliothecal aspects of the Library, I think that Gregorian and his executive troika of Andrew Heiskell, Bill Dietel, and Marshall Rose, were simply not interested in the arcana of library management and had other priorities than the Library as library. I may be wrong, but I have had a long time to think about it. Twenty-six years later I had an opportunity to express my view of the situation in a letter to *The New York Times*, published in its Thursday Styles section on October 18, 2012. My letter responded to an article in that section (October 11, 2012) called "The Education of Tony Marx," an account of the problems the relatively new NYPL President would face following the renaissance of the Library under his three immediate predecessors:

Sir: It was appropriate for "The Education of Tony Marx" (October 11, 2012) to appear in Thursday Styles since much of the remake of the library has been a triumph of style over substance. I can't speak for post-1986 administrations, or for the branch libraries, but I was Andrew W. Mellon Director of the Research Libraries in the first five years of the renaissance your article describes. Although there were many exciting developments in that period, and much to praise, it cannot be said that much of the private funds coming in flowed in the direction of our readers or the library services we provided for them. The suggestion that "scores of new curators were hired" is, as far as I can recall, pure fantasy verging on mythmaking for a period when we had started consolidating service points in order to reduce librarian and technical positions. Many positions were added in the Development Office, the Special Events department, and a much expanded exhibition program, but not for librarians. Federal grants to the Research Libraries provided new positions for special projects which were helpful to the Library, but were a drain on already overburdened staff, and only indirectly helpful to our readers.

Your article does capture the social and financial striving of the Library at that time perfectly, and its many successes in those areas. But the purpose of the Library is just that, to be a Library, not a place of public or private entertainment. I personally thought the priorities were out of whack when I left in 1986. I hope Marx can achieve a better balance; the new storage facilities are a step in the right direction.

David H. Stam
University Librarian Emeritus
Syracuse University

The news from NYPL since that letter appeared has been most discouraging and it seems unlikely that Marx can or desires to achieve a better balance.

I had every incentive to depart on good terms, and despite NYPL's many vicissitudes over the past 25 years since I left, I have remained a loyal and supportive alumnus, even though the much vaunted new and improved management was in my opinion a public relations chimera. Digitization has changed the whole field in many ways, but whether NYPL is a better research library today than it was before its so-called Renaissance I can't begin to fathom, but I doubt it. Every age has to develop its own hopes, fears, and even myths. I am not hopeful about the fate of the Research Libraries under the new regime and the Central Library Plan. Most disheartening for the Research Libraries was the reintroduction in May 2013 of that superfluous intermediate level of management with the appointment of a Chief Library Officer.

Other ironies abound. I declined to apply for the librarianship at Brown University because I knew my friend Paul Mosher was in the running. He didn't get the job but soon went to the University of Pennsylvania instead. A few years later Gregorian became President of Brown, where we just might have come together again if I had applied and been selected by Brown back in 1985 when I was rather desperate to leave NYPL. Gregorian is now (in 2013) the President of the Carnegie Corporation of New York, and at roughly my age must be approaching retirement. We have been out of touch for some time.

In interviews at Duke, which used the Dewey classification system, I managed to alienate a military historian on the search committee who couldn't believe that sound scholarly work could be accomplished in a non-Dewey library. I responded that a great deal of sound scholarship was coming from the best universities and libraries in Europe, most of which used no subject classification at all. Duke had several million volumes classified in the Dewey Decimal Classification, and I told the search committee that the Library would have to convert the whole collection to Library of Congress classification, the sooner the better. Duke chose to appoint Jerry Campbell who made no such threat. Ten years later he was replaced by David Ferriero who carried out the necessary reclassification. Another ten years and David became NYPL's Mellon Director, my successor thrice removed and soon a close friend. He is now the Archivist of the United States.

One other irony: my move to Syracuse confused my librarian colleagues, just as Gregorian's move to NYPL confused his academic colleagues. Neither of us seemed to be taking the right path up the greasy pole of success in our respective fields. It worked out for both of us.

The Gladys Krieble Delmas Foundation
1983 to 2011

Stepping back a few years, I have to record another significant personal development during my NYPL years. One Trustee member of the Committee on the Research Libraries in the early 1980s was Gladys Krieble Delmas, an amazing lady and fellow smoker who had started a Foundation in 1976 dedicated to improving the scholarly status of Venetian history in the English-speaking world. Her view was that Renaissance historiography was unfairly partial towards Rome and Florence to the neglect of her beloved Venice, a city where she and her husband, Jean Paul Delmas, spent a number of months every year. While Gladys was alive the Foundation's sole purpose was to provide grants to American and Commonwealth scholars to study various aspects of the history of Venice and to do so in Venice. Hundreds of fellowships for the study of Venetian history while in Venice, over twenty a year (often more) for over thirty years, have by all accounts redressed the imbalance.

Gladys Krieble was a handsome and cultivated Vassar graduate of 1934 who went on to study at Newnham College, Cambridge, and the Sorbonne before marrying Jean Paul Delmas, a French businessman. Gladys's father, Vernon Krieble, was a professor of chemistry at Trinity College, Hartford, Connecticut, who in 1953 invented an industrial adhesive that became Loctite, spawning a multi-national company that now produces everything from Super Glue to silicones, epoxies, and acrylics. Gladys and Jean married in 1937 when she was at the Sorbonne, and went on to spend the war together through some very hard times in Paris. A recent book alleges that she was part of a French collaborator's circle during WWII but we've found no evidence to suggest any such connections.[67] They lived in Latin America after the war, where she was a radio correspondent for Radio Canada and the French National Radio. She also wrote for various magazines including *The New Republic*. Although she had a comfortable youth and excellent education, her wealth came later in life, mainly in the form of Loctite stock. At her death in 1991 she held nearly 900,000 shares; between her death and the settling of her estate the share value had increased by over $8 a share thanks to an impending takeover, a considerable boon to the Foundation's portion of her estate.

Gladys began her association with the Library as a volunteer in the Rare Book Room, primarily treating leather bindings. Her job was to resuscitate dried out bindings with a beeswax salve known as British Museum Compound, a preservation solution no longer on the approved list of treatments, replaced by an acrylic wax known as SC600. Sometime in the mid to late 1970s the Library sponsored a luxury tour of major libraries in Ireland in which Jean and Gladys participated. That led to an invitation for her to join the Board of Trustees and as a Trustee she took her role very seriously and far from uncritically. During her lifetime she gave over $4 million to the Library (not through her Foundation but from what she called her "privy purse"), and her bequest added an additional $5 million. Since then the Foundation has continued to support the Library, particularly the Performing Arts Research Center (subsequently renamed) but on a much more modest scale.

She was a harsh critic of NYPL Board members who wanted to charge our users and of those who wanted to foster the sale of library assets, and she was a strong advocate of longer hours, financing one evening a week for a number of years through $1 million annual grants. Her motivation was very clear: to make the Library accessible to working people at times when they were not at work. I remember vividly one NYPL Board meeting where one Trustee, John Gutfreund, suggested that,

---

[67]   Glass, Charles. *Americans in Paris: Life and Death under Nazi Occupation* (New York: Penguin Press, 2009) p. 249-55, 270, 323, where her name is consistently misspelled as Delmass.

given our financial straits, it was wrong to be giving away our services free and called for charges to be instituted. When Gladys heard that, she pounded on the table, said "over my dead body," and pointed to the inscription above the fireplace in the Trustee's Room: "The City of New York has erected this building for the free use of all the people." She was particularly critical of the Library's Development Office which she felt cultivated social standing over humane values, and that they bombarded her with wasted mail and postage to give her information she already had. She was unconvinced by their argument that it was cheaper to leave her on the lists than remove her name. In 1989 when Gregorian resigned to become President of Brown University, she was sorely disappointed that the Library appointed a Jesuit, Timothy Healey, S.J., as his successor, causing a considerable reduction in her bequest to the Library. By that time Jean had died (1988), she had begun to lose interest in such battles, and she did not live to see the next succession when Healey died in office.

Her Foundation had a Board of three Trustees, including Patricia Labalme and her personal attorney. When Gladys discovered in 1982 that her Attorney/Trustee had embezzled money from her, she created an instant Board vacancy which she asked me to fill. Her reasons were that she liked my values, that I had a good understanding of humanities institutions, and that I was young enough to outlive her and Patsy Labalme. I suggested that she also wanted someone with whom she could share an ashtray. I accepted thinking it both an honor and a pleasant duty of reading Venetian proposals once a year and enjoying a delightful annual meal with our hard-working advisory panel. The Venetian program has continued unabated since her death in 1991 but with half of her estate coming to the Foundation we quickly expanded our mission to include programs in the Performing Arts (Joseph Mitchell), Humanities Scholarship (Patricia Labalme), and Research Libraries and

Archives, including the history of the book (David H. Stam).[68] We all shared responsibility for the Venetian program, with Patsy Labalme as first among equals, although we had no hierarchy among the three Trustees. Another early decision at our first retreat in 1992 was that all decisions would be unanimous and that we would not employ program officers, but would accomplish the work and pleasure of grantmaking ourselves. That was inspired partly by Gladys's principle of keeping administrative costs at a minimum, but also by our own wish to have the intellectual stimulation of following the growth of Venetian studies, as well as new developments in humanities scholarship, archival practices, and book history, and not least for all of us the growth of performing arts in New York City. Gladys had enjoined us to "have fun" and we wanted to have the pleasures of grantsmanship. We also were determined to spare potential grantees needless work and tried to make our proposal process as easy and unbureaucratic as possible. Not all of our administrators have fully understood this desideratum. The programs that we developed were primarily based on the founder's interests (including Jean's) and

---

[68] At the time of our reorganization in 1992, Joe Mitchell was a partner of the law firm of Reid and Priest, from which he resigned that year to join the Fan Fox and Leslie R. Samuels Foundation full time, and he is now President and Chairman of the Samuels Foundation. Gladys's friend Patsy Labalme was Associate Director of the Institute for Advanced Studies in Princeton. When she retired she became a Visitor in Historical Studies at the Institute where she continued to work on her edition of the *Diaries of Marino Sanudo*. By this time I was the University Librarian at Syracuse University. Over the past twenty years we have had the help of only three fulltime Office Administrators, Kathy Heins, Shirley Lockwood, and Rachel Kimber.

secondarily on the expertise of the founding Trustees.[69] Patsy Labalme died in 2002 and was succeeded by George Labalme, just as Deirdre Stam succeeded me in 2011 when the Veterans Administration officially declared me unemployable.

My colleague Joe Mitchell used to say (perhaps still does) that when you become a part of the philanthropic world you've had your last bad meal and your last honest conversation. Foundation work does involve hearing a lot of special pleading and active acts of concealment, but I've found in almost thirty years with the Foundation that we have developed some remarkable friendships, chief among them my Trustee and Advisory Board colleagues but also among people in our grantee institutions. The question about the latter is whether those friendships can survive beyond our ability to provide funding to their institutions, or beyond their connection to the Foundation. Some associations just fade away or die out, especially when the initiative is one-sided, but others continue to thrive. Our favorites are three people from Glimmerglass Opera with whom we have stayed in touch long after their retirements: Paul Kellogg, Bill Oliver, and Michael Willis represent for us the golden days of Glimmerglass Opera and we keep these friendships alive to keep the spirit of that time alive. Kellogg's honorary degree at Syracuse was a

---

[69]   Although the Foundation is named for Gladys alone, its assets include the estate of Jean Paul Delmas by bequest. One of the libraries visited on their Irish trip in the 1970s was Archbishop Marsh's Library, a beautiful and intact seventeenth-century library connected to St. Patrick's Cathedral in Dublin, the Protestant Cathedral later made famous by Dean Jonathan Swift. When I told Jean that I would be lecturing in Dublin in the fall of 1987, he asked me to visit Marsh's Library and give him some confidential advice on whether he should help fund a conservation bindery there. I did and was impressed by the library, by their famous reader cages where readers had been locked when reading Marsh's books, by the collections, by its irrepressible Director, Muriel McCarthy, and by the obvious need for conservation treatments. With a grant from Jean Paul Delmas of $250,000 the Library built what they called the Delmas Bindery, a three-level affair created *ex nihilo* out of a narrow light shaft. Jean would not have approved of the naming of the bindery, since he wanted anonymity in all his philanthropic activities. Some people infer that the funding and name came from the Foundation, but in fact it was only built with the help of Jean's quarter million.

high point, but we get together with Bill and Michael two or three times a year, for the last twelve years at the Skaneateles Festival, our annual August chamber music festival in the beautiful lake town of Skaneateles near Syracuse. I've embarrassed Bill often by citing him as the best development officer I've ever worked with. Paul we see less frequently but always with pleasure.

Others from the fund-raising world that have meant a lot to us in personal as well as professional ways are Jackie Davis of the Performing Arts Library of NYPL, Bill Lynch of the Brooklyn Academy of Music, Norton Owen from Jacob's Pillow and the Dance Heritage Coalition, Michael Ryan of Columbia (recently relocated to the New-York Historical Society). Some friendships began before my Foundation work began and continue even now that my role in grantmaking has ended.

Deirdre and I first went to Italy together in June of 1994, encouraged by Patsy Labalme and Andrew Heiskell to join the centennial commemoration of the American Academy in Rome. Now that I was out of the Library and a part of the Delmas Foundation, Heiskell was much friendlier. It was an amazing introduction, with the centennial dinner at the Vatican hosted by the Agnellis, presided over by Adele Chatfield-Taylor, with a private viewing of the Sistine Chapel for 220 guests, drinks in an open cloister, and dinner in the sculpture gallery, each of the guests seated between two people who shared at least one language. Among others we met the Librarian of the Vatican, an erudite and engaging Irishman named Father Leonard Boyle who later ran afoul of the Vatican hierarchy but was a serious and generous scholar. We also had an architectural tour of St. Peter's, given by an eminent member of our Delmas Advisory Board, Henry Millon, then at the National Gallery but previously the Director of the Academy. We went on to Florence and Venice and did some Delmas business in all three cities, but the highlight was the Vatican party. It was all so deliciously secular. One final image on the eve of our return home: sitting in a luxurious Roman hotel room, watching the O. J. Simpson slow-speed chase—June 13, 1994.

On our first official visit to Venice a few years later the Trustees threw a party at the Monaco Hotel for grantees then working in Venice and other friends. Among them was Jonathan Del Mar, the son of the famous British conductor, Norman Del Mar, and himself a conductor, musicologist, and editor of the new and ongoing Ur-edition of Beethoven. He was there working on a street guide to Venice with the help of a Delmas grant from our Commonwealth program. As the party warmed up we got on the subject of the doubled bassoon parts in the second movement of Béla Bartók's *Concerto for Orchestra*. When Deirdre joined us we fecklessly serenaded the room with a hummed version for three. When his guide was published he sent us an inscribed copy complete with the opening bars. In due course we met his wife, Annabell Gallup, the Southeast Asian curator at the British Library, and their sons, and we've tried to see them whenever we've been in London over the past fifteen years.

Little did I know how sitting on the other side of the fund-raising table would influence my professional work, and vice versa. Both Joe and Patsy made a point of telling me how valuable my experience as a library administrator was in evaluating research library proposals, an insider's view that many foundation executives lack, just as many fund raisers lack any real knowledge of their institutions. Similarly, Patsy Labalme's familiarity with Renaissance history and scholarship was a valued asset for our Humanities program. Much of what the Foundation funded through the research library program dealt with Special Collections, with a special emphasis on making archival collections more accessible through finding aids and other tools, including standards of archival description.

The first decade of the Foundation's work was a period of dire predictions of the death of the book, the development of electronic alternatives, and a growing obfuscation over the importance of the physical attributes of books. As a result, with Patsy Labalme's encouragement, I decided to include within the research library program a subsection to counter what we called "the war against the codex." There was plenty to support, given the typical forecasts of the demise of the codex, often kindled by self-serving cyber-entrepreneurs. Paradoxically but not incidentally, it also had been a time of growing interest in the history of the book, the development of national histories of books and libraries, and new scholarly centers and groups studying books as physical objects. At the heart of these movements was our long-time friend Ian Willison, a general editor of *The Cambridge History of the Book in Britain*, formerly a curator of printed books at the British Library, later a Senior Research Fellow, School of Advanced Studies, University of London, and a 2006 recipient of the CBE.[70] The Delmas program gave modest grants to promote these programs by helping to sponsor related conferences (some of them organized by Willison), and by encouraging centers for the book in the Library of Congress and in a number of American states. We also helped to advance the growth of SHARP (the Society for the History of Authorship, Reading, and Publishing), a group of like-minded scholars of bookish themes whose annual conference became one of our most rewarding academic venues, and a source of new friendships. Its founding and growth is almost exactly coterminous with the expanded Delmas Foundation programs, another lucky accident.

We've met many fascinating scholars through SHARP, including several of its leaders: Jonathan Rose, Simon Eliot, Robert Patten, and Leslie Howsam. On a 1999 bus ride in Madison, Wisconsin, we met fellow SHARP members Tim Rix, longtime Director of Longmans, and his friend and able editor, Annabel Jones. We saw them often over these years in Williamsburg and in London, until Tim's sudden death in 2012. Another good colleague and book historian is Bill Bell from the University of Edinburgh's Centre for the History of the Book which he directed until 2012. We first met him at the Williamsburg SHARP conference in 2001 where he gave a paper on the catalogue of the library aboard the *Discovery* on Robert Falcon Scott's first Antarctic expedition (1901-1904) voyage, a paper he is just now readying for publication. In 2003 I spent a couple of weeks as the guest of Bell's Centre for the History of the Book at the University of Edinburgh (painfully watching the start of the Iraqi War). We attend SHARP conferences as often as we can, most recently in Philadelphia in July 2013, and both Deirdre and I have given papers at SHARP meetings. The Foundation gave a number of grants to provide fellowships helping young scholars attend and present at SHARP conferences, a program later assimilated by the organization and funded by conference registration fees. Most gratifying was a 2007 regional conference on the history of the book in Venice which we worked out with Simon Eliot and a few of our Delmas fellows. Bob Patten was a particularly enjoyable SHARP President to work with, and

---

[70]   See the Willison festschrift on his 75th birthday, *The Commonwealth of Books: Essays and Studies in Honour of Ian Willison*, edited by Wallace Kirsop (Melbourne, Australia: Monash University Centre for the Book, 2007).

thanks to him the Delmas Foundation is handsomely acknowledged on the Society's web page. Other grants in this area have concerned printing and typographic history, exhibition catalogues, bibliophilic journals, and a program at the Folger Library for undergraduates using rare books. Our hope in all this is to help foster the next generation of book people.

It was a lucky break for me that I happened to be on hand at the time Gladys needed a new Trustee, and that Gladys herself had started her relationship to the Library as a volunteer in the Rare Book Room. My last task before retiring from the Foundation in October 2011 and becoming Trustee Emeritus was to prepare a comprehensive list of all grants made by the Research Library Program, a total of nearly six hundred from 1993 to 2011 for approximately $12 million, with something over $5 million going to archival standards and archives processing.[71]

All grant-giving represents some degree of guesswork and certainly some grants fail to deliver on their promises. We sometimes joked that, according to our grantees' final reports, we had never sponsored an unsuccessful conference. Some grants do not work out and it is refreshing when the grantees are candid about the failures. Some reports are needlessly modest though there seemed to be a rule that the smaller the grant the greater the gratitude. And there were many where the results were very gratifying. Let me cite examples from each of our programs.

In the Humanities program I would cite the large early grants which Patsy Labalme supported for the major humanities centers of the country to help secure their future or bolster their success. Included among them were the National Humanities Center in North Carolina, the American Council of Learned Societies, the Institute for Advanced Studies in Princeton, the American Academy in Rome, and a number of others. In our early days, when we were flush with funds but little known and generally beneath the philanthropic radar, it was easy for us to make six-figure grants and until the end of the century these grants made a great impact, no longer possible at such large amounts. Our asset portfolio sank badly during the financial crisis, just at a time when our help was needed more than ever, particularly in the performing arts. From a high of $75 million the assets now seem to have stabilized at just over $40 million

---

[71] The Foundation has posted this work on its website <www.delmas.org>.

for the past five years. (It's important to note that we've also been able to distribute over $40 million in our twenty years of grant giving.)

In the Performing Arts program, I think that our support of dance companies in New York City has been pivotal, especially for the New York City Ballet and the Paul Taylor Dance Company, but also for some of the smaller companies as well. Here we also began some collaboration among our programs where the Library program helped support the archival organization of these companies and the Humanities Scholarship program would also contribute toward appropriate goals.

One very gratifying success was the Glimmerglass Opera production of Monteverdi's *Incoronazione de Poppea* in 1994 with Jane Glover conducting, countertenor David Daniels as Nerone, and Dana Hanchard as Poppea. The production was a great triumph for Glimmerglass and for us as substantial sponsors. Two years later the production went to the Brooklyn Academy of Music for several performances, just at the time when Paul Kellogg became Director of the New York City Opera (while retaining his Glimmerglass post). Years later David Daniels told us that that production was the lynchpin of his career, and a spectacular career it has been, including the 2013 Metropolitan Opera production of Handel's *Guilio Cesare*.

Within the Research Library program, I think it safe to say that the archival world's work in EAD, encoded archival description, would not have proceeded so quickly or gained international recognition without our support. It's a complex and technical topic dealing with national and international standards for the description of archival collections through what are known as online finding aids. The resulting standards have been widely adopted and continue to be enhanced. The Library Program has been honored by the New York Archivists Round Table in 2005 for outstanding support of archives, and by the Society of American Archivists with its J. Franklin Jameson Advocacy Award in 2010. I retired from the Foundation in October 2011, succeeded by Deirdre C. Stam, who had been designated as my successor from the time of our organization in 1992. After a life-time in related fields she is well-qualified for the work and has already brought some welcome changes, particularly in grant evaluation and in computing requirements.

Another Transition: Syracuse University
March 1986 to August 1998

Our move to Syracuse was the result of another very coincidental but fortuitous circumstance. In 1985 I received a small NEH Travel to Collections grant to pursue my Leigh Hunt project of reconstructing his library, books which he normally annotated quite fully. The trip brought us to Special Collections at universities in Philadelphia, Delaware, Athens and Columbus (Ohio), Bloomington, Toledo, Cleveland, Buffalo Public Library, Cornell University, and Hamilton College, all having Hunt books I wanted to see.

I had not intended to include Syracuse University on the Hunt itinerary but at lunch at the Cornell hotel school that summer, during a break from my research, I happened to see Lou Martin, Cornell's Librarian and about to move to the Linda Hall Library, and Donald Anthony of the Syracuse Library who had just left his Directorship to move to Special Collections. Following Anthony's kind invitation, the next day we stopped in Syracuse en route to Hamilton College. While I visited with Anthony and worked on some Hunt material, Deirdre visited the School of Information Studies and later reported that some interesting things were going on there and that there were a couple of faculty vacancies that she might consider. I already knew that the head librarian position was open and that Pat Battin was advising the University in its search. On returning home I told Pat of our interest in Syracuse and asked her to nominate me for the job. In the end Deirdre and I both applied, as it turned out successfully: she received an offer a week or two before I did. I took over as University Librarian in March 1986 (despite a fair amount of staff opposition) and Deirdre joined the faculty that autumn. Another thin thread of chance or fate?

At Syracuse, on my second interview, a one-day trip on a dreadful stormy Thanksgiving Sunday 1985, Vice Chancellor Gershon Vincow told me that he'd received seventeen letters from library staff members protesting my candidacy (from major concerns to trivial quibbles, and a couple with accuracy), but uniform praise from the faculty I'd seen or who had heard my talk about how the research done by librarians can help them better understand their users and their own mission. Vincow's candor gave me insights into how I'd come across to staff and I would have been grateful to Vincow for that, even if he hadn't offered me the job. Because of severe weather, it took me forever to get home to Pelham and I wondered whether the auguries were misaligned.

When I received the offer from Syracuse, I called the Chair of the Newberry's search committee, the President of the Library, Harold Byron Smith, to tell him about the offer, that I was tempted to take it, but thought I should check about the status of their search. He said he was sorry to report that I hadn't made it even to their short list, but that his committee wanted me to know that I got "very high marks for candor." They went on to hire another historian with no knowledge of either librarianship or fundraising.

A number of NYPL Trustees sent farewell good wishes, one kind enough to say it was good news for me but terrible news for the Library. "What about us?" An emeritus trustee said he was unhappy for the Library about my departure "because you brought a civilized intelligence to the management, not just of the Research Libraries, but of the institution as a whole, and that, sir, is not easy to replace." Another, Diane Ravitch, asked me confidentially to tell her the back story that I've described above. Robert Menschel, a Trustee of both NYPL and Syracuse, called to encourage me to take the Syracuse job. These clearly were not the Trustees who forced on Gregorian the reorganization that I found unacceptable.

On February 25th, 1986, Gregorian and Chairman Andrew Heiskell threw a delightful farewell party for us, Gregorian presented me with a scarce book, Leigh Hunt's *Critical Essays on the Performers of the London Theatres, including General Observations on the Practice and Genius of the Stage* (London, 1807), by some thought to be the first English work of dramatic criticism. I reciprocated with a gift for the Prints Division of an etching of a bassoonist by Felicien Rops, and a volume of his libidinous drawings. A few days later son Wendell and I headed to Syracuse for a short period of bachelorhood in a condo near the campus, a renovated schoolhouse in which I had sublet an apartment stage-right of the school auditorium. Over the next few months I came to know and enjoy the occupants of the adjoining stage-left apartment of British historian Peter Marsh and his German wife Constanza. We fantasized how we might perform Pyramus and Thisbe with our porous and far from soundproof wall. Deirdre finished her teaching at Columbia's Library School in June, while staying in an East 81st Street apartment loaned to us by Gladys Delmas for three months. In June Deirdre joined me in Syracuse, and on July 15, 1986, we closed on our present home two miles east of the University.

We have lived in that house at 2400 Euclid Ave ever since, a place I've enjoyed immensely though Deirdre has not always been equally enthusiastic, especially in winter. When remembering what a wreck the house was when we moved in, I can't blame her for her doubts. We bought it from a locally-renowned artist and sculptor, Rodger Mack, then Director of the School of Art. He and his wife were in the midst of an ugly divorce and when his wife threw him out the house suffered badly from neglect and abuse, boarded windows, leaky roof, squirrels, insufficient light, and an unsuitable floor layout. It took about six months living with carpenters to complete the initial repairs and renovations, but we'd made enough money on the timely sale of our Pelham home that for tax purposes we had to put quite a bit into the improvements.[72] The result was visually attractive and an excellent venue for large parties. The largest, I think, was over eighty people—one colleague described our parties as "hospitality as administrative tool."

I felt that Syracuse was a good match from the beginning, the satisfactions many, the results tangible, and the disappointments few. Although not among the very best of research universities, it had the feel of a unified institution, less feudalized into departmental silos than most universities I knew. We soon learned that throughout the world, many of the people we met would have some kind of Syracuse connection, from relatives of children or grandchildren who went to Syracuse, to the Thai shop keeper in Chiang Mai, Thailand, who seeing my SU cap sang out, "We're No. 1."

---

[72] Syracuse in 1986 was the first time since Marlboro College that we began to feel financially comfortable. The combination of the house sale, accumulated vacation and sick leave pay, a timely inheritance, a higher salary in the new job, and a city with much lower costs for everything gave us some latitude, though we remained a fairly thrifty family. Our children were almost out of college and graduated without debts. Deirdre had full-time employment and eventually the Delmas Foundation added some income and a source of free performing arts entertainment. It has often struck us that our lives appeared more prosperous than they really were because so much of our social cum professional travel and entertainment was covered by the institutions we worked for. I once boasted to Gladys that we had enough frequent flyer miles to fly to India first class. She said I should remember that when we disembarked we would no longer be first class.

I developed strong faculty friendships and my new administrative colleagues sought my opinion, a refreshing change from NYPL where I had been marginalized by the administrative juggernaut. The library staff gradually came to accept my leadership. On my second day I attended the memorial service for a staff member I had never met, the Latin American specialist named Dan Cordiero, who had recently died of AIDS. The ceremony made me feel as though I had been instantly integrated into my new family. Several faculty made me feel particularly welcome. Intellectual historian Joseph Levine, a walking absent-minded professor, was a constant luncheon companion for years, a bookman devoid of preciosity and full of good sense, if a bit obsessive in his book collecting. Peter Marsh was a Canadian who was our modern British historian, in later years the ranking scholar of the Chamberlain family of Birmingham, England. He retired to that city in the early 2000s where we've visited him a few times. Ambassador Goodwin Cooke became an instant friend as my most consistent and evenly-matched squash partner. Goody was a State Department veteran who had many posts around the world: Ottawa, Rome, Belgrade, Pakistan, and as the chief ambassador to the Central African Republic. David Tatham of the Fine Arts Department and a Winslow Homer specialist, with his wife Cleota Reed, a specialist in ceramic tiles, became part of our circle of friends who made Syracuse a more intimate place than New York could ever be.

Within the year I began to be heavily recruited for a job at Harvard as Harvard College Librarian, the main operating officer of the Harvard libraries, under the University Librarian, political scientist Sidney Verba. Six or seven years earlier soon after I returned to NYPL I had some preliminary interviews for the same position at Harvard when historian Oscar Handlin was University Librarian, but we both agreed then that my service ethos was incompatible with Harvard's isolation from the greater world of library users. In this second round I simply was not interested, though Deirdre, a Radcliffe alumna, was clearly disappointed with the absence of this particular ambition. My stance on the issue led to one of the best putdowns I've received in a long life replete with putdowns. During the conversations Verba telephoned to ask the reasons for my lack of interest (I had known him earlier from some ARL and CRL connections and at one conference had punned on his name with "*in Verba veritas*"). I gave him a few facetious reasons like not wanting to leave the sculpture garden that came with our Rodger Mack home, and that they couldn't afford to move. Then we had this dialog:

Verba: Just what is it about Syracuse that you like so much?
Stam: I'll tell you frankly. I like Syracuse because it's not smug.
Verba: I'm sure you have a lot not to be smug about.[73]

I didn't tell him the main reason, that I had enough of being No. 2, that I'd spent too much time as No. 2 to academic historians and social scientists, educating them in subjects they didn't really care about, and that I was really enjoying the relative freedom of being the recognized leader at Syracuse and putting it on the library map. (Incidentally, the best boss I ever had was a meteorologist, George Benton at Johns Hopkins, who left Hopkins in 1978, the same year I did, to be lead scientist and associate administrator at the National Oceanic and Atmospheric Administration. The best for me were defined as being there when needed, and willing to learn but not interfering in affairs they knew little about, i.e. professional librarianship. Vincow was also quite strong in this respect. Many of the Deans did not agree: Vincow had been a Dean, but never a Librarian.)

Harvard too has some things not to be smug about. When Deirdre, as a Harvard/Radcliffe alumna, received a letter from Harvard's Presidential Search Committee in 1970, she somewhat puckishly nominated Margaret Mead as a potential successor to Nathan Pusey. The acknowledgment letter assured her that his [sic] candidacy would be carefully considered.

---

[73] I'm told that Winston Churchill said something similar about Clement Attlee: "He has a lot to be modest about." My most classic putdown was from a dog. I knew a Wheaton girl in Newport in 1955, and again in Norfolk in 1957 during my Navy days. She was a sexy five-foot minx nicknamed Mocker. We were driving in Norfolk in the summer of 1957 and she was asking me what I would do when I got out of the Navy. As I recall her brother was a Navy pilot, and thus the reason for her visits to these Navy towns. I said that I had no idea what I'd do, all I knew was that I needed a life filled with beauty. No sooner had I uttered those saccharine words than her dog in the backseat threw up, causing a paroxysm of laughter that gave meaning to her nickname. I never saw her again after that date and read recently that she had died.

One lucky break came shortly after I arrived in Syracuse, an offer from Jim Haas of the Council on Library Resources (CLR) to provide an intern to work with me for a year at CLR expense in a program to help prepare librarians for top administrative posts. My intern was to be Jeff Horrell, then the art librarian at Dartmouth, someone Deirdre had known from art library circles (ARLIS/NA), and she shared my excitement at the prospect. What I found in Jeff was an instant confidante, a sounding board outside the Library structure off whom I could bounce developing ideas and get honest reactions. He arrived in October 1986 but had already joined us for a library retreat at Blue Mountain Lake in the spring when about fifty Library staff participated in exploring ideas for what the Library needed most at that transition point.

Although the Library was underfunded, as most such libraries are, at Syracuse I felt I had solid support from Chancellor Melvin Eggers and Vice-Chancellor Vincow for needed programs, including automation, their support helped no doubt by my parsimonious approach to library management. Like NYPL, we suffered periods of retrenchment, most notably after Chancellor Kenneth "Buzz" Shaw replaced Eggers, when I was charged with reducing library personnel costs by almost twenty per cent. In preparation for these cuts Buzz had one-on-one sessions with each of his top administrators, the deans and department chairs on the academic side, and people like me responsible for a variety of administrative units. In my session I chose to ignore the Library needs by responding to rumors that the School of Music was a candidate for closure. I simply told him that I did not want to be part of a university without a school of music, and if it were to close I would have to consider my options. He responded that unfortunately I was in a small minority of people who cared. Whether I had any influence on the decision, I don't know, but in the end the School was saved by some modest cuts and a couple of voluntary retirements including the professor of organ and the head of the School, or so I understand. I also fended off a recommendation to shut down the Library's Belfer Audio Archive, though we did lose three of its four staff members. It celebrated its 50th anniversary in October 2013 and is thriving under Dr. Jennie Doctor.

By the time we got to Syracuse I had accumulated a large number of TWA frequent flyer miles, and with the help of Calcutta historian Robert Crane and his wife Lakshmi, and of my library colleague Gurnek Singh, we began planning a trip to India and Egypt for May of 1988. The trip was an eye-opening experience concerning a country and people to which we had given little attention. Our itinerary in the very hot months of May and June was mainly urban: Bombay (Mumbai now), New Delhi, Agra, Calcutta, Cairo, and Luxor. In Bombay we visited the Tata Institute on the edge of the Arabian Sea and some hospitable physics colleagues of the Syracuse physics department. We also took a day trip to the caves of Elephanta Island and their extraordinary sculptures. In New Delhi we visited the Library of Congress office running a program called PL 480 which distributed South Asian publications to American research libraries, and experienced the luxury of seeing diplomatic duties from the Consular compound—duties so onerous they required golfing outings at sunrise, before the heat of the day prevailed. We also made an excursion to Agra and the Taj Mahal, a monument that clearly justifies the hype surrounding it. On that trip we developed our own criteria for five-star monument status: one that takes the breath away.

In Calcutta we paid a courtesy call to the National Library and Kalpana Dasgupta, the Number 2 assistant chief and a Syracuse School of Information Studies graduate. Kalpana gave us an extensive and fascinating tour of the Library where Gurnek Singh had once worked on the Indian National Bibliography. (Gurnek later contributed the entry on the National Library to my *International Dictionary of Library Histories*.) And we had many other adventures in what was in effect a librarians' Busman's Holiday.

After the oppressive heat of India we flew in early June from Mumbai to Cairo, arriving on a bright clear and cool day to a holiday atmosphere and celebrations of the end of Ramadan. The visit was notable for two people. In Deirdre Stam, the erstwhile Egyptologist, I had the best possible guide to Egyptian antiquities, both in museums and in the Nile Valley. The other was our host in Cairo, Donald Jay, who had retired from NYPL to return to a position he had earlier held as head of the Cairo office of the Library of Congress, which like the New Delhi program, was responsible for distributing Middle Eastern publications to US research libraries with funds from Public Law 480 (PL 480). Our first-day tour of the Pyramids and the Sphinx was amazing for the colorful *joie de vivre* of the people. We later visited the Egyptian Museum in Cairo, some major Islamic sites, and then a trip to Luxor and the Valley of the Kings. We returned to Syracuse tired but refreshed.

In my experience of over thirty years of top administrative library positions, librarianship was no sedentary profession. Management by walking around was one of my habits, whenever I was at the home base. Automation itself created a need for greater collaboration among so-called stakeholders, and that in turn created a greater need for travel. I foolishly conjectured that my move to Syracuse would reduce my travel requirements. Within a few years of arrival in Syracuse, I found myself on the boards of three national organizations and a number of local and regional library organizations. I had simultaneous three-year terms with the Association of Research Libraries (six meetings per year, mostly in Washington), the Research Libraries Group (another six Board and Committee meetings, often at Stanford); and I was elected to the Research Division of the American Historical Association (another three meetings annually). I was always acutely aware of the dangers of being or appearing to be an absentee landlord; in fact our Syracuse friend and scholar Antje Lemke once chided me for being away too often. Perhaps she was right, but I rationalized that amount of travel as helping to put Syracuse on the bibliothecal map and as our contribution to national and international librarianship. But before 9/11 air travel was often a pleasure. Now I dread even the thought of flying.

One problem for a library like Syracuse is its isolation from the wider world of librarianship and scholarship. We did have a Friends group known as the Associates of the Syracuse University Library, and we tried to use the meetings of that group to introduce both staff and friends to new people and new ideas. In retrospect our roster of visitors was exceptional. Among librarians it included Mary Anne Scott, Director of the National Library of Canada; Alan Fern, Director of the National Portrait Gallery; Eric Ormsby, Librarian of McGill University and an expert on Persian manuscripts; and Emmanuel Le Roy Ladurie, the great French historian and Director of the Bibliothèque nationale in Paris (1987-89). Ladurie stayed with us at our home and was a delightful and amusing guest. He told a joke about some Frenchmen in a hot air balloon lost over foggy Norway. For a moment the mist cleared and revealed someone in an open field below:

"Where are we?"
"You are in a hot air balloon."
"Must be a librarian; he knows the facts but not the meaning."

As a Polar historian I naturally speculated on whether that story was a French sendup of the disastrous Swedish balloon expedition to the North Pole of Salomon Andrée in 1897, or perhaps a spoof on Ladurie's rather brief library career.

Visiting British librarians included the Librarian of Eton College, Paul Quarrie; Alex Wilson of the British Library; the afore-mentioned Ian Willison, quite often after his retirement from the British Library; and David Vaisey, Bodley's Librarian from Oxford, successor to Robert Shackleton. To name just a few others, there was Stephen Green, head of the Newspaper Library at the BL; Alice Prochaska, by then the Head of Special Collections of the British Library and before she became Yale University Librarian in 2001; and David McKitterick, Librarian of Trinity College Library, Cambridge. In addition to their more formal talks, these visitors would often meet with staff in more intimate seminar settings to compare policies, practices, and problems. On occasion they would travel back to New York City with me, good opportunities for long conversations on books and libraries. We also had Robert Warner, Archivist of the United States, Leonard Gold, Chief of the Jewish Division at NYPL, Nicholas Basbanes, bibliomanic historian, and, as noted earlier, Lola Szladits of NYPL's Berg Collection. I was simply taking advantage of my wide contacts in the worlds of scholarship and libraries to try to engage the interest of the staff in alternate ways of applied librarianship.

Like NYPL, despite lean resources we managed to make many useful acquisitions during my twelve years at Syracuse. It was our dear friend, Antje Bultmann Lemke, who helped orchestrate the acquisition of a significant group of Albert Schweitzer papers from Schweitzer's daughter, Rhena Schweitzer Miller. Antje was a Professor of Information Studies at Syracuse, and on her retirement had helped persuade Deirdre to become her successor as the School's resident humanist. She is now in her 90s, suffering some form of dementia, but in her prime a lively advocate of libraries, book arts, human rights, and many progressive causes. The daughter of eminent German theologian, Rudolf Bultmann, she gave a good portion of her father's papers to the Library. Her connections with Schweitzer came through her friendship with Rhena, her membership in the Schweitzer Fellowship in Great Barrington, Massachusetts, frequent visits to the Schweitzer Hospital in Haiti, and her 1990 translation of Schweitzer's *Out of My Life and Thought*, published by the Johns Hopkins

University Press. Mainly through her efforts, the Library successfully raised sufficient funds to add the Schweitzer papers to our collections. A well-equipped classroom in the Syracuse Library's Special Collections Research Center, sponsored by the Associates of the Syracuse University Library, now honors Antje.

Another room on the same floor honors University Trustee and *New York Times* columnist William Safire, a proud late-1940s SU dropout who retained his loyalty to the University until his death in 2009. After the Bronx High School of Science, he spent two years at SU and worked on the student radio station (WAER) before joining the *Herald Tribune* in New York. I wonder what he would have made of Virgil Thomson, who also wrote for the *Tribune* at that time, but I never asked him. Although we differed on almost all things political (except our opposition to gambling), I liked Safire a great deal and enjoyed his company and conversation. Deirdre and I once had breakfast with him in the Army and Navy Club in Washington shortly after she became the first person at the University responsible for the nascent Web. "You're my first web mistress," was his cryptic comment. I once teased him in a public introduction for his permissive attitude toward split infinitives. He responded by claiming it was the first time he'd ever been attacked as a liberal. At any rate, the gift of two of his major collections, on language and linguistics and on the British writer William Cobbett, together with his help in getting funds from the Dana Foundation both for the Safire Room and for the cataloguing of the collections he gave, were very welcome additions.

Several major additions to the Benjamin Spock papers were made during my time. I once took him and his wife Mary to a basketball game in the Carrier Dome, a game we watched from Chancellor Eggers' box. Some wag said to me afterwards that the spectacle of our students in the Dome should have given Spock pause about the effects of his permissive revolution.

Some minor part of the archives of John A. Williams, an African-American novelist and Syracuse native, were acquired during my time at Syracuse. His most famous and bestselling book was *The Man who Cried I Am*, but he wrote a number of other novels, short stories, and poetry, as well as the libretto for an opera called *Vanqui*, with poems from his *Safari West*. I say minor because he had already given the bulk of his papers to the University of Rochester Library. In the 1980s he became somewhat disillusioned by Rochester's administration of his collection and thus gave his papers from the 1960s to Syracuse, his alma mater. Through that acquisition we became good friends with John and his wife Lori, visiting quite often in New York City, their home in Teaneck, New Jersey, and at their beautiful farm in Central New York. John taught at Rutgers University from which he retired in 1994. With a Delmas discretionary grant I helped get *Vanqui*, by composer Leslie Burrs, staged by Opera Columbus, and it saw some excerpted concert performances but never achieved the wide success that John hoped for. We last saw him at home about 2006 when he was entering the early stages of dementia and he was angry about it. Fortunately, the rift with Rochester was healed when a new curator came, and the rest of his post-1968 archives went there and are well catalogued in Rochester's online catalogue.

One very major addition was in fact the recovery of stolen materials and previously donated materials from the John Mayfield collection. Mayfield was a true eccentric, the son of Earle Bradford Mayfield, a US Senator from Texas who won election in 1922 as a prohibitionist and who was labeled the KKK candidate. Not much is known about his son John, his education, or his occupations. He is known to have driven a bookmobile for the Montgomery County, Maryland, Library System. It was his book collecting that brought him to the attention of Chancellor William Pearson Tolley who appointed him as curator of the Mayfield Library in 1961 as part of a deal to bring his collection to Syracuse. The collection included some important papers of Eugene O'Neill, many 20th-century first editions, very significant manuscripts and letters of Algernon Swinburne with multiple copies of his *Atalanta in Calydon* (a first edition supposedly limited to 100 copies, although Mayfield assembled 107 of them on a bibliographical whim, including one given to Syracuse by George Arents and then misappropriated by Mayfield). Mayfield retired unhappily from Syracuse in 1971 and returned to his home and wife in Bethesda, Maryland, returning to Syracuse frequently to steal parts of the collection for re-gifting to Georgetown, and probably renewed tax deductions.

When I was the Librarian at Johns Hopkins, I had met Mayfield at a meeting of the Baltimore Bibliophiles sometime around 1975. I asked him about the rumors I'd heard of interesting bibliophilic activities in Syracuse, and he responded with a non-committal "we're having a lot of fun up there." Only later did we learn that the fun he was having was weekend raids to Syracuse to steal the best of the collection. The Syracuse deal with Mayfield for the gift of his collection had been consummated in 1964 with considerable fanfare. In the Syracuse entry of my *International Dictionary of Library Histories*, I gave this account of the Mayfield affair:

> . . . for most of the decade [the 60s] he served as a scout for archival and book gifts to the University. Only after his death in 1983 did the library discover that, following his retirement in 1971, Mayfield had systematically removed large portions of the collection, first to his Washington, DC, home and subsequently by gift to the Georgetown University Library (also in Washington, DC). Included in the transfers were important university holdings that he as curator of rare books and manuscripts had moved into the Mayfield Library. A later claim that the Mayfield Library had only been placed at Syracuse on deposit was never taken seriously, given Mayfield's own hoopla over the gift. A combination of extensive detective work and delicate diplomacy finally brought the most valuable of these missing materials back to Syracuse in 1989, including the Swinburne manuscripts, portions of the Dorothy Thompson collection (which Mayfield had helped to bring to the University), several Lord Byron letters, and many modern first editions.

The Lord Byron letters actually were not part of the Mayfield Library but much earlier gifts to the SU Library, manuscripts that Mayfield had subsequently stolen and given for tax purposes to the University of California at San Francisco which graciously acknowledged our claim without any fuss. The same was not true of Georgetown whose librarian, Joseph Jeffs, merely said that they would return anything which we could prove to be ours. Mark Weimer, Chief of our Special Collections, then known as the George Arents Research Library, was really the hero of this story, for he did most of the sleuthing required by that cavalier statement.

Curiously, all this was happening just at the time that Vartan Gregorian was leaving NYPL for the Presidency of Brown University. I volunteered to represent Syracuse at Greg's Inaugural ceremonies in Providence. His successor at NYPL had already been appointed, Timothy J. Healey, S.J., who was at the Inaugural ceremony representing Georgetown as its outgoing President and President-Designate of NYPL. I knew Healey from a Middle States Accreditation visit to Syracuse in 1988 when Healey chaired the committee and took a special interest in the Library. At Brown a year later, we had this conversation:

Stam: Tim, before you leave Georgetown, you have to help resolve the problem of the stolen materials that you have from Syracuse.

Healey: I'm not sure I can help. You see I have to deal with his [expletive] widow. I think the perfect solution would be for each of us to present our Mayfield collections to the Berg Collection at NYPL.

Stam: That's no help at all. We'll have to keep working at it.

What seemed to break the logjam, though I wasn't really sure, was the appointment of Susan Martin as the new University Librarian at Georgetown. I'd known her for some time (she had been my successor at Hopkins), and it appeared to me that she was much more interested in new technology than these arcane materials and was happy to let them go without a fight. Mark Weimer and I made a one-day trip to Washington later that year, picked up a good amount of the more portable materials from Georgetown, and settling back on the return flight, shared a very happy high five. Within the year Deirdre began teaching at Catholic University so we rented a truck to move her things to Washington, and with Wendell's help collect the significant parts of the Mayfield

Collection. We were happy to leave the political papers of his father at Georgetown.[74]

One of the choice items among the returned material was a beautiful pastel portrait of Sinclair Lewis by Peggy Bacon. It was from the Dorothy Thompson collection, solicited for Syracuse by Mayfield, and had been delicately framed by Georgetown, not knowing they didn't own it. It hung in my office for the next nine years, but was sent to the University Art Collection by my successor, Peter Graham, who understandably preferred his wife's art work on his office wall.

Probably the most extensive and expensive addition to the collections in my time was the gift-purchase acquisition of the papers and books of Joyce Carol Oates, class of 1960, as well as those of her classmate and friend, writer Robert S. Phillips, two very complementary collections. We had been receiving material from her since 1972 but this was the bulk of her archive as of 1990, as well as the archives of *Ontario Review*, a literary journal edited by her husband, Raymond S. Smith. As any reader of American fiction will realize, the Oates papers are huge and three or four supplemental acquisitions have been made since the first large tranche in 1995.

---

[74] This sad saga deserves another paragraph. I was truly appalled to learn from the internet that Georgetown University Library in 2009 had mounted a Swinburne exhibition honoring the late John S. Mayfield, claiming that Mayfield had "amassed the largest private collection of the poet's works." The exhibit brochure also praised him for the bibliographical feat of collecting 107 copies of Swinburne's *Atalanta in Calydon*. A sullied achievement as some of the copies were stolen from Syracuse and in any case it was a pointless exercise. Since we at Syracuse were fairly certain ten years earlier that the whole of the Swinburne collection had been returned, this news came as a bitter disappointment and can only reflect disingenuous if not deliberately deceptive behavior on the part of Georgetown authorities. The brochure describing the exhibition does not list the items exhibited so it is difficult to judge the damage. To sort out this complicated subject would require a good deal of further research, including study of Mayfield's tax records, but I fear there is no one left to do it, some of the records are no doubt lost, and no one is left to make the study given the length of time past. The exhibit pamphlet does give some additional information on Mayfield's life of which we were unaware. See http://www.library.georgetown.edu/sites/default/files/Gallitrifoldpdf.pdf

On the assumption that I should at least ascertain the existence of such a large collection, I flew to Newark on a snowy day in the early 1990s, drove to Princeton and met her husband at a warehouse on the east side of town to see most of the unopened boxes containing the collection, and then followed him through a snowstorm around the city to their home on the western side of Princeton. After giving me a diet cola, she pointed out a dresser filled with diaries and I took her gesture as an invitation to examine them. When I picked up one volume she protested self-consciousness, and said I'd be welcome to examine them when they were in Syracuse, an invitation I've never taken up. A selection of those diaries was about to be published in the *New Yorker*, so I wasn't sure what the fuss was about.

During the visit she also asked if I had ever read any of her work, and my proud answer that I'd read at least half a dozen of her novels was clearly a disappointment. I've read another half dozen in the intervening twenty years but never keeping up with her enormous output. She also asked whether I had known Vartan Gregorian when I worked at NYPL: "Don't you love him. He gave me a great big hug, and said, come to Brown; we'll pay you twice as much as Princeton." Gregorian had a great need to impress and be liked, and occasionally came out with outrageous lines like that. In an hour or so I departed through the snow storm for the Nassau Inn and a very welcome drink with my former colleague Bill Joyce who had moved to Princeton after I left NYPL.

I imagine that the unhappiness among Special Collections staff, caused both Joyce Carol Oates and Bob Phillips to become disaffected with my successor at Syracuse, Peter Graham, and they appeared to support the cabal that wanted him fired. I personally felt a strong ethical conviction that I should have no part of anything critical of my successors (after all I had left the job on retirement and it was their turn). A few years after I retired, I happened to see Oates in a Princeton restaurant and went to greet her. She was cordial but asked, "Are they going to get rid of that successor of yours?" I could only parrot my true view that it wasn't an issue appropriate for me to address in any way.

[*Coda: I've neglected to mention that my career had been built around retrenchments. There wasn't much to retrench at Marlboro—it would have cost more to lock the doors at night than it was to maintain our honor system. At the Newberry in 1971 we had to reduce the staff by 10% and I managed to do that with some hard feelings but as humanely as possible. Hopkins didn't really face their budget problems until around the time of my departure. At NYPL it was practically an annual exercise to develop various scenarios for retrenchment, dependent on the current threats from City Hall and where we were in relation to union contracts. But the biggest hit was at Syracuse in 1991 when all our Deans were under attack for living in "a cloud cuckoo land" of overspending, to quote the new Chancellor, Buzz Shaw. My response was to make a conscious choice to reduce those units of the library that did least by way of direct services to faculty and students. That meant the library administration, where we eliminated one Associate University Librarian position that I personally assumed to save one large administrative salary; the Special Collections staff which lost a number of lines partially made up with soft money; and our Belfer Audio Laboratory whose Director, Bill Storm, quit in anger, taking two other staff with him, though I believed strongly that he could have raised funds for those positions. The point is that all this pain gave me some managerial credibility with my bosses if not always with my staff or constituents.]*

My twelve years as University Librarian at Syracuse were not without their tragic aspects. Two such events stand out, the destruction of Pan Am 103 in 1988, and the death of Meseratch Zecharias in 1997.

Passengers aboard Flight 103 on December 21, 1988, included thirty-five Syracuse students (including some Library workers) returning from a semester abroad in London. Term was just ending and our students were heading home for their holidays so the mourning on campus was somewhat muted and a good chance to reflect on the loss and plan a memorial service for January 18, 1989. I still come to tears when I remember that event in our indoor stadium, the Carrier Dome. Over 15,000 people attended and few could have been unmoved. The Syracuse Symphony Orchestra, conducted by Kasuyoshi Akiyama, performed the "Nimrod Variation" from Elgar's *Enigma Variations*, and several Syracuse University choral groups combined with the Symphony to perform sections of Mendelssohn's *Elijah* and Mozart's *Requiem*. Eloquent but brief laments were given by Chaplain Richard Phillips, novelist Douglas Ungar representing the faculty, Governor Mario Cuomo, Senator Daniel Moynihan, and Chancellor Melvin Eggers. All were affecting in different ways and somehow the whole tragedy brought the campus together for a time—never have I been so proud of an institution to which I belonged.

Meseratch Zecharias, age 52, was a much-loved reference librarian and subject specialist from Eritrea who was murdered by her son, probably while he was in a drug-induced state. The effect on the Library staff was devastating. Thanks largely to the pastoral work of our Associate University Librarian for Reader Services, Carol Parke, an Episcopalian lay counsellor, we somehow weathered the trauma. For the very emotional funeral service I joined several other staff in participating, and at a further memorial service in Hendricks Chapel I offered a brief eulogy. Her death still seems inexplicable.

One irony of my time at Syracuse was that its vision when I came in 1986 was to reach what we called "the next tier of excellence" among research universities, irreverently known as NTOE, to be seen as equals among the likes of Duke, Northwestern, Emory, and others. Thus I was hired as someone thought to be a hotshot research librarian, and it was true that I enjoyed a fairly high status in the ARL community. That vision of the University became quite murky during my first four years and then pretty much disappeared in the early days of the Buzz Shaw administration when the vision was rearticulated "to be the leading student-centered research university," equally irreverently dubbed SCRU by skeptics. The emphasis was completely refocused on the undergraduate as customer/consumer, with the research component getting little more than a perfunctory pat on the head. We did our best to argue that there was no better laboratory for a student-centered research university than our Special Collections, and we did have some success in demonstrating that potential.

As to the undergraduate consumer, Shaw introduced a management scheme already alluded to, TQM or Total Quality Management, which he rechristened as SUIQ. On the office wall before me as I type in July 2013 is a handsome poster depicting the campus quad, the text of the vision statement quoted above, and a signed inscription from Buzz reading "David, many thanks for your contributions to reaching our vision, Buzz." I've not yet figured out how to react to that except to say that SUIQ did bring an emphasis on good service quality that should have been there at the outset.

The process of shifting from research priorities to undergraduate pampering continues long after my retirement, and reached its nadir in 2011 when the University, reading the handwriting on the wall, withdrew from the Association of American Universities (AAU), knowing that the Association was about to disqualify us because of an insufficient research agenda and a dearth of research funding. Nancy Cantor had become our new Chancellor in 2004 bringing an emphasis on town-gown relations and a new mantra of "Scholarship in Action." Like so many times in my life what was promoted as scholarship was really public relations. But in retirement and with a convenient home in the History Department, I was able to pursue my own *vita contemplativa* over the *vita activa*. Much criticized though she was by the faculty, in Cantor's defense I can say that she did the only two things I asked of her, bringing the Paul Taylor Dance Company to Syracuse for both residencies and performances with the Syracuse Symphony, and for helping to bring the Shen Wei Dance Company to campus. Cantor has announced her resignation from Syracuse for 2014 and is moving on to head Rutgers University's Newark campus.

During my twelve years at Syracuse, the longest job I ever held, I had the privilege of presenting for honorary degrees a number of distinguished individuals who were or became good friends: librarian and musicologist Carleton Sprague Smith, opera composer Carlisle Floyd, opera manager Paul Kellogg, and Tudor historian and philanthropist Vernon Snow. Also among them was Dorothy Porter Wesley, the doyenne of African-American bibliography, someone who was told as a youth that blacks had no history, and who spent her life disproving that contention.

The tradition at Syracuse is to hold a Commencement Eve dinner for all graduating students and their parents in the Carrier Dome, usually for about 2000 people, with the honorary degree recipients getting the podium for a few inspirational words. In 1989, Dorothy Porter Wesley was in her mid-80s, both in age and probably in weight as well. Since she was quite frail and wearing very high heels, I escorted her hand in hand to the podium. With the klieg lights blazing, she began in a tremulous voice, to some hushed concern from the audience: "As you can see, I'm a very old lady and I want you to know that I'm suffering from an incurable disease; at least I've never heard of a cure, or met anyone who has been cured. [Gasps.] I'm a bibliomaniac. [Pause.] I love books." She won the audience, and then walking with her around campus after Commencement the next day, one could feel the strength that our African-American students drew from her example. Her self-description as bibliomaniac sums up a good deal of my life too, and it's humbling to think that little if any of what I've accomplished and recorded here would have happened if poor eyesight, no doubt due to excessive early reading, hadn't prevented a potentially promising career as a naval officer.

One surprising arrival in Syracuse was an old friend, Robert Wedgeworth, a librarian with whom we had long associations. He was Executive Director of the American Library Association when I first met him in the 1970s. He had been Dean of the Columbia School of Library Service when Deirdre taught there in 1985, and saw it through until the school closed in 1992. He then spent six years as Librarian at the University of Illinois, several of them overlapping as President of IFLA (International Federation of Library Associations) before a short-lived retirement in 1999. He came to Syracuse in 2002 as President of Laubach Literacy International which soon merged with Literacy Volunteers International to become Pro Literacy International, a merger that he helped orchestrate. For some reason Syracuse is a center for literacy movements and the Syracuse University Library the center for archives of adult education and literacy organizations. We knew Bob in all of his various capacities since ALA and enjoyed his presence in Syracuse. We were especially pleased when he received an honorary Doctor of Humane Letters degree from Syracuse in 2008.

Another friend and *sui generis* bibliomaniac in Syracuse cannot pass unnoticed. It was Professor Mary Marshall who regularly brightened our lives during our first fifteen years in Syracuse until her death at 97 in 2000. Mary was the daughter of a Presbyterian minister who also had been President of Connecticut College. She graduated from Vassar College in 1924 and earned her Yale doctorate in English Literature (medieval her specialty) in 1932. She spent some time teaching literature to cowboys in Montana after Yale, and then a few years at Colby College between then and her appointment as "the token skirt" in the Syracuse English Department in 1948. Her passion was drama in general and Shakespeare in particular, and she retained her memory of texts, plots, casts, directors, and all things dramatic well into her nineties.

Mary "retired" as Professor Emerita (the first woman full Professor in our College of Arts and Sciences) in 1970, starting a second career two years later in "adult education," teaching drama in our University College and guiding and participating in theatre trips to London for many years. A coterie of devoted friends and students formed around Mary and repeatedly took her courses. In her declining years those friends formed a Mary Circle, assuring that every evening at cocktail hour someone would be there to pour the bourbon.

At her 85th birthday party I learned that she had regularly attended the Metropolitan Opera when she was a student at Vassar in the twenties, but that she had never been to its new building at Lincoln Center, opened in 1966. Only half facetiously I offered to take her there for her 90th birthday, thinking it a fairly unlikely prospect. But she reminded me every year and in 1993 we had our date. We drove down with my daughter Kathryn as chaperone, stayed at the University's Lubin House on East 60th Street, and had a grand time. The opera was Mozart's *Magic Flute*, observed from the 6th row center orchestra. I do not exaggerate in saying she was like a transported child. On the trip home I promised to take her to the New York City Ballet for her 95th birthday, but halfway through the year I told her that I thought we had better accelerate the schedule. "I think that would be very wise." So we made the same trip for her 91st, this time with Deirdre, for a performance of *Sleeping Beauty*. The coup at this performance was a backstage tour during intermission where we circled the back of the stage from stage left while the set was being changed. At the very back of the stage she said that she could see where this was leading, namely over to Peter Martins, famed dancer and then head of the New York City Ballet, at stage right where he was primed to be charming and they chatted with great animation for over five minutes before we rushed back to our seats. Gladys Delmas had been very generous to the NYCB, and Peter had good reason to be grateful. Mary survived for another seven years but was no longer able to travel. Contemporary legend has it that her last words to her doctor were: "I'm going now, and this time you can't stop me."

Chapter IV

"The Abbreviation of Time"
September 1998 to December 2013

"It will turn out fine in the end. If it's not fine, it's not the end."
From the 2012 movie, *The Best Exotic Marigold Hotel*

Busier than Ever
September 1998 to the Present

I'd like to say a word about how my working life as a librarian ended exactly forty years after my library assignment on the *USS Galveston* and how I plunged into retirement. At some point in 1994 during a London trip I happened to run into Richard Landon of the University of Toronto Library on the portico of the British Museum and British Library. He told me that he was enjoying a British Library Non-Stipendiary Fellowship, not very lucrative but very helpful in easing access to the BL and its extraordinary book and manuscript holdings. He suggested that I might enjoy one too. I did apply for and receive one of those fellowships to pursue my project of reconstructing Leigh Hunt's personal library. The fellowship helped persuade my boss, Gershon Vincow, that the honor should not be declined and that I should have a considerable amount of research leave in the next year.

Although I did not relinquish my job, the fellowship enabled me to spend four or five three-week periods in London during 1995-1996, working both at the British Library and the London Library. During one visit I had an epiphany that it was time to stop working for wages and shift my focus to my own work and the archival pleasures of reading other people's mail, while spending other people's money for the Delmas Foundation. Our own finances were at last in decent shape, Deirdre was gainfully employed, TIAA pension funds looked healthy, and some additional income from Foundation work seemed to make retirement feasible. Although both my boss and my wife were reluctant, I did retire in August 1998 at age 63 and turned to other things. By early 2000 Deirdre and I had agreed to curate a major Polar exhibition for the Grolier Club, scheduled for December 2005. Deirdre's subsequent employment running a rare book librarianship program at Long Island University's Palmer School of Library and Information Science at its Manhattan site oriented us much more toward New York City. For the next decade a modest apartment in the City allowed us to take full advantage of the performing arts pleasures afforded by our Delmas Foundation connections. For most of the period we averaged well over one hundred performing arts events per year. Completion of my *International Dictionary of Library Histories* in 2001 and preparation of the exhibition over the next five years made adjustment to retirement easy and regret-free.

Another irony of my library career is that for the last twenty years (1978-1998) I'd been at unionized institutions and generally had good relations with the union leaders. Although I'd been picketed lots of times, particularly on Fifth Avenue and in Harlem, the only day in which I'd been running a library during a strike was the last day of my career, August 31, 1998. The next morning my former colleagues were picketing outside the Library when my successor, Peter Graham, newly arrived from Rutgers, brought them a good supply of donuts. I thought that a good omen. Less so was a Hail and Farewell party on Labor Day at Randy Ericson's home to welcome Peter and bid me adieu from the Library. It was an oppressively hot and muggy evening, ending with a "derecho," a storm which cut a narrow but very destructive path through Syracuse and beyond, including our house and yard which lost about ten trees and suffered more damage. Fortunately, Kathryn's then husband Suthin Munawet and her step children were staying with us and Suthin was very handy with our chain saw. Peter Graham's time at Syracuse was not always easy and unfortunately he succumbed to cancer after only six years in office. It's a weird experience to be predeceased by one's successor.

It's an axiom of library administration that institutional responsibilities and personal collecting often involve implicit or blatant conflicts of interest, and must be avoided. Book collecting librarians are particularly vulnerable to this temptation. Deirdre and I had lots of books in our personal accumulation over the years, but with one exceptional subject, they were not bought as a coherent attempt to build a collection, create an investment, or qualify for membership in the Grolier Club. Rather they reflected whatever subjects we had worked on throughout our lives or which happened to interest us: English and American literature, art history, bibliography, British church history, John Calvin, Egyptology, philosophy of history, and Polar studies. I made a personal exception to the proscribed rules for library administrators, namely in collecting the work of and about Leigh Hunt (1784-1859). My self-serving rationalization was that such collecting was not in conflict with the institutions I worked for, and that the books would go eventually to some public institution that would take care of them. That collection now comprises about eighty works by Hunt, including many first editions and variants, one book owned and annotated by Hunt himself (I had given another Hunt-owned and signed book to the University of Iowa), and a rather spotty collection of works about him. Now, toward the end of 2013, we are looking for a home for that collection, at a time when interest in Hunt seems to be rising. Our other significant collection, the Polar collection, was mainly put together in retirement and that too is now seeking a home. Negotiations have begun. Although it's difficult to give up books that meant a lot to us, or which we meant to read but haven't, we are now ambivalently looking for good places for our collections with only moderate progress so far.

Amusements in Retirement
1998—The Present

When I was still collecting Leigh Hunt I bought the book alluded to above, a copy of *Amusements in Retirement; or, the Influence of Science, Literature, and the Liberal Arts, on the Manners and Happiness of Private*

Life. By the Author of the "Philosophy of Nature." Second Edition, by Charles Bucke, a copy owned and lightly annotated by Hunt. It joined a growing collection of our books intended for retirement reading, including an almost complete run of *History and Theory* with its often impenetrable prose. I've made some perceptible but small progress on the accumulated reading matter in the last fourteen years of retirement, though I've yet to read Bucke's *Amusements* and only a little of *History and Theory*. An additional ten shelves of books and journals on the philosophy of history continue to gather dust in the "barn," a converted garage/studio that serves as our book depository.

Retirement from Syracuse also meant retirement from the Board of Governors of the Research Libraries Group, a Board that I had served for twenty years with only a brief break. At my RLG farewell obsequies in June of 1998 I received the usual plaque and clock, a tie, and a Leigh Hunt first edition. A few weeks later I received a personal letter from Jim Michalko, the President of RLG as it then was (it subsequently merged with OCLC), which was a tribute beyond my just deserts but which I still cherish:

> July 13, 1998: You didn't know it then so let me tell you now. This organization has the mission it does and has continued to pursue it across many changes in higher education, technology and libraries because of you and your example. In the early days it was your leadership and more recently because of your example and the reminders you provided. Scholarship in the humanities and social sciences is honored in the breach and the current generation of library directors (mine, unfortunately) doesn't stand up in its defense in the meaningful ways they should. An outfit like RLG is always going to struggle—we've made the poor and demanding our special focus. It would have been very easy to drift away. Whenever that was the danger you spoke up. You reminded people why this is important and it was worth soldiering on. For that, RLG, libraries, and the scholars who don't know you are in your debt.

That seemed to me high praise indeed, but it also reflected my tendency to provide the lone dissenting vote on many issues. Nonetheless, I gratefully filed his encomium away for subsequent discovery and disillusionment. RLG was developed to concentrate on the needs of scholarship and provide for the needs of research in a collaborative framework. When RLG merged into OCLC in 2006, although some of that research emphasis remained, the original *raison d'être* was greatly diminished. The greatest misfortune for me personally and I imagine for many other scholars was the loss of RLIN, the Research Libraries Information Network, the best tool for scholarly research that I had ever used. It was replaced by OCLC's WorldCat, a huge but far less sophisticated tool that master bibliographer Donald Krummel once described as "the Walmart of bibliography." I attended the "celebration" of the merger, held at the New York Public Library in June of 2006; to me it seemed the celebration of the death of a dream. I was only glad that RLIN survived long enough for me to complete my *International Dictionary of Library Histories* and for us to complete our Polar exhibit, *Books on Ice*, two works that consumed much of my first eight years of retirement and would have been much more difficult without RLIN.

My appointment as University Librarian at Syracuse in 1986 gave me the sense that I'd found a home for the rest of my life. My retirement in 1998 confirmed the end of my constant itinerancy, though it also marked a period of extensive travel (Iceland, Britain, Italy, China, and Thailand, all in the first year). While it is fair to say that Deirdre faithfully supported my career choices, sometimes suggesting others, she never languished as the bored suburban housewife. As the subsidiary bread winner, she obligingly followed me around until Syracuse when the children were grown and mostly out of the nest. Let me take a moment to summarize what she did after we left Marlboro in 1967. We arrived in Chicago with three children under three, a maternal handful by any account, but not enough to stop her art historical pursuits at the Art Institute of Chicago. After some curatorial work in the Prints and Drawings Department she served as an Assistant to the Museum's Directors, Charles Cunningham and John Maxon, before becoming Assistant Curator for Classical Art, building on her Institute of Fine Arts Masters degree in Egyptology.

During my five years at Johns Hopkins, Deirdre taught art history at the Bryn Mawr School while adding two master's degrees to her resumé, one in Education from Hopkins, and another from Catholic University in Library Science. Her first library job after the latter degree was as a reference librarian at the Baltimore County Public Library in

Towson, Maryland. Our longer eight-year period in New York provided opportunities for greater variety and her timing was perfect in that her first assignment was at the Metropolitan Museum of Art as special coordinator to the Tutankhamen blockbuster exhibition that opened soon after we arrived. Her duties included everything from assisting in the unpacking of the exhibition objects to arranging housing for visiting Egyptian dignitaries. She interviewed for a job as administrative assistant to the Museum President, but lost interest when he asked such now illegal questions as what time she could get to work after getting children to school, and whether she had to prepare dinner for her husband every night. She then spent a year as reference librarian and art history bibliographer at the SUNY Purchase Library, when she also took on a part-time job as Executive Director of the Bibliographical Society of America whose President was then Marcus McCorison. Seeing a real library career in the offing, she left Purchase, hardly her favorite job, to start a doctoral program at Columbia University's School of Library Science, a degree she completed in what seemed a record four years, with a dissertation on the information-seeking practices of art historians. For our last two years in New York she was teaching in the School. In the following years she alternated teaching with administration at a variety of institutions: Syracuse University, the Museum Computer Network, Catholic University of America, the New York Center for the Book, and Drew University, retiring finally from Long Island University.

Our work with Terry Belanger and Rare Book School helped Deirdre engage more heavily in the world of rare books and special collections. In 2001 Michael Koenig, Dean of the Palmer School of Information Science at Long Island University, asked Deirdre to develop a program in rare book librarianship to be based in Manhattan at NYU's Bobst Library. Briefly, it led to the most fulfilling time of her professional life, nine years of stimulating students, an extensive network of connections in the book world, and an impressive number of publications including our co-edited *Books on Ice*. For the longer story someone should persuade her to write her own memoirs. By 2011 Deirdre had become quite experienced in the art of retirement, and this time made it permanent, apart, that is, from her new duties with the Delmas Foundation and consulting for the Sultanate of Oman in 2012 and 2013.

My major preoccupation in the first three years of retirement, 1998 to 2001, was the editing of an *International Dictionary of Library Histories* for the Chicago publisher, Fitzroy Dearborn. One of the editors there had floated the idea to Marty Runkle, Director of the University of Chicago Library and a close friend, and he in turn put them in touch with me. I accepted the challenge having only a vague idea of the difficulties of keeping about 200 contributors on track and under control, of editing every article, especially those written by ESL beginners, combining historical analysis with a reasonable amount of institutional public relations, and trying to maintain a fair balance among the many famous libraries under consideration. The result was a two-volume, 1100-page reference work of some inevitable unevenness published in September 2001, shortly after 9/11. It could never have been done in such a short time without email. Just before publication Fitzroy Dearborn had been negotiating their acquisition by Oxford University Press, a possibility that abruptly ended with 9/11. Thus it languished a bit in a publisher's limbo, although it was named one of NYPL's Best Reference Books of 2001. Three years of near full-time labor for $10,000, royalties of about $700, and six free copies can rightly be called a labor of love, and I did love it. Come to think of it, that nearly equals my total salary for my first three years at NYPL. I spent a great deal of time formulating my thoughts on library history for the introduction to the work, a sobering analysis of the perilous condition of libraries in their history of success and failure, the inevitable decay, and the constant hopes that they represent. I wrote it in August 2001, just as the Taliban were destroying various Buddhist icons, and I related that desecration to the fate of libraries.

In its dedication I paid tribute to some of the many people who had helped me in forming my views of librarianship, many of them already deceased:

Dedicated To the Memory of **Gladys Krieble Delmas (1913-1991)**
And to my own colleagues and mentors who believed, with me, in the sharing of knowledge, its preservation, and dissemination:

Robert Allen	Richard Macksey
Patricia Battin	Joseph C. Mitchell
Timothy H. Breen	Paul Mosher
Richard W. Couper	Alice Prochaska
Arthur Curley	Thomas Ragle

David V. Erdman	Robert Shackleton
Vartan Gregorian	Lacey Baldwin Smith
Warren J. Haas	Deirdre C. Stam
Donald W. Krummel	Lawrence W. Towner
Patricia H. Labalme	James M. Wells
Antje B. Lemke	Walter Muir Whitehill

Alexander Wilson.

All of these friends and colleagues appear somewhere in these memoirs. I sent a copy of the dedication page to each of the surviving dedicatees. Among the pleasing responses was a formal note from Gregorian, then at Brown University, with a handwritten postscript: "You are wonderful!" Somehow it reminded me of my relationship to my father.

One serious amusement came in 2000 by way of an invitation from Terry Belanger to conduct an external review of Rare Book School in Charlottesville, Virginia. Deirdre and I had had long associations with Belanger, going back to my days at NYPL and hers at Columbia's School of Library Science where she had been Terry's student and later his faculty colleague. Terry had founded Rare Book School at Columbia in 1983, an institute with a close relationship to the Book Arts Press, the bibliographical laboratory Belanger set up at the School in 1972. Over the years we both developed a real affection for that sometimes curmudgeonly character, an erstwhile fellow bassoonist. When Columbia in its dubious wisdom decided in 1990 to close the Library School where RBS had started, an angered Belanger took the opportunity to seek a new venue for RBS. In 1992 he was appointed University Professor at the University of Virginia where he moved the whole school, its presses, its tools, and its teaching collections, every lock, stock, and barrel. It is surprising today to realize that RBS has survived and thrived at the University of Virginia for twice as long as it struggled at Columbia.

Our sense was that in 2000 Belanger was feeling some intimations of mortality as he approached 65 and had experienced the death of a close friend. In effect he asked us to advise him on the future of a School that was largely his own creation and for which he did everything, from curricular decisions to coffee making. At the time there was an outside possibility that RBS could move to Long Island University if a sizable endowment might be dedicated to the School. I quote from the beginning of our report:

> The consultants were invited by Terry Belanger (TB), Director of the Book Arts Press and the Rare Book School (BAP/RBS), to examine the operations of the Press and School, to elicit local and national opinion about the school, and to make recommendations for BAP/RBS intended to assure its survival and viability in the near term as well as to outline potential scenarios for the post-Belanger era. We spent the period from September 10 to September 14 [2000] in Charlottesville, observing the extent of the facilities and programs, interviewing many University of Virginia affiliates of the program (UVA administrators, faculty, librarians, etc.), the staff of the Press, the Director himself, local book dealers, and regional supporters. In addition we met with several members of the organization's Board and Advisory Committee in other venues, communicated with persons in other academic institutions who are involved with BAP/RBS issues from a variety of perspectives, corresponded by email with a number of faculty and students of RBS, and explored every avenue of opinion accessible to us.

Our pro bono effort was amply rewarded by a week of good food and wine, a great deal of intellectual stimulation, and a wonderful print, now hanging in a downstairs bathroom, of a typewriter made up of all sorts of bassoon parts. The report had a number of recommendations, some of which Terry implemented, a few of which he ignored, and a couple more of which re-emerged after Terry was succeeded in 2009 by Michael Suarez, S.J. One fairly obvious one was to obtain IRS 501.c.3 nonprofit status as a charitable institution, dropping the misleading name of the Book Arts Press. Previously, fund-raising had come through an informal friends group, called at first the Friends of the Book Arts Press, and later the Friends of the Rare Book School. One disadvantage of this recommendation for Terry was that it meant a possible loss of control to a Board of Directors required by the law for non-profit organizations. We strongly urged that RBS remain in Charlottesville as a bibliographical milieu and support system that was unlikely to be matched elsewhere.

Both those recommendations were accepted and both the charitable status and the Virginia location are the case today.

Another recommendation, that RBS become more intimately connected to the academic side of its University, particularly with its undergraduate community, saw less progress before Terry's retirement as Director in 2009. Perhaps it was a part of our recommendations that was both more time-consuming and less congenial to him, especially after he became a MacArthur Foundation Fellow in 2005, a new source of funding which he used to great advantage for the well-being of the School. His successor, Michael Suarez, no doubt chosen in part to address that need for greater integration, appears to us to have helped further to integrate RBS within the University. He too has become a friend. As a former lacrosse player at Bucknell and sometime coach at LeMoyne College in Syracuse, Michael flew up to Syracuse for a day in 2011 and again in 2013 to attend Hopkins vs. Syracuse lacrosse matches, and, ever the teacher, he gave us game-long tutorials in that fascinating sport.

Retirement did not mean leaving the lecture circuit and, without seeking speaking engagements, they continued to pour in for twelve years. Beijing in 1998 on preservation; Brown University in 2000 on Special Collections; Copenhagen, Anchorage, and Fairbanks, Alaska in 2002, Edinburgh in 2003, all on Polar reading; Ottawa in 2004 on Arctic Survivals (a preservation paper with John Dean); a Rare Book School talk at the Grolier Club in early 2006; the Linda Hall Library in Kansas City, Missouri, in May 2006; Research Society for Victorian Periodicals in Richmond, Virginia, in 2007 on polar expeditionary periodicals; a joint appearance in Toronto in 2008 on shipboard reading, to name several. It all came to an end in April 2012 after a particularly ineffective talk I gave at the University of Southern Illinois in Carbondale. I had been invited for four days as part of an Antarctic series and I had a fairly good paper on Antarctic reading prepared. But it was misapplied to the audience, only one of whom knew much about the subject matter, and as Deirdre said I kept interrupting myself with digressions.[75] I knew I'd committed the unpardonable sin of boring other people. Furthermore my speech was beginning to be affected by ALS and Deirdre rightly told me it was time to stop. She now gets the invitations and that's fine with me.

To return to our Marlboro classicist of 1964-65, Geoffrey Fallows, I can recount a fascinating trip with him in 2002. We kept up consistently with Geoffrey over many years, getting to know his wife Caroline whose warmth and candor were so refreshing, following the fortunes of their two daughters in London and Newcastle, and making frequent reciprocal visits to all of our homes and educational institutions, the last being Syracuse in the US and the Camden School for Girls in the UK. One winter around 1995 we drove to Stratford for a performance of *The Spanish Tragedy*, the play in which Geoffrey had played a starring role at Marlboro 35 years earlier. A few months after Caroline died in 2001, under the guise of business we spent ten days with Geoffrey in the UK, visiting Shrewsbury School, the Lake District and Dove Cottage, Stratford, and Winchester School. My Delmas-related idea and the excuse for the trip was a project to fund some conversations between librarians of English public schools with significant rare book collections and their American private school counterparts, discussions which I thought could help exploit their collections by educating their students in the fascinating world of books. At Shrewsbury, where both Nicholas Barber and Geoffrey had been students, we found a sympathetic audience; at Winchester despite their splendid collections, we did not. Nothing ever came of the idea, but we thought we were providing excellent distractions for Geoffrey in his period of mourning. He was happy to introduce us to his beloved Lake District where he had often hiked with Caroline on school vacations. At Dove Cottage we had some fascinating discussions with Director Robert Woof about their needs for which the Delmas

---

[75] For years in public talks I had quoted a line from Justice Felix Frankfurter to the effect that he had only two problems in public speaking, "that I depart from my text, and that I return to it," and now I was caught in the same problem. I once told that to Doris Kearns Goodwin when she was visiting the Seward House Museum in Auburn, New York. When she volunteered that her husband had clerked for Frankfurter, I told her she should feel free to steal the line as I had, a rather cheeky response in that she had recently been involved in a plagiarism controversy.

Foundation might be helpful. But Woof had some other visitors that week from the National Lottery Heritage Fund from which Dove Cottage was seeking a large capital grant, and Woof thought it best to keep these two potential funders apart. The leader of the Lottery group was our friend Michael Smethurst (another fellow smoker), recently retired from the British Library where he had been Alex Wilson's successor and the main person responsible for moving the Library to its new St. Pancras site. You can imagine Deirdre's surprise when she ran into Michael's wife Mary in the gift shop. We did eventually all get together for a meal, having a good laugh about Robert's stratagem. Dove Cottage eventually got both their grant from the Lottery fund to build a new building and, much later, a grant from the Delmas Foundation to help process their growing archival collections, unfortunately the latter after Woof had died.

Despite some inconveniences occasioned by an outbreak of foot and mouth disease, we went on from there to Stratford for an enchanting weekend house party at the Stratford home of Philip and Jane Rylands. We had met the Rylands in Venice, where Philip is the Director of the Peggy Guggenheim Museum, and had met several times over grants to improve their library and over other mutual interests. Jane was an American from Perrysburg, Ohio (a town we had visited often), who had spent several years as Peggy Guggenheim's assistant; she has also published two volumes of short stories with Venetian settings. Their house in Stratford, a converted B and B, was a five-minute walk from Stratford's main stage and on our first night there we walked over to see the *Duchess of Malfi*. The following day, a Saturday, we crossed the street to visit the Shakespeare Institute in the former home of English novelist Marie Corelli, and after lunch the Shakespeare Birthplace Trust. Dinner that night was a grand affair with numerous guests: Benet and Joyce Hytner, the parents of Nicholas Hytner (until recently the head of the National Theatre), Peter Holland, Geoffrey, and the Stams. Joyce was a fund raiser for a number of arts organizations, including the Old Vic. Peter Holland, Director of the Shakespeare Institute, was there with his American wife from Notre Dame—he followed her to South Bend that same year and is now an Associate Dean at the University. I can't remember who else was there, but with those guests plus the Rylands and Geoffrey, it made for a very lively table.

At that time the Rylands had a son in Winchester School and that connection gave us the contact we needed for our visit to that aristocratic bastion two days later. We found a beautiful campus, some fascinating collections (partly thanks to Lord John Eccles,[76] the Second Viscount Eccles and husband of Mary Hyde Eccles, both fellow Grolierites), one Sterne scholar very interested in the library, but an aristocratic smugness that we found irritating. Our trip ended in London with a Conor McPherson play, *Port Authority*. We prided ourselves that we had provided some relief for Geoffrey in a difficult time, only to learn soon afterwards from the characteristically taciturn Geoffrey that he was already courting Caroline's best friend, Johanna, a fellow nurse after whom one of the Fallows children is named, and whom Geoffrey would soon marry. We were very happy for them. We saw them twice in 2010, first in July at Ted and Mary Wendell's summer home in Maine, and in October in Boston at Ted's 70th birthday celebration. Geoffrey now has Parkinson's disease and is adjusting to it much as I am to ALS.

Two years later (2003) we had a very odd experience related to the Rylands. Because of our Venetian connections a fairly good friend had arranged for us to have dinner in New York with John Berendt, author of *Midnight in the Garden of Good and Evil* (1994), who was then working on a book about Venice that would be published as *City of Falling Angels* (2005). Berendt was from Syracuse, had gone to Nottingham High School just down the hill from our house, was an important writer, and was interested in Venice, so we expected a stimulating evening. We felt ambushed half way through the meal when we realized that the purpose of this meeting was to get quotable dirt on the Rylands, whom he regarded as part of the evil influences of Venice, and especially Jane's relation to the Ezra Pound estate and legacy. It gradually became clear that he was planning to do for Venice what he had done to Savannah, wreak havoc and leave town. Deirdre was seated next to Berendt and endured

---

[76] Lord Eccles attended both Winchester School and Magdalen College, Oxford, and began book collecting and selling at an early age. Alongside its earlier collections, his gifts to Winchester make its Library even more impressive. He was a minister in various Tory governments and spear-headed the move to create a British Library separate from the British Museum. In 1973 he became the BL's First Chairman. We had lunch at the Princeton Club early in the 1980s when he reminisced about the early years of the BL. I recall that he was particularly pleased by the appointment of Alex Wilson as General Director.

the thrust of his attack, but across the table I could overhear some of his questions such as "why do you like them?" When published the book had a brief mention of the Delmas Foundation and a long hatchet job on the Rylands, but we gave him no ammunition to be used against our friends.

Another worthwhile endeavor of the early twenty-first century led in turn to the most painful incident for me of that decade. Shortly after my *International Dictionary of Library Histories* was published in 2001, Patsy Labalme informed Joe Mitchell and me by conference call that she had just been diagnosed with pancreatic cancer with its usual grim prognosis. She was most concerned that she would not be able to finish her major project, a substantial selection from the Diaries of Marino Sanudo (1466-1536), the lodestar of Venetian patrician history of the period. When she voiced her worry I told her that I had just finished a major editorial project, was then uncommitted to other projects, and that I would be glad to help in any way I could. I told her that the disadvantage was that I was not a Venetianist, but that the corollary advantage was also that I was not a Venetianist and thus could represent a more general audience.

Patsy jumped at the offer and for the next year until her death in November 2002 I worked almost fulltime on successive versions of the book. We were in frequent email correspondence over the manuscript, and I made four trips to New York to work with her on the book. I read drafts of every chapter at least three times, and worked very hard to track down some very obscure references for the bibliography. Despite the usual editorial differences between editors, she had nothing but gratitude and praise for my work. Her last note to me became her farewell:

> Sept. 5, 2002 David—Henry just brought to my hospital room your work on Ch. VIII. I've been frustrated in not being able to organize my ongoing work and this looks like just what I can do! Many thanks! . . . Love to you both—Patsy

I wrongly assumed that I would continue this labor of love after Patsy's death, assuring the timely appearance of the volume, and assisting Patsy's two specialist collaborators, Laura Sanguineti White and Linda L. Carroll, in seeing it through the Johns Hopkins University Press.

With her death Patsy was succeeded as Delmas Trustee by her widower, George Labalme. Within a month I was saddened by his action of removing me from the Sanudo project, probably because he did not understand the extent of my contribution, and by his finding some new advisors (very good ones, I should say) to complete the book. The work was published in 2008 as *Venice, Città excelentissima: Selections from the Renaissance Diaries of Marin Sanudo* (edited by Patricia H. Labalme and Laura Sanguineti White; translated by Linda L. Carroll) by the Johns Hopkins Press.

A much happier development of my first ten retirement years was engagement with the Polar Libraries Colloquy, a group I had joined several years before but had been too busy to attend. The PLC holds a biennial conference and in September 1998 I went to my first meeting, in Reykjavik, Iceland, en route to some Delmas Foundation activities in Venice. Three people were there who very helpfully mentored me in my newly chosen field of Polar history: Philip Cronenwett of the Stefansson Library at Dartmouth College; William Mills, Librarian of the Scott Polar Research Institute in Cambridge; and David Walton of the British Antarctic Survey, bookseller and publisher of Bluntisham Books. After a brief nap on arrival I flew to the north coast city of Akureyri late the same day in time for a two-day conference on Vilhjalmur Stefansson, honoring the establishment of the Stefansson Institute at the University of Akureyri. The day-long bus trip back to Reykjavik was narrated by a geologist from the University of Iceland who beautifully described the great variety of landforms we were passing through. A trip a few days later during a break in the conference took us to Thingvillir and to Geyser and sealed my fascination with Iceland, its history and its sagas. Ten years later I was able to return with Deirdre, just before the Icelandic bubble burst.

Subsequent meetings of the PLC that we both attended were held in Winnipeg, Copenhagen, Ottawa, and Rome; and Edmonton, which I attended alone in 2008. Each had its own high points, for us the post-Winnipeg train trip to Churchill on Hudson Bay, in Rome the banquet at the American Academy in Rome. The meetings themselves tended toward boilerplate librarianship but the corridor conversation and the shared fellowship made the conferences worthwhile and we regret missing the more recent sessions as diminished mobility and competing events limited our attendance. I particularly value the friendships formed through PLC, particularly David Walton, William Mills, and Kjell Kjar from northern Norway, a student of the *Belgica* expedition and a true explorer of expedition history in Svalbard.

It was on our thirty-six hour train trip from Winnipeg to the Hudson Bay village of Churchill in 2000 that I hatched the project that has consumed much of my time since, only briefly interrupted by the writing of this memoir. On that trip I was reading Sir John Franklin's *Journey to a Polar Sea* in a tidy hardbound German pocket edition when I ran across this passage: "I, therefore, issued directions to deposit at this encampment the dipping needle, azimuth compass, magnet, a large thermometer, and a few books we had carried, having torn out of these, such parts as we should require to work the observations for latitude and longitude." This fairly simple throwaway line raised for me the question of what Polar explorers read during the downtime of their adventures. With whatever downtime I had, I began the search for any sources that might indicate the reading of explorers: journals, diaries, memoirs, logs, autobiographies, biographies, letters, official reports such as the Arctic Blue Books. Deirdre too joined in the search with her casual reading of explorers north and south.

The first product of these searches was a paper we gave at the 2002 Polar Libraries Colloquy called "Silent Friends: the Role of Reading in Polar Exploration." We went on to deliver and publish a number of papers on the subject, and it was the inspiration of the deliberate pun in the title of our Grolier exhibition called *Books on Ice: British & American Literature of Polar Exploration.* We eventually mounted in December 2005 a show based on our own collection but borrowing heavily from Special Collections on the East Coast, and for one item, a Franklin relic, from the National Maritime Museum in Greenwich, England.[77] The exhibit included not only books about Polar exploration but a good number of books that had been taken to the ice and even produced on the ice or on expeditionary ships.

Apart from the exhibit, we had the most fun with a piece called "Bending Time: The Function of Periodicals in Nineteenth-Century Polar Naval Expeditions," which we delivered in 2007 to the RSVP (Research Society for Victorian Periodicals). It was published in the Winter 2008 issue of *Victorian Periodicals Review*, replete with enough

---

[77]   For an account of our experience in preparing the exhibition, see "Innocents on the Ice: the Evolution of an Exhibition," *Gazette of the Grolier Club*, n.s. 57 (2006 [i.e. 2007]) p. 50-60.

typos to be worthy of expedition printing. We've thought from time to time that we might bring our various Polar essays together in a volume tentatively entitled "The Book Cultures of High Latitudes." We have since that Hudson Bay trip in 2000 accumulated a very large data base of exploration reading that badly needs synthesis, what I hope will turn into a rather large online "Anthology of the Polar Reading Experience."

William James Mills, Librarian of the Scott Polar Research Institute, was an officer of Polar Libraries Colloquy (PLC) when I became active in the group. Meeting him for the first time in Iceland, it seemed a case of instant friendship based on shared interests in not only Polar studies, but books more generally and music (William was a talented lutenist). Then an almost stereotypical Cambridge donnish type, he shocked us all by marrying a Taiwanese woman he'd recently met on an Antarctic lecture tour. A few years after their first child he announced on the PLC website that they had produced twins, "two new PLC members." He died in 2004 of cancer but he spent his last three years parenting not only his twins, but also the twin volumes of his *Exploring Polar Frontiers: a Historical Encyclopedia, with Contributions by David Clammer, Sir Ranulph Fiennes, Jenny Mai Handford, Rear Admiral John Myres, Geoff Renner and David Stam* (Santa Barbara, 2003). I had written one modest contribution to his encyclopedia, a piece on expeditionary libraries, so I was more than surprised to find my name on his title page in such celebrated company. Earlier he had written a short article on "Polar Libraries" for my *International Dictionary of Library Histories* (Chicago, 2001), a piece which ended with some comments on the "library" at Elephant Island, that penultimate site of the Shackleton saga. We also developed a strong relationship through the Delmas Foundation which helped support some of William's favorite projects including the preservation of Frank Hurley's *Endurance* photographs and the development of SPRI's "Virtual Shackleton." He is missed still, but I am reliably informed that his widow and three children are thriving.

Retirement in 1998 released me from the moral constraint on personal collecting and it has been a late-life learning experience. Crucial to the planning of the Grolier exhibition, scheduled for December 2005, was a chance meeting in 2002 with an eminent London dealer/collector, Richard Kossov, who had assembled one of the world's finest collections of Antarctic materials, published its catalogue, and then dispersed his collection. He could admiringly be called a condition fetishist, his aim to acquire materials exactly as they were intended when leaving the printer's hand, pristine copies with perfect dust jackets, unblemished decorated bindings, unopened where possible, etc. He candidly told me that he did not sell to libraries because of the harm they often perpetrated against the near-perfect copies he worked so hard to find, what we came to call God's copies.

Frankly, quite apart from the need to bring such standards to the planning of the exhibition, the lesson for me was a hard one. I had spent almost thirty-five years as a library administrator, devoted to wide dissemination of the texts of human civilization, proclaiming the gospel of access, promoting preservation through conservation of the originals and the production of copies in microform or digital surrogates, and paying more than lip service to the importance of the physical artifact. I believed and still believe that our most powerful recruitment tool for both collectors and librarians is to let students handle the rare and beautiful and get the palpable sense of history which the originals can convey. But retirement and becoming a "collector" in the bibliophilic sense has lent new perspectives on these questions—for us, as we considered items for the exhibition and sometimes for our own collection, the artifact began to take on equal importance with the text itself, so that an ex-library copy without dust jacket would no longer do, nor would paperbacks or remainders.

Perhaps I exaggerate my own prior philistinism, but the moral stands: librarians have a lot to learn from collectors and dealers. Perhaps the ethical proscription against personal collecting by librarians needs some modification so that every library leader be advised, permitted, or even required to have at least one obscure non-conflicting area of collecting which will help him or her better to understand the values and motivations of both their donors and special collections staff. I'm being less than half facetious.

One research project which caused me a great deal of work and gave me even greater pleasure was for a talk I gave at a Philadelphia conference called "North by Degree" in May 2008. I had been working for some time on the archives of the Explorers Club dealing with the Lady Franklin Bay Expedition at Fort Conger in northern Ellesmere Island, led by Lt. Adolphus W. Greely of the Army Signal Corps. This was one of two contributions of the United States to the first International Polar Year scheduled for 1881-83 and intended to gather simultaneous scientific observations throughout the Polar world, both Arctic and Antarctic. Apart from the success of the expedition's scientific work, Greely's command was memorable in two respects, the importance of its books and library to the expedition, and the disaster that followed the failure of two relief vessels to rescue Greely's 25 men. Only six survived to be rescued in 1884 after a horrendous winter. My essay, called "Congering the Past: the Books of the Lady Franklin Bay Expedition (1881-1884): Before and After," was published by the American Philosophical Society in October 2013, five years after the talk was delivered, avoiding the posthumous publication that I was anticipating. By contrast, an article I published in Mystic Seaport's online journal *Coriolis* was submitted in March 2012 and after peer review was published in June of that year, winning Mystic Seaport's Morris Prize for their best article of the year.[78]

Now, fifteen years into retirement, I would describe myself as a full-time Polar historian, concentrating chiefly on the reading of Polar explorers, diverted for the moment by recovered memories. (In 2012 I took a personal sabbatical from Polar studies to write these autobiographical memoirs.) Our writing and speaking on Polar subjects has created a set of relationships to Polar writers, enthusiasts, scientists, now many of them good friends. I can't begin to describe them all but will name a few: Northern Pacific fur trade expert, John Bockstoce of South Dartmouth, Massachusetts; Jeff Clarke of Portsmouth, New Hampshire, a doctor who has made Ellesmere Island and the Greely expedition his own sovereign territory; Doug Wamsley, a lawyer from Ridgewood, New Jersey, who has a canny ability "to make his own luck" in finding and buying obscure but important Arctic archives; Russell Potter of Providence, Rhode Island, prolific writer and commentator on all things Arctic; and Fritz Nelson of the University of Delaware and now of Milwaukee, Wisconsin, who combines his field of permafrost with a deep interest in the archives that provide so much of the history of the Arctic and Antarctic.

---

[78] "The Lord's Librarians: The American Seamen's Friend Society and their Loan Libraries, 1837-1967. An Historical Excursion with some Unanswered Questions." *Coriolis: An Interdisciplinary Journal of Maritime History* III (June 2012) p. 45-59, Appendix p. i-xiv (Published online by Mystic Seaport Museum, and awarded its Gerald E. Morris Prize for best *Coriolis* article of 2012-13).

Greenland's Icy Mountains and Beyond
Summer 2007

I reserve for individual treatment Robert Bullock of the New York State Archives Partnership Trust and the now retired Public Relations Officer of the 109th Air Wing of the New York Air National Guard, Scotia, New York. I first met Bob at an informal business lunch in Syracuse with Chris Ward, New York State Archivist, where we were discussing possible grants from the Delmas Foundation. In the course of the meal, I casually mentioned our interest in the Polar Regions and something about our exhibition. Here again the thin line of chance crossed my path, and I learned to my uninformed amazement that the 109th Wing was the chief contractor with the National Science Foundation for logistical support to NSF scientific programs in Greenland and Antarctica. A fleet of C-130s, the Hercules or Herks, equipped with skis, did the heavy lifting in both domains.

We kept in touch and a few years later Bullock was planning his annual press week for the Greenland program and invited me to join the expedition and write about it. After a Sunday afternoon polo match in Saratoga Springs and a night at his home there, we woke early to get to the air base in good time. We left Scotia, a suburb of Schenectady, early on a crisp and clear Monday morning in June, flying over Quebec and Labrador, across the Davis Strait to Kangerlussuaq on the Greenland west coast at about 67° N. (I had not been in Schenectady since August 1955 and naturally I felt that life was coming full circle since my youthful visit fifty years before.)

The Herk is a lumbering and cumbersome craft, the passenger cabin equipped with four parallel rows of webbed seating facing inward from behind the flight deck to the front of the cargo hold. There was a large pipe for a pissoire at the front of the main cabin, and a curtained toilet at the back by the open cargo deck. What civilians would call the chief steward was here called the loadmaster. Windows were few and at a premium but most of the newcomers to the trip spent some time on the flight deck seeing the spectacular views. Despite the minimal comfort, passengers (military, scientist, press corps) managed to sleep or read, eating snacks that each had brought along (roughly the level of service we experience on domestic airliners today). The six-hour flight brought us to the small town of Kangerlussuaq at the end of Greenland's longest fjord,

Søndre Strømfjord. The town itself was dominated by the airport that served both military and commercial purposes.

Among a few tourist-like activities was a thirty-mile car trip to the Wallace Glacier, where our Danish tour guide and host, who had been in Greenland for twenty-three years, described how the face of that glacier was now reduced in height by about a third since he had arrived. Near the glacier face we dined *al fresco* on grilled fish and muskox T-bone steaks. We had two C-130 flights to the interior icecap planned for the week. One, to a weather station called Raven (which also served as an NSF research site), was routine and uneventful, and we returned early enough to take our late afternoon trip to the glacier. (It was the week of the summer solstice and night was no more than a couple of hours of twilight and dawn.) The goal of the second trip was to a place called Summit, a major scientific station for meteorological and ice core studies, atop two miles of ice in the frozen heart of Greenland.

The second trip, planned for Wednesday, was delayed by weather at Summit, though we were experiencing warm and sunny days at sea level. The delay was fortuitous because we were free to do whatever we wished on that day. I took in the small museum devoted to the importance in World War II of the airbase at the end of Søndre Strømfjord (i.e., Kangerlussuaq) as a crucial supply base. In the afternoon I visited a building housing an outfit called KISS (Kangerlussuaq International Science Support), dedicated to scientific research in Greenland. As always, I was checking out their modest library facilities when I learned that a well-known and occasionally controversial author on Antarctica, Sara Wheeler, had just arrived from two weeks at Summit.[79] I told someone there that I would like to meet her, that I had used her book called *Terra Incognita* in my honors classes at Syracuse, and left my card and room number at my digs in the Muskox Inn.

An hour later she knocked at my door, an attractive and self-confident woman of forty-five or so. We took a walk and then sat for about an hour in front of the KISS building, where she was waiting for the same van trip to the glacier that we had taken the day before. I learned that after three

---

[79]   Wheeler is a very good writer who is regarded by some of the Polar professionals as too popular and too self-centered to convey more than her personal experience of the polar regions. She had no wish to be or emulate any *jafa*.

books devoted to southerly Polar topics, she was changing her focus to the Arctic. We talked about some of the more fascinating stories of Arctic exploration lore, about useful books that were not overly academic, and even talked about our families. Her book was published in 2009 as *The Magnetic North: Travels in the Arctic Circle*. She was leaving the next day for Svalbard, another stop on her adventures above the Arctic Circle. We met briefly the next day at the airport and compared notes on our mutual experiences of Summit and the glacier. Meeting her left a much more favorable impression than many of her Antarctic colleagues and writers had led me to expect.

The trip to Summit was without doubt one of the most exciting adventures of my life; I can't think of a comparable one ever and to me it illustrates again that familiar thin line of chance. Unbeknownst to me, I was already showing symptoms of amyotrophic lateral sclerosis or ALS. It was diagnosed the following year, but in spring of 2007 I appeared normal enough and I got my cardiologist's approval for the trip. For the Summit trip we were required to wear what seemed to me extremely heavy weather gear. The first problem of that day was that I was barely able to get the clothing on, having lost a great deal of my arm strength to the unrecognized atrophy. But Bob Bullock was good enough to help me and for the rest of the day-long trip kept a careful eye on me.

The coastal areas of Greenland are extremely beautiful, but inland all scenery is absent above the undifferentiated icecap; the scene is without features of any kind, no visual clues to help identify where in this unearthly world you might be. One pilot compared flying over the icecap to flying inside a ping-pong ball, where one could not trust visual sight to tell altitude or assess the horizon. Landing must be completely instrumental. But we did land without incident at roughly 11,000 feet and amid horizontally blowing snow at about 0°F. I did a half-assed job of bundling up and disembarked with Bob, the first goal being one of the research buildings about 100 meters distant. Before getting very far I was having trouble breathing so Bob prudently determined that I had better get some help from the base medic at Summit's main building. He put me on a skidoo (snowmobile) and whisked me off to the dining hall where a kind medic put me on oxygen, gave me a field version of an EKG, checked my vital signs, and let me try to relax and regain some composure. As it happened, the couch where I was recovering was in a corner of the dining hall where the small base library was located. Within ten minutes we were told we had to make an emergency departure before the storm made flying impossible, but I wouldn't leave until I got a few pictures of what I took to be one of the world's highest libraries.

When we got back to the plane someone determined that the best place to keep me hooked up to an oxygen supply was on the flight deck, so I made a shaky climb up five or six ladder steps and settled down in the back of the cabin enjoying the high of pure oxygen. In the cabin were the pilot, co-pilot (a woman), navigator, and engineer. With the wind blowing fiercely the ice runway required rather constant preparation. Our first attempt at takeoff was aborted halfway down the icy runway and we returned to the starting place. There the navigator or engineer stepped off the plane to attach jet-assisted takeoff (or JATO) canisters to help in liftoff. It seemed like a nail biter as the runway flags flashed by but this time we were soon airborne over a vast sea of pure white.

Within ten minutes I was quite comfortable and no longer in need of oxygen. The C-130 flight deck is a very noisy place where communication requires a headset with some sort of speaking apparatus. I was set up with one of these and soon we five on the flight deck were having a long discussion on the history of Greenland. From the beginning of the trip I had been dubbed The Professor, and now they wanted to know what I had to say. Fortunately I had just been teaching my honors course, "Polar Heroes: Myths and Realities," which included quite a bit about Greenland. For over an hour we held this seminar in the sky, dealing with everything from the first population of Greenland, the coming of Christianity, the role of missionaries, and the disappearance of the Nordic colony around 1400, to the present-day politics of the island. It was very stimulating for me, exposing some of my many areas of ignorance, but it all ended when we flew out from above the icecap and began seeing a real landscape and icescape of glaciers and rivers, muskoxen frightened by the engines, the sight of fjords from within, the delight of very colorful coastal villages, the excitement of a mock landing at Jakobshavn without touching down, a final pass over the coastal land and its accompanying icebergs, and then returning to Kangerlussuaq. There I was met by the base medic, given further tests including another EKG and being a bit shaky again, advised to sleep it off. What a trip!

I've often told a story about a Danish friend, the librarian of the Dansk Polar Center in Copenhagen, Vibeke Sloth Jakobsen, someone very familiar with Greenland (in fact our tour guide at the glacier claimed

263

to know her). I once told her that Abraham Lincoln's Secretary of State, William Seward, while acquiring Alaska, also wanted US expansion to extend by purchase to Greenland and even Iceland.[80] Her retort: "if only we'd sold you Greenland and kept the Virgin Islands." Greenland has a raw beauty but it's a financial sinkhole and often a political liability for the Danes.[81] I wrote up accounts of the trip for the Syracuse alumni magazine and for the publication of the Polar Libraries Colloquy.

Naturally enough, Deirdre was envious of the trip and we tried to balance the books later that summer with a two-week trip to the northern peninsula of Newfoundland and the southeast coast of Labrador. We had been invited by our friends George and Margaret Sollish and ever since we've been glad that we accepted. The Labrador portion of the trip made the deepest impression with our coastal visits to Red Bay, a sixteenth-century Basque whaling station, and to Battle Harbour where Robert Peary brought news of his North Pole endeavors. It all fit in with our idea of the North.

Friendships Predominate

To return to more temperate climes, in the summer of 2008 I was invited by Beverly Lynch to give a talk at the California Rare Book School (CALRBS) that turned out to be an autobiographical exercise called "Luck is the Residue of Design, or Vice Versa, or Not: My Life in Special Collections." Unfortunately the announcement of my talk neglected to include the sub-title so no one knew what I'd be talking about. Nonetheless I had a good audience and that bit of navel-gazing helped me get over my reluctance to write these memoirs, self-indulgent as it seemed.

---

[80] See Brainard Dyer, "Robert J. Walker on acquiring Greenland and Iceland," *Mississippi Valley Historical Review*, 27 (September 1940), p. 263-66.

[81] This situation may be changing in the second decade of the 21st century, as international companies vie for mining rights and project contracts. See "As Investors Flood Greenland, China Has a Big Role," *Wall Street Journal* (August 23, 2013) p. 1 and 10.

But my trip to California caused another disconcerting though fortuitous incident. For a few weeks before my trip I had been trying to arrange an appointment with a Syracuse neurologist and I thought I had been quite clear about when I would be away. Meanwhile my regular doctor, Ray Forbes, told the neurologist that my condition was getting worse and I should see him soon. Their office took that as a demand for an emergency appointment and scheduled me right in the middle of my trip. Before I left I told them that wouldn't work and I'd call from Los Angeles for another appointment. When I called the following Monday I was told in no uncertain terms that they no longer considered me their patient and they would no longer serve me. I had no idea that patients could be fired and was quite upset, especially when I received their certified letter of severance, and when I learned from Forbes that they attributed this misunderstanding on their part to my "patient arrogance." A few months later with my ALS correctly identified, I figured out that the earlier doctor had missed the diagnosis and I came under much better hands, both with Dr. Jeremy Shefner and subsequently with the Veterans Administration which had determined that ALS was a service-connected disability, and thus making me eligible for their medical care.

My diagnosis came as something of a shock but not one to cause me any undue emotion. As Deirdre said in our next holiday letter, "David is not one to rail against his fate." But there was one moment that winter that moved both of us to tears or at least took our breaths away. One of the first symptoms of my newly diagnosed disease was the inability to deal with buttons. Some time that year we attended a performance of *King Lear* at the Brooklyn Academy of Music, with Derek Jacobi as Lear. In the last act, on his deathbed, Lear speaks a couple of lines we'd never noticed before, though we'd seen the play many times: "Pray you, undo this button: thank you, sir". To both of us it demonstrated the sheer depth of Shakespeare's humane understanding and his sense of human mutability.

New friends brightened my retirement years a great deal, most notably fellow Syracuse retirees Donald Meinig and Edwin Bock. The friendship with Meinig was something of a surprise because our one interaction while we were still working was a conflict. The Bird Library renovation of 1991 helped solve some service problems but exasercated the space problems, in part because the building codes required wider aisles than we had when the Library opened in 1972. Thus we were desperate for space and one alternative was to replace very large but brittle periodicals and serials with microform surrogates, before the age of mass digitization. One such replacement on microfiche was the *Congressional Record*, a great space killer going back to the 1780s. The problem we had was that the earliest years were in very good condition and should never have been discarded (shades of my earlier Hopkins debacle).

At the time Meinig was working on the third volume of his four-volume *magnum opus* on the *Shaping of America*. Don was no friend of technology, whether cameras, microfilm and microfiche readers, or computers. In his 1992 Haskins lecture he self-deprecatingly said that his "colleagues aptly sum me up as the man with the quill pen in an age of word processing." The prospect of dealing with these volumes on microfiche and the awkwardness of locating index references through a jumble of fiche was too much for him, as he let me know in no uncertain terms, making a good case for needing the hard copies. I somewhat rectified the dispute by advertising our willingness to trade the newly-acquired microform set for a hard copy in relatively good condition. We were able to make a deal with the State Library of Kansas in Topeka, obviously another library needy for space. When the hard copies arrived we were then able to house most of this huge acquisition on empty shelves of the History Department's new seminar room where Don could have easy access from the nearby Geography Department. We did keep the excellent early hard copy sections in Bird Library where they would also be accessible. Don was quite right about our cavalier disposal of the set, and he was able to use the replacement set for completion of his great work. Another deaccessioning fiasco.

By the time I moved to Eggers Hall and the SU History Department in 1998, Meinig was finishing his final volume. We would meet in the corridors of Eggers Hall and chat about mutual interests that included the geography of the Arctic, reading discoveries, a few mutual friends, and music. Soon we were having sporadic lunches that became somewhat more regular after his wife Lee suddenly died in 2010. For months after his fourth volume was completed, boxes of his books would appear outside the Geography Department, free for the taking. I searched many of these titles against the Library catalogue to be sure that the Syracuse Library had copies, sending those the Library lacked to the gift department. Then I took some for myself. He gave the best part of his collection to the Osher Library at the University of Southern Maine in

Portland, an attractive and well-equipped facility that we visited in 2010 with a number of other map-minded people. I told Don recently that Deirdre and I were now going through the same process, looking for homes for our more important collections, and by extension giving away some books which he had once owned. I commend his Haskins lecture: he ends his short memoir by saying, like me, that he was "one of the lucky ones"; my *felix culpas* are his "chance determinants," in his case supported by an enduring Anglican faith.[82] He is one of Syracuse's greatest scholars, though no longer an active one.

Edwin Bock had a very long career at Syracuse from 1963 to 1997, and somehow managed to spice it up with a variety of assignments. The National Academy of Public Administration, of which he is a fellow, describes him as "Professor Emeritus of Public Administration, Maxwell School of Citizenship and Public Affairs, and Professor of Political Science and Public Administration, Syracuse University; President, Inter-University Case Program, Inc.; Former Assistant Director, New York Office, Public Administration Clearing House." He taught at the Salzburg Global Seminar on Sociology in February1949, and was also a visiting professor there in February 1965 in their session on American Public Administration.

Bock was from Westwood, New Jersey, where, in addition to his Syracuse domicile with his wife George, he still maintains his parental home with its easy access to New York City, and not far from where I grew up in Paterson. He graduated from Dartmouth College in the class of 1943, where he had been editor of *The Dartmouth*, and he had interviewed Senator H. Styles Bridges on the afternoon of Pearl Harbor, December 7, 1941, with the interview published that evening in an extra edition of *The Dartmouth*. Bock celebrated his 70th class reunion in October 2013. On the internet is an interesting oral history interview about his Dartmouth years and especially his editing life there. He claims the interview needs editing and fact checking.[83]

---

[82]   Donald W. Meinig. *A Life of Learning* (New York: American Academy of Learned Societies, 1992).

[83]   See http://www.dartmouth.edu/~library/rauner/archives/oral_history/worldwar2/transcripts/Bock_Edwin.pdf?mswitch-redir=classic

After a few years in the Army, at war's end Bock went on to study at the London School of Economics, University of London. In 1949 he married his wife George, an aspiring student at the Royal Academy of Dramatic Arts. They stayed in London until 1952, imbibing ballet, books, and beer (*nomen est omen*). His professors at LSE were Harold J. Laski in Political Science and Edward Shils, later of Chicago, in Sociology. While in England he published a pseudonymous book called *Americans in Glasshouses* (1950) under the name of Leslie James. It's an effective send-up of British upper crust attitudes towards the postwar Yanks, in my view a bit too kind to the Yanks and the Brits. He thought the pseudonym necessary because he believed that a book implicitly critical of his own professors would not enhance his reputation at LSE. Copies of both the British and American editions can be found on the web at reasonable prices. I now have an association copy neatly inscribed by Leslie James.

Back in New York by 1952, Bock worked for the Public Administration Clearing House before becoming President of the Inter-University Case Program, a consortium of 60 graduate schools interested in doing case studies on how governments actually work. When that organization moved to Syracuse University in 1963 he moved with it and became a Professor of Political Science in the Maxwell School of Citizenship where he worked for over thirty years. For his first ten years at Maxwell he spent the winter months in India working with the Ford Foundation-sponsored Indian Institute of Public Administration. He is also the prime mover and first reader of these memoirs, no doubt a heavy burden.

Why we didn't meet when we both worked at SU and before we both retired I can't guess, but we did meet shortly after. Whatever the case over the last ten or more years he has become my best friend in Syracuse and we now have a fairly regular routine of semi-monthly luncheons mainly to explore our combined lives of over 170 years. In 2003, when I learned of his book collecting interests and saw some of his collection, I asked whether he would like me to sponsor him for membership in the Grolier Club. At the time he said he had some health issues that had to be resolved before he could consider that commitment. I let the question rest for three years before bringing it up again, and this time he agreed to go ahead. At his admissions interview he was asked why at his age (then about 86) he would want to make the required investment in the Club. His answer was that he believed that he was now mature enough to take his books seriously. I've been delighted by his engagement in Club activities, attending events far more often than most non-resident members. Virtually all Grolier members are certifiable OCD obsessives and Bock's interests focus primarily on his century's post-WWI British history and literature, with special passion for the life and works of Anthony Powell and T. E. Lawrence and he is active in their respective societies. Those writers are not a large part of my intellectual world, though I'm always pleased to read Bock's latest dramatic efforts, whether based on Powell's most minor characters or his major narrator. Ed's other passion, which I do share, is for dance and particularly ballet, his more for the Royal Ballet (London) and the Frederick Ashton school of choreography, while mine is more for the New York City Ballet and George Balanchine, as already noted. If we have occasion to attend dance performances together, whether in New York or Syracuse, we do, as we have whenever Shen Wei Dance Company or the Paul Taylor Dance Company have performed in Syracuse.

Bock has always been, to me at least, a bit opaque about his political views, preferring to drill out such information about his friends and even from strangers without much self-revelation. I gave him an opportunity to express himself directly; by way of response he sent this passage from *Pilgrim's Progress*:

> "But when Christina came to the Slough of Despond, she began to be at a stand; for, said she, This is the place in which my dear Husband had like to have been smothered with mud. She perceived also, that notwithstanding the command of the King to make this place for Pilgrims good, yet it was rather worse than formerly: So I asked if that was true? Yes, said the old Gentleman, too true: For that many there be, that pretend to be the King's Labourers, and that say they are for mending the King's Highway, that bring dirt and dung instead of stones, and so mar instead of mending."

He then ended with the concluding sentence of Bunyan's classic:

> "Shall it be my lot to go that way again, I may give those that desire it an account of what I Here am silent about; mean time,

I bid my Reader *Adieu.*" (London: Pickering, C. Whittingham, 1849).

Good luck to all when that time comes. Meanwhile, what I would add about Edwin Bock, in addition to his enigmatic politics which appear to me to lean slightly to the rational right (he admits to reading the *Wall Street Journal*), is that he has an infinite capacity for curiosity. When I asked him in his reading of this manuscript to identify any passages that he found especially boring, his rejoinder was that he didn't bore easily, and the character of his inquisitorial conversation suggests as much. "What was the color of her hair when you last saw her?" "Who was the soloist?" "What did they serve at the Vatican dinner?" Some of his questions seem boringly inventive to me and they do challenge one's memory of what may have been.

Invariably his questions lead back to his interlocutor, and in my case to my own growing fascination with boredom. When I was well into my reading and research into what Polar explorers read to cope with their own *ennui*, I accidentally ran across a provocative quotation from Kierkegaard: "boredom is the root of all evil."[84] Much to Deirdre's indifference, I began to see boredom all around me, especially in the great fiction that I've been reading in the past few years: *Madame Bovary*, *Anna Karenina*, Isabel Archer in *Portrait of a Lady*, *Ivanov* in the Chekhov play of that name, as well as other Chekhov plays, the wildly mercurial Poa Yu in *Dream of the Red Chamber*, to name a few. I even found one commentator who claimed that the sexual conquests of *Gilgamesh* were provoked by boredom. Often boredom is attended by depression and suicide, as it was for some explorers, with or without boredom. I don't find that Robert Falcon Scott was bored, but he certainly was often

---

[84] "Boredom is the root of all evil. Strange that boredom, in itself so staid and stolid, should have such power to set in motion. The influence it exerts is altogether magical, except that it is not the influence of attraction, but of repulsion." in "The Rotation Method," *Either/Or*, trans. by David F. Swenson and Lillian Marvin Swenson (Princeton, NJ: Princeton University Press, 1959) Vol. I, p. 281ff. From a fairly large body of literature, see Lars Svendsen, *A Philosophy of Boredom* (London: Reaktion Books, 2005), and Patricia Meyer Spacks, *Boredom: The Literary History of a State of Mind* (Chicago, IL: University of Chicago Press, 1995).

depressed and, as the leader of his fatal expedition, had to suppress it. I know I was lucky in that I learned in the Navy never to go anywhere without some printed matter. I haven't had a boring job since my first few months at NYPL in 1959, and I don't watch television, the greatest of boredom traps.

To return to my narrative, I should say a word about the Paul Taylor Dance Company, another preoccupation of mine during the 1990s and 2000s. The Delmas Foundation has supported this company consistently since our expansion in 1993, not only with grants for their performing season but also with funds for the preservation archiving of their work, one of our rare exceptions to a no preservation policy. But I had a wider interest in the company relating to Syracuse. When I arrived in 1986 a strong tradition of visiting dance and ballet companies to Syracuse was nearly dead, with only a visiting holiday *Nutcracker* surviving to this day.

In a meeting around 1994 with Ross Kramberg, Executive Director of the Taylor Company, I suggested that we might work toward including an annual visit on the subscription series of the Syracuse Symphony Orchestra, providing Taylor with live music instead of his accustomed tapes. When John Tomlinson, now the Executive Director, joined that meeting he dismissed the idea by saying "there's no interest in dance in Syracuse," I asked that they give us another chance and then let the idea rest. It gained new life when our Dean of the College of Arts and Sciences, Catherine Newton, told me that she wanted to commission a Paul Taylor dance to honor the School in which Paul Taylor had been a student and from which he received an honorary degree in 1986. To trim the story severely, that commissioned work, *Troilus and Cressida (Reduced)*, was premiered in Syracuse in 2006, and has become one of the Company's show closers. A much darker second commission from the University, *Brief Encounters*, premiered here in 2009 and gained rave reviews from Alistair Macaulay of *The New York Times* and others. The Company and Taylor 2 have now visited Syracuse often and Tomlinson has told me that I made it all possible by my persistence, by obtaining some modest funding, and by engaging Chancellor Nancy Cantor in the project, leading her in turn to join the PTDC Board.

Although Deirdre worked in New York City for most of the first decade of the twenty-first century, my retirement and more recently hers gave us opportunities to renew our sometimes neglected Syracuse friendships, especially with former Ambassador Goodwin Cooke and

Barbara and with David Tatham and Cleota Reed. Goody and I played squash regularly for nearly twenty years, ending with our simultaneous enhobblement early in this century; we now get together every couple of months to compare notes and check memories. Goody's uncanny ability to remember and quote much of his lifetime reading, including most of Shakespeare, remains impressive. We'll always be grateful for the help he gave as an advisor to our son Wendell who was an International Relations undergraduate at SU.

David and Cleota usually spend three or four winter months in London where among many other things David has taught at the SU semester abroad program and where he finished work on his fourth and last book on Winslow Homer, *Winslow Homer in London: A New York Artist Abroad*, published in 2010. Their assiduous pursuit of the performing arts, both in London and in Central New York is akin to our own, for them especially with opera. The rest of the year is filled with their hospitality and friendship. In December 2012, that included a celebration of David's 80th birthday and the publication of his own memoir, *Sketches from Memory: Family, Friends, and Ancestors . . .* , privately printed in 80 copies. The concluding "Note on the Author" quotes the entry on David on the website of the Department of Art and Music Histories (q.v.), concluding "To this it might be added that David Tatham was born in Wellesley, Massachusetts in 1932, that he has been a Red Sox fan since birth, and that he married Cleota Reed in 1979 after a whirlwind courtship of three years." We are proud to be counted among their "great friends."

Other warm friendships abroad have also enriched our portion of the twenty-first century, including John and Julia Boyd, Cel and Bill Phelan, Neil Chambers, Bill Bell, Margaret Benton, and many others. In March of 2003 Deirdre and I spent two weeks working at the Scott Polar Research Institute in Cambridge, the days devoted to our Polar studies and exhibit preparation but many nights and some lunches involved meeting current and potential Delmas Foundation grantees, including Newnham College (which Gladys Krieble attended), Girton College, Corpus Christi College, the University Library, and Scott Polar itself. Among the potential grantees was Churchill College where we attended a fascinating dinner party hosted by the Master, John Boyd, and his wife Julia. John was the former British Ambassador to Japan and on the Boards of both the British Museum and of Dove Cottage. At dinner Deirdre sat next to Julia and learned about her latest project, a biography of Dr. Elizabeth Blackwell, America's first female physician and graduate of an antecedent school of Syracuse University. Since Julia wished to learn more of Blackwell's Central New York connections, we arranged a visit a few months later, beginning a series of inter-connections, a talk about Blackwell that I arranged for Julia at the New York Academy of Medicine, a large birthday party for me and about 25 of our British friends at their London house near Victoria Station, and a week-long stay at that house when they were away. The last time we saw John and Julia was at a party that the Prochaskas and we hosted at Alice's London flat in late September of 2011. We'd love to see more of them, but travel is not as effortless as it once was.

That September visit to England for that reason was probably our last. That's a distressing thought because we have been so often and have so many friends there, among them Cel and Bill Phelan. Several years ago Alice and Frank Prochaska invited the Phelans to dine with us and we immediately found lots of common interests. At the time both couples had daughters in St. Paul's School for Girls in Brook Green. The Phelans are from Kilkenny, Ireland, both educated at University College Dublin, and when we first knew them they had started their London business of exhibition planning and management called Event Communications, Ltd. They were very helpful to us in informal advice on our 2005 exhibition at the Grolier Club, giving us the principle that first we had to determine what story we wanted to tell, and the rest would follow. But much earlier, in 2001, shortly before 9/11, they invited us for a weekend of opera in Wexford, Ireland, three obscure operas in a rather formal setting. I'll spare the reader the details except to say it was such a delightful trip that at the very least it required reciprocation, something we arranged the following summer in Syracuse, Skaneateles, and again three operas, this time at Glimmerglass Opera in Cooperstown. They also introduced us to Richard Kossov, an American lawyer turned London book dealer of travel literature and Polar materials, from whom we purchased a major item for our exhibit and from whom we learned a great deal.

During our stay at the Boyds' London house on Elizabeth Street in 2004, when the Boyd's were away, the house was otherwise occupied by their daughter and several of her graduate school colleagues from the Princeton University Philosophy Department. During the desultory conversations of that week one stands out, with a young man who told us that his suite mate during his senior year at Harvard had written a senior thesis as a disquisition and a play about Earnest Shackleton. Since we were indefatigable in tracking down unusual Polar materials, I was determined to locate the writer, Brett Egan, and get a copy of his work. It wasn't easy but I tracked him down in New York working as General Director of the Venice Music Festival.

After I learned that Brett had spent some time at McMurdo Sound and visited the historic huts there, courtesy of the National Science Foundation, we arranged a date to meet at his New York office to see the films he had taken on the ice. He himself never told us that while at McMurdo he had directed a production of *A Midsummer Night's Dream*. Nor did he tell us that the NSF had awarded him an Antarctic Service Medal. Though he never showed us his Antarctic work for Harvard, we hit it off well and quickly moved to other interests in the performing arts.

Over the next five years Brett would regularly make time for our growing friendship and we would meet over lunch or drinks three or four times a year. Next thing we knew Brett had become Executive Director of Shen Wei Dance Arts in 2006, shortly before Shen Wei was awarded his MacArthur Fellowship. Paul Kellogg, our friend from Glimmerglass Opera, and at the time the head of New York City Opera, was Chair of the Shen Wei Board and invited us to a party honoring Shen Wei's new fellowship, the first of several occasions when we spent time with the choreographer. Sometime in 2007 Brett casually mentioned that Shen Wei Dance Arts was looking for a college campus with various rehearsal spaces where Shen Wei could make dances on his performers. When I asked him to consider Syracuse as a possibility, he encouraged me to raise the issue at the University. I knew that our relatively new Chancellor, Nancy Cantor, was interested in dance and so I boldly sent her an email telling her of the opportunity for both the University and the company. She simply replied "Let's go for it" and turned the arrangements over to her new University Presenter, Carole Brzozowski. What resulted was a three-week residency in the snowless March of 2009, followed in September by Syracuse performances of Shen Wei's new work, the third dance of his triptych *Re-*, that filled the downtown Landmark Theater three times. On one of those visits we first met Joan Wadopian, a dancer with the Company, starting another lasting friendship. We became very fond of Joan during the company's Syracuse gigs, partly because she's so much fun to be with, partly because she was so kind to our granddaughters, helping to foster their interests in dance, but only later did we discover that she and Brett make such a great couple. To our surprise and pleasure he married Joan in 2011, long after he left Shen Wei Dance Arts. In 2012 he engaged Deirdre in some library consulting work in Oman which has also helped keep us in touch.

I think Brett would be embarrassed by this much attention so I will desist. In 2009 he was ready for another move, this time to Washington, where he now works with famed impresario Michael Kaiser. As the Director of the DeVos Institute of Arts Management at the Kennedy Center, Brett is busier than ever, a couple of years ago as Acting Director of the Oman Royal Opera House (until recently a full-time job) in addition to his other duties.

Neil Chambers is another friend from Britain who we met through an unsolicited Delmas Foundation proposal, asking support for his edition of the correspondence of the great eighteenth-century English naturalist and bookman Sir Joseph Banks. We saw each other a few times in London when his project was housed in the Natural History Museum. What helped keep the friendship alive for ten years was our standing invitation to fulfill his long-time goal of drinking manhattans in Manhattan. Finally the goal was achieved in January 2013 with his first visit to the United States when we spent a couple of respectably bibulous evenings in New York City. He told us that our London party in September 2011 was a unique experience for him because every one of the twenty or so guests he spoke with had actually heard of Sir Joseph Banks.

Our other great friendship of the new century has been composer Charles Fussell, who in turn has helped foster other friendships. Sometime in the 2001-02 season Charles had one of his works, *Goethe Songs*, performed on a Society for New Music program in Syracuse with a very good Syracuse soprano named Janet Brown who had premiered the work in Boston. Neva Pilgrim asked if we could put him up for the few days of his visit. I was to be out of town but Deirdre said it was fine with her if he would be comfortable at home with a lone woman. I missed the performance but returned in time for his last evening at our house. Apparently he and Deirdre had been chatting all weekend, and the conversation continued long into that last night. We've had many composers visit our house in Syracuse—Lou Harrison, John Harbison, Ernst Bacon, Vali Reza, Andrew Waggoner, Daniel Godfrey (for three months, our "composer in residence"), Carlyle Floyd, to name a few—but none has led to the strong bond we have with Charles. Charles has even dedicated a composition to us, a duo for marimba and double bass called "Moonshine." Unfortunately he has not let us hear the work, claiming that its one performance was a "train wreck."

As an openly gay man who enjoys the company of women, Charles has fit right into our family and our circle, and in that summer of 2002 we began our now ten-year-old tradition of week-long visits to Central New York. It started with four days, including a Glimmerglass Opera performance and some chamber music at the Skaneateles Festival. Two years later we wanted Charles to meet other friends we had visited sporadically in the Adirondacks near Lake Saranac. George Pappastavrou, a pianist, was the Director of the School of Music when I arrived in Syracuse. Lex Dashnaw, a native of Lake Placid and also a musician, is now retired from his post as a performing arts administrator at Long Island University and a choral conductor. The youngest of "The Boys," as we've come to call them, is Doug March, a recently retired choral conductor in New York schools. These guys have been together for thirty years and more, and are consummate hosts in their rustically palatial farm in the shadow of Whiteface Mountain. George is permanently retired there, with time out for Florida each January. Lex and Doug still have a base in New York City but spend most of the summer at Cobble Spring Farm. Their farmhouse music room, complete with piano and harpsichord and a beautiful Rodger Mack sculpture called Pachelbel, can seat 100 people and we've attended performances to benefit the cottage near Saranac Lake where Béla Bartók spent his last three summers and wrote his *Concerto for Orchestra*, the *Viola Concerto*, and the *Third Piano Concerto*. We've come to call these visits our annual Gay Awareness Week, and thanks to Charles our friendship with the guys has blossomed further.

Charles knew Virgil Thomson well and is now President of the Virgil Thomson Foundation, with the bitter-sweet job of phasing out the Foundation. It is concluding its work by supporting some rather large projects, including a production of *Four Saints in Three Acts*. Charles would do well to produce his own version of Thomson stories and *bon mots*. My favorite: "Ned Rorem's *Diaries* just go in one eye and out the other." We were all pleased and excited to learn in April 2013 that the Library of America is planning a two-volume edition of Virgil Thomson's reviews and criticism, edited by Tim Page and substantially supported by the Thomson Foundation.

In the fall of 2011 Charles invited me to join him at a Met dress rehearsal of Debussy's *Pelléas et Mélisande* with Sir Simon Rattle conducting. It was a lush and beautifully articulated performance with one element that was unique in our experience. During the curtain call rehearsal, after Sir Simon had joined the singers on stage, he walked to the front of the stage to kiss the extended hand reaching out from the prompter's box.

We can usually find something new to do with Charles on each annual visit to Central New York and the Adirondacks. Our August 2012 week included a welcoming lunch in Utica with our daughter Kathryn and her friend, the Librarian of the Utica Public Library; an official Delmas visit to the Holy Trinity Seminary in Jordanville, a fascinating library and museum of the Russian Orthodox Church Outside Russia; a performance of Kurt Weil's *Lost in the Stars* at Glimmerglass; and dinner with Neva Pilgrim and friends, all in the first 36 hours. On the way to the Adirondacks we fulfilled a long-felt desire to see the Edmund Wilson house in Talcottville, New York, made famous by his book, *Upstate*. Disappointingly, no one was home, but it was an evocative visit. On that trip we also had the pleasure of drinks with Mrs. Peter Mennin, Georganne, a fine photographer and the widow of the former President of Juilliard, a prominent composer whose work I had long enjoyed. She has a summer home on the grounds of Melville Dewey's Lake Placid Club.[85] After three nights we hurried back to Syracuse for an outdoor concert at Brook Farm on Skaneateles Lake, featuring Ludwig Spohr's *Nonette*, which we'd never heard live. A typical Fussell visit, filled with non-stop musical talk—and we hope there will be more.

---

[85] For an excellent article on Melville Dewey, Central New York, and the Lake Placid Club, see Deirdre C. Stam, "Melville and Annie Dewey and the Communitarian Ideal," *Libraries & Culture: A Journal of Library History,* 24: 2 (Spring 1989), p. 125-143.

Chamber Music America
2003-2012

Apart from my scholarly work, some publications and lectures on Polar studies, hundreds of performing arts events, one highlight for me of the first decade of the twenty-first century has been membership on the Board of Chamber Music America. I learned about CMA first when David and Louise Robinson, founders and hosts of the Skaneateles Chamber Music Festival, won a CMA Distinguished Service award for their support of the Festival, and in 2002 when the Delmas Foundation gave a grant for the Cassatt Quartet (then the resident quartet of Syracuse University) to play a benefit concert for CMA at Merkin Hall in New York. The concert was a great success but didn't raise much money for a clearly needy organization. Through that concert, however, I met Margaret Lioi, the Executive Director, and learned a lot from her about the role of the organization in support of chamber music. Any reader who knows me at all will know of my passion for chamber music, even when only a listener or spectator. My interest was piqued by what I learned.

After a discreet lapse of time, Margaret asked me whether I would consider becoming an appointed member of the Board and asked if I could meet their requirements of attendance and engagement in Board meetings and giving or getting $5000 per year towards the CMA budget. So after a vetting by another Board member, Anthony Viscusi, over lunch at the Century Club, and after I cleared the idea of using Delmas discretionary funds with my fellow Trustees, I agreed to join the Board and attended my first meeting in 2003 and my first annual conference in January 2004.

CMA defines chamber music as music for ensembles of from two to ten players, one player per part, usually without a conductor. CMA membership includes ensembles, individual artists, presenters, educators, managers, composers, and many others involved in the field. The genres represented include jazz, contemporary, early music, and Western classical and include both vocal and instrumental music. Its support for these groups comes in both tangible ways, such as ensemble residency grants, commissions for new work, access to health and instrument insurance, and a series of prestigious awards, and in the less quantifiable areas of public relations, publicity, and advocacy.

When I joined the Board in 2003 it was in the middle of a tendentious debate over the appropriate role, if any, for jazz in the organization. The debate was triggered by receipt of very substantial multi-million dollar grants from the Doris Duke Foundation to support jazz ensembles and composers. The new funds far outnumbered the totals available for traditional classical chamber music: Haydn, Mozart, Beethoven, Mendelssohn, and Bartók string quartets, for example. The traditionalists, largely led by artist managers and presenters, argued that the large influx of money was distorting the mission of the organization and that it should get back to a more focused approach exclusive of jazz. There was also an erroneous claim that CMA wanted all its presenters to schedule jazz in their programs. In effect the Board had to decide between inclusion and exclusion and then convince the membership of the wisdom of their choice. I would also say what no one said at the time, that there was a subtle racial undertone to a debate which often started with a disclaimer of any animus against jazz. The Board, led by President Phillip Ying (violist of the Ying Quartet) and John Steinmetz (first bassoon of the Los Angeles Opera), came down solidly on the side of inclusion, helped by the fact that some brilliant jazz musicians had been recruited to the Board. It was a dead issue during the last half of my Board tenure, but could reemerge in a different form if or when significant funding for jazz ensembles or composers dries up. For myself I would add that while I had enjoyed jazz during my college years and a bit beyond, it had lost its hold on me, and only the educational benefit of coming to know fellow members like Stefon Harris, Billy Childs, and Rufus Reid has brought a new appreciation of this art form, a form as diverse and interesting as contemporary classical music.

Like most parts of my life and work, the real benefit of CMA Board membership was in friendships. I had long enjoyed just schmoozing with musicians, not only about their lives in music but as much about their lives as human beings. In that respect, CMA was as rich in friendships as I ever could have imagined. I had met bassoonist John Steinmetz when he came to the Skaneateles Chamber Music Festival in the early 2000s. He encouraged me to join the CMA Board when he was also a member and that has kept us in touch ever since. The 2012 summer issue of CMA's magazine, *Chamber Music*, has a splendid article by John on techniques of chamber music rehearsals, aptly called "Plays Well with Others."

In addition to Margaret Lioi and Chairman Louise Smith of Chicago, Judith Sherman was also on the Board of Chamber Music America when I came on. A much-recognized and much-honored record producer (including almost all of the Kronos Quartet's work), she and her extraordinary violinist husband Curtis Macomber have been stimulating and understanding friends and colleagues whom we first met in Skaneateles several years ago. They both work too hard and travel too much so we don't get to see (or hear) them as often as we would like.

Edward Surovell, a realtor from Ann Arbor, was also on the Board when I arrived. He sought me out at the outset because of shared interests in music, book collecting, libraries, and publishing practices. His collections of Michigan imprints, Native-American languages, Mormon literature, and some more esoteric subjects are impressive. With my sponsorship he joined the Grolier Club and we continue to meet there—we now have a three-year tradition of summer visits to Syracuse and environs, and in 2012 an additional Thanksgiving visit. He has had personal family experience with ALS and is splendid in his casual concern.

The normal tenure of Board members is two three-year terms, except for officers. Towards the end of my sixth year Margaret and the Board asked me to stay on as Chair of the Development Committee, a rather thankless task which I did as well as I could for another three years by which time it was clearly time to step down. At my last meeting in May 2012, I said that without being lugubrious about it I wanted the "In lieu of flowers . . ." ending of my obituary to read "send contributions to Chamber Music America, 99 Madison Avenue, Fifth Floor, New York, NY 10016." I still hope that happens, but if you respond make sure you have the right address when the time comes. My last Board meeting discussed an impending move.

More Amusements
2008 and Beyond

When I was diagnosed with ALS in November 2008, knowing it to be a fatal disease, I decided that I should spend a good deal of the rest of my life reading or rereading really great literature, trying to absolve my bibliophilic sins of omission. Balancing that desire with the wish to keep up with my Polar studies (seldom truly great literature) has not always been easy, but I have now read all the way through *War and Peace*.

Other reading has included *Tristram Shandy*, most of Montaigne, *Pride and Prejudice* and *Northanger Abbey*, Trollope's *Orley Farm* and *Barchester Towers*, *Don* Quixote, four of Sebald's indefinable works, Melville's trilogy of nautical novels, *Whitejacket* (naval ship), *Moby-Dick* (whaling ship), and *Redburn* (merchant marine ship), *Tom Jones*, Gibbon's *Autobiography*, *Madame Bovary*, and many others, most recently *Anna Karenina*.

But the five-foot shelf of classics gleaned from our accumulations of books remains constantly replenished as I replace books read with others still unread, or only partially so: *Ulysses*, *The Anatomy of Melancholy*, Gibbon's *Rise and Fall* (unabridged, though I confess to listening with fascination to a dozen CDs of an audio abridgement), Thucydides and Plutarch (abridged), *The Canterbury Tales*, *The Decameron*, and Don *Juan*, Wordsworth's *Prelude*, Boccaccio, Rabelais, etc., *ad infinitum* beyond any reasonable sell-by date. Occasionally it has been a chore for a fairly slow reader, but mostly this reading has been pure pleasure. It took me nearly a lifetime to get through *Tristram Shandy*, but I'm glad I finally did and to find that my own style can be Shandean. I attribute my slow reading to a lifetime of writing word by word, copy-editing word by word, and proofreading word by word. I don't know if the connection could ever be demonstrated, but any attempt at speeding up usually leads to utter failure of an attention deficit nature.

There are a few other Central New York boards I should mention, for example the Board of the Seward House Museum in Auburn, NY, a house museum in the home of Lincoln's Secretary of State, William Henry Seward, noteworthy for having been occupied by the same family for well over a century. I served on that Board for over fifteen years. Since Deirdre has been on the Board of the Oneida Community Mansion House in Sherrill, NY, during a part of the same period I was on the Board of Seward House, we have become acutely aware of the potential and problems of house museums. The latest plan of the Seward House Museum to sell a valuable Thomas Cole painting has caused something of a local kerfuffle, but seems to us a reasonable plan for an object that they are in no position to protect.

Another rewarding experience has been with the quite informal Board of the Society for New Music in Syracuse, founded by singer Neva Pilgrim forty years ago, and living on a miraculous shoestring ever since. I've been on that Board since we came to Syracuse, most of it as Vice President (for Life) on the condition that I not be asked to serve as President. At one point between jobs Deirdre did spend a year in that role. She played the same role for a year with the Syracuse Friends of Chamber Music, an excellent concert series founded in 1949 by Louis Krasner, a versatile composer and teacher who had commissioned and premiered the Berg *Violin Concerto* in 1934. Krasner had deposited the original manuscript in the Syracuse University Library, but sold it to Yale just before I arrived in Syracuse. When I met him in 1986 at my welcoming party, he told me that I had arrived just a little too late. That concerto has always meant a lot to us; we once heard a marvelous performance by Itzhac Perlman in Carnegie Hall. Deirdre's succinct critique: "too short." Jerome Robbins also made a dance on the Berg *Violin Concerto* called *In memory of . . .* , another beautiful version of the same work.

Our other Central New York musical affiliations have included the Skaneateles Chamber Music Festival, now co-directed by cellist David Ying and his pianist wife Elinor Freer. Scheduled each summer for the four weeks before Labor Day, the Festival is always an opportunity to meet musicians from around the country and abroad. Among those we came to know through the Skaneateles Festival were Hilary Hahn who at age twelve first came during the summer that Deirdre worked for the Festival; Andrés Cárdenes, concertmaster in Pittsburgh; violinist Curtis Macomber; bassoonist John Steinmetz of Los Angeles, pianist and festival director Robert Weirich, and all of the Ying family. Not least was composer in residence George Rochberg from the University of Pennsylvania whose *String Quintet* was dedicated to Gregorian. We attended the premiere in 1982 at Alice Tully Hall in New York with Gregorian and his wife (Rochberg had known Gregorian at Penn where Gregorian was Provost before coming to NYPL).

I've already mentioned Glimmerglass Opera, but other affiliations include the local classical music station, the Syracuse Symphony Orchestra (sadly bankrupted in 2011, but on the verge of new life two years later), New York State Baroque based in Ithaca but with regular Syracuse performances, and of course the School of Music at Syracuse University. The Central New York area has a rich and active musical life, far broader than such a relatively small community might expect, but its typically greying audience badly needs new blood.

I shouldn't forget the Book Arts Center at Wells College, Aurora, New York. I was on that Board for over fifteen years, having been nominated by Dick Couper. It represented a philosophy that I held strongly, that to get young people hooked early on the Book Arts was to hold their interest for life. It was for the same reason that we in the Delmas Foundation encouraged the Folger Library to develop undergraduate courses at the Folger to teach students the use and potential of primary resources, a program that continues successfully. The Wells program covers typography, bookbinding, book design, and production, and has attracted a loyal following. Funding is a different issue and is always difficult in a small struggling college. I resigned from the Board in spring of 2012 but for the time being Deirdre has taken over my role, as she did with the Delmas duties.

Over the years librarians and others often have told me that I seem to know everybody. If so, it's more people than I could possibly remember; I can say that long association with such library groups as ARL, RLG, IRLA, and my various boards, committees, and task forces, provided a very wide circle of colleagues and friends among a select group of librarians. I also served on ten or so library visiting committees across the country, from the Metropolitan Museum to Rochester, Chicago, and Stanford universities, and equal numbers of external review committees (British Columbia, Carnegie-Mellon, CUNY Graduate School, George Washington, Institute of Fine Arts of NYU, the Mercantile Library of St. Louis, Michigan, Northwestern, SUNY Binghamton, and Yale's Beinecke Library, among others). All these extended visits were opportunities for learning and for networking, although several evaluations led to what one might call regime change. Similarly, six decades of concert going and affiliation with musicians and musical groups, from the Board of Shriver Hall concerts at Johns Hopkins to the Society for New Music in Syracuse, and of course the Board of CMA, have provided a network of friends in the field of chamber music. On the other hand, my ignorance of popular culture is unparalleled! (Dan Traister challenges this assertion.)

I don't intend a Maugham-like "summing up" to conclude this lengthy excursion into my past, but one reflection I would like to share arises from the personal assessment such an exercise requires. Over the years I've often characterized certain types of managers as control freaks, never thinking of myself as one of those insufferable people. I now know better. Although I don't believe ambition was a major motivation in my life, I now see that my career was a lifelong search for independence and control, closely approached but never really achieved until retirement, a blissful period of freedom and productivity. That search was the reason I left both the Newberry Library and the New York Public Library, while both Johns Hopkins and Syracuse allowed a good deal of both freedom and control. With my disease, however, control is gradually slipping away, literally, from my fingers and hands. I am now increasingly dependent on Deirdre and both friends and strangers for help with the simplest of actions, from standing up to cutting my food to putting on a jacket. I could not be more fortunate in both wife and friends.

Intimations of Mortality
2012-??

Years ago in Edinburgh, while auditing the lectures of Professor A. Melville Clark, I was struck by his reference to the last sentence of Edmund Gibbons' *Autobiography*, I think in a lecture about human mutability: "I will not suppose any premature decay of the mind or body; but I must reluctantly observe that two causes, the abbreviation of time, and the failure of hope, will always tinge with a browner shade the evening of life." Those sentiments on the transiency of life were in keeping with my mood in that troubled and formative year. More congenial to my present mood in the evening of life fifty-eight years later are Gibbons' thoughts a few pages earlier:

When I contemplate the common lot of mortality, I must acknowledge that I have drawn a high prize in the lottery of life. The greater part of the globe is overspread with barbarism or slavery: in the civilized world, the most numerous class is condemned to ignorance and poverty; and the double fortune of my birth in a free and enlightened country, in an honourable and wealthy family, is the lucky chance of an unit against millions. (Oxford World Classics edition, Oxford, 1972 [1907], p. 220-21 and p. 217.)

"I repeat and confirm that I have not seen what I have seen
And that what has happened to me has not happened."
Cervantes. *Don Quixote*. Part II Chapter LXXII.

FINIS

Epilogue

The Origins of this Screed

"The *whole* of anything is never told"
Henry James. *Notebooks* (March 18, 1878)

On a bus tour in Beijing in November 1998, I was sitting with Gary Strong, then the Director of the Queensborough Public Library in New York City and now recently retired as University Librarian of UCLA. We were there to celebrate the 100th Anniversary of the Peking University Library where Chairman Mao himself had been employed as a student worker. Since I had just begun my work on *An International Dictionary of Library Histories* (2001), library history was much on my mind. As is the wont of many old farts in retirement, I was reminiscing to Gary about some events in my career when he interrupted to say that I really should write something about my experience of research library developments in the twentieth century so those memories would not be lost.

With that thought in mind, ten years later I responded to an invitation from UCLA to speak at the 2008 California Rare Book School (CALRBS) with the suggestion of an autobiographical talk about my life in Special Collections, claiming that Gary had to bear some responsibility for this self-indulgent navel-gazing. Beverly Lynch, the School's Director, welcomed the suggestion, and the resulting talk and unpublished paper was entitled "Luck is the Residue of Design: or Vice Versa, or Not: My Life with Special Collections," delivered in August 2008. Some small vestiges of that prose piece appear here.

Closer to home, shortly after retirement in 1998, I met Syracuse University Professor Emeritus of Political Science Edwin Bock who, after a few years of monthly lunch dates, began to press me to write something of my life, including some of the anecdotes I'd been telling him. This ridiculous idea gradually and insidiously crept into my subconscious, and emerged more fully with a talk at the 50th anniversary Charlottesville conference of the Rare Book and Manuscript Section (RBMS) of the Association of College and Research Libraries (ACRL) of the American Library Association (ALA) in 2009. The story is told above, but, in a word, I was chosen as one of the few attendees in 1959 still alive in 2009. Although *RBMS* declined to print my talk and I declined to let them publish it online, it represented another step in the evolution of this manuscript.

It doesn't seem quite right to refer to friends and relatives as peer-reviewers but this self-published work has had more than its share of candid readers. Terry Belanger, Ed Bock, Joseph Mitchell, Robert Patten, Deirdre C. Stam, James H. Stam, and Daniel Traister have all read the manuscript with care and to them I am extremely indebted. Several others, too numerous to recall, have read appropriate sections. Tammy R. Hnat-Comstock, the Maxwell School's training whiz, has rescued me from many computing glitches. Virginia Bartow, at one time head of the Arents Collection at NYPL and now cataloguer of special collections materials, a few years ago began quizzing me about various recollections of my NYPL years. She too has been a helpful stimulus to getting some of these recollections out in the open.

For a year beginning in spring of 2009, NYU historian Tony Judt began publishing a series of vignettes of his life. Produced in the harrowing circumstances of the late stages of his much more rapid ALS, they appeared first in *The New York Review of Books* and then collected in *The Memory Chalet*, published posthumously by Penguin Books in 2011. Although I never met him, he too was an inspiration, as was my friend John Western of the Syracuse University Department of Geography who maintained an almost daily email correspondence with Judt during the author's last year, something I feel privileged to have read. Their common bond was youthful trainspotting in the British Midlands in the mid 1950s, the same time that I was in Edinburgh watching from our New College Residence window steam engines passing through the Princes Street Gardens.

Another enabler over the past few years has been Dan Traister, master of book memory, and missionary to professional memory preservation. The symposium honoring him on his retirement in March 2012 alluded in its very title, "Memory/Reason/Imagination: Librarians and Scholars—Past, Present, and Future," to his concern for recording the memories of scholar librarians. He too has encouraged me to write some of my memories. I fear he's gotten more than he wished. What Dan does spectacularly well is to make connections between potential readers and the books they ought to read or at least know about. He illustrates R. S. Ranganathan's principles of "Every reader his book" and "Every book its reader" as well as anyone I know.

For me what has been most gratifying in my own long career has been making connections between books and people and also among people. We joke about it as social engineering but it boils down to friendships. I feel negligent in having left out so many stories of friends, colleagues, and even antagonists. To them I can only recommend that they capture their own. It's a worthwhile experience.

Appendix I

Dramatis Personae

The Stam Family: My Grandparents and Parents Generation

Peter Stam (my grandfather, 1866—1940, immigrant from Alkmaar, Holland (1890), contractor and Mission administrator. Wife: Amelia Yetge Willems (1867—1961), immigrant, born Rotterdam. Children: Peter, Clazina, Henry, Jacob, Harry, Catherine (d. age 1), John, Cornelius, Amelia.

Jacob Stam (my father, 1899-1972), Paterson, NJ, lawyer, Gideon, and lay preacher, and Deana Bowman Stam, Rochester, NY (my mother, 1901-1965). New York Law School. [86] Children:

---

[86] My brother Jim adds these details about Jacob Stam: "He probably took some graduate courses at Rutgers, but evidently went from grammar school to business college for such things as shorthand, typing, and accounting (in which subjects he excelled). To supplement the family income he was secretary to Frederick Beggs, Passaic County Surrogate Justice, who persuaded Jacob to get a law degree at New York Law School where he passed his bar exams before finishing his degree. When he married Deana Bowman, Jacob went into the legal business for himself. Despite Beggs' view that he would not make it on his own, Dad celebrated fifty years of practice shortly before he died amidst many encomiums. In his first year of practice he had handled his first million dollar estate, and soon Beggs's wife Vera, principal owner of Empire Piece Dyeing and Finishing Company, became his client. He served as the Company's lawyer, accountant, and eventually Secretary/Treasurer of the Board. It folded after WWII when Paterson's textile industries moved south, but we remember a wartime tour of the silk factory to see its parachute production."

1) *Paul B. Stam* (first son and my oldest brother, 1923), Durham, NC. Chemist, business man, lawyer. BS Wheaton College. PhD Princeton University; JD University of North Carolina. Wife: Jane Levering Stam (1925-2014). BS Wheaton College. Children: Karen, Paul, Carl, William.

2) *Ruth Stam Stevens* (first daughter and my oldest sister, 1926—), San Jose, Costa Rica. BA Wheaton College. Husband: Ladoit Stevens (1920-2011). Moody Bible Institute; BA Wheaton College. Missionaries, Latin American Mission. Children: Mary Beth, Daniel, David, born in US; Dean, Vernon Jay, Margaret, all born in Costa Rica.

3) *Juan Edward Stam* (second son and my second brother, 1928—), San Jose, Costa Rica. BA and MA, Wheaton College; STM, Fuller Seminary, Pasadena, CA; PhD Univ. of Basle. Missionary, Latin American Mission, and theologian. Wife: Doris Emanuelson Stam. BA Wheaton College. Taught Greek in Costa Rica and Nicaragua. Children: Robert Bruce, Rebecca, Richard, all born in Costa Rica.

4) *Mary Stam* (second daughter and my second sister, 1932—), Colorado Springs, Colorado. BA Wheaton College. Missionary in US and retired Comptroller of Young Life, Inc. Unmarried.

5) *David Harry Stam* (third son and fifth child, 1935—), Syracuse, NY. BA, Wheaton College; MLS Rutgers University; PhD Northwestern University. Librarian and historian: University Librarian Emeritus and Senior Scholar, History Department, Syracuse University. Wife: Deirdre Corcoran Stam (1940—). BA Harvard University; MA Institute of Fine Arts, NYU; MEd Johns Hopkins University; MLS Catholic University; DLS Columbia University. Children of David and Deirdre Stam: Julian Stam born February 23, 1964, Wellsboro, PA, private business man. Wife: Anja Plato. Kathryn Stam born October 31, 1966, New Hartford, NY. Associate Professor, SUNY-IT, Utica, NY. Child: Terrin Munawet, January 28, 1997. Wendell born October 31, 1966, Jackson, WY. Wife: Rachel Mancol Stam. Children of Julian and Anja Stam: Kristin born December 1, 1989; Maia Stam born April 13, 1993. Child of Wendell and Rachel Stam: Benjamin Stam, December 21, 2007.

6) *James Henry Stam* (fourth son and my third brother, 1937—), Ijamsville, MD. BA, Upsala College, East Orange, NJ; PhD Brandeis University. Scholar-in-Residence, Philosophy, American University. First wife: Liga Ziemelis Stam. BA Upsala College; MALS, Rutgers University. Children of first marriage: Andra, Ronald Karlis, Maira, Deana, Silvia. Second wife: Andrea Tschemplik (1961—): BA Upsala College; MA Philosophy, Bryn Mawr College; PhD Philosophy, Graduate Center of the City University of New York. Associate Professor, Philosophy, American University.

7) *Robert Philip Stam* (fifth son and my fourth brother, 1941—), New York, NY. BA Calvin College, Grand Rapids, MI; MA, English, Indiana University; PhD, Comparative Literature, UC Berkeley. University Professor, Cinema Studies, Tisch School of the Arts, New York University, and NYU Abu Dhabi. First wife: Gilda Penteado. Child: Gilberto. Second wife: Ella Shohat. MA Philosophy, Tel Aviv University; PhD. Professor of Art and Public Policy-Middle Eastern and Islamic Studies, New York University, and NYU Abu Dhabi.

Appendix II

Selected Publications of David H. Stam

"A Bibliography of the Published Writings of Harry Miller Lydenberg, 1942-1960," *Bulletin of The New York Public Library* 44 (1960).

Turgenev in English: A Checklist of Works by and About Him. Compiled by Rissa Yachnin and David H. Stam. With an introductory essay by Marc Slonim (New York: New York Public Library, 1962).

Wordsworthian Criticism 1964-74: An Annotated Bibliography. Compiled by David H. Stam. (New York: New York Public Library, 1974).

"British Studies at the Newberry Library," *British Studies Monitor* IV (Winter 1974).

"Leigh Hunt & *The True Sun*," *Bulletin of The New York Public Library* (Summer 1974) p. 436-453.

England's Calvin: A Study of the Publication of John Calvin's Works in Tudor England (Ann Arbor, University Microfilms, Inc., 1978).

"Scholarly and Research Services of Research Libraries," *ALA Encyclopedia* (Chicago: American Library Association, 1986). Revised from 1980 edition.

"'Prove All Things: Hold Fast That Which is Good'; Deaccessioning and Research Libraries," *College & Research Libraries* (January 1982), p. 5-13, from a speech given at the Brown University Conference on Deaccessioning, June 1981.

"Concluding Unscientific Postscript: Reflections on Selectivity from a Non-Technical Perspective," (from a Rockefeller Foundation Symposium on Scientific Information Systems, October 1982). In: *Selectivity in Information Systems*, ed. Kenneth S. Warren (New York: Praeger, 1985).

"National Preservation Planning in the United Kingdom: An American Perspective," *British Library R & D Report No. 5759*. (London: British Library, 1983).

"Think Globally—Act Locally: Collection Development and Resource Sharing," *Collection Building* (Spring 1983). Reprinted in *The Best of Library Literature*, 1984, and in *Collection Building Reader* (New York: Neal-Schuman, 1992).

"The Doors and Windows of the Library: Leigh Hunt and Special Collections," *The Life & Times of Leigh Hunt*, ed. Robert A. McCown. Iowa City, Friends of University of Iowa Libraries, 1985. Reprinted in *The Book Collector* (Spring, 1986). Reprinted in *The Best of Library Literature* (New York: Scarecrow Press, 1986).

"Finding Funds to Support Preservation," in *The Library Preservation Program* (Chicago, American Library Association, 1985).

"Collaborative Collection Development: Progress, Problems, and Potential," *IFLA Journal* XII, No. 1 (1986). Reprinted in *Collection Building* VII, No. 3 (1986). Translation appeared in *Bulletin des Bibliothèques de France* XXXI, No. 2 (1986). Also reprinted in *Collection Building Reader* (New York: Neal Schuman, 1992).

"Technology and African Studies: Preservation; The Research Libraries Group Approach to a National Problem," in *African Studies* (London, The British Library, 1986). British Library Occasional Papers 6.

"Cooperative Collection Development: The RLG Experience," in *Research Libraries: The Past 25 Years, the Next 25 Years* (Boulder, Colorado: Colorado Associated University Press, 1986).

"The Bibliography of Modern American Literature: Ein Beispiel für nicht-deutsche Literaturerschliessung," in *Bibliographische Probleme im Zeichen eines erweiterten Literaturbegriffs* (Weinheim, West Germany, DFG, 1988).

"Sharing Resources: Do We Have Valid Models?" in *Collections: Their Development, Management, Preservation, and Sharing.* ARL/SCONUL Joint Meeting, University of York, September 19-22, 1988 (Washington, Association of Research Libraries, 1989).

"*Plus ça change . . . : Sixty Years of the Association of Research Libraries.* October 22, 1992." (Washington, DC: Printed and distributed by the Association of Research Libraries, 1992) and accessible on its website, www.arl.org.

"The Questions of Preservation," in *Research Libraries—Yesterday, Today, and Tomorrow.* William J. Welsh, editor (Kanazawa, Japan: Kanazawa Institute of Technology and Greenwood Press, 1993) p. 303-318. (Presented at Kanazawa, Japan, in May 1984).

"'Can the Research Library Teach?' A North American Perspective on the Teaching Library," *The LIBER Quarterly*, VII (1997) p. 427-436.

"'A Glutton for Books': Leigh Hunt and the London Library, 1844-46," *Biblion*, New York Public Library, Spring (1998) p. 149-190.

International Dictionary of Library Histories. Edited by David H. Stam 2 vols. (Chicago/London: Fitzroy Dearborn, 2001) 1053 p.

"Libraries on Polar Expeditions," in *Exploring Polar Frontiers: a Historical Encyclopedia*, edited by William James Mills. (Santa Barbara, CA: ABC\ Clio, 2003.) Vol. I, p. 379-381.

"Towner, Lawrence William (1921-1992)," in *Dictionary of American Library Biography.* Second Suppl. (Westport, CT: Libraries Unlimited, 2003) p. 214-216.

"Arctic Survivals: the Restoration of Records Recovered from Lost Polar Expeditions," *Proceedings of the Twentieth Polar Libraries Colloquy, June 7, 2004*. Ottawa, Canada (with John Dean, Cornell University Library).

Books on Ice: British and American Literature of Polar Exploration. By David H. Stam and Deirdre C. Stam (New York: Grolier Club, 2005), xxi, 158 p. illus. Catalogue of an exhibition held at the Grolier Club, Dec. 5, 2005 to Feb. 4, 2006.

Obituary, Richard W. Couper. *Proceedings of the American Antiquarian Society.* Vol. 116, part 2 (Worcester, MA: AAS, December 2006).

"'Innocents on the Ice': the Evolution of an Exhibition." *Gazette of the Grolier Club*. New ser. 57 (2006 [i.e. 2007]) p. 50-60.

"Polar Libraries," entry for *Oxford Companion to the Book*. Ed. Michael Suarez et al. (Oxford: Oxford University Press, 2008).

"Bending Time: the Function of Periodicals in Nineteenth-Century Polar Naval Expeditions," with Deirdre C. Stam. *Victorian Periodicals Review* 41, No. 4 (Winter 2008) p. 301-322 [appeared in early 2009].

"Bibliography," in *Matthew A. Henson's Historic Arctic Journey*. Explorers Club edition of Henson's autobiography, with Introduction by Deirdre C. Stam (Guilford, CT: The Lyons Press, 2009).

http://www.nytimes.com/info/henry-w-howgate/ David H. Stam. "Henry W. Howgate," *New York Times Online*. Retrieved December 15, 2010.

http://www.nytimes.com/info/first-international-polar-year/: David H. Stam. "First International Polar Year," *New York Times Online*. Retrieved December 15, 2010.

http://www.nytimes.com/info/adolphus-w-greely/: David H. Stam. "Adolphus W. Greely," *New York Times Online*. Retrieved December 15, 2010.

"Bassett Jones, the Grolier Club, and the 1932 Polar Exhibition: Two Thousand Items and Counting," *Gazette of the Grolier Club*. Number 61 (2010) p. 41-54.

"'Dreadful to Behold': Frostbite on the 1910-1913 British Antarctic Expedition," *American Journal of Public Health*. (2010), vol. 100. p. 2364 (with Timothy de Ver Dye and Heather Lane).

"The Lord's Librarians: The American Seamen's Friend Society and their Loan Libraries, 1837-1967. An Historical Excursion with some Unanswered Questions," *Coriolis: An Interdisciplinary Journal of Maritime History* III (June 2012) p. 45-59, appendix p. i-xiv (Published online by Mystic Seaport Museum, and awarded its Gerald E. Morris Prize for best *Coriolis* article of 2012-13).

"'Congering' the Past: the Books of the Lady Franklin Bay Expedition (1881-1884): Before and After," in *North by Degree. New Perspectives in Arctic Exploration*. Susan A. Kaplan and Robert McCracken Peck, Editors. (Philadelphia, PA: American Philosophical Society, 2013) p. 239-256.

"The Library of Fort Conger: Lady Franklin Bay Expedition, Adolphus W. Greely, Commander." An essay and catalogue of the expedition library, a Word document accessible at the Explorers Club and Mystic Seaport Museum.

Book reviews in *Albion, American Nineteenth Century History, Choice, College and Research Libraries, Journal of Academic Librarianship, Library Resources and Technical Services*, and *Notes* (Music Library Association).

Index

The names in the following list are included to identify briefly most of the people mentioned in the text, many with a brief description of the person's role in the period of our primary interactions. All but a few of the people in the list I have met personally, some briefly, some frequently; exceptions are a few artists such as Thomas Kyd, Leigh Hunt, Ted Shawn, Ruth St. Denis, Igor Stravinsky, and a few other dead white men whose work entered into my library career in some way or another. The list also serves as a subject index to the book.

Aaron, Daniel: Founder, Library of America 169

Akiyama, Kasuyoshi: Conductor, Syracuse Symphony Orchestra 236

Aldridge, Frederick Stokes: Lt. Col. US Marines. Fleet Intelligence Officer, COMBATCRULANT 46, 55

Alston, Robin: Bibliographer, publisher, and editor 196, 199

Altick, Richard: Professor of English, Ohio State University 169

Anderle, Donald: Associate Director for Special Collections, Research Libraries, New York Public Library 162, 202

Anderson, Frances: Harlem resident and friend of New York Public Library's Schomburg Center for Research in Black Culture Antarctica 121, 192-3

Arbucho, Paul: Chief compositor, New York Public Library Printing Shop 70

Ash, Lee: Librarian, consultant, and editor, Subject Collections Association of Research Libraries (ARL) 132

Atkinson, Hugh: University of Illinois. University Librarian 154, 166

Atkinson, Ross: Associate University Librarian for Collection Development, Cornell University 166

Austell, Rhett: Trustee, New York Public Library 175

Austin, Gabriel: Reference librarian (New York Public Library and Grolier Club); Owner, Wittenborn Art Book Store. New York, NY automation 77, 133

Bacon, Ernst: Composer. Director, School of Music, Syracuse University 275

Bailey, Herbert: Director, Princeton University Press. Chair, Committee for Production Guidelines for Book Longevity 171

Baker, John Philip: Chief, Conservation Division, Research Libraries, New York Public Library 163

Baker, Nicolson: Novelist. Author of Double Fold and other works related to library preservation 164

Baldwin, John: Professor of Medieval History, Johns Hopkins University 148

Banks, Paul: Conservator, Newberry Library; Professor of Library Science, Columbia University School of Library Service; and University of Texas School of Information and Library Science 131, 140-3

Baraka, Amira (aka LeRoi Jones): African-American author and activist from Newark, NJ 190-1

Barber, Nicholas: First classics fellow, Marlboro College. Career in international shipping and in publishing. Chairman of the Board of Ashmolean Museum, Oxford. 95, 100, 109, 138, 251

Barker, Nicolas: Author, editor, The Book Collector. Deputy Keeper, Preservation Department, British Library 92, 132, 199

Baron, Hans: Renaissance bibliographer, Newberry Library. Author, The Crisis of the Early Italian Renaissance 139

Barth, John: Author and Professor of English, Johns Hopkins University 148

Battin, Patricia: Librarian, Columbia University; President, Council on Library and Information Resources. Doctor of Humane Letters, Syracuse University, 2000 164, 247

Beck, Sidney: Musician, conductor, and music curator, New York Public Library 77, 88, 94

Becker, Evelyn: Donor to New York Public Library. Wife of John Becker, composer 181

Beeman, Richard: Graduate Fellow, Newberry Library. Professor of American History, University of Pennsylvania 128

Behrendt, John C: Geologist. Participant in International Geophysical Year at Ellsworth Station, Antarctica: Operation Deep Freeze, 1957-58. President, American Polar Society 54

Belanger, Dian: Independent historian of Operation Deep Freeze 53-4

Belanger, Terry: Founder and Director of the Book Arts Press and Rare Book School, Columbia University School of Library Service, and University of Virginia) xi, 103, 198, 246, 248-9, 286

Bell, Bill: Professor of English, University of Edinburgh. Director, Centre for the History of the Book at the University of Edinburgh 218, 272

Bennett, Scott: Librarian, Milton S. Eisenhower Library, John Hopkins University. University Librarian, Yale University 166

Bennett, William: Chairman, National Endowment for the Humanities 120, 140

Benton, George: Vice President for Administration, Johns Hopkins University 225

Bentz, Dale: Librarian, University of Iowa, Iowa City, IA 169

Berendt, John: American author of books about Charleston, SC, and Venice, Italy 253

Blaney, Ann: Biographer of Leigh Hunt. Melbourne, Australia 169

Blom, Leo: Dutch violist and my uncle by marriage. Principle violist, Netherlands Radio Philharmonic, Hilversum, Holland 39

Bloustein, Edward J.: President, Bennington College, VT. President, Rutgers University 115

Bluhm, Heinz: Professor of Germanic Studies, Boston College 127

Boatrite, Harold: Philadelphia composer, and Professor of Music, Haverford College 58

Bock, Edwin: Professor of Political Science Emeritus, Syracuse University 265, 267, 270, 286

Bockstoce, John: Author, sailor, Arctic historian and traveler. South Dartmouth, MA 259

Boelzner, Gordon: Pianist, and Music Director, New York City Ballet 181

Bond, William: Librarian, Houghton Library, Harvard University bookbinding 132

Bowen, Jean: Chief, Music Division, Performing Arts Research Center, New York Public Library 179

Boyd, John: Master, Churchill College, Cambridge University. Board member, British Museum and Dove Cottage, Grasmere, England 272

Boyd, Julia: Independent author, London, England. Wife of John Boyd 272

Boyden, Roland: Dean, and Professor of English History, Marlboro College, VT 129

Boyle, Leonard, OP: Dominican. Chief Librarian, Vatican Apostolic Library 216

branch libraries *69-70, 73, 151, 175, 189, 206-7, 209*

Braudel, Fernand: French historian. Founding member of Annales School 132

Breen, Timothy: Professor of American History, Northwestern University, Evanston, IL 131, 154

Brelsford, Edmund: Professor of Languages, Marlboro College. Early music performer 101

Brown, Geoffrey: Drama director and teacher, Marlboro College 101, 105

Bryant, Douglas: University Librarian, Harvard University Library. Founding Director, American Trust for the British Library 98

Brzozowski, Carole: Dean, College of Visual and Performing Arts. University Presenter, Syracuse University 274

Bullock, Robert: President, Archives Partnership Trust, Albany, NY. Public Relations Officer, New York Air National Guard, 109th Wing, Scotia, NY 260

Bultmann, Rudolph: 35, 229, 309

Bundy, Edgar C.: Wheaton graduate. Anti-Communist evangelist 26

Butts, Calvin: Associate Pastor, Abyssinian Baptist Church, Harlem, NY 192

Calhoun, Keith: Farmer, Ontario, WI 136-7

Campbell, Frank: Chief, Music Division, Performing Arts Research Center, New York Public Library 88, 126, 179

Cantor, Nancy: Chancellor, Syracuse University 237, 271, 274

Cárdenes, Andrés: Violinist. Concertmaster, Pittsburgh Symphony Orchestra 282

Carpenter, Mary: Professor of English, Queens University, Kingston, Ontario 169

Carter, John: English book dealer. Author of works on book collecting, including ABC for Book Collectors 73, 91, 98, 188

cataloging 106, 109, 168

Chambers, Neil: Editor, correspondence of Sir Joseph Banks 272, 275

Chatfield-Taylor, Adele: President and CEO, American Academy in Rome 216

Cheever, John: Short story writer, novelist, and diarist 134

Childs, Billy: Jazz composer and pianist. Board member, Chamber Music America 279

Clarke, John Henrik: Professor of African-American History, Hunter College, CUNY 192-3

Coakley, William: Poet. Associate Editor, New York Public Library. Cogswell, James: First Librarian, Astor Library, New York, NY 94

Cole, John Y.: Founder and director, Center for the Book, Library of Congress 156

Cole, Robert: Bassoonist and my bassoon teacher. First bassoon, New York City Ballet Orchestra 78

collections 7, 70, 89-90, 129-30, 139-40, 162, 169, 172-3, 182-7, 197, 220-1, 229-30, 232-7, 250-3, 256-8

conservation 140-3, 158-9, 163, 171, 198-9, 215, 258

Considine, Bob: Controversial conservative journalist. His archives are in the Syracuse University Library 56

Cooke, Goodwin: Diplomat, U.S. State Department, Ambassador to Central African Republic. Professor, International Relations, Syracuse. My regular squash partner in Syracuse 17, 224, 271

Corbin, Sol: Trustee, New York Public Library. Attorney, Proskauer Rose 175

Couper, Richard W.: President, New York Public Library. Patron, Hamilton College Library 73, 174, 247, 296

Cowley, Malcolm: Author and critic 133-4

Crane, Robert: Professor of South Asian History, Syracuse University 226

Cronenwett, Philip: Special Collections Librarian, Dartmouth College 255

Crook, Arthur: Editor, Times Literary Supplement 133

Cropp, Martin: Third Marlboro classics fellow. Professor of Classics, University of Calgary, Alberta, CAN 100-2

Cunningham, Charles: Director, Art Institute of Chicago 82, 245

Curley, Arthur: Deputy Director, Research Libraries, New York Public Library. Director, Boston Public Library 162, 193, 201, 206, 247

d'Amboise, Jacques: Principle Dancer, New York City Ballet. Doctor of Fine Arts, Syracuse University, 2008 201

Daniels, David: Countertenor, Glimmerglass Opera 220

Dasgupta, Kalpana: Assistant Chief, National Library of India, Calcutta. 227

David Tatham: Winslow Homer Scholar. Professor of Art History, Syracuse University 224, 272

Davis, Natalie Zemon: Professor of History, University of Toronto, UC Berkeley, and Princeton University 138

Davisson, William P.: Book collector and Professor of History, Marlboro College, Vermont 104

deaccessioning 105, 171-2, 174-5, 187-8, 266, 293

Dean, John: Bookbinder, conservator, and preservation administrator, Newberry Library, Johns Hopkins University, and Cornell University 128, 138, 141-3, 250, 296

DeGennaro, Richard: Librarian, University of Pennsylvania; Director, New York Public Library; Librarian, Harvard College Library 132, 152, 158, 208

Del Mar, Jonathan: Conductor, Beethoven Editor. Son of English conductor Norman Del Mar 216

Delmas, Gladys Krieble: Trustee, New York Public Library Philanthropist. Founder, Gladys Krieble Delmas Foundation 64, 197, 211, 247

Delmas, Jean Paul: French businessman. Husband of Gladys Krieble Delmas 64, 211, 215

Demos, John: Professor of American History, Yale University 138

Dimunation, Mark: Chief, Rare Books and Special Collections, Library of Congress 7

Diringer, David: British linguist and historian of writing systems 132, 142

Doares, Juanita: Associate Director for Collection Management and Development, Research Libraries, New York Public Library 162, 190

Dodson, Howard: Director, Schomburg Center for Research in Black Culture, New York Public Library 193

Dunkin, Paul S.: Professor of Library Service, Rutgers University 74

Edmunds, John: Composer, music librarian, New York Public Library 181

Egan, Brett: Executive Director, Shen Wei Dance Company; Director, DeVos Arts Management Institute at the Kennedy Center, Washington, DC 274

Eggers, Melvin: Chancellor, Syracuse University 121, 226, 236

Eisenhower, Milton S.: President Emeritus, Johns Hopkins University 144, 153-4, 160

Eisenstein, Elizabeth: Professor of History, University of Michigan 130, 138

Eliot, Simon: President, Society for the History of Authorship, Reading, and Publishing. Professor of English, School of Advanced Studies, University of London 218

Emerson, Jane: Fourth Marlboro College classics fellow. Somerville College. Headmistress, Northfield School for Girls, Northfield, MA 100, 109

Erdman, David V: Scholar (Blake, Coleridge, Byron), editor, and Professor of English Literature at SUNY Stony Brook. Editor of Library Publications, New York Public Library 69, 248

Ericson, Randy: Associate University Librarian for Technical Services, Syracuse University Library; Librarian, Hamilton College Library   31, 242

Fallows, Geoffrey: Second Marlboro classics fellow. Master, Camden School for Girls, London   96, 100, 106, 251
Farrell, Suzanne: Principal dancer, New York City Ballet   201
Fasana, Paul: Associate Director for Technical Services, Research Libraries, New York Public Library; Andrew W. Mellon Director of the Research Libraries   162, 176
Ferguson, Frances: Professor of English, Johns Hopkins University.   148
Fern, Alan: Chief, Division of Prints and Photographs, Library of Congress. Director, National Portrait Gallery   183, 228
Ferriero, David: Librarian, Duke University; Andrew W. Mellon Director of the Research Libraries, New York Public Library; Archivist of the United States   188, 211
Finzi, John: Assistant Director for Collection Resources, Library of Congress   166
Fish, Stanley: Professor of English, Johns Hopkins University   148
Fitzgerald, Rita: Secretary to four successive Associate Librarians at the Newberry Library   136
Floyd, Carlisle: Composer. Professor of Music, University of Houston. Doctor of Music, Syracuse University, 1997   238
Foner, Eric: Professor of History, Columbia University. President, Organization of American Historians   176
Francis, Sir Frank: Director and Principal Librarian, British Museum   132
Fraser, Lady Antonia: Author and New York Public Library reader free will   164
Freeman, Robert: Director, Eastman School of Music, Rochester, NY   179
Freer, Elinor: Pianist. Co-Director, Skaneateles Music Festival, Skaneateles, NY   282
Fried, Michael: Professor of Art, Johns Hopkins University, and poet   148
Friedman, Hannah: New York Public Library, Supervisor who made me cut off a beard. Later, Head of Acquisitions, Research Libraries, NYPL   61
Fussell, Charles: Composer. Professor of Music, Boston University and Rutgers University   275
Fussler, Herman: University Librarian, University of Chicago   132

Gallup, Annabell: Southeast Asia curator, British Library. Wife of Jonathan Del
    Mar   217

Gardner, Philip: Navy yeoman, Washington, DC, librarian, Rockville, MD   48

Garfield, Bernard: Bassoonist. Principal Bassoon, Philadelphia Orchestra   93

Gehl, Paul: Curator, John M. Wing Foundation, Newberry Library   135

George, Carolyn: Photographer and former dancer, New York City Ballet   201-2

Giacchino, Aldo: City planner. Clerk typist, New York Public Library   80

Gideons   4, 7, 9

Gladys Krieble Delmas Foundation   197, 211

Glover, Jane: Conductor, Glimmerglass Opera   220

Gold, Leonard: Chief, Jewish Division, New York Public Library   229

Goldthwaite, Richard: Professor of History, Johns Hopkins University   148

Goodwin, Doris Kearns: Popular author and radio commentator   251

Gordan, John. Chief, Berg Collection, New York Public Library   89, 91, 93,
    160, 197

Gordan, Phyllis: Trustee, New York Public Library, collector, philanthropist
    160, 175, 183

Graham, Billy: Evangelist and leader of the Billy Graham Evangelistic
    Foundation, Charlotte, NC   4, 7, 16, 19, 25, 27, 91, 97

Grailcourt, Charles: Professor of Economics, Marlboro College   96, 110

Green, Stephen: Chief, Newspaper Library, British Library, Colindale   229

Greene, Jack: Professor of American History, Johns Hopkins University
    Chairman, Johns Hopkins 1973 Library Search Committee   144

Greenland   11, 260-4

Gregorian, Vartan (Greg): President, New York Public Library; Brown
    University; Carnegie Corporation   73, 76, 121, 140, 174-5, 191, 232,
    235, 248

Grolier Club   92, 161, 178, 186-7, 242-3, 250, 256-9, 268, 270, 273, 280, 296-7

Grounds, Rev. Vernon: Family minister, Paterson, NJ   10

Gutfreund, John: Trustee, New York Public Library. Financier   212

Haeger, John: Director of Program Coordination, Research Libraries Group   167

Hahn, Hilary: Violinist extraordinaire   282

Hall, David: Sound Engineer. Chief, Rodgers and Hammerstein Archives of
    Recorded Sound, Performing Arts Research Center, New York Public
    Library   179

Handlin, Oscar: Historian. Harvard University Librarian   178, 224

Harbison, John: Composer, Professor of Music, Massachusetts Institute of Technology, Cambridge, MA   275

Hardison, O. B.: Director, Folger Shakespeare Library, Washington, DC   139

Harley, J.B. (Brian): Cartographer and editor, with David Woodward, of The History of Cartography   137

Harper, Conrad: Trustee, New York Public Library; Attorney, Simpson Thatcher & Bartlett, New York, NY   160-1, 175

Harris, Stefon: Jazz musician. Board member, Chamber Music America   279

Harrison, Lou: Composer   275

Harvard University Library   107

Hass, Warren J. (Jim): University Librarian, Columbia University, and President, Council on Library Resources   165

Healey, Timothy (Tim), S.J.: President, Georgetown University. President, New York Public Library   188, 208, 213

Hedgeman, Anna: Harlem resident and friend of the Schomburg Center for Research in Black History, New York Public Library   192-3

Heetderks, John: Wheaton classmate from Grand Rapids, MI   23, 28

Heiskell, Andrew: Trustee and Chairman of the Board, New York Public Library. Chairman, Time Inc.   176-7, 209, 216, 222

Hershey, Johanna: briefly my successor as Librarian at Johns Hopkins   153

Higham, John: Professor of History, Johns Hopkins University   148

Hindel, Leonard (Lenny): Bassoonist, Metropolitan Opera and New York Philharmonic Orchestra   78

Hoey, Lorraine: Wheaton College, IL, student. Editor. Wheaton Record   26

Holland, Peter: Director, Shakespeare Institute, Stratford, UK   252

Holmgren, Edwin: Director, Branch Libraries, New York Public Library   175, 207

Howsam, Leslie: President, Society for the History of Authorship Reading, and Publishing. Professor of English, University of Windsor   218

Hugo, Harold: Scholarly printer, Meriden Gravure Company, Meriden, CT   104

Hunt, Leigh: Nineteenth-century English author   130, 133, 146, 169, 184, 221-2, 241, 243-4, 293-5, 299

Hurley, Cheryl: President, Library of America   169-70

Hutson, Jean Blackwell: Chief, Schomburg Center for Research in Black Culture, New York Public Library   190, 192

Hytner, Joyce: Development consultant, Old Vic Theatre. Mother of Nicholas Hytner, Director, National Theatre, London   252

Independent Research Library Association (IRLA) 120
Isaac, Rhys: Australian historian of 18th-century U.S. 132

jafa 146, 261
Jakobsen, Vibeke Sloth: Librarian, Dansk Polar Center, Copenhagen, Denmark
    263
Jammes, André: Parisian rare book and manuscript dealer 132
Jay, Donald: Associate Director for Public Services, Research Libraries, New
    York Public Library 162, 227
John Becker: Composer and Professor of Music, Northwestern University
    180-1
Jones, Annabel. English editor, Longmans 218

Kazin, Alfred: American author 182
Keating, Rusty: Marlboro College nurse and part of our circle of friends 96
Kellogg, Paul: Artistic Manager, Glimmerglass Opera, Cooperstown, NY;
    General and Artistic Director, New York City Opera. Doctor of Fine
    Arts, Syracuse University, 2001 215, 220, 238, 274
Kenner, Hugh: Professor of History, Johns Hopkins University 148, 150-1
Kilby, Clyde: Professor of English, Wheaton College, IL 28
Kirstein, Lincoln: Founder, New York City Ballet 179, 201
Kjar, Kjell: Polar historian, Tromsø, Norway 255
Koenig, Michael: Dean, Palmer School of Information Science, Long Island
    University, Brookville, NY 246
Kolvoord, Robert: Proprietor, Old Settler Book Bookshop, Hillsboro, NH 108
Kramberg, Ross: Executive Director, Paul Taylor Dance Company 271
Krasner, Louis: Violinist. Professor of Music, Syracuse University. Founder,
    Syracuse Friends of Chamber Music 282
Krummel, Donald: Associate Librarian, Newberry Library. Professor of Library
    Science, University of Illinois. Musicologist and bibliographer xi, 245
Kvam, Roger. Wheaton College, IL, student. Editor, Wheaton Record 26
Kyd, Thomas: Elizabethan playwright, author of The Spanish Tragedy 110, 299

Labalme, George: Trustee, Gladys Krieble Delmas Foundation 215, 254

Labalme, Patricia (Patsy): Venetian historian. Trustee, Gladys Krieble Delmas Foundation 213

Landon, Richard: Director, Thomas Fisher Rare Book Library, University of Toronto 64, 241

Lavery, Sean: Principal dancer, New York City Ballet 202

Le Roy Ladurie, Emmanuel: Historian. Director, Bibliothèque Nationale, Paris 228

LeClerc, Paul: President, New York Public Library 73, 176, 188, 205

Lee, Sul: Director, University of Oklahoma Library 172

Lemke, Antje Bultmann: Professor Emerita of Information Studies, Syracuse University. Daughter of German theologian, Rudolf Bultmann 229

Lenox-Hooker, Catherine: Interim Director, Schomburg Center for Research in Black Culture, New York Public Library 193

Lerner, Gerda: Professor of History, University of Wisconsin. President, Organization of American Historians 175

Levine, Joseph (Joe): Intellectual historian. Professor of History, Syracuse, NY 224

library automation 63, 129, 144, 153

Line, Maurice: Director-General, British Library Lending Division, Boston Spa, Yorkshire, UK 198

Lioi, Margaret: Executive Director, Chamber Music America xi, 278, 280

Longacre, Richard: Political scientist. Provost, Johns Hopkins University 156

Lydenberg, Harry Miller: Director, Reference Department, New York Public Library 72-4, 293

Lynch, Beverly: Professor of Information Studies, UCLA. Director, California Rare Book School (CALRBS) 264, 285

Lyons, Louis: Boston newscaster. Kipling Fellow, Marlboro College, VT 99

Mack, Rodger: Sculptor. Professor of Art, Syracuse University 223, 225, 276

Macksey, Richard: Professor of Humanities, Johns Hopkins University xi, 148, 150, 247

Macomber, Curtis: Violinist, Manhattan String Quartet 280, 282

Maddox, Alton H.: African-American Attorney for Schomburg Coalition 192

Mandelbaum, Maurice: Professor of History, Johns Hopkins University 148

Marsh, Peter: Professor of History, Syracuse University 222, 224

Marshall, Mary: Professor of English, Syracuse University 239

Martins, Peter: Principal dancer and Ballet Master, New York City Ballet   201-2, 240

Marx, Anthony: President, New York Public Library   73

Mason, Francis: Deputy Director, Pierpont Morgan Library. Dance critic   161

Maxon, John: Director, Art Institute of Chicago   245

Mayfield, John: Collector of Swinburne and modern firsts. Curator, Mayfield Library, Syracuse University Library   65, 231

McGann, Jerome: Professor of English, Johns Hopkins University; California Institute of Technology; and University of Virginia   148

McKitterick, David: Librarian, Trinity College, University of Cambridge   132, 145, 229

McLuhan, Marshall: Canadian philosopher of communication theory   132

Meiggs, Russell: Classicist, Balliol College, Oxford. Kipling Fellow, Marlboro College   99

Meinig, Donald: Historical geographer. Professor of Geography, Syracuse University   265

Mekeel, Herbert: Minister of First Presbyterian Church of Schenectady, NY   34

Menschel, Robert: Trustee, New York Public Library, Syracuse University. President, Museum of Modern Art. Senior Partner, Goldman Sachs   222

Metcalf, Keyes: Harvard University Librarian; Chief, Reference Department, New York Public Library; Consultant for Marlboro College Library   107

Miller, Rhena Schweitzer: Daughter of Albert Schweitzer   229

Millon, Henry (Hank): Architectural historian. Director, Center for Advanced Studies in Visual Arts, National Gallery of Art; Member, Delmas Venetian Advisory Board   216

Monter, William: Professor of History, Northwestern University   131, 144

Morgan, Paul: Curator, Bodleian Library, Oxford, and liaison to College libraries   145

Morison, Stanley: Typographer of Times New Roman, and friend of Newberry Library   91, 132, 200

Morris, James: Program Officer, Andrew W. Mellon Foundation.   171

Morris, Robert: Archivist, Schomburg Center for Research in Black Culture, New York Public Library   191-3

Mosher, Paul: Vice-Provost and Director of Libraries, University of Pennsylvania, and Vice-Chair, RLG Committee on Collection Management and Development   166, 168, 201, 210, 247

Muller, Stephen: President, Johns Hopkins University   154, 161

Munawet, Suthin: Former husband of daughter Kathryn Stam and father of grandson Terrin Munawet   113, 122, 242

Munby, A.N.L. (Tim): Fellow and Librarian, King's College, Cambridge   132

Nash, Ray: Professor of Graphic Arts and Design, Dartmouth College   97, 104
Newman, Charles: Author, Editor of Tri-Quarterly, and Professor of English, Johns Hopkins University   148
Newman, Morris: Bassoonist and bassoon teacher, New York. Also recorder and krumhorn player   78
Newton, Catherine: Dean, Faculty of Arts and Science, and Professor of Earth Sciences, Syracuse University   271

Oates, Joyce Carol: Author. Syracuse University: BA, 1960. Professor of English, Princeton University   234-5
Oberlin, Russell: Countertenor, New York, NY   78
Ong, Walter J., S.J.: Professor of English, St. Louis University, Chicago, IL   132
Ormsby, Eric: Historian. Librarian, McGill University, Montreal, Quebec, CAN   228
Ostvold, Harold: Chief of the Reference Department, New York Public Library   84, 94
Oswald, Genevieve (Gigi): Founder and first Chief, Dance Collection, New York Public Library, now the Jerome Robbins Dance Collection   179
Owen, Norton: Archivist, Jacob's Pillow Dance Festival, Beckett, MA   203, 216

Pappastavrou, George: Pianist. Director and Professor Emeritus, School of Music, Syracuse University. Bloomingdale, New York   276
Pargellis, Stanley: Historian. Director and Librarian, Newberry Library   76, 139
Parke, Carol: Associate University Librarian for Reader Services, Syracuse University   237
Patten, Robert: President, Society for the History of Authorship, Reading, and Publishing. Professor of English, Rice University   xi, 218, 286
Paul Taylor Dance Company   220, 238, 271
Pearson, Lennart: Bronx, New York, and City College transfer to Wheaton. Also classmate and roommate, New College, University of Edinburgh   29, 33-4, 60
Peckham, John: Assistant to Harold Hugo, Meriden Gravure Company, Meriden, CT   104

Pforzheimer, Carl J., Jr.; Collector and financier. Trustee, New York Public
   Library   184-5

Pforzheimer, Carol F.: Trustee, New York Public Library   184

Phillips, Robert S.: Author, Syracuse University: BA 1960. Professor of English,
   University of Houston   234

Pilgrim, Neva: Founder and Music Director, Society for New Music, Syracuse.
   Professor of Music, Colgate University   182, 275, 277, 281

Pocock, John: Professor of History, Johns Hopkins University   148

Polacek, Richard: Librarian, William H. Welch Medical Library, Johns Hopkins
   School of Medicine   64, 144, 160

preservation   7, 74, 108-9, 111, 120, 129, 140-3, 158-9, 164, 170-2, 198-200,
   250, 257-8, 271, 294-5

Prising, Robin: Actor and author of Goodbye, Manila   94

Prochaska, Alice: Historian, Librarian, Administrator   173, 198, 229, 247

Prochaska, Frank: Historian and classmate   146, 148, 273

Quarrie, Paul: Librarian, Eton College, UK   229

Ragle, Tom: President, Marlboro College, VT   xi, 96, 98, 100-2, 106, 108, 110

Rago, Henry. Editor, Poetry. Chicago, IL   128

Ratcliffe, Frederick: University Librarian, University of Cambridge   198

Ravitch, Diane: Educator. Trustee, New York Public Library   222

Ray, Gordon: President, John Simon Guggenheim Memorial Foundation.
   Trustee, New York Public Library   160, 177

Reagan, Ronald: President of the United States   120, 140

Redon, Odilon: French symbolist painter. Deirdre Corcoran's Harvard thesis
   topic   81

Reed, Cleota: Ceramics historian. Wife of art historian David Tatham   224, 272

Reid, Rufus: Jazz bassist. Board member, Chamber Music America   279

Reiman, Donald: Scholar, Editor, Shelley and His Circle   169, 184

Research Libraries Group (RLG)   158

Reza, Vali: Composer, Professor of Music, University of Pittsburgh   275

Rice, Howard, Jr.: Assistant Librarian, Princeton University Library, and donor
   to Marlboro College Library   105

Richnell, Donald: Director-General, Humanities and Social Sciences, British
   Library   199

Roberts, Denis: Librarian, National Library of Scotland   167

Robinson, Charles: Professor of English, University of Delaware, Newark   169

Rochberg, George: Composer. Professor of Music, University of Pennsylvania
64, 282

Roloson, Robert: Chicago collector and donor to Newberry Library   130

Rose, Jonathan: President, Society for the History of Authorship, Reading, and
Publishing. Professor of History, Drew University   218

Rose, Marshall: Trustee, New York Public Library. New York realtor.   209

Rosenthal, Albi: Oxford Rare Book dealer   132

Rosenthal, Robert: Curator of Special Collections, University of Chicago Library
132

Rosenthal, Samuel: Trustee, Newberry Library   129

Roth, Elizabeth: Head, Print Collection, Research Libraries, New York Public
Library   162

Rushdie, Salman: Author, Satanic Verses, inter alia   171

Ruzicka, Rudolph: Typographer and book designer, Hanover, NH   105

Ryan, Michael: Director, Rare Books and Manuscripts Library, Columbia
University   191, 216

Rylands, Jane: American author of Venetian stories. Wife of Philip Rylands   252

Ryskamp, Charles: Director, Morgan Library and the Frick Collection, New
York, NY   139

Safire, William: Trustee, Syracuse University, and donor. Columnist, New York
Times   230

Savelle, Max: Professor of American History, University of Washington, Seattle,
WA   138

Schenck, Andrew: Associate Conductor, Baltimore Symphony Orchestra   149

Schlereth, Thomas: American historian, University of Notre Dame   128

Schlosser, Leonard: President, Lindenmyer Paper Company. Chair, Board of the
Conservation Center for Art and Historic Artifacts, Philadelphia, PA
171

Schuman, Henry: Oboist. Conductor, New Cecilia Chamber Orchestra   78

Schwantner, Joseph: Composer. Professor of Music, Eastman School of Music,
Rochester, NY   179

Scott, Mary Anne: Director, National Library of Canada, Ottawa, CAN   228

Segal, Martin E.: Business consultant and philanthropist. Chairman, Board,
Lincoln Center for the Performing Arts   175

separation of church and state   4, 9

Serkin, Rudolf: Pianist; Founder and Director, Marlboro Music Festival, Marlboro, VT   115

Shackleton, Robert: Bodley's Librarian, Montesquieu scholar, and book collector 104, 138, 146, 154, 229, 248

Shaw, Edward: President, Research Libraries Group, Stanford University.   64

Shaw, Patrick: Chicago architect and child sculptural model   128

Shen Wei: Founder and Artistic Director, Shen Wei Dance Arts. MacArthur Fellow   238, 269, 274-5

Sherman, Judith: Record producer, New York. Board member, Chamber Music America   280

Shils, Edward: Professor, Committee on the Social Sciences, University of Chicago   268

Siegel, Ernie: Director, Enoch Pratt Free Library, Baltimore, MD   64, 161

Sills, Beverly: Soprano, New York City Opera. Chair, Lincoln Center Council 179

Singh, Gurnek: South Asian Bibliographer, Syracuse University Library   226-7

Skipper, James: President, Research Libraries Group   165

Smethurst, Michael: Director-General, Humanities and Social Sciences, British Library   64, 147, 167, 252

Smith, Carleton Sprague: Chief, Music Division, New York Public Library. Syracuse University, Doctor of Humane Letters, 1987   121, 238

Smith, Harold Byron: Industrialist. Chairman of the Board, Newberry Library, Chicago   222

Smith, Herman Dunlop: President, Marsh & McLennan Insurance Company. Chairman of the Board, Newberry Library   136

Smith, Lacey Baldwin: Professor of British History, Northwestern University, and my dissertation advisor   129, 131, 146, 248

Smith, Louise: Business consultant. Chicago. IL. Chair of the Board, Chamber Music America   xi, 280

Smith, Raymond S.: Editor, Ontario Review. Husband of Joyce Carol Oates 234

Snow, Vernon: President, John Ben Snow Foundation. Professor of History, Syracuse University. Doctor of Humane Letters, Syracuse University, 1996   238

Snyder, Henry: Editor and Director, English Short Title Catalogue in North America. Professor of History, Louisiana State University and University of California at Riverside   196

Sparrow, John: Warden, All Soul's College, Oxford University. 145

Spock, Benjamin: Pediatrician and author 56, 230

sports 8, 17, 20, 31, 113, 177

St. Denis, Ruth: Dancer. Co-Founder of Denishawn Dance Company and Jacob's Pillow Dance Festival, Beckett, MA 202-3, 299

Stam, Deirdre Corcoran: Art historian, librarian, professor, wife vii, 125, 290

Stam, James H.: Philosopher, professor, brother 286

Stark, Lewis M.: Chief, Rare Book Division, Reference Department, New York Public Library 76

Stefansson, Evelyn: Widow of Vilhjalmur Stefansson 87

Stefansson, Vilhjalmur: Canadian/American Arctic explorer, author, and book collector, Dartmouth College 87, 255

Steinmetz, John: Bassoonist, Los Angeles Opera. Board, Chamber Music America 279, 282

Stevenson, Allan H: Scholar of watermarks, Chicago, IL 128

Stewart, Ruth Ann: Assistant Director, Schomburg Center for Research in Black Culture; Assistant Director for External Services, Research Libraries, New York Public Library 162

Stokowski, Leopold: Conductor, American Symphony Orchestra 38

Stravinsky, Igor: Composer 182, 299

Suarez, Michael, S.J.: Director, Rare Book School, Charlottesville, Virginia 249

Sverdlove, Dorothy: Chief, Theater Division, Performing Arts Research Center, New York Public Library 179

Syracuse University Library 54, 56, 65, 83, 109, 228, 230, 239, 282

Szladits, Lola: Curator, Henry W. and Albert A. Berg Collection of English and American Literature, New York Public Library 75-6, 182, 197, 229

Tanselle, Thomas: Bibliographer. Retired Vice-President, John Simon Guggenheim Foundation 131, 170

Tauber, Maurice: Melville Dewey Professor of Library Service, Columbia University; Consultant on Library Technical Services 132

Taylor, Jane: Bassoonist and my first bassoon teacher. Founder and mainstay of the Dorian Quintet 78

Taylor, Paul: Dancer, choreographer, and founder, Paul Taylor Dance Company. Doctor of Music, Syracuse University, 1986 220, 238, 269, 271

Tedeschi, John: Reformation scholar and curator of Special Collections, Newberry Library   136, 139

Thomas, Sarah: Successively head librarian of Cornell University, Oxford University, and Harvard University. Graduate student worker in the Hopkins library when I was Librarian there   153

Thomson, Virgil: Composer. Music critic, New York Herald Tribune   230, 276
tobacco   63-4, 70

Tomlinson, John: Executive Director, Paul Taylor Dance Company   271

Towner, Lawrence W. (Bill): Director and Librarian, the Newberry Library, Chicago, IL   129, 248

Traister, Daniel: Rare book librarian, New York Public Library and University of Pennsylvania   xi, 173, 286

Tribolet, Harold: Manager, Department of Extra Binding, R.R. Donnelly & Sons, Chicago, IL   131

Truesdell, Clifford: Professor of Rational Mechanics, Johns Hopkins University   155

TULIP 18

Ungar, Douglas: Novelist and Professor of English, Syracuse University and University of Nevada, Las Vegas   236

Vaisey, David: Bodley's Librarian. Oxford University   229

van Haaften, Julia: Curator of Photographs, New York Public Library. Also, Museum of the City of New York   183

Verba, Sidney: Harvard University Librarian and Professor of Political Science, Harvard University   224

Vincow, Gershon: Professor of Chemistry. Vice Chancellor for Academic Affairs, Syracuse University   221, 241

Wadopian, Joan: Dancer, Shen Wei Dance Arts. Wife of Brett Egan   274

Wadsworth, Charles: Pianist. Founding Director, Chamber Music Society of Lincoln Center   179

Waggoner, Andrew: Composer, Professor of Music, Syracuse University   275

Wallis, Helen: Cartographic historian. Chief, Map Division, British Library   132

Wallis, Victor: Political scientist, Berklee College of Music, Boston, MA 77, 86-7

Ward, Chris: Archivist, New York State, Albany, NY 260

Warner, Robert: Archivist of the United States. Professor of Library and Information Science, University of Michigan, Ann Arbor, MI 56, 229

Weber, David C.: Director, University Libraries, Stanford University. RLG Board of Governors 166

Wedgeworth, Robert: Librarian, University of Illinois. President, Pro Literacy International. Doctor of Humane Letters, Syracuse University, 2008 239

Weimer, Mark: Director, George Arents Research Library, Syracuse University 232-3

Weirich, Robert: Pianist. Artistic Director, Skaneateles Music Festival, Skaneateles, NY 282

Wells, James M.: Associate Director, Custodian, John M. Wing Collection of Printing History, Newberry Library, Chicago, IL 248

Wesley, Dorothy Porter: African-American Bibliographer, Howard University. Doctor of Humane Letters, Syracuse University, 1989 238

Wheeler, Sara: Polar author. London, England 261

white gloves 159

Whitehill, Walter Muir: Director and Librarian, Boston Athenaeum (aka Mr. Boston). Trustee, Marlboro College 248

Williams, John A.: African-American novelist 230

Willis, Michael: Press relations officer, Glimmerglass Opera, Cooperstown, NY 215

Willison, Ian: Book historian and librarian, British Library. CBE 132, 217-18, 229

Willoughby, E. E.: Shakespearean scholar and librarian, Newberry Library and Folger Library 134

Wilson, Alexander (Alex): Director-General, Humanities and Social Sciences, British Library 248

Wilson, Douglas: Jefferson and Lincoln Scholar. Professor of Professor and Librarian, Knox College, Galesburg, IL 136

Wilson, Edmund: Author and inspiration for the Library of America 170, 277

Winogren, Blanche: Harpsichordist. Wife of Sidney Beck 94

Wolf, Edwin, 2nd: Director, Library Company of Philadelphia 139

Wolff, Tobias: Fiction writer and Professor of English, Syracuse University, and Stanford University 171

Wood, Thor: Chief, Performing Arts Research Center, New York Public Library 103, 179

Woodring, Carl: Professor of English, Columbia University 169

Woodward, David: Cartographic historian, Newberry Library and University of Wisconsin, Madison, WI. Editor (with Brian Harley) of The History of Cartography 137

Woof, Robert: Director, Wordsworth's Dove Cottage, Grasmere, UK 251

Woolley, Samuel: Trustee, New York Public Library 175

Wray, Wendell: Chief, Schomburg Center for Research in Black Culture, New York Public Library 191-3

Wynne, Marjorie: Curator of Manuscripts, Yale University Library and Beinecke Library 76, 197

Ying, David: Cellist, Ying Quartet. Professor of Cello, Eastman School of Music, Rochester, NY. Co-Director, Skaneateles Festival, NY 282

Ying, Phillip: Violist, Ying Quarter. President, Chamber Music America. Chair, Chamber Music Department, Eastman School of Music, Rochester, NY 279

Yuan, Frank: Wheaton classmate and travelling companion 31

Zukofsky, Louis: American Poet 150, 180

Zukofsky, Paul: Violinist. Contemporary music specialist. Son of Louis Zukofsky 150

Zdanis, Richard: Johns Hopkins University. Associate Provost 151, 152

Edwards Brothers Malloy
Thorofare, NJ USA
October 25, 2016